Media Studies

Media Studies

Key Issues and Debates

Edited by
Eoin Devereux

SAGE Publications
Los Angeles ▪ London ▪ New Delhi ▪ Singapore

SAGE Publications Ltd
1 Oliver's Yard
55 City Road
London EC1Y 1SP

SAGE Publications Inc.
2455 Teller Road
Thousand Oaks, California 91320

SAGE Publications India Pvt Ltd
B 1/I 1 Mohan Cooperative Industrial Area
Mathura Road, New Delhi 110 044
India

SAGE Publications Asia-Pacific Pte Ltd
33 Pekin Street #02-01
Far East Square
Singapore 048763

British Library Cataloguing in Publication data

A catalogue record for this book is available from the British Library

ISBN 978-1-4129-2982-0
ISBN 978-1-4129-2983-7 (pbk)

Library of Congress Control Number: 2006935377

Typeset by C&M Digitals (P) Ltd, Chennai, India
Printed in Europe by the Alden Group, Oxfordshire
Printed on paper from sustainable resources

For Joe and Gavin

Contents

Contributors

Eoin Devereux is Senior Lecturer in Sociology at the University of Limerick, Ireland.

Kim Akass and Janet McCabe

Kim Akass has co-edited and contributed to *Reading Sex and the City* (IB Tauris, 2004), *Reading Six Feet Under: TV To Die For* (IB Tauris, 2005), *Reading The L Word: Outing Contemporary Television* (IB Tauris, 2006) and *Reading Desperate Housewives: Beyond the White Picket Fence* (IB Tauris, 2006). She is currently researching the representation of motherhood on American TV and is co-editor of the new television journal *Critical Studies in Television* (Manchester University Press) as well as (with McCabe) series editor of 'Reading Contemporary Television' from IB Tauris.

Janet McCabe is Research Associate (TV Drama) at Manchester Metropolitan University. She is author of *Feminist Film Studies: Writing the Woman into Cinema* (Wallflower, 2004), and is co-editor of *Reading Sex and the City* (IB Tauris, 2004), *Reading Six Feet Under: TV To Die For* (IB Tauris, 2005), *Reading The L Word: Outing Contemporary Television* (IB Tauris, 2006) and *Reading Desperate Housewives: Beyond the White Picket Fence* (IB Tauris, 2006). She is managing editor of the new television journal *Critical Studies in Television* (Manchester University Press) as well as (with Akass) series editor of 'Reading Contemporary Television' for IB Tauris.

Michael J. Breen

Michael J. Breen is Head of Department, Media & Communication Studies and Joint Director, Centre for Culture, Technology and Values at Mary Immaculate College, University of Limerick, Ireland. His primary research has been in the area of media effects, analysis of media content, and the role of media content in public opinion formation. He is particularly interested in the influence of communications media and technological change on individual beliefs, attitudes and values, and on the formation of public attitudes and values. His publications include 'Fear, Framing and Foreignness' (with Eoin Devereux and Amanda Haynes), *International Journal of Critical Psychology*, 16, Spring 2006 and 'Citizens, Loopholes and "Maternity Tourists": Media Framing of the 2004

Citizenship Referendum' (2006) (with Amanda Haynes and Eoin Devereux) in Corcoran and Peillon (eds) *Uncertain Ireland*. Dublin: IPA.

John Corner

John Corner is Professor in the School of Politics and Communication Studies at the University of Liverpool. His books include *Television Form and Public Address* (Edward Arnold, 1995), *The Art of Record* (Manchester University Press, 1996), *Critical Ideas in Television Studies* (Oxford University Press, 1999) and a number of edited works, most recently, with Dick Pels, *Media and the Re-Styling of Politics* (Sage, 2003). He has just co-authored a book on the history of British current affairs television and is currently researching on documentary aesthetics and on recent shifts in media-political relations.

David Croteau and William Hoynes

David Croteau is a former Associate Professor (retired) in the Department of Sociology at Virginia Commonwealth University and the author of *Politics and the Class Divide* (Temple University Press, 1994). William Hoynes is Professor of Sociology at Vassar College and the author of *Public Television for Sale* (1994, Westview Press).

Croteau and Hoynes are co-authors of *By Invitation Only: How the Media Limit Political Debate* (1994, Common Courage Press); *Media/Society: Industries, Images and Audiences* (3rd edn, Pine Forge Press, 2004); and *The Business of Media: Corporate Media and the Public Interest* (2nd edn, Pine Forge Press, 2005). They are co-editors, with Charlotte Ryan, of *Rhyming Hope and History: Activists, Academics, and Social Movement Scholarship* (University of Minnesota Press, 2005).

Natalie Fenton

Natalie Fenton is a Senior Lecturer in the Department of Media and Communications, Goldsmiths College, University of London. She has researched and published on a range of issues in relation to the role of the media in the formation of identities and democracies. Examples of this work include *Mediating Social Science*, with Alan Bryman and David Deacon (Sage, 1998), *Trust and Civil Society*, with Fran Tonkiss, Andrew Passey and Les Hems (2000

MacMillan; *Media and Cultural Analysis: Critical Interrogations*, with Jim McGuigan, Graham Murdock and Michael Pickering (Sage, Forthcoming). She is particularly interested in media and civil society, in particular, the relationship between the media and social/political mobilisation and transnational social movements.

Amanda Haynes

Amanda Haynes is a Lecturer in Sociology at the University of Limerick, Ireland. Foremost among her eclectic research interests is the reception and integration of immigrants, particularly the role of the mass media in this process. Amanda's most recent publications include 'Don't Rock the Geo-Political Boat' *Media and Migration*, Dialogue Series VI, UCSIA, University of Antwerp, 2006; 'Fear, Framing and Foreigness' (with Eoin Devereux and Michael J. Breen) *International Journal of Critical Psychology*, 16, Spring 2006 and 'The Glass Ceiling in IT' *Encyclopaedia of Gender and Information Technology* (Eileen Trauth, ed. Idea Group Inc, 2006).

Joke Hermes

Joke Hermes is Professor of Applied Qualitative Research in Public Opinion at INHolland University, Diemen/Amsterdam, Netherlands. She is co-editor of the *European Journal of Cultural Studies*. Her most recent publications include: *Rereading Popular Culture* (Blackwell, 2005); '"Ally McBeal", "Sex and the City" and the tragic success of feminism' in *Feminism in Popular Culture*, edited by Joanne Hollows and Rachel Moseley (Berg, 2006, pp. 79–96); 'Citizenship in the age of internet' in the *European Journal of Communication*, 2006, 21: 295–309, 'Father knows best? The post-feminist male and parenting in 24' in Steven Peacock (ed.) *Reading 24. Television Against the Clock* (IB Tauris, 2007). Email: joke.hermes@inholland.nl.

Kevin Howley

Kevin Howley is Associate Professor of Media Studies at DePauw University (Indiana, USA). He is author of *Community Media: People, Places, and Communication Technologies*, (Cambridge University Press, 2005). His work has appeared in the *Journal of Radio Studies; Journalism: Theory, Practice, and*

Criticism; Television and New Media and *Social Movement Studies*. Dr. Howley also produces documentary videos including, most recently, *Victory at Sea? Culture Jamming Dubya* (2004).

Peter Hughes

Peter Hughes lectures in media studies at La Trobe University, Australia, where he teaches media research, documentary film and television and new cultural technologies. He is editor of the online journal of media and history, *Screening the past*, http://www.latrobe.edu.au/screeningthepast. Recent publications include: 'The media, bushfires and community resilience' (with Peter B.White), in *Disaster Resilience: An Integrated Approach*, D. Paton and D. Johnston (eds) Springfield, Ill: Charles C. Thomas, 2006 'Battling ferocious flames: Bushfires in the media'(with Cohen, Crez and White), in *The Australian Journal of Emergency Management*, 21, no. 1: 50–5 2006, 'Navigating the archives', *Southern Review*, 38, no. 1: 69–80 2005, 'Power and misrepresentation' in *After Mabo. Australian Screen Education* no. 38: 123–5 2005, and (with Ina Bertrand) *Media Research Methods: Institutions, Texts, Audiences*, Basingstoke, New York: Palgrave, 2005.

Karim H. Karim

Karim H. Karim is the Director of the School of Journalism and Communication at Carleton University in Ottawa, Canada. He has been a visiting scholar at Harvard University and a senior policy analyst in the Canadian government's Multiculturalism Program. He won the inaugural Robinson Prize for excellence in communication studies for his book, *Islamic Peril: Media and Global Violence*, (Black Rose Books, 2001). Dr. Karim is currently leading a research project on Muslims in North America and Europe. He holds degrees from Columbia and McGill universities.

Jenny Kitzinger

Jenny Kitzinger is Professor of Media and Communication Research at the School of Journalism, Media and Cultural Studies, Cardiff University. She specializes in research into the media coverage, and audience reception, of social, health and scientific issues. She has also written extensively about sexual violence. Her most recent book, *Framing Abuse: Media Influence and Public Understanding of Sexual Violence Against Children*, was published by Pluto Press (2004). Jenny is also co-editor of *Developing Focus Group Research: politics, theory and practice* (Sage, 1999) and co-author of: *The Mass Media and Power in Modern Britain* (Oxford University Press, 1997); *Great Expectations* (Hochland and Hochland, 1998) and *The Circuit of Mass Communication in the AIDS crisis* (Sage, 1999). She is currently working on a book with colleagues about *Human Cloning in the Media* (Routledge, 2007).

Jeroen de Kloet and Liesbet van Zoonen

Jeroen de Kloet is Assistant Professor at the Department of Media Studies at the University of Amsterdam and coordinator of the Amsterdam branch of the International Institute for Asian Studies. His publications include 'Sonic Sturdiness: The Globalization of "Chinese" Rock and Pop', in *Critical Studies in Media Communication*, 2005, 22(4): 321–338 and 'Saved by Betrayal? Ang Lee's Translations of "Chinese" Family Ideology', in P. Pisters and W. Staat, *Shooting the Family: Transnational Media and Intercultural Values*, pp. 117–132. Amsterdam: Amsterdam University Press (2005). See also http://home.tiscali.nl/jeroendekloet.

Liesbet van Zoonen is professor of Media and Popular Culture in the Department of Communication at the University of Amsterdam. Her most recent book is *Entertaining the citizen: when politics and popular culture converge* (Rowman and Littlefield, 2005).

Sonia Livingstone

Sonia Livingstone is Professor of Social Psychology, Department of Media and Communications, London School of Economics and Political Science. She has published over 100 articles and chapters on the subject of media audiences, focusing on audience reception of diverse television genres, with recent work focusing on children, young people and new media, especially the internet. Her books include *Making Sense of Television, Mass Consumption and Personal Identity, Talk on Television, Children and Their Changing Media Environment, The Handbook of New Media, Young People and New Media, Audiences and Publics*, and *Harm and Offence in Media Content*. Sonia's webpage is www.lse.ac.uk/collections/media@lse/whoswho/sonialivingstone.htm

Greg Philo

Greg Philo is Professor of Communications and Research Director of the Glasgow University Media Group. His most recent books include (with David Miller) *Market Killing*, Longman, 2001; (with Mike Berry) *Bad News from Israel*, Pluto, 2004 and *Israel and Palestine: Competing Histories*, Pluto, 2006.

Pamela J. Shoemaker, John Hyuk Lee, Gang (Kevin) Han and Akiba A. Cohen

Pamela J. Shoemaker is the John Ben Snow Professor at the S.I. Newhouse School of Public Communications, Syracuse University. Her recent books include *News Around the World: Practitioners, Content and the Public* (with Cohen, 2006); *How to Build Social Science Theories* (with Tankard and Lasorsa, 2004); *Mediating the Message: Theories of Influences on Mass Media Content* (with Reese, 1996); *Gatekeeping* (1991); and the edited volume *Communication Campaigns about Drugs: Government, Media, Public* (1989). She is co-editor of the journal *Communication Research*, and former president of the Association for Education in Journalism and Mass Communication.

John Hyuk Lee is Assistant Professor at Central Michigan University. His recent publications include 'The role of scene in framing a story: An analysis of scene's position, length and dominance in a story' (with Y.J. Choi, 2006) in *Journal of Broadcasting and Electronic Media*; and 'Influence of poll results on the advocates' political discourse: An application of functional Analysis debates to online messages in the 2002 Korean presidential election' (with Y.J. Choi, and C.H. Lee, 2004) in *Asian Journal of Communication*.

Gang (Kevin) Han is Ph.D. candidate at the S.I. Newhouse School of Public Communications, Syracuse University. His book chapter 'A comparative study of international news coverage in China and Japan: People's Daily and Asahi Shimbun, 1982–1998' (with G. Zhang) in *Mass media and East Asia after the Cold War* was published in Tokyo, Japan in 2005. He has also published a number of research articles in leading journals in China.

Akiba A. Cohen is Professor of Communication at Tel Aviv University in Israel. In addition to the book co-authored with Shoemaker, above, he is author or co-author of *Media, Minorities and Integration: The Arab and Russian Communities in Israel* (with Adoni and Caspi, 2006); *The Holocaust and the Press: Nazi War-Crimes Trials in Germany and Israel* (with Zemach, Wilke and Schenk);

Global Newsrooms, Local Audiences: A Study of the Eurovision News Exchange (1995); *Framing the Intifada: Media and People* (edited with Wolfsfeld, 1993); *Social Conflict and Television News* (with Adoni and Bantz,1990), and *The Television News Interview* (1987). He served as president of the International Communication Association and is an elected Fellow of the Association.

Phillipa Smith and Allan Bell

Philippa Smith is Projects Manager for the Institute of Culture, Discourse and Communication at AUT University in Auckland, New Zealand. With previous experience as both a journalist and public relations executive in both the United Kingdom and New Zealand, Philippa returned to academia to attain her MA in Communication Studies at AUT University which she passed with First Class Honours in 2003. In 2004 she received the AUT School of Communications Studies award for excellence in Post-Graduate Research and in the same year was also a recipient of the AUT Vice-Chancellors award for excellence in team research in the Television Violence in NZ project. Philippa has a particular interest in discourse analysis in relation to national identity and has presented papers at a number of conferences in this area. Currently she is involved in research into new media and the Internet. Allan Bell is Professor of Language & Communication and Director of the Institute of Culture, Discourse and Communication at Auckland University of Technology, New Zealand. He has led a dual career combining academic research with journalism and communications consultancy. He has published many papers in academic journals and edited collections, and authored or co-edited five books including *The Language of News Media* (Blackwell, 1991), *Approaches to Media Discourse,* with Peter Garrett (Blackwell, 1998) and *Languages of New Zealand,* with Ray Harlow and Donna Starks (IPG, 2005). He is co-founder and editor of the international *Journal of Sociolinguistics.*

Denis McQuail

Denis McQuail is Emeritus Professor and Honorary Fellow at Amsterdam School of Communication Research, University of Amsterdam. A renowned scholar, he is the author of numerous books including *McQuail's Mass Communication Theory* (5th Edn.) published by Sage in 2005.

Foreword

Field Observations on Media Studies
Denis McQuail

Media studies has been a recognised field of research and teaching for more than thirty years, although it has resisted attempts at clear delineation and boundary drawing. To some extent, this resistance stems from its intrinsic character as an open field of inquiry, without the ambition to present itself as a scientific discipline. It makes no exclusive claim to its typical subject matter or to certain theoretical propositions. Its subject matter is both diverse and continually changing and there is an element of deliberate *bricolage* in the adoption of suitable concepts and theoretical ideas. The topics and manner of inquiry require a close engagement with human experience and do not privilege any particular perspective on the nature of experience.

Despite this deliberate embracing of indeterminacy, the field cannot avoid acquiring a certain profile in the eyes of those who view it, even if it does not possess any profile that is generally acknowledged from within. In addition, the field has a place in a larger historical context of media, culture and society at a given place and time and a more restricted context of other branches of study of media in various aspects. As a larger project, it is given certain meanings by observers as well as participants, according to what it seems not be as well as what it seeks to be. For the most part we rely for our understanding of what it is about on its actual pre-occupations and its works as they are presented from time to time. The forms of presentation are diverse, but not least important have been a succession of readers and anthologies, with which it has generally been well served. There has been a succession of authoritative and stimulating collections, testifying to the fertility of the soil although without providing the equivalent of a handbook of agriculture. In some respects, this reflects an intrinsic characteristic of the field - that it should not seek to construct any new paradigm to replace the dominant paradigm that it sought to dismantle. In this it is republican in spirit rather than monarchist, even if it is not completely egalitarian and celebrates its own saints and heroes. Underlying the reluctance to claim any exclusive identity is a fairly central guiding principle, one that elevates the media as they are performed, experienced and understood over other considerations. Everything that bears on the nature of this central focus is in a state of flux, depending on historical and cultural context and on the uncertain incidence of events.

The present volume is a worthy addition to this tradition of representing ongoing work and thinking in media studies, one which takes us across the boundary of a century against a background of changing culture and changing media. It brings the reader up to date with current lines of theory and new directions in research and it has been carefully structured to focus on the central issues in the field, following a common format of explication and illustration, reflecting a distinct editorial perspective. It has a mixture of elements, combining illustrative analyses of things observed with methodological and theoretical discussion. As such it provides an interesting object of contemplation for those who would like to have at least a provisional map of the field and a guide to its flora and fauna. It has always been possible to do this with the literature appearing as media studies, but arguably by now a stage of maturity has been reached that gives this more point. The aim of the following remarks is to offer one view of the nature of the field, not quite from the outside, but without claiming the specific identity of a practitioner.

One might begin with the paradigm of inquiry that has been for the most part rejected – what media studies is not or would prefer not to be. It is arguable that the field has arrived at a point comparable that where the study of 'mass media' once began in the early decades of the last century. At that time the unplanned cultural and social influence of a range of popular forms of communication, in print, film, sound and graphic images drew the attention of a highly disparate set of observers, with backgrounds in anthropology, sociology, education, journalism, politics, the arts. There was no dominant discipline and no dominant paradigm to give a home or guidance to the individuals so moved, although there was a shared fascination with novel features of the phenomena. These features included especially their immense popularity (at a time when the masses were feared and democracy viewed ambivalently) and their dissonant relation to established systems of aesthetic and moral judgement and to the social regulation of such activities. These two basic features were potentially related, since by the reigning standards of arts and morals, it has often seemed difficult to make sense of the overwhelming appeal of the popular arts without invoking some form of personal or social pathology. Many observers were led either towards identifying deficits of personality or environment in the 'fans' of 'mass culture' (itself by definition defective) or some problematic condition of society that provided a fertile ground for cultural weeds. In reaction, others were led to defend the mass of the people from the disdain of the high-minded and even to find cultural merit and personal rewards for the hard pressed populace, or excuses in social conditions that could always be remedied.

These very mixed responses crystallised, under a variety of influences that reflected the nature of industrial mass societies and the state of the human sciences at the time, into a search for the *effects* (as distinct from the causes) of typical features of mass media and mass culture. For the most part this search tended to focus on potentially harmful effects on individuals, in keeping with the general supposition that mass culture belonged to the unregulated and disorderly sphere of social life and with the utilitarian principle (and fact of life) that any organized inquiry required justification in terms of some social problem that might be alleviated by the findings. If not in search of solutions to problems (or explanations of failure and breakdown), research was directed at instrumental purposes of persuasion, marketing, propaganda and beneficial (for the source at least) public information. There was little space in the spectrum for inquiry that was not governed by such criteria of relevance, seeking to describe and understand the new cultural landscape, with an open mind as to explanation and valuation.

This situation was accentuated and perpetuated by the prevailing conditions of academic inquiry, with a clear split between the scientistic and applied model of research and the descriptive, speculative and analytic modes of inquiry embraced by the institutional world of humanities and the arts that retained traditional criteria, having weathered the storms of modernism. It took the emergence of critical theory and the birth, or rebirth, of an appreciation of popular culture (there was more to appreciate in all senses) well after mid-century to shift the balance against the older established order shaping research into media. In any case, these few remarks serve to explain what was deficient in the older paradigm, quite apart from its very dominance, which encouraged both arrogance and selective ignorance. The rejected elements of the old paradigm were its over-emphasis on a search for effects (largely chimerical in any case), its instrumentalism and scientism, and (often) behaviourism), its superficiality in respect of what should be the main element in media study (the media themselves in all their aspects). Apropos of the search for 'effects', it can be added that this was based on a misconceived notion of communicative 'power' as something within the control of sources and actualised in 'messages', rather than the outcome of a mutual relationship between all those involved and largely outside planned direction as well as being unpredictable in outcome.

There is no longer much debate about the relative merits of an old or a new paradigm (it is not be found in this book), both having largely gone their separate ways or been hybridised, but there is no harm in recalling that there still could be one. Some of the 'key issues and debates' that are dealt with in the following chapters do inevitably reflect some of the perennial arguments of the founding period between various factions in social sciences and humanities, although there is now less debate within the field. One internal matter of debate that does raise its head concerns differences between culturalist and political economic approaches, although in this instance, it is a matter of a continued tension between the two intellectual movements that gave rise to the field in the first place, one stemming from critical theory, the other from a wish to explore specific aesthetic and cultural performance and experience in new ways.

If the once dominant paradigm was rejected as unsatisfactory, what essentially has media studies come to offer in its place or as an alternative? Here subjective perception and interpretation have to serve in place of any to give an objective account. At the centre of the newly opened field is the 'work of art' (artefact), text, or cultural product, whether film, song, television drama or other genre, selected for attention primarily on grounds of the quality of 'popularity', in turn indicated either by size, range, generality or longevity of appeal or by intensity of attraction to a relatively small group. There are no firm criteria for distinguishing or ranking such potentially deserving objects of attention although, in effect, any aspect of media output can be involved if it raises (or answers) questions of interest or opens doors for wider exploration. An object of inquiry can be considered under several perspectives, the most important dimensions being threefold: the manner of its *construction*; the 'performance' involved; and its reception. These are usually all related or relatable but each can lead independently in different directions. The first dimension of the essential text as constructed in the work or symbolic form leads into considerations of; language signification; the representation of 'reality'; questions of genre; possibly also issues of aesthetics and ethics. Taken further, the trail takes us towards systems and organization of production, publicity and marketing, including matters of finance, politics and industry structure. Somewhere along the way, at different points, there are by-ways into matters of technology and media theory.

The dimension of 'performance' refers potentially to any aspect of the enactment of the work as selected, but most generally to the relationship that develops between a person or persons at source and an actual or envisaged audience, a relationship that extends over space and time, although most salient and intense at a moment of contact. The perspective of author, performer, actor, musician, designer, etc. is what is primarily at issue, both in respect of intention and intended meaning and effect, but also related to the role being enacted, with varying degrees of self-consciousness. The self-chosen persona or self-image of the creator/actor as well as the adopted or allocated role provides a path in a given instance that also leads to questions of the social context and oganization of production, linking up with issues raised by the chosen form and content. These remarks are not intended to imply any particular distinction between types of cultural production, although they have to be made at some point. In particular, the general question of performance arises more or less equally in relation to information, entertainment, religion or artistic expression, even though the 'performance' at issue is extremely various. This gives to media studies a more or less unlimited field of potential inquiry and potentially some escape from traditional categorizations and valuations that might close questions before they can be answered. Even so, this aspect of media studies probably gives more difficulty than others just because it transgresses a number of familiar assumptions, not least about what counts as 'media'.

The third dimension noted above, that of reception, deals also with relationships and meanings, especially the relationship between work and performer on the one hand and 'receiver', as defined by various categories, on the other. Most commonly the latter involves a distinction between individual persons, groups identified in some way that matters to members (whether as part of their identity and what they bring to a communication experience, or as a group of fans, with otherwise disparate or irrelevant characteristics) and media audiences that are perceived and identified as 'targets', 'markets', or a set of spectators that happens to assemble (or be encountered or engineered).

Reception is itself a broad notion encompassing elements of 'performance' on the part of receivers, with a variety of possible roles, depending on genre and circumstance and many different routines and acts that make up the business of what would be called 'media use' or 'behaviour' within the other paradigm. The question of 'meaning' is central to reception, partly because it is the nearest that media studies usually comes to the issue of 'effects' (leaving aside the fact that reception itself is the main effect). Even the traditional notion of media effects pays attention to the question of how content is 'made sense of', although usually with some preconception of what that sense actually is, derived from other sources. Cultural content and performance are not considered to be without effects, but these depend not only on the determination of the 'objective' observer, but on the understanding and also purpose on the part of a 'receiver'.

The relationship element in reception embraces the issue of involvement with the source and performer, questions of reciprocity and response and relationships within an 'audience', according to distinctions briefly indicated. The process of reception is not primarily a matter of momentary choice by, or of 'impact' on, individuals, but a broader notion that takes account of subsequent reflection, conversation and interactions with other 'receivers'. This also takes inquiry along other pathways, since the potential relationships and the way they are engaged in is often secondary to established social and group circumstances and background. What is referred to above as an 'object of inquiry' in media studies, is not reducible to objects or behaviours. More relevant are larger cultural and social entitities.

Much more detail and qualification could be added to this avowedly media-centric view of the field and in this compressed form it may seem more a caricature than a true representation. But it should still contain enough truth to help clarify the differences between media studies and its once dominating 'parent' (without meaning to exclude other views of that relationship). It remains to address a number of other issues arising from a perusal of the contents of this volume, with their indications of the current state and direction of the field. It should be evident why media studies does not really need to claim a specific disciplinary identity of the kind imposed by once modern systems of the academy. Even the term 'interdisciplinary' can be misleading, since this takes at face value older divisions, including their sometimes exclusive and limiting claims. Even so, the above account makes clear that almost all questions raised in the field can well lead into territory that is claimed by specific older branches of study. The field of study is so complex that it would be foolish not to benefit from the potential and perspectives of other existing frameworks of knowledge and inquiry. There is no reason to waste much time on boundary disputes and none is wasted in the collection that follows.

The matter of methods and methodology has not been referred to, although it is clear from the nature of the questions as framed above that there is an emphasis on the depth and detail of information required, requiring the application and, even more, the further development of what are called 'qualitative' methods. These have to be able to uncover meanings and patterns in diverse and interrelated types of 'information', itself a quite inadequate term in this context. The primacy of various types of 'discourse analysis' and of equally diverse kinds of 'ethnography' is very evident in work done. There is little place for quantification as a central methodological principle, as in traditional social sciences, since counting is an extremely imprecise way of recording 'quality'.

The variety, range and scale of the potential subject matter of media studies is huge and untameable by reduction to numbers. On some matters the need to generalize at some points has to be faced, if only to fulfil the performance expected of the graduates of 'media studies'.

This exploratory excursion into somewhat difficult territory, guided by the contents of this book as a reminder of the many fruits of media studies, has returned with a result that may be unnecessary or unwanted, in the shape of a rough sketch map and the conclusion that there is a not so unfamiliar landscape out there. In passing, it is worth noting that the sketch that has been essayed here should not be visualized in terms of straight lines, arrows and points, with a hierarchy of features indicating or derived from a definite structure. Instead, we should picture a very complex, indeterminate and organically changing ecology of elements. There are links of causation and logical principles, but a great deal is circumstantial, unpredictable and constantly being invented, changed or reversed. Because of this and the very scope of the potential terrain, there are many uncertainties, especially about the choice and formulation of objects of study as well as about how best to study them. Progress in these matters does not depend on having some overall plan, and there is no expectation of achieving certain knowledge or completion in any sense. Even so, as with all academic fields (and more so than most), it is not easy to keep pace with change and media studies has vulnerable areas for this and other reasons. Amongst these, my own candidates would relate to three areas of particular uncertainty and challenge (by no means all neglected in this volume), namely questions to do with: issues of media essentialism; technology in many respects; citizenship and democratic politics; the boundaries, or lack of them, between the study of what can be conceived primarily as 'communication' and the related territories and matters where communication does not seem central, for instance the areas of sport, leisure, travel and material consumption. On final reflection, it has to be said that this personal view does reflect an unintentional bias towards communication as a central focus or process and perhaps a flawed or potentially misleading guide.

Denis McQuail
University of Amsterdam

Acknowledgements

The editor would like to thank Julia Hall, Gurdeep Mattu and Ian Antcliff at Sage (London); Brian Keary, Amanda Haynes, Michael Breen and Anne McCarthy, John Logan, Carmen Kuhling, Ellie Byrne and Paula Dundon at University of Limerick; Ger Fitzgerald, Sarah Moore, Niall McGowan, Leo Halpin, Michael O'Flynn and Sandra Loftus for their friendship. Special thanks to Liz, Joe and Gavin for being very good.

Introduction

Eoin Devereux

A note to the student

Welcome to *Media Studies: Key Issues and Debates*. Your textbook brings together the expertise of both firmly-established and newly-emerging scholars who have interesting and insightful things to say about the contemporary mass media. Taken collectively, the contributors to this textbook have a vast amount of experience as teachers, researchers and practitioners in the field of media analysis and production. Working in diverse geographical locations, their contributions make use of illustrative materials from both 'old' and 'new' media that are timely, up-to-date and relevant. The iPod, *The Sopranos*, *Big Brother*, blogging and 'Street Newspapers' are just some of the better-known examples discussed. The illustrative materials in this textbook draw upon a mixture of well-known globalized media texts as well as ones which are specific to particular localities.

Coming from a variety of academic disciplines and approaches (cultural studies, communications studies, sociology, social psychology, political economy, Marxist, feminist and post-structuralist, to name just a few) the contributors to *Media Studies: Key Issues and Debates* make use of a wide range of theoretical and methodological tools, yet they all share a commitment towards ensuring a critical understanding of the mass media in a social context. Media globalization and technological changes are actively creating an even more complex media landscape which serves to underline many of the long-standing issues and debates within media analysis, as well as creating new kinds of questions particularly about audience agency and, indeed, whether the notion of 'mass' media is in itself becoming redundant.

In bringing this group of scholars together my instructions to them were simple yet challenging. I asked each contributor or team of contributors to write a student-friendly and accessible chapter on their particular area of expertise. I also requested that each chapter would begin with a clear definition or definitions of its key concepts; it should provide the student reader with a comprehensive overview of the current state of play in the field; use interesting and geographically diverse examples from a variety of media settings; and provide clear guidance in terms of future study and research. It is my firm hope that you will apply many of the insights contained in this book to your own everyday experiences of the mass media and that this will result in a deeper and more critical understanding of the media-saturated environment in which most of us now live our lives. Furthermore, it is hoped that this textbook will be a starting point for you in terms of going further with your own studies and analysis of the media either at post-graduate level or in your professional lives.

A basic pedagogic principle underlies the organization of *Media Studies: Key Issues and Debates*. It is one of learning by *reading, thinking* and *doing*. This involves:

1. Reading about a particular issue.
2. Thinking carefully about the possible theoretical and methodological options we may have at our disposal if we wish to push the boundaries in terms of how a particular media phenomenon is best understood.
3. Developing the confidence to apply the theoretical concepts and methodological approaches discussed in this textbook in order to understand more about media organizations, media producers, media content and media audiences.

With this in mind, each of the book's 16 chapters contains the following:

- A definition or definitions of the key concept(s) being examined.
- A discussion providing you with a comprehensive overview of the key debates, which are currently taking place amongst researchers.
- Boxes and tables containing up-to-date illustrative materials and data.
- Detailed case studies.
- Useful chapter summaries.
- A 'Going Further' section at the end of each chapter in which the authors provide you with an annotated reading list for further research and study.
- Student activities which ask you to apply the chapter's concept(s) to a range of media. The student activities include model essay or exam questions and short projects which allow you and your fellow students to put theory into practice by applying specific concepts to an array of media content, media technologies or media contexts.

A number of the chapters contain actual detailed examples of how researchers engage in textual, discursive or ideological analyses of specific media texts.

These step-by-step examples of content analysis will prove invaluable to the student reader who is keen to engage in his or her own analysis of a media text.

Organization of the textbook

In some respects, compiling a media studies textbook is not too far removed from the processes involved in the production of other forms of media content, for example, a radio/television news programme or a magazine or newspaper. All of these activities involve the active selection (and de-selection) of content in order to fit within the particular theme or focus that a producer or editor has in mind. Your textbook is no exception. The commissioning and selection of the chapters for *Media Studies: Key Issues and Debates* was shaped by two related sets of concerns. First, I was interested in including contributions that had a focus on investigating the media in a *social context*. Second, I commissioned chapters, which took account of the tripartite model of media analysis focusing on the *production, content* and *reception* of media texts (See Devereux, 2003 for an elaboration). This holistic approach to media analysis recognizes the importance of examining media texts in terms of their initial production context, their content and their reception by audience members. The production, content and reception model asks us to place the initial creation or production of a media text, the contents of the text and its reception by audience members on an equal footing. All three approaches are complimentary and, taken together, they offer us the best chance to understand the mass media more critically.

The sequence of chapters in this textbook follows the production, content and reception model, as do many of the book's individual contributions. A further unifying theme of all 16 contributions to this textbook is the recognition that the social world continues to be a divided and unequal world. Inequalities in terms of class, disability, ethnicity/race, gender, region and sexuality are all of significance in terms of shaping access to, and the experiences of, the mass media. The mass media are inextricably bound in the perpetuation of unequal relationships of power. All is not lost however, as many of the contributions to this textbook demonstrate – there are an increasing number of possibilities open to audience members in terms of exercising their agency and countering dominant discourses or ideologies. While Habermas's public sphere may just be a tantalizing possibility, there is some evidence to suggest that in an age of media globalization and conglomeration more modest public sphericules are emerging.

Key themes

Media Studies: Key Issues and Debates begins with an essay by Natalie Fenton in which she examines the long-standing tensions between critical political economy and cultural studies approaches to media analysis. Recognizing the importance of the production, content and reception model, Fenton demonstrates that there are significant benefits to be gained by combining elements of both approaches. In appreciating the sociological significance of the media we need to examine both the powerful forces, which shape media content, and the hermeneutic or interpretative work engaged in by audience members. The textual turn so much favoured within cultural studies approaches can benefit greatly from questions emanating from the political economy tradition and vice-versa.

The vast power of global media conglomerates is the focus of the following two chapters. David Croteau and William Hoynes adopt a critical political economy perspective in examining the implications of the increased levels of ownership concentration and conglomeration within the global media industry. Michael J. Breen, working from a Marxist perspective, takes this theme further in attempting to decipher the hyperbole surrounding new media and new media technologies. While both chapters point to the possibilities that new media technologies offer *some* audience members to become media producers themselves, these possibilities have to be set against the sheer magnitude of the 'Big 5' multi-media conglomerates and the reality of the global digital divide which still persists (see Bagdikian, 2004).

Much student work within the field of media studies begins with the analysis of content. Analyses focused on ideology have fallen out of favour with many, to be replaced with an emphasis on *discourse*. The following three chapters (Chapter 4, 5 and 6) explore a range of methods which are used by media researchers in order to understand more about the intricacies of media content. How we approach the analysis of media content is evidently the site of considerable debate and controversy within the field. Should we examine media content on its own or should such analyses be undertaken in the light of analyses of production and reception?

Phillipa Smith and Allan Bell explain what discourse analysis is all about. They highlight the many pitfalls which are endemic to analyses of content focused on the increasingly popular (but difficult) method of discourse analysis. Using an exemplary case study of print media coverage of whaling in New Zealand, they demonstrate how discourse analysis can be best utilized.

Both Greg Philo and Jenny Kitzinger argue for the continued importance of examining media texts in terms of their production, content and reception. Philo takes issue with discourse analysis in Chapter 5. In writing about the work of the Glasgow University Media Group he restates the importance of recognizing the ideological dimensions of media content. Focusing on the contentious issue of embryo research, Kitzinger discusses the usefulness of frame analysis. Both contributors make a convincing case for an approach to media content that gives equal weighting to the production, content and reception of media texts.

The divided and unequal make-up of the post-modern social world has already been commented upon. Both Amanda Haynes (Chapter 7) and Joke Hermes (Chapter 8) examine the media's role in the perpetuation of unequal relationships of power. In discussing how the mass media represent ethnicity and 'race', Haynes demonstrates how media content assumes 'whiteness' and in many instances still manages to 'other' ethnic minority and majority groups. Haynes points out, however, that there are positive signs in evidence with the growth of media content made by and for ethnic minorities – a theme explored in greater detail in Chapter 16 by Karim Karim on diasporic media audiences. Hermes discusses the representation of gender in both fictional and non-fictional media settings. While changes are evident within some forms of media content, where the complexities of sexuality and gender are acknowledged, a hetero-sexist hegemony is found to still prevail.

John Corner and Pamela Shoemaker and her colleagues revisit two long-standing issues within media analysis; namely questions surrounding power and newsworthiness. Corner, in Chapter 9, examines the changing relationship between media power and political power. He shows how changes have occurred in how politicians use the media to promote themselves. These changes have gone hand-in-hand with new styles of journalistic practice as well as changing expectations amongst citizens. Shoemaker et al. (Chapter 10) discuss the debates surrounding the concept of newsworthiness. Drawing upon a major international study they argue for the continued use of the concept of 'proximity' as well as the need to make use of the concept of 'scope'.

The contributions by Peter Hughes (Chapter 11) and Kim Akass and Janet McCabe (Chapter 12) focus on texts and textual analysis and genre. Using a highly detailed case study of the renowned BBC documentary *Big Al*, Hughes painstakingly demonstrates how a textual analysis of a single media text may be undertaken. Akass and McCabe show how the concept of genre may be used to great benefit in undertaking textual analysis. Using a number of examples from mainstream US (and globalized) fictional television series, they show how an increasingly sophisticated (and fruitful) form of textual analysis has come to the fore. Both textual and genre analysis allow us to examine the complexities and ambiguities of media texts either as a stand-alone method or in conjunction with an analysis of production and/or audience readings.

The final four chapters focus on audiences and reception. All four share a positive view that media audiences are capable of considerable agency. In Chapter 13 Sonia Livingstone examines the interplay between the adoption of new media technologies in the home (and in the bedroom in particular) and the forging of identities in adolescence. Jeroen de Kloet and Liesbet van Zoonen are also concerned with identity politics in Chapter 14. They explore the world of those audience members who are often pathologized within media and popular discourse – the fan. Fandom is shown to have important performative and localizing dimensions.

In the penultimate chapter, Kevin Howley discusses how, in the context of a shrinking (or non-existent) public sphere, some audience members engage in the production of their own media texts for wider circulation amongst marginalized groups. Such media content may challenge the hegemonic order and is a concrete example of audience agency at work. Karim Karim's chapter on diasporic media audiences (Chapter 16) provides further evidence of this kind of activity. Globalization has resulted in the formation of hybrid identities. The technological developments, which underpin media globalization, also mean that migrant or diasporic audiences can participate in alternative media cultures, which are created by, and for, the diaspora themselves.

References

Bagdikian, B. (2004) *The New Media Monopoly*. Boston: Beacon Press.

Devereux, E. (2003) *Understanding The Media*. London: Sage.

Bridging the Mythical Divide: Political Economy and Cultural Studies Approaches to the Analysis of the Media

Natalie Fenton

DEFINITIONS

Critical Political Economy is based upon a concern with the structural inequalities of production and the consequences for representation and access to consumption. By placing issues of economic distribution at its centre, it prioritises the relationship between the economy and forms of democratic politics.

Cultural Studies foregrounds the analysis of popular cultural practices over dominant or elite cultural practices. It emphasizes the social agency of individuals and their capacity to resist social determination and dominant cultural agendas.

Introduction

The process of making sense of the world and taking meaning from the things that surround us is one of the main reasons why people are fascinated with the role of the media in society. This is largely because of the centrality of the symbolic to media content and form – quite literally what do media images mean for the way we interpret and evaluate the world? In other words, how meaning has been thought to be relayed, consensus achieved and change considered possible through the media. How to come to terms with symbolic imaginings and to understand their place in our world draws on a wide range of theory from a range of disciplines that often disagree on the emphasis given in each approach; the balance of power between the producer, the audience and social and economic structures; the centrality of the media to social processes and the appropriate means to carry out research. This chapter considers the way meaning has been theorized in relation to the media in two key approaches that have often been pitched one against the other: political economy and cultural studies.

Political economy and cultural studies are considered to be the two main theoretical approaches in media studies and they have enjoyed a relationship of antagonism on several levels. Put crudely, political economy views the media as promoting the dominant ideology of the ruling classes: in spite of their liberating potential, the media of modern mass communication have contributed to the creation of new levels of social stratification – communication classes which in turn engender new forms of domination. The mass media are an obstacle to liberation and overwhelm all other forms of non-mass media.

A cultural studies approach starts with the basic argument that the mass media gives us citizens of the media: people who are able to manipulate imagery and information for their own ends, to build their own identities and local politics from the vast array of mediated bits and pieces they have at their disposal. Through this, social and political agency occurs offering the possibility of oppositional political projects emerging. Traditionally political economy has tended to read the state and other superstructural forces from the specific configuration of capital at any one time and insists that this is the starting point of social analysis. Cultural studies reminds political economy that the substance of its work, the analysis of communication, is rooted in the needs, goals, conflicts, failures and accomplishments of ordinary people attempting to make sense of their lives. Cultural studies has recognized the energising potential of multifaceted forms of social agency, each of which brings with it dimensions of subjectivity and consciousness that are vital to political praxis. Often this has been displayed through research that focuses on media consumption (see below), but cultural studies conceptions of power have a tendency to be rooted in individual subjectivities, their identities and collective action rather than as political economy would have it, structured in the institutions of society.

Although the two approaches have often been seen as entirely contrasting with irreconcilable differences (see for example, Garnham, 1995; Grossberg, 1995) this chapter argues that in practice such distinctions can be less clear-cut and there is much to be gained from embracing the differences where they do exist and moving towards a dialogic inter-disciplinarity. In sum, I will argue that debates from both camps are required to inform a thorough analysis of the role of the media in society. In other words, structural inequities must be taken on board, along with cultural complexities of consumption, to resist a simplistic retreat to either.

Considering the divide: conflict and continuity

The apparent conflict between political economy and cultural studies has been rehearsed on several occasions. It is depicted variously as the disagreement over how to theorize power and culture: between scholars who hold on to a Marxian premise of labour/class in socio-relational analysis (political economists) and those who reject this approach (culturalists); as a split between studies of production (political economy) and studies of consumption (cultural studies); as the attempt to study the social totality (political economy) and those who renounce the possibility of ever achieving such grandiose aims; and/or as economic reductionism (all social relations boil down to economic determinants) versus cultural specificity. Each criticism masks work in the field that is inclined to acknowledge and appreciate the necessary continuities between the two.

Kellner (1989) states that the Frankfurt School of the 1930s was the first to incorporate both culture and communications in a critical social theory of mass communications. Much like many media studies departments today, by combining political economy of the media, cultural textual analysis, and audience reception studies the Frankfurt school theorists worked through theories of mass production, commodification, standardization and massification. In the work of Adorno and Horkheimer (1979) we see a political economic analysis based on the industrialization of the mass media into a *culture industry*. Other theorists in the Frankfurt School also looked at the audience and a close consideration of how ideology is carried out through the media and other public institutions (see the work of Benjamin, 1973). There was, of course, much disagreement and debate between them but they existed side by side, each enhancing the critique of the other and between them they provided a systematic approach to the media that included political economy and socio-cultural approaches.

Kellner (1989) maintains that the inter-disciplinary approach of the Frankfurt School integrated political economy and cultural studies within the context of capitalist society and the manner in which culture and communications were produced and the roles they played. However, as critical social theory transformed over time into cultural studies, there was a shift away from some of the foundational pretexts of the first generation of scholars of the Frankfurt School. In short, the idea of the 'culture industries' as ideological and manipulative was questioned (Kellner, 1998), and later rejected as the belief in oppositional cultural practices increased. Similarly, class, which has always been at the core of political economy approaches, became less central to critical studies as other cultural signifiers, such as race, gender, nationality and audience identities, were brought to the fore. This development led to a movement away from the audience position as constructed by the text, towards the examination of the pleasures of the actual audiences. It was the political move by feminist media theorists to focus on women's pleasure that first prompted conceptions of the audience as active. Combined with the work of Birmingham's Centre for Contemporary Cultural Studies (CCCS), in particular, that of Stuart Hall, the active audience paradigm came into being.

Stuart Hall's article *Encoding and Decoding in Television Discourse*, which was first presented in the early 1970s, provided the impetus for active audience studies. Hall believed that more attention should be paid to the 'practice of *interpretative* work' in the decoding of televisual signs by audiences and, in particular, how that reception frequently involved the 'active transformation' of meaning. He predicted that such a realisation promised '... a new and exciting phase in so-called audience research, of a quite new kind' (Hall, 1993: 94).

So, as an antidote to a life condemned to ideological slavery came the active audience. Active audience theorists have stressed that audiences are capable of arriving at their own decisions about the meaning of a media text. In other words, meaning does not reside within the text, or at least not exclusively so. Many also stress that texts are 'polysemic', that is, they are capable of more than one interpretation (e.g. Ang, 1985; Radway, 1984). Polysemy refers to the potential for multiple meanings to be taken from one text, thus allowing ambiguity and interpretative freedom. Textual determinism was rejected and ambiguity and interpretative freedom heralded as intrinsic to significatory systems. This marked an unbridgeable divide between political economy and cultural studies that is challenged below.

Political economy

Political economy was developed in the late 1960s through a concern with the increasing role of private businesses in cultural production. Golding and Murdock (2000) made a distinction between traditional political economy and critical political economic approaches to the media by highlighting four key differences:

- Critical political economy sees the economy as interrelated with political, social and cultural life rather than as a separate domain.

- It is historical, paying close attention to long-term changes in the role of the state, corporations and the media in culture.
- Critical political economy is centrally concerned with the balance between private enterprise and public intervention.
- A critical approach goes beyond technical issues of efficiency to engage with the basic moral questions of justice, equity and the moral good.

In their own words, a **critical** political economy:

> ... sets out to show how different ways of financing and organising cultural production have traceable consequences for the range of discourses and representations in the public domain and for audiences access to them. (Golding and Murdock, 1991: 15)

Critical political economy is especially interested in the ways that communicative activity is continuously structured by the unequal distribution of material and symbolic resources. Classically, theorists adopting this approach point to the fact that media production has been increasingly commandeered by large corporations and moulded to their interests and strategies. In recent years we have seen a push towards privatization and the declining vitality of publicly-funded cultural institutions. The expansion and growth of commercialization has inevitably pushed smaller-scale operations out of business or into consolidation with larger companies. Newspapers have merged into each other or into other groups in order to stay alive as they try to survive in an ever more competitive market place. General economic conditions will also influence the product of the media industries. The production output of the mass media is concerned both with commodities and creation, the balance is precarious and framed by the general economic context within which production takes place. In periods of economic stringency the criteria of cost effectiveness are likely to be the deciding factor of output, the result being a systematic rejection of the unpopular and unprofitable and a reversion to tried and tested formulae with a proven market. Critical political economists argue that the nature of the mass media cannot be adequately considered apart from more general economic changes, which in turn require a historical perspective which will locate changes in the mass media within the general context of the processes of industrialization.

Part of the debate within critical political economy focuses on issues of ownership and control of the media. Having power in or control over media is argued to impact upon the capacity to determine or influence the contents of the media products and meaning carried by them. This has grown out of a strictly Marxist perspective which states that the class which has the means of material production at its disposal has control, at the same time, over the means of mental production. The fact that culture is produced and consumed under capitalism is fundamental to understanding inequalities of power, prestige and profit. Early work in the field was concerned to address the extent to which the cultural industries serve the interests of the rich and powerful. Since these early Marxist days, theories have developed so they are no longer structuralist theories of power, which are now thought to be too simplistic in their notions of a direct transmission of the ruling ideology to subordinate groups (as in the likes of Miliband, 1977 and Althusser, 1971). Now the focus is on ideas and concepts which people use to make sense of the world and are to some extent dependent on the media. In other words, the frameworks offered by the media are articulated by the nexus of interests producing them. A critical political economy looks at the intentional action (by owners, editors etc.) and structural constraints (such as resources of time and money), at each level of the production process.

In *Manufacturing Consent*, published in 1994, Herman and Chomsky propose a mass media propaganda model for a modern Western liberal democratic society, in which cultural mechanisms for the maintenance of the status quo are less overt, but not less effective, than in systems such as totalitarian dictatorships.

> The mass media serve as a system for communicating messages and symbols to the general populace. It is their function to amuse, entertain, and inform, and to inculcate individuals with the values, beliefs, and codes of behaviour that will integrate them into the institutional structures of larger society. (Herman and Chomsky, 1994: 1)

Herman and Chomsky's propaganda model is based on media 'filters', through which information must pass before it can reach the public. The first filter, limitation of media ownership, is the result of a process of consolidation that began in the nineteenth century, (Herman and Chomsky, 1994: 2). By 2000, there were ten major players in the global entertainment and media industries: Disney, General Electric, AOL-Time Warner, Sony, News Corporation, Viacom, Vivendi, Bertelsmann, AT&T, and Liberty Media. (McChesney, November 2000) Though not all of these are dedicated media companies, all develop, produce and distribute a plethora of disparate cultural products in many countries through countless corporate entities.

> ...the dominant media firms are quite large businesses; they are controlled by very wealthy people or by managers who are subject to sharp constraints by owners and other market-profit-oriented forces. (Herman and Chomsky, 1994: 12)

In free market societies, cultural products are also likely to pass through the advertising filter, which links the entertainment industry with other sectors. Through their public association with media producers, advertisers gain an interest in the company's content:

> Advertisers will want, more generally, to avoid programs with serious complexities and disturbing controversies that interfere with the 'buying mood'. (Herman and Chomsky, 1994: 17)

This influence commonly functions pre-emptively: the sensibilities of the advertiser are taken into consideration by the media company prior to the screening of contentious material.

Another focal question for the critical political economy of communications that engages with the moral dimension of this approach is to investigate how changes in the array of forces which exercise control over cultural production and distribution limit or liberate the public sphere (Habermas, 1989). The ethical impulse lying behind the creation of the public sphere, of inventing a space where citizens may meet and discuss as equals, is premised on the desire to establish the conditions for living in a truly democratic society. Critical political economy is concerned to explain how the economic dynamics of production structure public discourse by promoting certain cultural forms over others. Theorists in this approach argue that what is happening is a narrowing of the range of discourses which inhibits a full understanding of the complexities and ambiguities of our social conditions. For example, in the UK it is argued that the increasing privatization and commercialization of public space has lead to an abundance of the dominant, cheap transatlantic forms of story-telling which excludes or marginalizes a whole range of discourses.

Hesmondhalgh (2002) emphasizes the important point that not all political economy of the media is the same. Within political economy there are subgenres. Work by Schiller (1989), Herman and Chomsky (1994) and McChesney et al. (1998) catalogues and documents the growth in wealth and power of the cultural industries and their links with political and business allies. Like the early work in the field, these theorists have been criticized for proposing a very simplistic, top down model of power that assumes the lack of sophistication of a conspiracy theory – those who possess power and wealth will seek, by every means possible, to retain and extend it, most often successfully. This is an equally unsophisticated reading of their work but nonetheless a certain strategic tenacity is stressed.

Critics of the McChesney, Schiller, and Herman and Chomsky camp foreground complexity, contestation and ambivalence in terms of explaining the cultural industries. Rather than assuming a straightforward and direct relationship between wealth and power, other factors are considered such as the professional ideology of journalism that establishes the codes and conventions of news-making and allows for contradiction within industrial commercial cultural production. The roles and working conditions of cultural workers are taken into account, as are the processes of consumption beyond a simple product exchange relationship.

A distinct lack of emphasis on investigating the audience or the consumer has been signalled as a lack of concern with, or disbelief in, the agency of the individual. A closer reading of political economy refutes this critique. Free market economics argues that the best way of ensuring adequate distribution and production of commodities is through the market. The more people want, the more they will buy and thus the logic of the market will prevail; the necessary and the strong will survive, the unnecessary will die. This sort of consumer sovereignty approach is present in political economy but the critical political economist is more likely to stress the more sophisticated processes of tracking audience choice and interpretation of taste and trends within markets and how this data then impacts upon the media product.

The work by du Gay et al., (1997) on the development of the Sony Walkman as a cultural product reveals that through the monitoring of consumption and market research, the design of the Walkman was modified from a stereo with two headsets to one with a single headset. This illustrates how production and consumption are indelibly connected. The technology was not simply produced as a finished artefact which then had an impact on consumption – consumer activities were crucial to the introduction, modification and subsequent redevelopment and marketing of the product.

In a critical political economy, audience responses to texts are related to their overall location in the economic system. This approach stresses that nobody has access to a complete range of cultural goods without restriction. Political economy tries to explain these constraints by recourse to material, social and cultural barriers. For example, communications and facilities rarely come for free, their access is dependent upon a person's spending power and disposable income is significantly different between different groups in society. For political economists the shift in the provision and distribution of cultural goods from being public services to private commodities signals a substantial change in the opportunity for different groups in the population to have access to them. As long as access is associated with cost then those who can gain access will be those with the financial capability – income will determine ones ability to function fully in the public sphere.

Cultural differences are also relevant to readings of media texts. The meanings of mediated imagery are tied to a community and its shared experiences and to the actual ability of individuals to actively interpret it. This ability may depend on many things not least educational and cultural capital, national, local and personal socio-economic realities. Work by Fenton et al. (1998) illustrates that social class and educational achievement are critical determinants of audience responses to news texts. In this analysis the reader can effect the reading process, can resist the 'preferred reading' (i.e. that which appears dominant in the text) up to a point and to that end is an active agent. Yet agency is limited by structure. The danger of a political economic approach is that it paints a picture of a culture industry in which monolithic corporations rule supreme, manipulating consumers and infiltrating our consciousness to the extent that they could almost be considered totalitarian in their aims, reach and impact. The corporate machine dominates all discourse. Any competing discourses that challenge the status quo are either appropriated by the corporate machine for commodification or squeezed out of existence. Escape from the prison-house of the ideology of production becomes nigh impossible.

A critical political economy approach to the media has shifted away from the assumption of such a mechanistic economic determinism but continues to stress that power can be challenged and lessened only by political means. They argue that theories which ignore the structure and locus of representational and definitional power and emphasize instead the individual message's transformational capability, present little threat to the maintenance of the established order. Critical political economists are happy to accept that 'the text is different as produced and as read' (Mosco, 1996: 260) but they also maintain that the producers are, on the whole, motivated by profit and audience share and will do whatever they can to increase their capital. So, despite protestations to the contrary, critical political economy does attempt to take account of audience activity but it does so within a broader context of social and economic structures.

Work such as this challenges the idea that culture and the economy are separate discrete spheres operating frequently in a relationship of antagonism. Instead it prefers to stress the blurring or fusing of these boundaries – the mutual constitution of economy and culture. Research in this vein is concerned with the cultural dynamics of capitalism and markets as well as questions of representation, identity and meaning.

Cultural studies

Cultural studies is cross-disciplinary and embraces social theory, cultural analysis and critique in an academic project that draws on the humanities, sociology, social policy, social psychology, politics, anthropology, women's studies and social geography among others. At its core is a concern with a critique of the configuration of culture and society with its sight fixed firmly on social transformation.

> British cultural studies situated culture within a theory of social production and reproduction, specifying the ways that cultural forms served either to further social domination or to enable people to resist and struggle against domination. It analyzed society as a hierarchical and antagonistic set of social relations characterized by the oppression of subordinate class, gender, race, ethnic, and national strata. Employing Gramsci's model of hegemony and counterhegemony, it sought to analyze 'hegemonic', or ruling, social and cultural forces of domination and to seek 'counterhegemonic' forces of resistance and struggle. (Kellner, 1989: 28)

The Birmingham Centre for Contemporary Cultural Studies, now disbanded, was *not* – as many have criticized cultural studies in general as being – ahistorical, particularist, or idealist. Rather its work was more often materialist, analyzing socio-historical conditions and structures of domination and resistance. Kellner (1989) notes that its work could be defined by its attempt to critique the crucial political problems of their age. The early focus on class and ideology derived from their acute sense of the oppressive and systemic effects of class in British society and the struggles of the 1960s against class inequality and oppression. Studies of subcultures in Britain sought out new counter cultures and examples of people acting as agents of social change during a time when it appeared that sectors of the working class were being integrated into the existing system and conservative ideologies. The period of Thatcher's government starting in 1979 and stretching to 1994 raised new issues of conservative populism. The focus on feminism was influenced by the feminist movement, while the turn towards race was motivated by the anti-racist struggles of the day.

In other words, the focus of British cultural studies at any given moment has been determined by the struggles in the contemporary polity. Their studies of ideology, domination and resistance, and the politics of culture, directed cultural studies towards analyzing cultural artifacts, practices, and institutions within existing networks of power and of showing how culture both provided tools and forces of domination and resources for resistance and struggle. This was an important political direction that shifted emphasis from the effects of media texts to audience uses of cultural artifacts. This led to a direct focus on audiences and reception, areas that had been neglected in most previous text-based approaches to media.

Feminist researchers in particular reacted against the simplistic conception of the process of mass communication as one of linear transmission from sender to receiver to claim that female audiences play a productive role in construct-ing textual meanings and pleasures. Women do not simply take in or reject media messages, but use and interpret them according to their own social, cul-tural and individual circumstances – the audience is involved in making sense of the images they see – the message does not have the total monopoly on meaning. Audiences are seen as actively constructing meaning so that texts which appear on the face of it to be reactionary or patriarchal can be subverted. In the case of Ang (1985) the subversion comes through the pleasures that are gained from it. The world of fantasy is the 'place of excess where the unimag-inable can be imagined' (Ang, 1996: 106).

This stimulated further examinations of the role of the active audience in relation to (among others) television programmes (Ang, 1985; Corner et al., 1990), romantic fiction (Radway, 1984) and comics (Barker, 1993). The audience was no longer conceptualized as a collection of passive spectators but as a group of individuals who can see the hidden text of a cultural product for what it is and is not. The corollary of this was that as individuals have the capacity to undermine the intended meaning of texts, they can therefore subvert the rela-tions of power within which they are located (Fenton et al., 1998).

Active audience theorists in media studies have been criticized on several counts, often by political economists, of relativism gone mad – as an interpre-tative free-for-all in which the audience possesses an unlimited potential to read any meaning at will from a given text. Morley (from within the tradition of cul-tural studies) has criticised the neglect in most active audience research of 'the economic, political and ideological forces acting on the construction of texts' (1993: 15). By drawing attention away from the media and texts generally as instruments of power, they have been accused of a lack of appreciation of wider political factors and hence of political quietism (Corner, 1991) and ideological desertion. Ang and Hermes, (again a cultural studies theorist) (1991) object to the growth of active audience studies on broadly similar grounds. For them, the problem is that writers who applaud and revel in the ability of audiences to sub-vert texts, and hence to expropriate power, fail to give due recognition to the immense marginality of that power within a wider context. Therefore, the celebration of the active audience and of its subversive powers inflates the significance of the moment of audience reception.

Despite the misgivings noted above and now recognized by many within cultural studies, the achievements of cultural studies are plenty. They have argued that ordinary, everyday culture needs to be taken seriously and in doing so it has forced us to refine our notion of the problematic term 'culture'. In this process it has challenged essentialist assumptions of culture as a bounded, fixed thing and encouraged a consideration of culture as a complex space where many different influences combine and conflict (Hesmondhalgh, 2002: 39). Through its focus on the concept of culture and how notions of culture are represented in media texts it has emphasized the exclusion and marginalisation of the less powerful in society. It has also forced cultural theorists to acknowledge their role as researcher and the politics of speaking from a particular subject position.

By bringing to the fore issues of subjectivity, identity, discourse and pleasure in relation to culture, it has obliged us to take account of the nature of mediated discourse and recognize the exclusion of some voices to the preference of others. It has made us appreciate the politics of pleasure in the text and how meanings can be delimited and circulate in society.

Holistic approaches to the media

Recently, there have been studies that accept the benefits of each approach and seek to embrace both in an attempt to account for the social totality of production, content and reception of the media. As a result of a growing awareness of the framing power of texts and an understanding that the text must be viewed in relation to hegemonic culture, more circumscribed accounts of audience activity have emerged that seek a re-acknowledgement of the role of texts and production in a political economic context. These studies suggest that differently located audiences may derive particular interpretations of texts, but that the text itself is rarely subverted. In other words, the essential power of authors to frame audience reception is accepted; audiences do engage in interpretation but that interpretation is subject to the denotative structure of the text. In this manner, ideology remains a crucial reference point. Examples of research which reveal this orientation include Kitzinger's (1993) research on AIDS in the media, Corner et al.'s (1990) study of the representation of the nuclear energy industry and Fenton et al.'s (1998) study of the representation of social science in the media. In these analyses the reader can effect the reading process, can resist the 'preferred reading' (i.e. that which appears dominant in the text) up to a point and to that end is an active agent. Yet agency is limited by structure. As Tudor (1995: 104) says, 'the remarkable capacity of human beings to construct diverse meanings and take a variety of pleasures from texts is matched only by the equally remarkable degree to which those meanings and pleasures are common to large numbers of people'.

While we now have a huge amount of research about the audience reception of a host of different types of text, it is difficult to gain an impression of its overall impact and significance. What is really crucial, as Schiller (1989) and Ang and Hermes (1991) suggest, is the overall impact of cultural products. We may find that the conservative underpinnings of a number of episodes of a particular soap opera shown to focus groups is not specifically imbibed by them, but it is the overall interpretative impact of a host of different media and cultural products that is crucial, not any one isolated media or text. Similarly, the themes and issues that are absent in the messages inscribed in texts are as important and potentially more significant than what is actually present. Therefore, inviting audience members to reflect on television programmes or newspaper articles and then deciding whether the inherent texts are polysemic or whether audiences decode in terms of the preferred reading are limited research strategies since the silences in the texts are likely to be marginalized by the researcher's and the audience's emphasis on the text as such and on the use of it by the latter (Fenton et al., 1998).

Box 1.1   The best of both worlds: using an holistic approach

An approach that aimed to take account of both political economic and cultural studies concerns was adopted in *Mediating Social Science* (Fenton et al., 1998). In an attempt to make sense of the nature of communication and social agency, the research made strenuous efforts to adopt a holistic approach to the study of the media. In order not to prioritize one particular phase of communication (and by implication the power of one type of agency), a number of potential definers of meaning including social scientists as sources, journalists, funding bodies, public relations departments and the general public as audience were examined. This research included: analysis of the policy environment

(Continued)

of higher education and the need for social scientists to be seen to be proactive in gaining media coverage; analysis of the journalist–social scientist's relationship including the professional dynamics of the newsroom; analysis of the news texts themselves; and analysis of audience's responses to the news items. Key to the latter was the question of how much freedom and autonomy audiences have to undermine the intended meaning of texts and subvert the relations of power within which they are located. This research suggests that the capacity to establish voices (both by news sources and audiences) in opposition to the status quo is restricted and contingent on many factors. Traditional mass media are unlikely to provide a means by which oppositional voices can be relayed to audiences and enhance critical, rational understanding. The researchers analysed responses to newspaper, television and radio news reports of social scientific research to reveal a marked consistency between intended meaning at the point of production and audience understanding and interpretation of the text. This is not to say that audience members passively deferred to the text – on the contrary, they found substantial evidence of independent thought and scepticism. However, the 'distinctiveness of decoding' occurred when evaluating the text rather than at the point of interpretation. Resistance to the message did not lead to a renegotiation of it. It was interrogated but not expanded. Two reasons are given for this interpretative closure. The first relates to the genre of the text being analysed. Hard news reporting is governed by a range of mechanistic, narrative conventions that are intended to generate a denotative transparency to inhibit potential readings. For example, it is a genre where prominence and frequency of appearance are reliable indications of significance *and* signification. Most news-consumers are conversant with the rules of this presentational game and construct their readings according to them. As such, news is a peculiarly 'closed' form of actuality coverage whose polysemic potential is circumscribed. There is none of the *interpretative* room to manoeuvre that is such an evident and essential facet of other forms of fictional and factual genres. The second reason for this interpretative closure relates to the nature of the subject matter being reported. For example, one of the news reports under study is about a remote and esoteric issue (false memory), which, although its broader implications resonate with the audience, remains beyond their direct personal and professional experiences. This, it is argued, is a situation where we find the most acceptance of media definitions and the power of the audience is at its most limited. It is also the point at which the social structural factors of educational and cultural capital carry the most interpretative significance (Fenton et al., 1998).

Holistic approaches to media research establish that interrogating the role of the media in society does not start or stop with the interpretation of it by audiences or the analysis of it as a text. Although audiences are active, their activity is still subject to a number of structural constraints. The media messages matter because they make some interpretations more likely than others. The cultural capital that audiences bring to media texts are not uniform - different people from different social backgrounds will have different social and interpretative tools at their command. By ordering the distribution of cultural tools as well as cultural products, social structure serves as a constraint on the process of making meaning. Cultural consumption is a social act; it is always affected by the social context and the social relations in which it occurs. In other words, audiences may be active producers of meaning but the process takes place in conditions and from commodities that are not of our making. Once the role of production passes to the consumer, as in much alternative media production, the nature of the beast changes but it is still circumscribed in the social structures from which it emerged. It is not suffice merely to celebrate agency/resistance or to detail the structures of power. We must always attend to the dialectical relationship between agency and structure, cultural production and consumption.

The struggle over meaning takes place between the process of production and the act of reception – both of which are determined by their place in a wider social, political, economic and cultural context. Choices made by the audience must be looked at within the social context of their daily life and the content itself must be interpreted according to the social and political circumstances of its production.

Box 1.2   Understanding *Big Brother*

A good example of the inter-play between structure and agency, as well as being a modern multimedia phenomenon, is the television program *Big Brother*. Devised by Jon De Mol in the Netherlands and launched in 1999, *Big Brother* has become one of the most successful franchises in television history (Hill and Palmer, 2002). *Big Brother* is a combination of various genres, in particular documentary, game show and soap opera, designed to maximize audiences. It is a live game show where contestants, previously unknown to each other, are

(Continued)

put in a house for usually nine weeks under constant televisual surveillance and each week nominate a member of the household for eviction. The nominees for eviction are voted on by the viewing public. The winner is the final remaining housemate who receives a cash prize. The format has been imported into several countries and adapted to suit their own national characteristics.

The game function was enhanced by live feeds and continual access via digital television. In the UK the website's live coverage has itself been re-mediated and broadcast every hour on the 'Global Media Interface' giant screen in London's Leicester Square. In Germany there is a *Big Brother* magazine. The multimedia relay often in real time made it a major talking point. In the UK the press (both tabloid and broadsheet) ran front page headline stories on the various characters involved. The program elicited an enormous amount of comment, discussion and evaluation by almost everyone: in the press, on public transport, on social occasions and in households. Extracting one form of media display for critical attention could not capture the extent of the inter-textual experience that *Big Brother* had become. Scannell (2002: 277) explains that this talk was not accidental but a structural feature of the show's relational totality of involvements.

> ... to consider what it was that elicited such a 'discursive ferment' is to get to the heart of the program's core-structure as an event invented for television. The program invited, indeed demanded, that not only should it be watched on a daily basis but that it should be talked about ...The more you watched the program the more you knew about all the inmates, their personal traits and the way they interacted with each other. Just as in soap opera the more you watched the more expert you became in evaluating character and behaviour as time went by.

This reveals that the text of *Big Brother* is crucial in assessing audiences' relations to it, both in terms of genre and in terms of narrative structure. As Scannell (2002: 273) notes: 'a range of different time spans and horizons were cleverly utilized by the designers of *Big Brother* to build momentum, to create involvement'. Scheduling to fit the context of our own daily lives was also crucial: 'If the pivotal time in the week is Friday evening, as that which is most looked forward to, then using that night as the weekly program-climax meshed perfectly with the time structures of daily life "out there" in the real world' (Scannell, 2002: 273).

Big Brother offered the possibility of participation through voting and interactive websites. It had an ever-expanding frame of reference prompted by its popularity, descriptions of the live exits (when voted-off participants left the house to be welcomed by thousands of cheering and booing fans), the anticipation of audience behaviour (predicting voting strategies) and the developments in the house. This was further augmented by constant references on news programs, chat shows, breakfast television, in the press and on the internet. It offered the possibility of engaging in gossip networks of an extensive nature – allowing the moral evaluations of the character and actions of others. As Hill notes (2002), one of the most compelling reasons for watching *Big Brother* was that everyone else was watching it and talking about it.

Big Brother has also been described as symptomatic of a particular social period that introduces what Corner (2002) has called a 'postdocumentary culture': A period in which audience expectations, social affiliation and modes of cognition and affect combine with the objective factors of a multi-channel and intensively commercialised television industry. The funding of documentary is threatened by the commodity status of all programmes in a television marketplace that is radically changed in terms of production and consumption. This cultural turn has been argued to be part of an evolution to a more voyeuristic, narcissistic and carnivalesque society (Mathijs, 2002) demanding that any future documentary project in television will need to reconfigure itself strategically within the new economic and cultural contexts.

The economic context of *Big Brother* was played out in a global media marketplace. Selling a format that can be locally produced is hugely economically successful – it reduces the costs of production and the risks associated with new programming. *Big Brother*'s global performance points to a strong and often remarkable market share. During the first series in the Netherlands, up to six million viewers tuned in to watch an intimate moment between two contestants. In Germany the first series was so successful that a second was commissioned immediately followed by a third. Other countries followed: Portugal, Spain, Belgium, Switzerland, Sweden, UK, America, Australia, Argentina. All, apart from America and Sweden, achieved a huge increase in market share for their respective television companies. In the UK, Channel 4 had the best Friday night ratings in its history. For the first series 67% of the population watched *Big Brother* at least once. More than seven million viewers telephoned Channel 4's hotline to vote for the winner; the website received three million page impressions each day, which made it Europe's top website during the summer of 2000 (Hill, 2002). Put simply, the *Big Brother* format was eminently marketable, cheap and came with the promise of delivering audiences.

(Continued)

What such an example reveals is that *Big Brother* cannot be understood if we insist on analysing it as a programme on its own. Rather it must be seen as a stage of development in the history of documentary and entertainment; as a televisual event and a website, news source, chat show fodder etc.; as a global product for a mediated world where the driver is profit and market share. We could not hope to understand its place in our world by focusing on either the viewer's enjoyment or the damaging influence of a particular ideology chosen apparently by the producer to be relayed through the text. Both pleasure and ideology are constantly at work when we consume culture and the dilemma of how to understand the tension between them is at the centre of progressive cultural theory. As Corner (2002: 268) says in relation to *Big Brother*:

> In assessing it, we should neither simplify nor forget the relationship between its representational system and its commodity functions. By 'performing the real' with such strategic zeal, framing its participants both as game players and as television 'actors', it has helped mark a shift in the nature of television as a medium for documentation. Perhaps it marks a shift, too, in the nature of that broader sphere, a sphere where vectors both of structure and agency combine to produce experience, that John Hartley (1996) has suggestively dubbed 'popular reality'.

Part of the appeal of Big Brother is in the tension between engaging with the real (this is what people really do when you watch them 24 hours a day) and the televisual (a mediated unreality); the ordinary and the extraordinary. Not content with creating celebrities the format was exploited further with the extension of the brand to Celebrity Big Brother, where all the contestants are minor celebrities. In January 2007 Celebrity Big Brother created a public relations storm by inviting into the house a former Big Brother contestant turned celebrity Jade Goody, a young, white, working class woman. There ensued a clash between Goody and Bollywood actor Shilpa Shetty that resulted in the show being criticised as racist. The broadcasting regulator, Ofcom received 46,700 complaints, the most it has ever received with the majority being sent by email. The event created an international furore that was debated in all the major national news outlets and even discussed in the House of Commons during Prime Minister's Question Time. In the public debacle that followed Carphone Warehouse, one of the programm'es major sponsors, withdrew its £3m sponsorship. To understand the nature, scale and impact of this media event requires an understanding of the race, class and gender politics of the time; the global multi-media reach of the product; the changing nature of national identity; the commercial imperatives that underpin all production as well as the role of new technology and the role of the interactive audience. The Jade Goody/Shilpa Shetty racism row brought into sharp relief the fact that cultural production and cultural consumption are determined by and intricately embedded within social, economic and political contexts.

Conclusion

To talk of one dominant ideology related directly to economic power implies an improbably coherent, controlling, argument-free ruling class that forces the rest of us to go along with its interests. Mass media texts can, however, still be understood in ideological terms, as forms of communication that privilege certain sets of ideas and neglect others. Those who argue that media texts include contradictory messages that at once present the dominant ideology but also undermine it, point to the challenge of newer politics based on gender, ethnicity and sexuality that reveal a society of difference both in terms of identity and interpretation. Cultural studies teaches us that difference is ever present albeit incorporated into mainstream culture in a way that is unchallenging rather than radical. It also teaches us that power is not uniform nor is it uniformly applied and accepted. But while inequality and difference is ever more apparent the concept of ideology still has a central role to play in suggesting connections between media and power. The approach of critical political economists insists that we retain a critical edge in our analytical prevarications and provides us with the means to be politically discriminate.

The struggle over meaning takes place between the process of production and the act of reception – both of which are determined by their place in a wider social, political, economic and cultural context and both of which are subject to constraints. Choices made by the audience must be looked at within the social context of their daily life and the content itself must be interpreted according to the social and political circumstances of its production. To focus largely or exclusively on the structure and content of media messages and attempt to read off the impact of these messages cannot possibly interrogate the consequences of mediated culture (Thompson, 1990). So, rather than just looking at how the mass media may exert an ideological or hegemonic effect on the behaviour and attitudes of individuals, it is crucial to consider the functioning of the mass media within the larger sociological perspective of culture, social structure and social groups. It would be foolish to ignore that we still live in deeply unequal capitalist societies, driven by profit and competition operating on a global scale. It is also undeniable that we live in a media dominated world with many different ideas and identities in circulation at any one time. We need to understand the former to appreciate the latter. It is vital to appreciate the relation between individual autonomy, freedom and rational action on the one hand and the social construction of identity and behaviour on the other. There may be a struggle between competing discourses but it is far from being a free-for-all. To understand the role of the mass media in society we need to consider it in its social entirety – however difficult that may seem.

Summary

- Political economy and cultural studies approaches to the media have historically been seen as divergent and antagonistic in the ways in which power and culture is theorized and the appropriate means of researching media, communication and culture.
- Critical political economy seeks to reveal how forms of financing and organizing cultural production has consequences for public discourses and representations and the public's access to them within a broad context of social and economic structures. It begins from the standpoint that we live in deeply unequal capitalist societies, driven by profit and competition operating on a global scale. It tries to show how this impacts upon the constitution of the public imagination.
- Cultural studies puts ordinary, everyday life at the centre of research and foregrounds issues of subjectivity, identity, discourse and pleasure in relation to culture. While acknowledging the broader structural concerns of political economists, cultural studies also points out the many different ideas and identities in circulation at any one time that offer the potential for social and political agency.
- Many studies have recognized that keeping political economy and cultural studies in distinct camps fails to take account of the complexity of communication and culture. By attempting to combine the socio-economic and political concerns of political economy (the macro-context), with the agency and subjectivity of cultural studies (the micro-context), researchers are beginning to address issues of media, culture and society in their social entirety.

GOING FURTHER

On the Frankfurt School:

Adorno, T. and Horkheimer, M. (1973) 'The Culture Industry: Enlightenment as Mass Deception' in *Dialectic of Enlightenment*. London: Verso.

Benjamin, W. (1973) 'The Work of Art in the Age of Mechanical Reproduction' in *Illuminations*, London: Fontana.

On political economic approaches to media and communications:

Golding, P. and Murdock, G., (1991) 'Culture, Communications and Political Economy' in J. Curran and M. Gurevitch (eds) *Mass Media and Society*. London: Edward Arnold.

Mosco, V. (1995) *The Political Economy of Communication*. London: Sage.

Schiller, H. (1989) *Culture Inc.* New York: Oxford University Press.

On cultural studies approaches to media and communications:

Hall, S. (1980) 'Cultural Studies: two paradigms' in P. Scannell (ed.) *Media, Culture and Society*. London: Academic Press.

McGuigan, J. (1992) 'Populism and Ordinary Culture' in *Cultural Populism*. London: Routledge. pp. 13-44.

Williams, R. (1965) 'The Analysis of Culture' in *The Long Revolution*. Harmondsworth: Penguin. pp. 57-70.

On the conflict between political economy and cultural studies:

Ferguson, M. and Golding, P. (eds) (1997) *Cultural Studies in Question*. London: Sage.

Garnham, N. (1995) 'Political economy and cultural studies: Reconciliation or divorce?' in *Critical Studies in Mass Communication*, 12: 62-71.

Grossberg, L. (1995) 'Cultural studies vs. political economy: Is anyone else bored with this debate?' in *Critical Studies in Mass Communication*, 12: 72-81.

Holistic approaches to the study of media and communications:

Du Gay, P., Hall, S., Janes, L., MacKay, H. and Negus, K. (1997) 'The Production of the Sony Walkman' in *Doing Cultural Studies: The Story of the Sony Walkman*. Milton Keynes: The Open University Press.

Fenton, N., Bryman, A. and Deacon, D. with Birmingham, P. (1998) *Mediating Social Science*. London: Sage.

STUDENT ACTIVITIES 1:1

1   Go back to the work of the Frankfurt School and focus on the critique of the culture industry proposed in the writings of Adorno and Horkheimer.

Consider the questions:

- What aspects of Adorno and Horkheimer's argument in 'Enlightenment as Mass Deception' could be characterized a political economic analysis and why?
- Are Adorno and Horkheimer's arguments useful when analyzing cultural production today?

2. In political economy having power in or control over the media implies the capacity to determine or influence the contents of media products and meanings carried by them.

   Consider the questions:

   - What are the key concepts from the tradition of 'critical political economy' of the mass media? How have these been used as a means of understanding cultural production and media organizations?
   - Why do political economists continue to stress questions of ownership? Is there a link between the ownership of the mass media and the dissemination of messages?
   - What is meant by commodification? How does the process of commodification impact upon cultural producers and their audiences? Is it possible to resist commodification?

3. In cultural studies, being a consumer infers social agency, having the capacity to resist dominant social relations and ultimately change them.

   Consider the questions:

   - What is the relationship of culture to the economy in the suggested further readings for cultural studies above?
   - How is the audience conceived?
   - Where does power reside?

4. The conflict between political economy and cultural studies is longstanding and well documented but may finally be wearing thin.

   Consider the questions:

   - What are the main points of contention between the two approaches?
   - Have there ever been attempts to overcome this theoretical divide?
   - What are the potential difficulties in combining the best of both theories?

5. This chapter argues that understanding mediation and communication requires a radically contextualized and dialogic inter-disciplinary approach.

Task: Consider the iPod as a cultural product. Try to do a political economic analysis of the iPod. Think about who produces it, how it is produced, who buys it, what legislation is relevant to it, the technological infrastructure it is part of. Now try to do a cultural studies analysis. Think about who uses it and for what purposes, the role it plays in an individual's sense of self and identity formation. Now think about the complex of power relations involved in producing, buying and using something like an iPod. Where does power reside?

References

Adorno, T. and Horkheimer, M. (1979) *Dialectic of Enlightenment* translated by J. Cummings. London: Verso Editions.

Althusser, L. (1971) 'Ideology and the State' in *Lenin and Philosophy and other Essays*. London: New Left Books. pp. 123–73.

Ang, I. (1985) *Watching Dallas: Soap Opera and the Melodramatic Imagination*. London: Methuen.

Ang, I. (1996) *Living Room Wars: Rethinking Media Audiences for a Post-modern World*. London: Routledge.

Ang, I. and Hermes, J. (1991) 'Gender and/in Media Consumption' in J. Curran and M. Gurevitch (eds) *Mass Media and Society*. (2nd edn.) London: Routledge.

Barker, M. (1993) 'Seeing how far you can see: on being a fan of *2000 AD*', in D. Buckingham (ed.) *Reading Audiences: Young People and the Media*. Manchester: University of Manchester Press.

Benjamin, W. (1973) 'The Work of Art in the Age of Mechanical Reproduction' in *Illuminations*. London: Fontana.

Corner, J. (1991) 'Meaning, Genre, Context: The Problematics of Public Knowledge in the New Audience Studies' in J. Curran and M. Gurevitch (eds) *Mass Media and Society*. London: Edward Arnold.

Corner, J. (2000) 'What Can We Say about Documentary?' *Media, Culture and Society* 22(5): 681–8.

Corner, J. (2002) 'Performing the Real: Documentary Diversions' *Television and New Media*' 3(3): 255–69.

Corner, J., Richardson, K. and Fenton, N. (1990) *Nuclear Reactions: Form and Response in Public Issue Television*. London: John Libbey.

du Gay P., Hall, S., Janes, L., MacKay, H. and Negus, K. (1997) 'The Production of the Sony Walkman' in *Doing Cultural Studies: The Story of the Sony Walkman*. Milton Keynes: The Open University Press.

Fenton, N., Bryman, A. and Deacon, D. with Birmingham, P. (1998) *Mediating Social Science*. London: Sage.

Garnham, N. (1995) 'Political economy and cultural studies: Reconciliation or divorce?' *Critical Studies in Mass Communication* 12: 62–71.

Golding, P. and Murdock, G. (1991) 'Culture, Communications and Political Economy', in J. Curran and M. Gurevitch (eds), *Mass Media and Society*. London: Edward Arnold.

Golding, P. and Murdock, G. (2000) 'Culture, Communications and Political Economy', in J. Curran and M. Gurevitch (eds) *Mass Media and Society*. (3rd edn.) London: Edward Arnold/New York: Oxford University Press. pp. 70–92.

Grossberg, L. (1995). 'Cultural studies vs. political economy: Is anyone else bored with this debate?' *Critical Studies in Mass Communication* 12: 72–81.

Habermas, J. (1989) *The Structural Transformation of the Public Sphere: An Inquiry into a Category of Bourgeois Society*. Cambridge: Polity.

Hall, S. (1974) 'The television discourse: encoding and decoding', *Education and Culture*, 25: 8–14.

Hall, S. (1980) 'Encoding/decoding', in S. Hall, D. Hobson, A. Lowe, and P. Willis (eds), *Culture, Media, Language*. London: Hutchinson.

Hall, S. (1993). 'Encoding, decoding' in S. During (ed.), *The Cultural Studies Reader*. London: Routledge. pp. 90–103.

Hartley, J. (1996) *Popular Reality*. London: Arnold.

Herman, E. and Chomsky, N. (1994) *Manufacturing Consent: the political economy of the mass media*. Vintage: London.

Hesmondhalgh, D. (2002) *The Cultural Industries*. London: Sage.

Hill, A. (2002) 'Big Brother: The Real Audience', *Television and New Media* 3(3): 323–340.

Hill, A. and Palmer, G. (2002) 'Big Brother', *Television and New Media* 3(3): 251–54.

Kellner, D. (1989). *Critical Theory, Marxism and Modernity*. Cambridge: Polity Press.

Kellner, D. (1998). 'Communications vs. cultural studies: Overcoming the divide'. *http://www.uta.edu/huma/illuminations/kell16.htm* Accessed March 2006.

Kitzinger, J. (1993) 'Understanding AIDS: researching audience perceptions of Acquired Immune Deficiency Syndrome' in J. Eldridge (ed.) *Getting the Message: News, Truth and Power*. London: Routledge.

Mathijs, E. (2002) 'Big Brother and Critical Discourse: The Reception of Big Brother Belgium', *Television and New Media* 3(3): 311–22.

McChesney, R. (2000) *Rich Media, Poor Democracy*. New Press: New York.

McChesney, R., Meikdins Wood, E., Bellamy Foster, J. (1998) *Capitalism and the Information Age: the political economy of the global communication revolution*. New York: Monthly Review Press.

Miliband, R. R. (1977) *Marxism and Politics*. Milton Keynes: Open University Press.

Morley, D. (1993) 'Active Audience Theory: Pendulums and Pitfalls', *Journal of Communication* 43: 13–9.

Mosco, V. (1996) *The Political Economy of Communication*. London: Sage.

Mosco, V.and Wasko, J. (eds) (1988) *The Political Economy of Information*. Madison: University of Wisconsin Press.

Murdock, G.and Golding, P. (1981) 'Capitalism, communication and class relations' in S. Cohen and J. Young (eds) *The Manufacture of News*, second edition London: Constable.

Radway, J. (1984) *Reading the Romance: Women, Patriarchy and Popular Literature*. Chapel Hill: University of North Carolina Press.

Scannell, P. (2002) 'Big Brother as Television Event', *Television and New Media* 3(3): 271–82.

Schiller, H. (1989) *Culture Inc*. New York: Oxford University Press.

Thompson, J. (1990) *Ideology and Modern Culture*. Cambridge: Polity.

Tudor, A. (1995) 'Culture, Mass Communication and Social Agency', *Theory, Culture and Society*, 12: 81–107.

Wasko, J. (2001) *Understanding Disney: The Manufacture of Fantasy*. Cambridge: Polity.

The Media Industry: Structure, Strategy and Debates

2

David Croteau and William Hoynes

DEFINITIONS

Conglomeration: The process of corporations purchasing other companies and thus becoming much larger and usually more diverse, often to include both media and non-media firms.

Globalization: The distribution of media products across national boundaries; large media conglomerates now own and distribute media across the globe.

Horizontal integration: An ownership structure in which one conglomerate owns or operates different kinds of media (for example, movie studios, television networks, music labels and radio stations), concentrating ownership *across* the different segments of the media industry.

Vertical integration: An ownership structure in which one conglomerate owns or operates all aspects of production and distribution within a single segment of the media industry; for example, movie studio, talent agency, movie theatres, DVD manufacturing plant and video rental stores.

Introduction

The media industry has undergone significant structural change, growing to become a pervasive and increasingly influential force in society. These structural changes are linked to the strategies pursued by the major media players as they respond to pressures from investors for short-term profits. In turn, these structural changes and industry strategies have raised significant questions and prompted key debates about the role and future of media.

This chapter sketches out some of the ways that the structure of the media industry has changed. We link these changes to the strategies adopted by media conglomerates, and consider some of the debates that have arisen as a result. Our examination of the contemporary media industry draws largely from a political economy approach to the study of media, a theoretical perspective that Natalie Fenton has explored in Chapter 1.

Industry trends

The last quarter century has been marked by dramatic structural changes in the media industry. Some of the most significant include growth and integration, globalization, and concentration of ownership, each of which we take up separately.

Growth and integration

Recent decades have seen expansive media growth. Not only is the number of media outlets available via cable, satellite, and the Internet greater than ever but the media companies themselves have been growing at an unprecedented pace. In large part, this growth has been fueled by mergers. In 1983, for example, the largest media merger to date had been when the Gannett newspaper chain bought Combined Communications Corporation – owner of billboards, newspapers, and broadcast stations – for $340 million (about $677 million in 2006 US dollars). In 2000, AOL acquired Time Warner – a $166 billion deal (about $191 billion in 2006 US dollars), worth over *282 times* as much!

Beyond sheer scale, one of the key differences in today's media companies is the wide variety of media they comprise. Today's media giants are likely to be involved in almost all aspects of the media: publishing, television, film, music, the Internet, and more. A conglomerate by definition consists of many diverse companies. A media corporation that is *horizontally integrated* owns many different types of media products, such as broadcast and cable television, film, radio, and the Internet – all different types of media.

Technological change has facilitated the involvement of media corporations in many different media. It used to be that each medium was a distinct entity;

all that has changed with the coming of the digital age. Digital data – the 1s and 0s that make up binary code – are the backbone of contemporary media products. With the transformation of text, audio, and video into digital data, the technological platforms that underlie different media forms have converged, blurring the lines between once-distinct media.

The convergence of media products has meant that media businesses have also converged. The common digital foundation of contemporary media has made it easier for companies to re-package the same content for different media. For example, it was a relatively small step for newspapers – with content already produced on computers in digital form – to develop online Internet sites that contain uploaded newspaper articles. Thus, newspaper publishers have become Internet companies. In fact, many media have embraced the Internet as a close digital cousin of what they already do. The music industry, to use another example, has responded to the unauthorized sharing and downloading of digital music files (early Napster, Kazaa etc.) by developing its own systems to deliver music via the web to consumers (iTunes, Rhapsody etc.) – for a fee, of course. The television and film industry's response to the sharing of digital files is not as fully developed but will likely follow suit. In 2006, for example, US television networks began offering single program episodes of popular television programs through iTunes for download onto color screen iPods. In addition, film studios are developing a new online distribution system which will permit audiences to purchase and download movie files shortly after theatrical release, although downloaded films can only be played on PCs and do not include all the DVD extras that are available through in-store distribution of films. The adult film industry is one step ahead of Hollywood, and has already developed a full-scale Internet distribution system that allows users to download pornographic films, burn the films onto DVD, and watch the films on a standard DVD player.

While horizontal integration involves owning and offering different types of media products, *vertical integration* involves owning assets involved in the production, distribution, exhibition, and sale of a single type of media product. In the media industry, vertical integration has been more limited than horizontal integration, but it has been playing an increasingly significant role. The supplanting of the advertiser-based 'broadcast model' by fee-based efforts has contributed to increased interest in more vertical integration. In the content versus conduit debate, as one *New York Times* profile put it, 'Now, many big media companies are concluding that it is more powerful to own both' (Schiesel, 2001: C1). Or as media pioneer Ted Turner colourfully explained, 'Today, the only way for media companies to survive is to own everything up and down the media chain ... Big media today wants to own the faucet, pipeline, water, and the reservoir. The rain clouds come next' (Turner, 2004).

Mergers and acquisitions, therefore, are often carried out to bolster a company's holdings in an attempt to become more strongly integrated, either horizontally, vertically, or both. The numerous mergers that have left an industry dominated by large companies have also produced an industry where the major players are highly integrated.

Globalization

Growth in the size and integration of companies has been accompanied by another development: the globalization of media conglomerates. More and more, major media players are targeting the global marketplace to sell their products.

There are three basic reasons for this strategy. First, domestic markets are saturated with media products, so many media companies see international markets as the key to future growth. Media corporations want to be well positioned to tap these developing markets.

Second, media giants are often in a position to effectively compete with – and even dominate – the local media in other countries. These corporations can draw on their enormous capital resources to produce expensive media products, such as Hollywood blockbuster movies, which are beyond the capability of local media. Media giants can also adapt already successful products for new markets, again reaping the rewards of expanding markets in these areas.

Third, by distributing existing media products to foreign markets, media companies are able to tap a lucrative source of revenue at virtually no additional cost. For example, a movie shown in just one country costs the same to make as a movie distributed globally. Once the tens of millions of dollars involved in producing a major motion picture are spent, successful foreign distribution of the resulting film can spell the difference between profit and loss. *The Island*, a 2004 action movie about cloning, was a bust at the US box office ($35 million), but earned $124 million in foreign box office receipts. Overall, US domestic box office totalled $9 billion in 2005, while movie ticket sales outside the US were $12 billion; Hollywood films accounted for at least 80% of box office outside the US (Booth, 2006: A12). As a result, current decision-making as to whether a script becomes a major film, routinely includes considerations of its potential for success in foreign markets. Action and adventure films translate well, for example, because they have limited dialogue, simple plots, and rely heavily on special effects and action sequences. Sexy stars, explosions and violence travel easily to other cultures. Similarly, animated films and television cartoons can be repackaged in various languages at a relatively low cost, which makes animated content attractive to global media companies seeking a cross-national audience. Comedies, however, are often risky because humour does not always translate well across cultural boundaries.

International revenues are making up an increasingly large percentage of the income of such companies as Viacom, Disney, Time Warner, and News Corp. For example, Viacom's MTV Networks International operates music, lifestyle or gaming channels in Austria, Belgium, France, Germany, Holland, Hungary, Israel, Japan, Poland, Switzerland and the UK, and MTV Networks programming is available in 167 countries. Similarly, Time Warner's Cartoon Network is among the leaders in children's television in the US, as well as in Latin America, Spain, Italy, India and the UK; Time Warner's CNN International continues to increase its global presence, with new CNN programs launched in Latin America and India in 2005. As a result, all major media conglomerates are now global players, representing a major shift in industry structure.

Ownership concentration

While individual media companies grow, integrate, and pursue global strategies, ownership in the media industry as a whole becomes more concentrated in the hands of these new media giants. The concentration of media ownership is a phenomenon that applies to the industry as a whole, rather than to a single media conglomerate. The fact that media conglomerates are getting larger does not necessarily mean that ownership is becoming more concentrated. Growth in media companies may just be a sign that the industry as a whole is expanding – as it certainly has in recent years. The real question is whether the revenues of the industry as a whole are being channelled to just a handful of companies.

Ownership concentration in any industry is often measured by determining the percentage of total revenue in an industry segment going to the top four and the top eight companies. These numbers are referred to as the 'concentration ratio', or 'CR', of an industry. CR4, then, refers to the ratio of revenue going to the top four companies in an industry. CR8 is a calculation of the same ratio for the top eight companies. A common threshold for declaring an industry highly concentrated is if the top four companies control 50% or more of the industry's revenue or if the top eight companies control 75% or more. The limited amount of work that has been done in this area suggests that most of the major media industry segments are highly concentrated, with the exception of newspapers (which fell just short of the 50% threshold) and local television stations (Albarran, 2003; Albarran and Dimmick, 1996). The same held true for the CR8 ratio. It is clear that some forms of media are more concentrated than others and that the level of ownership concentration can change. One of the reasons for variable concentration between media segments is the cost of entry. Publishing a magazine requires considerably less funding than launching a television network, to take just one example. As a result, large, big-budget media such as movies and television tend to be much more concentrated than lower-cost media, such as various forms of publishing and radio.

In the various editions of his book, *The Media Monopoly*, and most recently, *The New Media Monopoly* (2004), Bagdikian has also shown the dramatic increase in the concentration of media ownership. Back in 1983, when the first edition of his book was published, Bagdikian argued that 50 media firms controlled the majority of all media products used by American audiences. Over the years, Bagdikian tracked the remarkable decline in the number of firms controlling the media. By the 2004 edition of his book, he wrote that just five global conglomerates – Time Warner, Disney, News Corp., Viacom and Bertelsmann – 'operating with many of the characteristics of a cartel, own most of the newspapers, magazines, book publishers, motion picture studios, and radio and television stations in the United States media' (2004: 3).

Structure and strategy

Structural change is a means, not an end, for major media firms. Media companies grew, became more integrated, and developed a global presence to more effectively carry out some basic business strategies. While we discuss various strategies individually, it is clear that these are often overlapping approaches that make up an overall integrated business strategy. Major media corporations pursue these strategies to accomplish three general goals. First, media giants seek to maximize profits. This simple truth is the heart of any analysis of business strategy within the media industry. While the strategies discussed here have been popular in recent years, they will continue to be so only if they remain profitable. Structural changes have facilitated the use of new strategies that place a premium on profits. As once-distinct media companies have been transformed into collaborative divisions of single corporate conglomerates, one effect has been increased pressure to improve profitability. What might have been a respectable profit margin in a particular segment of the industry may now be unacceptable when compared against other divisions of the company.

Second, some of the structural changes have enabled companies to reduce costs by improving efficiency and streamlining departments. Efficiency can improve when conglomerates more fully utilize and combine assets into an integrated media strategy. Also, announcements of mergers and acquisitions are often accompanied shortly thereafter by layoffs, as redundant personnel are cut after the consolidation of key functions. Keeping costs low, relative to revenue generated, is a central goal of any for-profit business, including media companies.

Third, conglomeration has enabled companies to pursue various business strategies geared to reducing risk. In seeking to ensure continued profits, companies often try to control the environment in which they operate by reducing uncertainty and minimizing expensive competition. By doing so, they can better ensure lower costs and higher profits. One or more of these three general goals lies behind all of the specific strategies discussed.

Economies of scale: taking advantage of size

The most obvious change in the media industry's structure has been the growth of the major media companies. While there are notorious difficulties involved in managing such vast global enterprises, companies also enjoy some distinct advantages when they grow to be such large media players.

One advantage is that they can afford to develop more expensive projects because they control or have access to enormous amounts of investment capital. By 2003, the *average* cost of a single Hollywood film exceeded $63 million, while the average cost for that year's top seven movies topped $102 million (Germain, 2004). Only a select few companies can afford this sort of risky investment. Other very expensive areas of the media business – such as national television networks – are also accessible only to a few megamedia corporations. That means competition in some very lucrative areas of the media business is limited to only a few corporations that develop huge war chests of resources. Such limited competition helps to ensure the profitability of these ventures, despite their enormous costs.

A second advantage of size is that media giants have the resources to advertise and promote a product with expensive, multifaceted campaigns. For example, the cost of major advertising and promotion often amounts to an additional 50% of a movie's entire production cost. For studios, therefore, it is important to carefully pick and choose the films to receive big-time promotion. Usually, such support goes to films featuring well-known box office stars aimed at teens and young adults – the industry's best customers. Studios launching such expensive projects cannot afford to experiment with risky, unproven efforts. Instead, major Hollywood movies tend to follow a few select formulas with records of past success, such as the action-adventure genre. Coupled with stars that are proven box office draws, such formulaic films are the trademark of a 'Hollywood' production. In the end, studios hope that a big investment, following a proven formula and combined with heavy promotion, will result in substantial profits. This strategy is largely unavailable to smaller competitors.

A similar strategy is also used in other fields. Publishers have increasingly turned to their own version of the blockbuster strategy, increasingly relying on 'big name' authors and books. In recent years, as a direct result of consolidation in the media industry, pressure has increased to make book publishing as profitable as other forms of media. To achieve these profit goals, publishers have focused their resources and attention on a few titles they believe may become bestsellers. A handful of celebrity authors receive huge advances, while lesser-known authors receive minimal pay. Meanwhile, while focusing on these 'big books', some publishers have been known to slash the overall number of books they publish and keep in print, especially reducing the number of 'mid-list' books that can be costly to promote but are not likely to become bestsellers, and 'serious' titles that reach a more limited readership.

A third advantage of size is that companies can develop economies of scale. Traditionally, economies of scale refers to the fact that the cost of producing individual units of a product (books, CDs etc.) declines as the volume of sales goes up. The investment in studio time, for example, remains the same whether a CD sells 3,000 copies or a million copies. Even the per-disk cost of actually manufacturing the CD can go down if larger quantities are produced. The bigger the sales, the less, per unit, the production and manufacturing costs are, because those costs are spread over many more units. This translates into more profit for the media company and is one advantage of the global strategy pursued by the big media firms. For media conglomerates with the capacity to promote heavily, it is more efficient to develop and support major hits with sales in the millions than it is to produce many products with much smaller sales. Products that reach smaller niche audiences are not likely to be as profitable.

A fourth advantage of size is the ability to withstand short-term losses. Despite following previously successful formulas, the reality is that for every blockbuster hit there are dozens of movies – or books or other media products – that make little or no money. Here too, being bigger is an advantage. Only a major conglomerate can afford to absorb the cost of an expensive media flop and still keep on making movies while they wait for the next megahit. Smaller companies, of course, cannot afford such a capital-intensive strategy.

Synergy: exploiting integration

Synergy is the idea that separate entities working together within a conglomerate can achieve results that none could obtain individually. In other words, the whole is greater than the sum of its parts. Maximizing synergy, therefore, is taking advantage of multiple media holdings to develop or promote a single project with many different facets. In this way, media conglomerates seek to maximize the benefits they can obtain from owning many different media firms.

One element of synergy involves developing and packaging a single concept for various media. A children's story, for example, may be packaged as a comic book, movie, soundtrack, television cartoon series, and computer game – each adding to the popularity of the other. By doing this, media conglomerates can take advantage of simultaneous revenue streams, thereby generating as much profit as possible from a single idea. It is now routine for executives from a conglomerate's different divisions to meet specifically to develop ideas that can be used across media. In fact, some companies base executive bonuses in part on how well managers can create ideas that are exploitable in this way (Orwall and Lippman, 1999). The result is that project ideas now often live or die based on how well they can be exploited across media – rather than just how 'good' they are on their own terms.

A second aspect of synergy involves cross-promotion – promoting a single concept via various media. Turning the notion of artistic creativity on its head, companies now often strive to develop an idea that can be successfully marketed, rather then trying to market an interesting idea. For example, after Disney bought the ABC television network, periodically some of the plots for the network's favorite sitcoms involved the characters vacationing at Disney's theme parks. Synergy can be seen most starkly in 'blockbuster' media projects that can quickly seem to saturate society. The popularity for a media product generated by cross-promotion can further be exploited by lucrative licensing deals with other companies. Consequently, conglomerates, with their enormous resources and diverse holdings, have an advantage in developing and promoting projects in ways that smaller competitors simply cannot match.

Of course, synergy does not always work. Some recently merged companies have found it difficult to coordinate efforts across various media – book publishing and movie making, for example – that sometimes have vastly different norms of operation and dramatically different industry cultures. The prominent failure of the AOL–Time Warner merger is one such example. Assumptions about the efficiency of synergistic relationships have also been challenged at times. Most often this has occurred when a division of a huge conglomerate is forced to do business with another of the conglomerate's companies, even though the same work might be more efficiently done by an outside company. Still, despite such setbacks, the profits associated with a successful synergy project are a strong inducement for companies to keep trying.

Segmentation and specialization: the rise of niche media

Most companies that make consumer products operate in a single market: they produce goods that are sold to consumers. Media industries are different because they often operate in a 'dual product market'. That is, they sell two separate products to two completely different sets of consumers. The first market involves the selling of media content (books, videos, CDs etc.) to audiences of readers, viewers and listeners. The second market involves selling the attention of audiences (as measured by ratings, circulation etc.) to advertisers. Because some media depend so heavily on them for survival, advertisers are media's most important customers by far. While consumers and advertisers are two separate markets, they are closely related. TV ratings are directly linked to advertising revenue. Attracting a large audience to a television programme allows the networks to charge more for advertising time on that programme. The bigger ratings numbers translate into more advertising dollars. Some advertisers paid over $2.5 million for a 30-second commercial during the 2006 Super Bowl because, in recent years, more than 130 million people watched at least part of the game.

However, ironically, one of the ways that big media conglomerates can take advantage of their size is by thinking small. That is, rather than simply targeting large audiences, media giants are now more likely to use new technologies to develop niche products aimed at specific market segments. Niche audiences are important to media companies because they can be sold to advertisers at a premium. When advertisers choose where to place their messages, they are usually interested in reaching fairly large audiences. As a result, they pay more for advertising time on a television programme or in a newspaper that has more viewers or readers. But more importantly, advertisers are interested in reaching the 'right' audience – those with sufficient income in the demographic group most likely to purchase the advertisers' products. By using specialized media products to segment the audience into specific demographic groups, media companies can more efficiently meet the needs of advertisers.

Some forms of media, such as magazine publishing, have long had significant niche audiences. However, some forms of media have always been wholly aimed at a single large mainstream audience. Broadcast television, with its limited channels, is a good example of an industry that used to rely on this approach almost exclusively. But the widespread adoption of cable and satellite has significantly changed television marketing. Audiences have slowly migrated to cable, with its cacophony of competing channels with relatively low-cost programming usually aimed at niche audiences. This requires a fundamentally different marketing strategy than the 'old' broadcast networks used in the past.

For media companies, the strategy of focusing on specific niche markets can be financially risky because it places all of a company's eggs in one basket, so to speak. If music videos become less popular, and your company's cable channel plays only music videos, you are in trouble. However, the solution to such dangers comes, again, from conglomeration. Major media companies generally do not own *single* cable channels. Instead, they usually own many different channels, either wholly or partially. That way, the media company can profit from specialized niche marketing via any single channel, as well as simultaneously enjoy the security benefits of diversification because of the overall mix of audiences tuning into its collection of holdings. For decades, this has been the situation in the magazine industry, where major media companies own an array of different titles.

The Internet offers advertisers the promise of being the ultimate medium for audience segmentation. Not only is the Internet highly fragmented with niche specialty interests, but a consumer's moves on the Internet can be electronically tracked via 'cookies' and spyware – placed on a user's computer, allowing a website to identify return visitors and monitor their use of the Internet. Sites that sell items, such as Amazon.com, can track a user's purchases, enabling customized advertising based on an individual user's past purchases to be presented to that user when he or she next visits the site. Buy a couple of mystery novels at such a site and, on a return visit, you are likely to be greeted by suggestions and advertising for more books in this genre. Thus, this technology allows for marketing based not on a person's demographic characteristics, but on their specific interests and past market behaviour. This is the ultimate in niche marketing. While the particulars vary by medium, the basic dynamic in all of these segmentation and specialization efforts is the same: offer a specialized media product to a particular audience segment to generate more interest from advertisers who want to reach this audience. The result has been an explosion in media products – cable channels, magazines, Internet sites – that obscures for consumers the concentration of media ownership. With so many choices available to consumers, it is usually difficult to realize that, more and more, a select few media giants are controlling many of these choices.

Globalization: reaching the global market

As we noted earlier, to varying degrees, all the major media companies have become global media players. This has meant structural transformations in how the corporations are organized. But it has also produced significant changes in the strategies companies employ to achieve maximum profitability and reduce risk.

One basic change is the increasing reliance by media companies on international revenues. In addition to pursuing basic economies of scale via expanded global markets, media giants have also set their sights on international revenues because market expansion is likely to be greatest in developing countries outside of the US and Europe.

Meanwhile, there are portions of the globe where media corporations see much more potential for rapid expansion. For example, News Corporation has probably been the most aggressive in pursuing a global media strategy becoming, in its own words, 'the world's most international media provider' (News Corporation, 2003). Beginning with a base in newspapers in both Australia (where it owns over 100 papers and controls more than two-thirds of all newspaper circulation) and Britain (where it owns the prestigious *Times* and *Sunday Times*, as well as the tabloid *News of the World* and *The Sun*), News Corporation has expanded to all forms of media. Its US holdings include, most notably, the Fox network, more than 30 television stations, Twentieth Century Fox studios, several cable channels (Fox News, FX, Fox Movie Channel, Speed Channel, National Geographic Channel etc.), HarperCollins book publishers (with over 20 imprints), DirecTV satellite television, *TV Guide*, and the *New York Post*, among many others (See Figure 2.1).

Filmed entertainment	20th Century Fox
	20th Century Fox Espanol
	20th Century Fox Home Entertainment
	20th Century Fox International
	20th Century Fox Television
	Blue Sky Studios
	Fox Searchlight Pictures
	Fox Studios Australia
	Fox Studios Baja
	Fox Studios LA
Television	FOX Broadcasting Company
	Fox Sports Australia
	Fox Television Stations
	FOXTEL
	STAR
Cable	Fox Movie Channel
	Fox News Channel
	Fox College Sports
	Fox Sports En Espanol
	Fox Sports Net
	Fox Soccer Channel
	Fox Reality
	FUEL TV
	FX
	National Geographic Channel
	SPEED
	Stats, Inc.
	Sun Sports
Direct broadcast satellite television	BSkyB
	DIRECTV
	FOXTEL
	SKY Italia
Other assets	MySpace.com
	National Rugby League (Australia)
	News Outdoor Group
Magazines and inserts	Big League
	Inside Out
	Donna Hay
	ALPHA
	News American Marketing
	SmartSource
	The Weekly Standard
	Gemstar - TV Guide International, Inc.

Newspapers	Australia & Asia	United Kingdom
	Daily Telegraph	News of the World
	Fiji Times	The Sun
	Gold Coast Bulletin	The Sunday Times
	Herald Sun	The Times
	Post-Courier	Times Literary
	Sunday Herald Sun	Supplement
	Sunday Mail	
	Sunday Tasmanian	
	Sunday Times	
	The Advertiser	United States
	The Australian	New York Post
	The Courier-Mail	
	The Mercury	
	The Sunday Mail	
	The Sunday Telegraph	
	Weekly Times	
Books	Harper Collins Publishers (various imprints)	
	Amistad	
	Avon	
	Ecco	
	Greenwillow Books	
	HarperCollins Publishers Australia	
	HarperCollins Canada	
	HarperCollins Children's	
	HarperCollins UK	
	Harper Perennial	
	HarperTorch	
	Harper Audio	
	Regan Books	
	William Morrow	
	Zondervan	

Figure 2.1 News Corporation Select Holdings, 2006

However, its global media holdings are far more extensive. News Corporation has been especially successful in satellite television services, including full or partial ownership of the British Sky Broadcasting (BSkyB), Sky Italia, Sky Latin America, Australia's FOXTEL, China Networks Systems, and Japan's SkyPerfecTV, among others. News Corporation also owns all or part of 90 different television channels, including Sky TV channels distributed through much of Europe. It has TV and radio stations in the US, Europe, and India;

elsewhere, News Corporation owns publishing companies and other media interests. According to News Corporation's CEO, Rupert Murdoch, the company's satellite systems and television channels reach more than three-quarters of the earth's population (Gapper, 1997).

News Corporation has also cashed in on the global love of sports by owning valuable broadcast rights to sporting events, sports channels, sports venues, and even some professional sports teams. Fox first made a big splash as a competitor to the 'big three' networks in the US by obtaining the rights to broadcast NFL football games. The company went on to own regional sports cable channels in the US (Fox Sports Net), Star Sports (a set of sports channels in Asia), and Fox Sport Noticias in Latin America, among others. News Corporation's ownership of sports franchises has included the preeminent British premiership soccer club, Manchester United, and half of the Australian National Rugby League. In the US, it owned (and later sold) the Los Angeles Dodgers baseball team, has minority ownership in both the New York Knicks NBA basketball team and the New York Rangers NHL hockey team, has an option to purchase 40% of the Los Angeles Kings (NHL) and 10% of the Los Angeles Lakers (NBA), and owns 40% of Los Angeles' Staples Center.

News Corporation has used these vast holdings to develop a global strategy that reproduces a successful media model around the world. Thus, its satellite television services, along with some of the channels distributed over those services, have become staples in Europe, Latin America, Asia and elsewhere. News Corporation has also focused much of its attention on areas of the globe that have been less developed in terms of media infrastructure. It is in Asia and Latin America that the company has staked its ground for long-term growth.

News Corporation represents one of the most developed examples of a global media strategy. However, a business approach without borders is now a common characteristic of the new media giants.

Joint ventures: reducing risk

As mentioned earlier, in pursuing profits, companies try to reduce the amount of risk and uncertainty they face in their business environments. We have already seen various strategies, including diversification, that are used to reduce risk. However, to conduct business, companies depend upon the cooperation of other organizations. So, while media conglomerates are competing in some areas, they have simultaneously developed an extraordinary level of collaboration and cooperation. The resulting set of strategic partnerships is often compared to the *keiretsu* (Auletta, 1997), a Japanese business model characterized by informal, collaborative associations between companies in related fields.

The tangled web of collaborative ventures is constantly changing. It is has been most extensive in movie projects, cable channels, and Internet ventures where the largest of the media companies often cooperate through joint ownership of projects. For example, A&E Television Networks, which operates cable's A&E channel, the Biography Channel, and the History Channel, is a joint venture between network 'competitors' NBC (General Electric) and ABC (Disney), along with the Hearst Corporation. The British version of these channels has an additional partner: News Corporation, the parent company of the FOX network! Such cooperation, which some argue is more like collusion, has become a staple of the industry.

Technology has played a role in the rise of collaborative ventures. As digitization and technological convergence have brought telephone, cable, Internet and software companies into each other's businesses, they often choose to collaborate, rather than compete, on new ventures. Such developments can blur the distinction between media, computer and telecommunications companies. In perhaps the most high profile of these ventures, software giant Microsoft teamed up with media giant NBC to create both a cable channel (MSNBC) and accompanying website (MSNBC.com). But NBC was not alone. All of the television networks, to use one example, have collaborative agreements or joint ventures with Internet companies. Thus, the 'new' media of the Internet have become just as fertile ground for joint ventures as the 'old' media.

Resulting debates

The media industry, then, has been undergoing significant changes as companies have grown, integrated and become global players. In turn, these new media giants have pursued a range of strategies meant to maximize profits for investors. There is broad agreement about these basic trends. However, the significance of these trends is a subject of intense debate. Below we briefly mention four of the key questions raised by these developments.

Is media power too concentrated?

In the growth of media conglomerates, some critics see the concentration of economic, political and cultural power in the hands of a few major corporate players. On the economic front, the growth in media conglomeration and concentration in ownership present potential threats to the basic functioning of the market. In market economies, competition spurs innovation and keeps prices down because consumers have choices and can take their business to a competitor if they find one company is charging too much, not providing the products and services consumers want, or not keeping up with innovations in the field. A media industry with heavy concentration of ownership reduces such competition. For example, the music industry has used limited competition to keep the prices of CDs artificially high. In 1996, the largest music companies, along with major music retailers, were subject to a class action lawsuit on behalf of consumers. The suit charged that the music companies had conspired to keep prices high, despite the fact that technological advances have made CDs cheaper to produce. After a two-year investigation, the US Federal Trade Commission ruled in May 2000 that the five biggest music companies (Time Warner, Sony, Bertelsmann, EMI and Universal) used illegal marketing techniques to artificially inflate prices and prevent retailers from offering discounts.

On the political front, large media conglomerates pose the potential for intervening in the political process of free democracies by using their media holdings to promote political candidates and policies, skewing news and attacking opponents. Critics of media consolidation point to former Italian Prime Minister and media mogul Silvio Berlusconi, whose media empire was instrumental in his rise to political power.

Culturally, large media conglomerates are the 800-pound gorillas that can dramatically influence a society's culture simply by the sheer scale and pervasiveness of their messages. Media have been accused of, among other things, contributing to a culture of violence, exploitative sexuality, bitterly divisive political discourse, sensationalism and the erosion of traditional values.

However, defenders of the media conglomerates counter that such concerns are misplaced and overblown. They point out that the explosion in media technologies and channels in recent years has resulted in more choice than ever for consumers. The concentration of media ownership is the natural byproduct of a maturing industry, as young startups and older, under-performing firms are consolidated into the business plans of mature but innovative companies. The rapid growth in media outlets, the constant shifts in consumer tastes, and the ever-changing terrain of the industry itself makes any apparent domination of the industry by a few companies an illusion. No one can control such a vast and constantly evolving industry. Neither can the industry control the political environment of democratic societies. Indeed, defenders argue, attempts by major media players to influence political dynamics eventually backfire and are simply not good business decisions.

Finally, on the cultural front, defenders of the industry charge critics with elitism, arguing that media content simply reflects the diversity of cultural experiences in society, with media companies responding to consumers rather than imposing preferences on unwilling citizens.

Are global media producing cultural imperialism?

One of the most dramatic and far-reaching debates occurring today involves the perceived impact of global media. With media content such as films, television programmes, and music videos criss-crossing the globe, the debate about the meaning and influence of global media is far from settled.

On one hand, some critics (Artz and Kamalipour, 2003; Herman and McChesney, 1997) note that the term 'global media' is a misnomer, since most media products receiving wide global circulation are produced in wealthy Western countries, especially the US. Instead of a global exchange of images and ideas, these critics point to a dramatically uneven flow, and see the global-ization of media as a form of cultural imperialism, in which Western ideas, values and interests seek to colonize the minds of citizens around the world. In some circles, the Western media are seen as undermining traditional cultures and promoting values and beliefs antithetical to local customs. Perhaps the most visible example of this perspective has come from Islamic fundamentalists who have condemned the role of Western media in their societies. In addition, these critics argue that expensive Western media content has a tendency to undercut local media, further enhancing the power of the major media conglomerates and undermining the potential for the development of successful local media content and companies.

Others, however, contend that the expansion of global media is challenging oppressive regimes and paving the way for free speech and expression. From this perspective, global media are engines of democracy, free markets and con-sumer power. Instead of imposing themselves on naïve audiences, those more sympathetic to global media conglomerates argue that media from the US and Europe are popular around the world because they connect with public tastes and desires across the globe. Enthusiasts for global media also point to new, hybrid media forms that emerge when media cross national and cultural boundaries, as media companies must adapt their products for local tastes and cultures. Supporters also suggest that global media are central players in the building of cross-national, global communities and a growing sense of global citizenship. Furthermore, the export of media may be more complicated, as when immigrants remain in touch with media from their home countries through the Internet and via satellite television channels. Finally, many argue that the spread of lower-cost media technologies is setting the stage for a more balanced flow of media as higher-quality production becomes accessible to more producers from a wider range of nations.

Is for-profit media undermining the quality of news?

With growing competition for advertising dollars and the attention of media audiences, and increasing demand for profits in all of a media conglomerate's different segments, there is considerable debate about the future of news.

The debate revolves primarily around the question of news quality and whether profit-oriented media conglomerates are willing to invest the resources that high-quality journalism requires. Some critics point to cuts in news budgets and, with the growth of news focused on the lives of celebrities and the world of entertainment, the decline in long-form documentary reporting on television in favour of inexpensive talking-heads cable news programme, and the generally weak commitment to investigative reporting, as signs that profit pressures are part of a dynamic that is undermining the quality of news. From this perspective, the growth of global media-entertainment companies not only weakens journalism, but blurs the boundaries between news and entertainment, creating lots of 'infotainment', but little useful news for active citizens.

While profit pressures on the news are widely acknowledged, not everyone agrees about the consequences. Some believe that news is becoming more audience-friendly, with new entertainment-oriented formats serving to attract the attention of a busy public. From this perspective, profit pressures may unsettle traditional forms of news, but will do so in response to public taste, with news reflecting what people want, instead of what elite critics think people need. Instead of news as a resource for citizens, these critics argue that news will be most helpful to people if it responds to consumer demand, just like any other product. Delivery of such a news product is significantly enhanced by niche outlets that can make available highly-relevant customized news for specialized niche audiences.

Conclusion: is the era of mass media over?

Mass media have been built on the model of a few large producers creating content to be consumed by a mass audience. As we have already seen, in recent years, the audience for media has been fragmenting as new technologies have enabled companies to target niche markets. So far, however, a few large producers have continued to dominate the media landscape. The power and influence of these major media conglomerates have been what concern many critics.

However, some industry observers point to two developments to suggest that these gigantic global corporations may soon become media dinosaurs. First, new technologies are enabling more people to become media producers, rather than merely consumers. Lower cost digital equipment is allowing for more easily accessible music recording, movie making, website construction, and much more. This DIY phenomenon is changing the media landscape, with new websites such as YouTube.com providing an online venue for people to upload, share and watch videos from around the globe. Second, the Internet is enabling new ways of distributing these new media products to substantial audiences. This involves the broadband capacities of the Internet and applications, such as BitTorrent, that enable easier downloading and distribution of large video and audio files. It also involves the growth of social networking websites where people can share their many interests, including favourite movies, music and more. Such networking, which has been enormously popular amongst teens and young adults, allows for unprecedented exposure and promotion for independent media products.

The result is an explosion of media content being produced outside of the major media conglomerates. Indie music, independent film and animation, weblogs, podcasts and independent news and commentary sites, are among the many media now being created by individuals who, in the mass media age, would have been solely consumers rather than producers of media. The influence of major media players will not disappear, but they will find themselves playing on a terrain populated by an ever-increasing number of media producers who will chip away at their share of the marketplace, leaving them with significantly less influence than in the past.

But wait, say critics, history has shown that the major media corporations are extremely adaptable and have the ability to absorb new media formats and turn them into profitable ventures under their control. Nearly all of the top Internet websites are operated by the same media conglomerates that dominate other forms of media. The podcast phenomenon began with independent producers but was quickly adopted by major media companies who issued content that became the most popular downloads – a theme further developed by Michael J. Breen in Chapter 3. The idea that small independent producers will be able to compete with the production, advertising and promotion capacities of major media conglomerates is simply naïve and underestimates the flexibility of the major media players. It also ignores the continuing success of many 'big budget' media products – the marketing and promotion of which the major media conglomerates have perfected – which are completely out of the reach of smaller independent media producers.

So have the structural changes that emphasize growth and conglomeration run their course? Will the next half century see the explosion of truly independent media challenging the traditional corporate players? Or will the resources and deep pockets of the major media enable them to retain control of the emerging media world – regardless of the form it takes? Such questions will continue to mark the debates regarding industry structure for some time to come.

Summary

- With continuing growth in cable, satellite and Internet-based content, the volume of available media has increased dramatically in recent years. At the same time, the major media companies have become large and highly diverse media conglomerates.
- The media industry is now a global industry; major media conglomerates emphasize a global marketplace as the arena for promoting and selling media products.
- Major media conglomerates enjoy distinct advantages associated with their large and diverse holdings, including access to capital for expensive productions, resources for multi-media promotion campaigns, and the ability to withstand short-term losses while waiting for the next blockbuster.
- Rather than targeting large 'mass' audiences, media conglomerates use new technologies to develop niche products aimed at specific market segments – offering specialized media products to a particular audience demographic to generate interest from advertisers who want to reach this specific audience segment.
- While media companies compete against each other for audiences and advertisers, they have also developed new forms of cooperation in the form of joint ventures and strategic partnerships aimed at reducing risk for the major media conglomerates.
- Key debates about the consequences of the emerging global media industry focus on the power of major media conglomerates, the influence of Western media that circulate throughout the world, and the impact of profit pressures on the quality of journalism.

GOING FURTHER

Baker, C. E.(2001) *Media, Markets, and Democracy*. New York: Cambridge University Press.
An analysis of the structural limitations of commercial media and the complex relationship between media, regulatory policy and democracy from a leading scholar of media law and policy.

Croteau, D. and Hoynes, W. (2006) *The Business of Media: Corporate Media and the Public Interest.* (2nd edn.) Thousand Oaks, CA: Pine Forge Press.
The authors' overview of trends in the global media business in the early twenty-first century.

Hamilton, J. T. (2003) *All the News That's Fit to Sell.* Princeton, NJ: Princeton University Press.
A leading media economist explores the economics of the news business, analyzing how information is transformed into a familiar news product.

McChesney, R. W. (2004) *The Future of the Media.* New York: Monthly Review Press.
A critical analysis of the crisis of US media and an impassioned call for reform of the media industries.

STUDENT ACTIVITY 2.1

Mapping Media Ownership
Figure 2.1 on pages 44–45 shows a selection of the holdings of one media conglomerate, News Corporation, as of 2006. In this assignment, you will explore two other media corporations, analyze their holdings and comment on what you find.

1. Choose two of the companies listed below to explore.
2. Use a search engine to find the company's main website. Visit the websites of the companies and carefully catalogue both their media and non-media holdings.
3. Make an 'ownership map' – a list of the companies and products owned by the two corporations, grouping the holdings by type of media.
4. Write a brief two to three page combined profile of your companies, drawing upon the key concepts from this chapter: conglomeration, globalization, vertical and horizontal integration, synergy, etc. Don't just repeat what you've catalogued in your 'map'. Many of the corporate websites include a recent company 'Annual Report', which can provide important insight into the company's business strategy and view of their holdings.

5. Finally, comment on what you've found. (Did you recognize some of the media outlets or products owned by your company? Were you surprised by anything you found? Explain.)

Major Media Conglomerates

Bertelsmann	Hearst Corporation
Clear Channel Communications	Sony Corporation
Comcast	Time Warner
The Walt Disney Company	Viacom
General Electric	Vivendi

References

Albarran A. B. (2003) 'US Media Concentration: The Growth of Megamedia' in A. Arrese (ed.) *Empresa Informativa y Mercados de la Communicacion*. Pamplona, Spain: EUNSA. pp. 63–74.

Albarran A. and Dimmick, J. (1996) 'Concentration and Economies of Multiformity in the Communications Industries', *Journal of Media Economics*, 9(4): 41–50.

Artz, L. and Kamalipour, Y. R. (eds) (2003) *The Globalization of Corporate Media Hegemony*. Albany, NY: State University of New York Press.

Auletta, K. (1997) 'American Keiretsu', *New Yorker* (20 October, pp. 225–227).

Bagdikian, B. (2004) *The New Media Monopoly*. Boston: Beacon Press.

Booth, W. (2006) 'Hollywood Caters to a Ravenous Global Appetite', *Washington Post* (27 May, p. A1, A12).

Gapper, J. (1997) 'News Corporation Raises Coverage', *Financial Times,* USA edn. (15 September, p. 23).

Germain, D. (2004) 'Production Costs Surge for Top Hollywood Studio Films', Associated Press. 23 March. Accessed via Lexis-Nexis.

Herman, E. S. and McChesney, R. W. (1997) *The Global Media*. London and Washington: Cassell.

News Corporation (2003) *Annual Report*. On-line: http://www.newscorp.com/Report2003/2003_annual_report.pdf

Orwall, B. and Lippman, J. (1999) 'Return of the Franchise', *Wall Street Journal*. 14 May, pp. B1, B6.

Schiesel, S. (2001) 'Media Giants: Overview: The Corporate Strategy; Where the Message is the Medium', *New York Times*. 2 July, 2001, p. C1. Accessed via Lexis-Nexis.

Turner, T. (2004) 'My Beef with Big Media', *Washington Monthly*. July/August. On-line: www.washingtonmonthly.com/features/2004/0407.turner.html Accessed 14 September, 2004.

Mass Media and New Media Technologies

Michael J. Breen

DEFINITIONS

New media: Recently evolved systems (in the last 10–15 years) for delivery of content to audiences. These media differ radically from traditional media in several respects: entry is cheap, the number of practitioners is limitless, geography is not a barrier, communication is a two-way process, and the audience has high power in terms of how and when content is consumed.

New media technologies: Those technologies which are involved in the creation, delivery and consumption of media content. These apply especially to digital media, such as digital satellite, Internet-linked PCs, MP3 players etc.

Introduction

When does the first fax machine date from? What about the idea of hypertext? Or 'the web'? It often surprises students to learn that Alexander Bain invented a machine capable of transmitting images over a fixed wire in 1843 (Samson, 2005). Bush, in 1945, conceptualized an encyclopaedia based on associations:

> The human mind ... operates by association. With one item in its grasp, it snaps instantly to the next that is suggested by the association of thoughts, in accordance with some intricate web of trails carried by the cells of the brain ... the speed of action, the intricacy of trails, the detail of mental pictures, is awe-inspiring beyond all else in nature. (Bush, 1945: 106)

He then goes on to suggest that a machine, which he called 'the memmex' could be created to utilize some of these ideas for information searching and retrieval from pre-existing databases. While much of Bush's ideas were impractical, the 'web of trails' is a good metaphor for Internet searching today.

Much of the commentary on new technologies is accompanied by hyperbole, not least of all from advertisers who aim to persuade end-users that the latest, must-have product can do what no technology has ever done before. This is, generally speaking, entirely untrue in that new technologies are almost always extensions or developments of existing applications, but which offer new advantages of various kinds. Undoubtedly there have been technological innovations that have revolutionized society, particularly the telephone, but much else of the technological revolution has been a rethinking of what has been thought before.

In this chapter our focus is on the question of technology in relation to mass media. While any worthwhile analysis of media issues must draw on the inseparable triumvirate of producers, content and audience, it is clearly of paramount importance to acknowledge and explore the role of new technologies in the shifting media landscape of the twenty-first century, precisely in terms of impact on that triumvirate. In this chapter, we initially consider the notion of new media and new media technologies, and then examine the impact of these on producers, content and audiences, before finally exploring some of the implications of this debate for the future media landscape.

Box 3.1   Key questions to bear in mind

This chapter has a sociological focus from a Marxist tradition, which examines new media from the point of view of social, economic and political power. In this respect students are encouraged to reflect on some core questions, many of which apply to mainstream media as well:

- What discourses are enabled by the new technologies?
- Whose voices are heard/not heard?
- What ideology dominates?
- Whose interests are served by the rise of the new media?
- Who is truly powerful in this arena?
- Has content changed?
- What is omitted from content?

- Who is excluded, who is absent or not represented within the new media content?
- Who is excluded from accessing such content?
- Is the power of the audience, individually or collectively, enhanced or diminished within these new media?

New media and new media technologies

For the purpose of this chapter, we make a distinction between new media and new media technologies, while accepting that such a distinction often gets blurred. New media are recently evolved media (within the last 10–15 years) for the delivery of content to audiences. Readers should note that this is a hotly contested definition and will find a significant debate across the Internet and in print as to the true definition of the term (see Box 3.2).

Examples of new media are digital satellite radio and television, online newspapers and books, online surveys, podcasts and blogs. Digital satellite radio and television have significant capacities beyond standard terrestrial radio and television. Satellite broadcasters can reach enormous audiences, because satellites have a large footprint (the amount of territory that an individual satellite can reach), as well as being able to carry hundreds of channels, unrestrained by the considerations of the availability of the broadcast spectrum, itself a scarce resource. Equally, satellite broadcasters are not constrained by the local law applying to terrestrial broadcasters, which sometimes leads local legislators to try and control the technology. When the Taliban took power in Afghanistan, it set out to rid Afghanistan of influences it considered contrary to Islam, including television sets, video recorders and satellite dishes (*Associated Press*, 12 July 1997). Satellite television is officially banned in Iran, but thought to be received by four million homes (*BBC News*, 8 May 2006).

New media technologies are advances in technology which have a direct bearing on the generation, location and consumption of mass media content. Examples include personal computers, mobile telephones, digital cameras, personal digital assistants (PDAs), MP3 players, iPods and computer networks, especially the Internet.

These media and the associated technologies are the locus of a great deal of academic research today, with several journals dedicated to the topics, for example, *New Media & Society*, *Convergence*, *Wired* and *Television & New Media*. As Silverstone put it, in the inaugural issue of *New Media & Society*:

> The technologies that have emerged in recent years, principally but not exclusively digital technologies, are new. They do new things. They give us new powers. They create new consequences for us as human beings. They bend minds. They transform institutions. They liberate. They oppress. (Silverstone, 1999: 10)

Five years later, in the fifth anniversary edition of the same journal, Lievrouw wrote:

> The continuities between conventional and new media have become more obvious, in contrast to the novelty, discontinuity, and breaks with the past that preoccupied new media scholars a decade ago. Technological change … (is) … an incremental process today, in which the latest innovations tend to be variations or elaborations of existing systems and infrastructures, rather than radical departures. (Lievrouw, 2004: 11)

Silverstone and Lievrouw are both correct; new media and new media technologies can be both transformative and radical. They are also, however, for the most part, the domain of large commercial interests, although the rise of podcasting and the blogosphere herald new, exciting, non-commercial and sometimes anarchic possibilities in the social use of ICTs. In order to come to a better understanding of these transformative and potentially powerful new media technologies, we turn now to a tripartite examination of producers, content and audiences, before turning to a reflection on the ongoing implications for society.

Box 3.2   New media: the contours of debate

New media is a contentious term as even the most cursory search of the Internet or a journal database will prove. While the term is primarily within sociological, communications or technological studies, it also has application within other disciplines such as art (see, for example, Manovich, 2003). Clearly the term is used by economists, political scientists, sociologists, engineers, as well as artists, musicians and social commentators.

In general, scholars writing on new media, while drawn from a variety of backgrounds, can be grouped in a number of different ways.

One approach is to examine scholarship along a continuum from Utopian to Luddite: Utopian are those scholars who embrace the new technologies as the ultimate salvation of the world. These include pioneers like Negroponte and Dyson.

The Net offers us a chance to take charge of our own lives and to redefine our role as citizens of local communities and of a global society. It also hands us the responsibility to govern ourselves, to think for ourselves, to educate our children, to do business honestly, and to work with fellow citizens to design rules we want to live by. ... I want to take away the mystery and the technical mumbo jumbo, so that you can see the Net for what it is: a place where people meet, talk, do business, find out things, form committees, and pass on rumours. ... Some of the capabilities are different from the so-called real world: Anyone can go online and publish something that can be read anywhere in the world; a child can write to a president; a Hungarian merchant can find a Chinese customer. Above all, the Net is home for people. ... The Net offers us a chance to take charge of our own lives and to redefine our role as citizens of local communities and of a global society. It also hands us the responsibility to govern ourselves, to think for ourselves, to educate our children, to do business honestly, and to work with fellow citizens to design rules we want to live by. (Dyson, 1997: 6)

On the extreme are technological neo-Luddites, who reject new technologies and new media, with expressions of concern about what these are doing to society and its future. These include such people as Joy, co-founder of Sun Microsystems.

We are being propelled into this new century with no plan, no control, no brakes. Have we already gone too far down the path to alter course? I don't believe so, but we aren't trying yet, and the last chance to assert control – the fail-safe point – is rapidly approaching. We have our first pet robots, as well as commercially available genetic engineering techniques,

(Continued)

and our nanoscale techniques are advancing rapidly. While the development of these technologies proceeds through a number of steps, it isn't necessarily the case – as happened in the Manhattan Project and the Trinity test – that the last step in proving a technology is large and hard. The breakthrough to wild self-replication in robotics, genetic engineering, or nanotechnology could come suddenly, reprising the surprise we felt when we learned of the cloning of a mammal. (Joy, 2000)

Most commentators and scholars are more centrist, with a balanced perspective between the advantages of technology and the inevitable social effects that follow from technological development and adaptation, including such scholars as Silverstone and Lievrouw.

A second approach is to evaluate the particular approach and application of the author. A political science approach can differ from that of a technological evaluation. Cohen-Avigdor is a communications scholar who along with Lehman-Wilzig (2004) developed a new approach to the life cycle of new media. Downey and Fenton are also scholars in mass communications who concentrate on the mechanisms by which political groups on the right and left advance their agendas (see Downey and Fenton, 2003). Howard is a political communications theorist who examines how epistemic communities or knowledge networks develop via the use of new media (2002). Kluver is a Singapore-based scholar who studies how citizens inform themselves using new media (2002). Reading is a feminist scholar who studies how the use of new technologies helps people to construct a different relationship to past history (2003). Media sociologists like Gitlin (1998) and Shoemaker take a sociological approach to new media, utilizing a much broader canvas than technologists, for example. Gitlin raises issues around the new media as a public sphere or public sphericules, a reflection of McLuhan's global village as compared to a globe of villages.

Habermas and the public sphere

Habermas conceived the public sphere (1962, 1989) as private individuals coming together as a mass public, participating in a debate about the structure and organization of society and coming to a considered public opinion (as opposed to a public opinion that was the result of economic, political or media manipulation).

'Public opinion' takes on a different meaning depending on whether it is brought into play as a critical authority in connection with the normative mandate that the exercise of political and social power be subject to publicity, or as an object to be moulded in connection with a staged display of, and manipulative propagation of publicity in the service of persons and institutions, consumer goods, and programs. (Habermas, 1989: 236)

In his view the formation of public opinion through open rational discourse is a key element of a participative democracy. This 'public sphere' wherein such a discourse takes place, is utterly dependent upon access, freedom, equality, legality and high quality participation by an engaged citizenry. Habermas suggests that the notion of public opinion has shifted in meaning, due primarily to the role of the mass media.

The concept of the public sphere itself has been challenged by many critics who see the fragmentation of social discourse as militating against any possibility of a single public sphere discourse. Gitlin (1998) and Goode (2005) argue that the utopian ideal of a single public sphere is replaced by a multitude of public sphericules wherein partisan public discourses occur without engagement of alternate viewpoints. These sphericules are encouraged by new technologies like blogs, chat rooms and list-servs such that the new medium of the Internet, far from being a unifying agency, serves to further fragment and divide society into small communities of self-interest.

The literature dealing with new media and new media technologies is vast. The main journals for locating such works from a media-oriented point of view are the *Journal of Communication*, *New Media & Society*, *Media Culture & Society*, the *European Journal of Communication*, *Journalism & Mass Communication Quarterly*, and the *Journal of Broadcasting & Electronic Media*.

Producers

In 1983, the men and women who headed the 50 mass media corporations that dominated American audiences could have fit comfortably in a modest hotel ballroom. The people heading the 20 dominant newspaper chains probably would form one conversational cluster to complain about newsprint prices; 20 magazine moguls in a different circle denounce postal rates; the broadcast network people in another corner, not being in the newspaper or magazine business, exchange indignation about government radio and television regulations; the book people compete in out-rage over greed of writers' agents; and movie people gossip about sexual achieve-ments of their stars. By 2003, five men controlled all these old media once run by the 50 corporations of 20 years earlier. These five, owners of additional digital cor-porations, could fit in a generous phone booth. ... Richard Parsons, chairman and CEO of AOL Time Warner. ... Michael Eisner, chief of Disney, Sumner Redstone, ruler of Viacom, formerly CBS ... News Corp's Rupert Murdoch ... (and) Reinhard Mohn, patriarch of the 168-year-old German firm, Bertelsmann. (Bagdikian, 2004: 27)

The above list constitutes Bagdikian's 'Big Five'. Since the early 1980s, Bagdikian has been documenting the shifting sands of media ownership in the US and has chronicled how more and more media outlets are in the hands of fewer and fewer owners. These are media emperors, and their empire extends far beyond the geographical boundaries of the US. They are also owners and controllers of much more than media outlets. As well as cross-ownership in many industries, they are all major players in new media and new media tech-nologies, with a very substantial Internet presence.

Box 3.3   More definitions

Mass medium: a medium designed to reach a very large audience, for example, newspapers, magazines, radio, television, books, sound recordings and film.

Common carrier: A telecommunications system which provides transmission ser-vices to the general public for a fee, for example, telephone services, Internet.

Internet: A world-wide system of networked computers containing data which is accessible and addressable by the general public.

Portal: An access point to the internet, for example, Google, Yahoo, CNN.

Cyberspace: A term coined by William Gibson (from cybernetics and space) to denote a metaphoric abstraction for the online world of computer networks, especially the Internet.

Blogosphere: The collective social network of all web-based logs (blogs).

Blog: A web-based log, published online, which reflects the opinions of the author, usually on specific topics of interest, and which bypasses the more nor-mal publishing routes (see, for example, www.blogspot.com, www.journals.ie, www.globeoflogs.com or www.britlog.com).

Table 3:1 Top visited sites in the US, UK, Australia and Germany by rank order (compiled from Nielsen data online, 2006)

	US	UK	Australia	Germany
Microsoft	1	1	1	2
Yahoo!	2	3	4	7
Time Warner	3	7	10	6
Google	4	2	2	1
eBay	5	4	5	3
News Corp. Online	6	8	6	
InterActiveCorp	7	9		
Amazon	8	6		9
RealNetworks, Inc.	9	10		
Walt Disney Internet Group	10			
BBC		5		
Telstra			3	
Aus Fed Gov			7	
Fairfax Digital			8	
Apple Computer			9	
United Internet				4
T-Online				5
Bertelsmann				8
OTTO				10

Table 3.1 shows the most visited sites in the US, UK, Australia and Germany. Interactive's Barry Diller was responsible for the creation of the Fox Broadcasting Company. Time Warner have a significant holding of Google's stock and also own AOL. Yahoo, owned by Softbank who have significant cable, satellite and other online interests, is led by Terry Semel, formerly of Warner Bros. Telstra is 25% owned by News Corp. To the extent that these corporations represent a major web presence, they are an indicator that the web is not an independent entity, and that it does in fact represent hegemonic media interests that are already major presences in non-digital traditional media worldwide.

When the original military focus of ARAPNET was lost, with the development of the open network NSFNET in 1990, the Internet as we know it today was born. A loose network of networks, with no individual agency or institution in control, it was seen as an excellent medium for free exchange of information and the expression of opinion. Its lack of organized structure meant that it was seen as having anarchic possibilities, somewhat outside conventional boundaries. In the 17 years since then, it is clear that much of what constitutes the core of Internet presence is, in fact, that of social convention, with the large scale domination of commercial content providers, especially the major media players.

One element of the Internet that retains the original possibilities of the early days is that of the blogosphere. The blogosphere is the collective term given to the entirety of web logs (blogs) that exist in cyberspace on a virtually unlimited selection of topics. The open nature of the Internet makes it a perfect medium for the individual blogger, with its ease of setup and maintenance, as well as ease of frequent access for a potential audience. Blogs are different from websites in two important respects: they do not require the sophisticated kind of tools that website creation requires (and can therefore be placed online immediately by somebody without web-authoring skills) and they universally allow for reader feedback. It is this latter dimension that lies at the core of the blogosphere, where the dialogic responses to a blog posting constitute as much part of the blog as the original post. This does hold out the possibility of making Habermas's 'public sphere' a reality, although some scholars have responded that it is more a case of many small weak public sphericules (see Box 3.2).

Blogs can often represent a counter-hegemonic view, rather than that of the mainstream. One such example (of poacher turned gamekeeper) is that of Ariana Huffington in the US who runs www.huffingtonpost.com as a blog with a focus on mass media, commentary and analysis. Others include the Daily Kos blog (www.dailykos.com) which offers a liberal commentary on US politics; Whispers in the Loggia (www.whispersintheloggia.com) – a Philadelphia-based blog run by a 24-year-old American with access to the Vatican authorities and insider information on Vatican affairs and www.samizdata.net which is a UK based blog whose authors self-identify themselves as 'a bunch of sinister and heavily armed globalist illuminati who seek to infect the entire world with the values of personal liberty and several property (sic). Amongst our many crimes is a sense of humour and the intermittent use of British spelling'.

Common to many of the blogs and the more mainstream commercial media presence is the possibility of downloading the material automatically to a personal computer, PDA or other storage medium for later consumption. One mechanism for doing this is RSS (sometimes called Really Simple Syndication) which allows subscribed users to be automatically updated whenever there is new or altered content on their favourite websites. This can also be done with specialist software such as Avantgo which achieves the same end. Behind RSS and Avantgo lie the principle of keeping the end-user engaged with the content, by maximizing the ease with which the user can receive the updated material. With the advent of mobile computing, and the increasing sophistication of mobile telephones and WiFi-enabled PDAs, this has become all the more important for content providers. New technologies allow end-users to carry a great deal of content with them; digital content weighs nothing of itself.

This latter development points up an important technology-led change for media producers. In the late 1990s, there was little significant difference in how publishers saw themselves, other than perhaps the provision of an online presence, sometimes with an online version of content as in the case of many newspapers, and often with an e-commerce gateway. At the beginning of the twenty-first century, that has changed. The core of this change is from traditional publishing to content provision. It is content that counts, not the medium in which it is delivered. Is it to a consideration of content that we now turn.

Box 3.4   A level playing field?

The statistics on Internet usage worldwide make for an interesting read. The table below shows the comparative usage across the continents, and reports both the level of Internet penetration within a country and as a percentage of world usage.

World Internet Usage as of 11 January 2007 (www.internetworldstats.com ©Copyright 2007, Miniwatts Marketing Group)

	Pop. in millions	% of world population	% of Internet penetration	% of world usage
Africa	933.45	14.2	3.5	3.0
Asia	3712.53	56.5	10.5	35.6
Europe	809.62	12.3	38.6	28.6
Middle East	193.45	2.9	10.0	1.8
North America	334.54	5.1	69.4	21.2
Latin America/ Caribbean	556.61	8.5	16.0	8.1
Oceania/Australia	37.47	0.5	53.5	1.7
WORLD TOTAL	6574.65	100	16.6	100.0

(Continued)

It is immediately clear that there is a great variety in the level of Internet penetration worldwide, and one immediately related to wealth. North America has the highest population penetration at 68.6% while Africa has the lowest at 2.6%. Although North America has only 5.1% of the world's population, it accounts for 22.2% of world Internet usage.

A Panos report in 2005 based on a study in rural parts of India (Gujarat), Tanzania and Mozambique found: 'Fewer than 2% of the people interviewed for the study mentioned the Internet, although Internet is available within reach of almost all the research areas (for instance, at Internet cafes in nearby towns). This finding is important for development organizations and governments who are concerned to increase the flow of information in rural communities. They should recognize that the Internet, for whatever reasons, has not become part of the daily lives of many rural people' (Panos Institute, 2005: 4).

We also know from work done by the Panos Institute (www.panos.co.uk) that four years into the twenty-first century only one rural-based African in a thousand has a telephone. Sub-Saharan Africa is home to 10% of the world's population, but has only 0.2% of the world's one billion telephone lines. In Burkina Faso, one of the world's poorest countries, a mobile call can cost half the daily wage of an agricultural worker. Only 2% of rural homes in Zambia have electricity, and in rural areas there is less than one phone per thousand people. While more than 17% of the population of low-income countries is under the age of 14, less than half the population of low-income countries has access to secondary education. It costs around $20 a month for a low volume Internet account in North America – and up to around $100 per month for a similar account in Africa.

Even the Internet's most ardent enthusiasts urge caution against making excessive claims for it in Africa. As the United Nations Economic Commission for Africa puts it. 'There are more radios per capita than telephone lines, let alone computers [in sub-Saharan Africa] ... Thirty-five of the 49 countries in the world which have less than one telephone per 100 people are in sub-Saharan African. So if the objective is to include more and more communities in the information loop, then radio, and not the Internet, is the technology of choice, and will be for quite some time to come' (da Costa, 1996, cited in Panos (1998: 2). Radio covers approximately 75% of Africa's population and television 40%. The Internet's 0.1% shows just how marginal a medium it still is, in terms of mass media provision on the continent.

Content

Under traditional media categories, content was delivered in textual, visual or aural forms. Consumers read newspapers and magazines, watched TV and films, listened to recordings or the radio. Those strict divisions no longer apply today. The Internet delivers hybrid content, in which aural, visual and textual forms can be intermingled in a multi-media format. Browsing *National Geographic* online for example, one can read the text, click on a hypertext link to be brought to a related story, see a short video, or hear a recording of related sounds. Hypertextuality means that web-based content is not presented in a linear fashion, but that the user is free to jump around according to personal preferences.

Until relatively recently, without a laptop computer, users were obliged to engage with content while at their own PCs. The advent of handheld technologies, such as PDAs or internet-enabled mobile phones, which are increasingly cheaper, more sophisticated and highly convergent, has changed that. Content can be consumed, like fast food, at the individual user's convenience. The nature of the device used to access the content may vary, and providers increasingly create alternate access points for different users. Reading content on a mobile telephone, with its typical 2×2inch screen, requires that content is tailored to match the output interface. Equally, because of cost in mobile telephony, users tend to be much more selective in deciding what content they want in advance.

This dimension of user selectivity of content is a critical change in consumption patterns. Watching television news or listening to radio news requires the user to be engaged in a direct linear fashion. The traditional user cannot fast-forward, pause, repeat or review the broadcast. Reading newspapers allows the user to jump around, but on opening a page the viewer is confronted with all the stories, headlines and photographs from which a selection may be made. In new media, these parameters no longer apply. New media content is non-linear, in that the user decides the direction in which to go. Increasingly the user can construct a personalized newscast, in which news of particular events is delivered digitally to a computer, PDA or other device. This of course means that many users are no longer exposed to the more normal broad swathe of news. A user interested only in celebrities may never get to hear a political story again. A news junkie may never again encounter a sports story unless it is mainstream news. A political maven may not even realize the World Cup is on, due to personalized constraint of news sources and elements.

When the video recorder was introduced, it quickly became evident that a major use was for time shifting: people could watch their favourite programmes at a different time to the broadcast time. Today, the advent of portable MP3 players and Apple's iPod have brought about a time and content shift of a different kind. In late 2006, Apple's podcasting website (www.apple.com/podcasting) boasted more than 20,000 available podcasts while a search for 'podcasts' on Google yielded 422,000,000 hits. In the US, ABC, CBS, NBC and NPR all have news podcasts available. In Ireland, RTE and the *Irish Emigrant News* offer podcasts, as do BBC and ITN in the UK, and ABC and SBS in Australia. Highly specialized podcasts also exist, such as the daily pray-as-you-go podcast from the Jesuit Media Initiative in London, or on male hair loss or learning the Mohawk language or real estate investments. At the heart of podcasting is user choice, made possible by new technology. Podcasts can be made available for download by any Internet user, utilizing podcast creation software which is freely available on the Internet.

Apple have recently introduced their iPod video which allows users to access and play video podcasts. Among Apple's offering are 2,000 music videos as well as ABC and Disney television shows. It is difficult to predict how well iPod video and its related types will succeed. There is a qualitative and quantitative difference in the experience of watching *The Sopranos* or *Saving Private Ryan* on the big screen compared to the relatively tiny screens of most mobile phones, PDAs or iPods. Whatever the outcome of portable video delivery, it is clear that users now have the ability to generate their own audio for personal use, in a manner which may well threaten radio in particular. The new technologies have made it a very simple matter to create aural content on demand, for usage on demand, without reference to a broadcaster's schedule. The increasing miniaturization of this technology, along with falling prices for solid-state memory, means that this possibility lies within most users' budgets. The full implications are as yet unclear. The reaction of the mainstream music companies to music sharing sites and to music sharing software (most obviously through legal action as was evidenced in cases pursued against both Napster and Limewire by the global multimedia conglomerates) is an indication of how strongly the threat is felt. Legal sites like (new) Napster (www.napster.com) and iMesh (www.imesh.com), who underline the importance of copyright and stipulate that their software cannot be used to share copyright materials, are dwarfed by the presence of sites offering free downloads of music in breach of copyright provision. The proponents of file-sharing will argue that all that is happening is that technological developments allow audience members to share music or video with one another freely. Multimedia conglomerates see this kind of activity as piracy, which deprives them and their artistes of large amounts of revenue which, they argue, is rightly theirs. Overall, however, the essential element of tailoring content in this fashion is that it offers increased agency to the audience, in which audience choice is the core component of consumption, as opposed to provided content. In view of that agency we now turn to a consideration of audience.

Audience

Never before have the public had such a wealth of information available to them. Google now indexes in excess of some three billion web pages. These are all available to users worldwide (with some exceptions like China where Google and other Internet providers have agreed to accept state censorship). The Internet represents such a volume of information that users need well developed searching techniques if they are not to be overwhelmed by the amount of material made available on any single general search. Equally, searchers need to be aware of specific search algorithms which privilege particular pages. But despite the volume of material, it is questionable whether or not the public today is better informed, more discursive, or more aware than in previous generations. If audience agency teaches us anything, it is that audiences want to be selective in their choice of material, not on the basis of education but rather on the basis of personal entertainment.

Music is a good example of this. Most consumers have distinct preferences in relation to music. Some might be fans of Morrissey, The Smiths and David Bowie while others might prefer Bach, Buxtehude and Brahms. Consider for a moment two such consumers, each with Internet access and a fast broadband connection. While both may use similar search techniques to download music into a portable player of their preference, it is highly unlikely that one will be downloading the same as the other. Even where musical tastes are more generic, audience agency is defined precisely in terms of the ability of the individual audience member to select content of choice. Given the constraints of time (one can only listen to a finite amount of music in the course of a day) and technology (even iPods have limits on the number of tunes they can hold), consumers choose what is both desirable and usable. In this respect, consumers have, to some degree, turned the tables on the producers. In the past, like Ford and his 'you-can-have-any-colour-car-as-long-as-it's-black' approach, mainstream media providers, with an eye to profit, produced what they wanted for mass consumption. Because it was oriented to a mass market, audiences took what came, and hoped they had sufficient of what they wanted. This was true of magazine content, newspaper stories, television programmes and radio play lists; the producer was the one who decided on the content reaching the consumer.

The new technologies, like podcasting, have changed that. Consumers can decide to hear/see/read only the materials they select in advance. Mainstream broadcasters cannot duplicate this. It is impossible, for example, for a terrestrial station to devote itself to Morrissey and The Smiths, with no other content. It would soon become bankrupt. It is, however, perfectly conceivable for a consumer to create a shuffle podcast of music only from Morrissey and The Smiths in lieu of that putative radio station and to utilize that for their listening pleasure. This self-created narrowcasting is what gives the audience agency. Audience members can control what comes in their direction, on demand – something not possible with conventional mass media processes.

Just as this is true of music, so it is also true of news. It is quite possible to the consumer to decide on a highly selective approach to news, such that there could easily be complete over-exposure or under-exposure to critical public issues. McLuhan's global village is replaced by care only for one's own self-defined village. Despite the inadequacies of contemporary news sources in dealing with issues like material deprivation, marginalization and profound social need, at least the extent of coverage of events like the Indonesian tsunami mean that the public worldwide are aware of the extent of what happened. A complete reliance on personalized narrowcasting (which is, admittedly, highly unlikely in the short term) would have serious detrimental effects in terms of the public knowledge base. This is not just important in its own terms of public awareness: it is critical for the citizens of a democracy to engage in discourse about the nature of the society in which they live. The lack of a political discourse is a danger in any democracy. There is a serious diminution of the public sphere because of a lack of common perspectives on key issues, driven by lack of exposure to those issues.

It must be said, of course, that audience agency of this type is not the most significant threat to the public sphere. Of far greater importance is the hegemonic domination of news sources, including the Internet, by the major corporations. Conglomerates and corporations control news worldwide. This has resulted in the commodification of news which reflects hegemonic commercial interests. A case in point is NBC in the US, which is owned by General Electric, which is itself a major player in the provision of nuclear power. It would be interesting for any student to research the extent to which NBC news has covered nuclear power issues, particularly from the anti-nuclear lobby. As a general rule, the sources of television news in the developed world represent the powerful and the wealthy. The Internet, for all its flaws and distractions, at least offers the potential of an alternate voice, albeit one that is not yet fully articulated.

Implications for the future

What does all of this mean into the future? Some things are clear, even without a crystal ball. Convergence will continue, and technologies will be developed that will allow all the various requirements of consumers to be met on a single device. It is quite conceivable that your next handheld will serve as a diary, Internet browser, mobile phone, digital camera, GPS, MP3/video player and personal computer with sufficient power and memory to handle the required applications seamlessly and swiftly. This will, of course, come at a cost, but the costs will come down over time. It is also possible that such devices will come to the consumer at a negligible cost in the future with the profits being made on the consumables: sound, video and text.

There are, of course, other costs. New media and new media technologies are often discussed without reference to some of the hidden costs that apply. Campbell and Breen, writing about the Internet in 2001, stated:

> A variety of promises have been made or at least implied in relation to the Internet. Its proponents make much of its ability to deliver the latest research from a wide variety of disciplines to millions of users. It is seen by some as the saviour of democracy, the social weapon that will destroy hegemony and prevent the political manipulation of society. Claims are frequently made that it will create a new and powerful voice for the people. The promises, extensive and seemingly limitless, are however often made without reference to any of the costs involved in the delivery of such a system. No technology has ever been adopted without social cost, and it is certain that, whatever the benefits, a communications technology as powerful and as 'revolutionary' as the Internet will exact a considerable cost from existing social structures. There is no such thing as a free lunch. The goods promised by Internet development have to be paid for in hard cash. These costs are not only financial, but also social and cultural. A few commentators have begun to count the cost. Some caveats have been forthcoming from neo-Luddites, ranging from a concern about a loss of writing skills, already evident from the use of spell checking in word processors and a tendency to streams of ungrammatical prose in e-mail, to a range of social ills, up to and including an Orwellian nightmare of excessive social control. (Campbell and Breen, 2001: 222)

These are important considerations in any debate on media and technology. We have little reason to believe that much has changed in this regard over the last five years, despite the very significant developments in technology and delivery. The ability of Google to permanently record all of an individual user's searches, the archiving of GMail users' email even after deletion, and the retention of users' usage records by ISPs are only some examples of how electronic fingerprints are left on the Internet by all users, often unawares.

Equally, there is the reality of Internet dominance by existing conglomerates. The extent of that dominance is a cause of great concern. There is a debate in the US Congress at present on the issue of 'net neutrality' which should be of major concern to all Internet users. In the current dispensation, all packets of information are treated equally. Some ISPs want to be able to privilege certain packets over others, based on end-user fees. The essential outcome of this would be total dominance of the Internet by those who can afford to pay the most to have 'their' packets out there. Lessig and Wu (2003) are the leading researchers on this topic. In a letter to the (US) Federal Communication Commission they wrote:

> A network that is as neutral as possible is predictable: all applications are treated alike. ... The value of network neutrality can be seen clearly in another context: the nation's electric system. ... When consumers buy a new toaster made by General Electric they need not worry that it won't work because the utility company makes a competing product. ... The uniformity of the electric grid is a safeguard against the risk of restrictions and uneven standards. ...
>
> The nation's broadband network is in its infancy, just now reaching tens of millions of users, like the narrowband Internet in the mid-1990s. At this critical juncture, the broadband networks, particularly those operated by cable operators, have imposed a confusing patchwork of contractual and technical restrictions, enforced in an unpredictable manner. ... Since every provider acts independently, neither developers nor consumers can predict whether a new, innovative application will be banned in certain parts of the country. It is as if a new toaster were to work well in Connecticut and California, but not in Wisconsin or Wyoming.

Lessig and Wu's primary fear is the creation of a multi-tier Internet, with those producers who can pay controlling content and those consumers who can pay having privileged access. This is in complete opposition to the ideal of the Internet at its inception. Much of what happens on the Internet today is about commerce: consumers pay for access to online newspapers, to specialist information sites, to download music and video. If the Internet is trundling toward a pay-per-use fee structure, it will be even more difficult for the developing nations of the world to get a foothold on the digital information ladder.

The concern of many is that big business, like the media conglomerates, is driven only by the profit motive, and this could become the only controlling factor behind the Internet, with money talking the loudest. Such a development would not be in the interest of social equality, would not add a whit to the development of a discursive public engaged in debate about the pursuit of democracy, would not increase access to voices from the margins, would not add to the quality or dependency of news, and would not be in society's best interests. On the other hand it would make the media conglomerates even more powerful, would allow capital to be the driving force of the Internet, would stifle marginal voices, would diminish public debate, would hasten the advent of pay-only media and would add significantly to social inequality around the globe.

Technological development should be at the service of all, not the privileged few. Already we have seen that some technologies are out of reach to those who cannot pay, like satellite radio and mobile telephony. The problem is that we are currently poised technologically with two potential routes: one in which producers control content through commercial access, and the other where the audience has access to content and creates its own channels according to its own desires. The former is an increasing reality while the latter is in danger to being only a virtual dream. New technologies and new media are engaging, enchanting and exaggerated. The challenge to society and to end-users is to be aware of the social and political costs of such technologies and their applications.

Conclusion

New technologies have a profound impact on the manner in which media content is produced, communicated and consumed. The erosion of the power base of the old media is likely to increase over time. Despite the relative increase in which new technologies can be harnessed by consumers with a potentially significant increase in audience agency, the dominance of old media conglomerates is likely to become an equivalent new media dominance. Just as old media rarely enter into an analysis of their role in political economy, nor in any invitation to audiences to engage in serious reflection on systemic social issues and contexts, so too new media and new technologies are even more focused on the immediacy of content, often in a triumph of style over substance. Consumers are rarely confronted with the ethical concerns of the digital divide, or the inequality of distribution of new technologies. Producers are likely to increase their efforts to create a two-tier Internet in which commercial content is likely to be privileged over ordinary content, with the inevitable results of majority control by commercial interests. Multimedia content, along with sexier new technologies, will most likely be widely promoted without much regard to the nature, quality or utility of content. New technologies are essentially amoral. It is in the usage of those technologies, by producers and consumers, that the real ethical questions lie. Students should be encouraged to ask an overarching question about new media, new technologies, producers and content: in whose interest is this being promoted, and at what political, economic and social costs?

Summary

- New media and new media technologies must be evaluated in terms of producers, content and audiences, according to standard criteria and aesthetic considerations. Some trends suggest a shift in power, from mainstream producers to selective audiences creating self-designed narrowcasts, but the extent and effect of this process has yet to be quantified. Content is king. In the end, the technology which delivers content to the end-user is irrelevant. The real issue is the content received and the use to which it is put.
- Two core questions which still remain are about the quality of content and the representativeness of content. Irrespective of how content comes to the end-user, it is important to ascertain its quality, something easier said than done. Equally, end-users need to reflect on how representative content is of the society in which they live. Despite the open nature of the possibility, content creation is still controlled by major commercial publishers. One significant danger of the new technology is that is distracts attention from core social issues, by allowing users to be focused on entertainment rather than information.
- The beguiling promises of new media technologies are unattainable for many due to the 'digital divide', with the consequence of society being further defined and divided between 'information rich' and 'information poor'.

GOING FURTHER

Bagdikian, B. H. (2004) *The New Media Monopoly*. Boston: Beacon Press.
For 20 years Bagdikian has documented the issues of mass media ownership and the power
   of the major conglomerates. His book is a *tour-de-force* that engages with major concerns

about mass media ownership and content over time, about the influence of economic factors on the (non)publication of content, and the privilege of the wealthy in terms of media access and control. In Chapter 3 he focuses particularly on the Internet and in his Afterword he deals with the failed 'big promise' of the new technologies.

Chomsky, N. (1989) *Necessary Illusions: Thought control in democratic societies.* London: Pluto Press.

Necessary Illusions is Chomsky's thoroughly documented and referenced attack on the mainstream US media as lacking independence, a scathing critique of the power of media corporations per se. In this book he raises core questions about citizenship, free speech and participatory democracy. Astute students should be able to apply the core theoretical components of his argument to new technologies as further evidence of the loss of independence and the rise of conglomerate power.

Lehman-Wilzig, S. and Cohen-Avigdor, N. (2004) 'The Natural Life Cycle of New Media Evolution – Inter-Media Struggle for Survival in the Internet Age', *New Media & Society*. 6(6): 707-30.

This is an excellent review of the evolution of new media from a historical perspective. There is emphasis on the effects of new media on older media formats using the development of the Internet as a case study, which the authors categorize as a 'multimedium' threatening all other traditional media.

Greenwald, R. and Kitty, A. (2005) *Outfoxed: Rupert Murdoch's War On Journalism.* New York: The Disinformation Company.

Greenwald and Kitty painstakingly research the Fox News Network as a prime example of a new mainstream medium with extensive reach via cable and satellite. The book demonstrates the extent to which one powerful voice (Murdoch's) can drive an entire media empire and in so doing can utterly distort the media landscape. Fox has a major share of the US news audience and its power of influence cannot be underestimated. This book is a prime example of Bagdikian's treatise on media monopolies in new and old technologies.

Lister, M., Dovey, J., Giddings, S. and Grant I. (2003) *New Media: A Critical Introduction.* London: Routledge.

This book is divided into five sections: New Media and New Technologies; New Media and Visual Culture; Networks Users and Economics; New Media in Everyday Life; and Cyberculture: Technology, Nature and Culture. It deals comprehensively with the history, culture and technologies of the new media, and situates them solidly against a theoretical framework.

STUDENT ACTIVITY 3.1

For both blogs and podcasts, carry out an Internet search to locate as many of each as you can find. Create a table indicating ownership, size, genre and frequency of update. Pay particular attention to commercial interests and see if you can document whether private individuals or major corporations predominate in each case.

References

Bagdikian, B. H. (2004) *The New Media Monopoly*. Boston: Beacon Press.

Bush, V. (1945) 'As We May Think', *The Atlantic Monthly*, July. 176(1): 101–108.

Campbell, P.B. and Breen, M.J. (2001) 'The Net, Its Gatekeepers, Their Bait and Its Victims: Ethical Issues Relating to the Internet' in E.G. Cassidy and A.G. McGrady (eds), *Media and the Marketplace: Ethical Perspectives*. IPA Press: Dublin.

Da Costa, P. (1996) 'The Internet – An African Perspective'. Paper presented at Friedrich Ebert Stiftung/International Development Research Centre Pre-conference Seminar – 16/17 October. Cited in Panos Media Briefing No. 2, London: Panos Institute.

Downey, J. and Fenton, N. (2003) 'New Media, Counter Publicity and the Public Sphere', *New Media & Society*, June. 5(2): 185–202.

Dyson, E. (1997) *Release 2.0: A design for living in the digital age*. New York: Broadway Books.

Gitlin, T. (1998) 'Public Spheres or public sphericules?' in T. Liebes and J. Curran (eds), *Media, Ritual and Identity*. New York: Routledge.

Goode, L. (2005) *Jurgen Habermas: Democracy and the Public Sphere*. London: Pluto Press.

Habermas, J. (1962, 1989) *The Structural Transformation of the Public Sphere: An inquiry into a category of bourgeois society*. Cambridge, Mass.: MIT Press.

Howard, P. N. (2002) 'Network Ethnography and the Hypermedia Organization: New Media, New Organizations, New Methods', *New Media & Society*, December. 4(4): 550–74.

Joy, B. (2000) 'Why the future doesn't need us', *Wired*, 8(4), April. (http://www.wired.com/wired/archive/8.04joy_pr.html)

Kluver, A. R. (2002) 'The Logic of New Media in International Affairs', *New Media & Society*. December. 4(4): 499–517.

Lehman-Wilzig, S. and Cohen-Avigdor, N. (2004) 'The Natural Life Cycle of New Media Evolution – Inter-Media Struggle for Survival in the Internet Age', *New Media & Society*. December. 6(6): 707–30.

Lessig, L. and Wu, T. *Ex Parte Submission in CS Docket No. 02–52. Submisison made to the FCC re Net Neutrality*. http://www.timwu.org/wu_lessig_fcc.pdf

Lievrouw, L. A. (2004) 'What's changed about new media? Introduction to the fifth anniversary issue of *New Media & Society*', *New Media & Society*, February. 6(1).

Manovich, L. (2003) 'New Media from Borges to HTML', in Wardrip-Fruin, N. and Mantfort, N. (eds) *The New Media Reader*. MIT Press.

Negroponte, N. (2000) 'From Being Digital to Digital Beings', *IBM Systems Journal*. 39(3–4): 417–18.

Negroponte, N. (2003) 'Creating a Culture of Ideas', *Technology Review*, February. 106(1): 33–4.

Negroponte, N. (2004) 'Beyond Telecommunications', *BT Technology Journal*, October. 22(4): 4.

Panos Media Briefing No 28 (June 1998) *The Internet and Poverty: Real Help or Real Hype*. London: Panos Institute.

Panos Institute (2005) *Telephones and Livelihoods: How Telephones Improve Life for Rural People in Developing Countries*. London: Panos Institute.

Reading, A. (2003) 'Digital Interactivity in Public Memory Institutions: The Uses of New Technologies in Holocaust Museums', *Media Culture & Society*, January. 25(1): 67–85.

Samson, I. (2005) 'Genius of a Crofter Boy', *Celtic Heritage*, Sep/Oct.

Surveillance Function', *Journal of Communication*, 46(3): 32–47.

Shoemaker, P. (1996) 'Hardwired for News: Using Biological and Cultural Education to Explain the Surveillance Function', *Journal of Communication*, 46(3): 32–47.

Silverstone, R. (1999) 'What's New About New Media?', *New Media and Society*, 1(1): 10–12.

Unravelling the Web of Discourse Analysis

Philippa Smith and Allan Bell

DEFINITIONS

Discourse analysis involves a close examination of text, including visual imagery and sound as well as spoken or written language. It is concerned with both the form of the text and its use in social context, its construction, distribution and reception. It aims to understand and elucidate the meanings and social significance of the text.

Introduction: why analyze discourse?

Defining 'Discourse Analysis' (DA) is a formidable task. Existing definitions are numerous and the term itself has been described as 'wide-ranging and slippery' (Taylor, 2001: 8). Our definition above attempts to encompass a wider application of this method, stressing that DA is not a 'one-size-fits-all' research tool for the many disciplines that have embraced it. However, if a more abstract interpretation is applied as in Devereux's definition of discourse as 'a form of knowledge' (Devereux, 2003: 158) then analyzing discourse can be seen to go beyond a pure examination of the words and images that constitute texts. Viewing discourse on a macro level leads to a greater understanding of the way in which it is constructed. Rather than being a search for answers, DA allows us to question, analyze and interpret beyond what may seem the preferred reading of a text, a concept used by Hall in relation to the active decoding of a text by the reader and discussed later in this chapter.

Box 4.1 Historical origins of DA

Van Dijk (1988a) provides a brief but useful review of the historical development of discourse analysis, linking its origins to classic rhetoricians such as Aristotle. The emergence of a contemporary form of discourse analysis through disciplines in the humanities and social sciences did not occur until the late 1960s and early 1970s but its roots are earlier. Van Dijk outlines influences such as Russian formalism, French structuralism, sociolinguistics, ethnographic approaches, text linguistics and psychology. Antonio Gramsci, Michel Foucault, Jacques Derrida, Ferdinand de Saussure, Mikhail Bakhtin and Vladimir Propp are just a few of the theorists who have influenced discourse analysis in some way.

Approaches

It is better to view DA as a range of approaches rather than a single practice (Taylor, 2001). The options include social linguistic analysis, interpretive structuralism, critical linguistic analysis, conversational analysis, genre analysis, ethnography of communication, genealogical analysis, discursive psychology, narrative analysis, literary analysis, content analysis, and the list could go on. Suffice to say that such a range of options can be overwhelming to someone approaching the field for the first time.

A factor common to all approaches is the analysis of language in use, with the methodology more likely to be qualitative than quantitative. The detail of analysis that qualitative research offers enables the deconstruction of language to reveal nuances and shades of meaning that go far beyond the benefits of a purely quantitative approach. However, as a consequence of the rise in the number of disciplines taking DA on board as an exciting and new methodology, several major strands are emerging (or perhaps rather, diverging), leading to disagreement amongst some academics over DA's parameters and application. From one perspective, the embracing of DA by so many disciplines has facilitated its diversity and acceptance as a research methodology. From another point of view, this also poses problems. When there is such diversity, how do you teach DA? How do researchers decide on what approach to adopt for a particular purpose? How do they assess what is the most applicable, reliable and fruitful type of analysis for their purpose?

Box 4.2 Comparing different approaches

Studies such as that by a group of New Zealand researchers at Victoria University of Wellington provide useful insights into how different approaches to DA might be applied. Stubbe et al. (2003) offer a comparison between conversation analysis, interactional sociolinguistics, politeness theory, critical discourse analysis and discursive psychology through applying these five approaches to the same text – a recording of a workplace conversation. The researchers found that while these analyses had common elements, each also highlighted different aspects of the interaction.

Linguistics can be considered the major source of DA, in particular European text linguistics (van Dijk, 1988a). Halliday's approach to linguistic description, systemic functional theory (1976, 1978, 1985), focused on the function of language and how people use it to exchange meaning. Moving from an abstract view of linguistics towards a more functional perspective led to the emergence of critical linguistics whereby choice of words and word combinations were seen to reflect ideological forces (Fowler et al., 1979). Critical linguistics however was later overtaken by social semiotics (Hodge and Kress, 1988) and critical discourse analysis (Fairclough, 1989, 1992, 1995; and van Dijk, 1993). Analyses of text can range from the micro-analysis of language features, such as lexical choices or syntactic forms, to a broader focus that looks at overall textual structures. These broader kinds of analyses have maintained the principle of linguistic analysis – that both language and discourse have a systematic nature that may be described through rules (van Dijk, 1988a). However, the search for meaning behind the social construction of words, sounds and images remains at the heart of modern discourse analysis, which aims to achieve a more whole and transparent view of the world through understanding dominance and power.

'Critical Discourse Analysis' (CDA) is the approach that has increasingly found most favour with academics across disciplines because of the attention it pays to the role of power in discourse. Wodak (2001: 2–3) defines CDA as being 'fundamentally concerned with analysing opaque as well as transparent structural relationships of dominance, discrimination, power and control as manifested in language ... three concepts figure indispensably in all CDA: the concept of power, the concept of history, and the concept of ideology'.

Box 4.3   Challenging CDA

Although a popular emergent research method, CDA has not been short of criticism and there are indications that it may take some time to reach a level of
consensus amongst academics. Hammersley (1997) suggests that CDA is over-
ambitious in its claim to not only understand discursive processes but also its
intention to evaluate discourse against a socio-cultural background and suggest
changes to address societal injustices. His view is that CDA takes a crude position on a variety of issues, recognizing, for example, only two parties in a
relationship – the oppressors and the oppressed – which can be unrealistic and
lead to the presentation of speculation as well-grounded knowledge. Widdowson
(1995) believes that because a text can be interpreted in different ways
depending on the world a person is from and what they bring to the text, CDA
can produce a prejudiced view as a researcher's preferred reading. He sees
this as being more partial interpretation than analysis and also criticizes CDA
for failing to distinguish text from discourse. Both these issues have been disputed by Fairclough (1996) in relation to his own research. Toolan's view (1997)
is that CDA is a meaningful tool to understand the ways that information and
communication (discourse) increasingly shape our lives. However, he highlights
several areas for improvement including the need for greater thoroughness in
CDA's textual analysis to strengthen the evidence in its argumentation.

From text to social context

The move from looking at discourse in a textual to a social context has encouraged
ideological and sociological approaches in DA and has appealed to social scientific
fields such as psychology and management studies. What discourse analysis brings
to such disciplines is a way of analyzing their research material and data 'more systematically and in more detail from a discourse perspective' (Fairclough et al., 2004:
3). The recognition of the relationship between discourse and power has also led to
greater critical analysis of texts. What we read, see and hear should not be taken
for granted. We are daily faced with a complexity of discourse – 'without discourse,
there is no social reality, and without understanding discourse, we cannot understand our reality, our experience, or ourselves' (Phillips and Hardy, 2002: 2). The
main concern here is the need to understand and be aware of certain discourses
that may mislead us in the construction of our identity and how we see ourselves.
Realistically, it would be impossible for individuals to constantly monitor the

multitude of discourses in their lives without verging on paranoia, but a degree of scepticism and analysis is called for.

Foucault's interest in the power play of specific discourses over society has influenced the postmodern connection between language and social structure (Devereux, 2003). This is echoed by Fairclough when referring to discursive practice contributing not just to the reproduction of society ('social identities, social relationships, systems of knowledge and belief'), but also to the transformation of society (1992: 65). Analysis of texts also enables identification of the representation, identity and stereotyping of groups and individuals. It allows for critical analysis, an awareness of persuasive language, and uncovers dominating social powers behind discourses. Such critical analysis might not solve problems, but it is a prerequisite that has the ability to identify and analyze situations, and perhaps suggest ways of alleviating or resolving them (Fairclough et al., 2004). The New Zealand Government, for example, recognized that promotional texts used by tobacco companies carried tempting lifestyle messages to influence, particularly, young people's behaviour and their attitudes towards smoking. As a result, tobacco and advertising sponsorships were banned in the 1990s (Health NZ, 2005).

A burgeoning of text types in society, largely brought about through developing technologies, compels researchers to seek understanding of social reality through analyzing the discourse of the texts and questioning them. Legal documents, advertisements, political and Government papers, company newsletters, propaganda leaflets, articles in newspapers, magazines and books, television, radio and film, music and lyrics, performing arts and more recently the Internet, mobile phones, mobile television and computer games: these are just some examples of the proliferation of texts. Added to this are the changing and merging of existing discourses through processes of globalization of discourses and discourse genres (Fairclough, 2001).

Box 4.4   Hall's encoding/decoding model

Although DA mainly seeks to analyze texts themselves, it is important to acknowledge that audiences can interpret media language (signs or codes) in ways that differ from what the creator of those codes intended as the preferred reading. The encoding/decoding model was put forward by Hall (1980) to make sense of factual or current affairs television, but it has also been applied to other forms of media. The model suggests that audiences are not passive, but capable of decoding messages according to their own social identity. The meaning of the text is seen as situated somewhere between its producer and its reader. Hall outlined three hypothetical interpretive codes possible for the reader when looking at mass media codes:

(1) 'dominant' where the encoder and decoder are similarly positioned;
(2) 'negotiated' where the decoder accepts some of the text's meaning but rejects others;
(3) 'oppositional' where a decoder creates his/her own version of the text with different intentions.

Obviously this presents a challenge for discourse analysts and is one of the criticisms of CDA referred to earlier. However Phillips and Hardy (2002) suggest that the complexity and ambiguities of DA can be dealt with, for example, by looking at the location of individual texts within larger bodies of texts and making reference to broader discourses.

In search of stabilization

While the surge of interest in DA is exciting, its rapid development in multi- and inter-disciplinary application can also create problems. Because discourse analysis continues to evolve, there is variation amongst researchers on how it is determined and used. Different theorists, whether concerned with linguistics, literature, film, cultural history or semiotics, may all have their own interpretation and use of discourse analysis (Paltridge, 2000). Perhaps DA is in an uncertain situation where diversification of its use will result in destabilization or inconsistency in its methodology. Or perhaps this is part of a process whereby the input of many researchers into theories and methods of DA will result in a greater understanding of its application and what it might accomplish.

A need for synthesis is expressed in Fairclough's book *Discourse and Social Change* which seeks to establish a 'method of theoretically adequate and practically usable' language analysis as a means to study social change (1992: 1). Van Dijk too emphasizes the need for 'explicit and systematic analysis' based on 'serious methods and theories' (1990: 14). Georgakopoulou and Goutsos (1997: 187) call for 'more constructive dialogue' between the various emerging approaches of discourse analysis to avoid the dangers that discourse analysis 'will come to mean loosely any work from diverse analytic perspectives with no common metalanguage, method or technical apparatus'. Development of a meta-language to enable discourse analysis to achieve a distinctive methodological status has already begun (Lee, 2005) and new academic journals have been launched, some recently, to respond to this situation (see the further reading section at the end of this chapter).

Ongoing debate, discussion and practice are essential in cultivating a common acceptance and understanding of how DA should be conducted. Antaki et al. (2002) argue that there are basic requirements for analysis, regardless of the particular type of analysis one undertakes. They point to a lack of support in the DA environment whereby researchers can test and refine methods among sympathetic colleagues, and claim this can lead to analytical shortcomings in the methodology. They state:

> Writers are not doing analysis if they summarise, if they take sides, if they parade quotes, or if they simply spot in their data features of talk or text that are already well-known. Nor are they doing analysis if their discovery of discourses, or mental constructs, is circular, or if they unconsciously treat their findings as surveys. (Antaki et al., 2002: 27)

However, other academics – particularly those working in a CDA framework – emphasize the responsibility of researchers to take sides and make an impact on social inequity by pointing out the power plays of discourse. Fairclough (1995) suggests that analysis of texts may be used to encourage people to move beyond reception of media texts to action in response to those communicative events, a call which is echoed by academics from other disciplines (see Willig, 1999).

In the interests of reliability and validity, research has traditionally made a point of emphasizing the impartiality and non-involvement of researchers. However, when it comes to discourse analysis, interpretation is an unavoidable issue in the investigation of texts. Silverstone (1981) analyzed the British television serial drama *Intimate Strangers* using a Proppian analysis based on Russian formalist Vladamir Propp's (1970) list of narrative functions, which he suggested formed a shared predictable pattern in all tales. Silverstone pointed out the difficulty of discussing an audiovisual text by way of writing. His analysis relied on his own description of the programme because there was no other way to convey the information. However, his acknowledgement that the study was based on his own interpretation did not detract from a meaningful discussion of the text. In our view, in situations where analysis can have an impact on social justice, the researcher has the right to reach through the opaqueness of texts and indicate 'real' meanings or power struggles as they see it. However, the researcher must also resist the temptation to become intimately involved and must support findings with theory and the evidence of other studies. Ultimately however, the audience/reader needs to be aware that they too have the right to accept, reject or negotiate the academic discourse with which they are faced and act as they see fit.

News discourse and why we should analyze it

The influence of the media in reflecting, constructing and expressing culture, politics and social life should not be underestimated. We are surrounded by media – it informs us, it is a window on the world – though whether the media reflects or constructs reality or both is a question central to discourse analysis. News is a creative process that takes raw materials (linguistic, social or historical determinants), works on them, and transforms them into 'a recognizable product which we accept as familiar' (Hartley, 1982: 7). Not only do news texts 'draw upon and recirculate discourses' (sometimes magnifying and privileging some), but they are also capable of promoting mythologies and false understandings (Burton, 2005: 292). Therefore a critical understanding of news discourse through analysis can demystify social meanings that in turn will contribute towards greater equity among people (Hartley, 1982). Alongside the growth and development of media have come more sophisticated means of media analysis (Devereux, 2003), and these offer different approaches to follow when analyzing news discourse, depending on what we are looking for and on what level.

News offers an ideal source of data from which we can learn about social meanings and stereotypes through its mode of language and communication (Bell, 1995). For example, within one text we might track the development of a narrative to determine the journalist's perception of the significance of the order of information that is presented. Is the journalist providing us with the most important facts first, or the most entertaining? In another example we might adopt a method to investigate whether there are patterns in the language of a text which promote a particular discourse in representing or stereotyping specific groups. Van Dijk's *Racism and the Press* (1991) is an extensive study on the reporting of ethnicity in mainly British and Dutch newspapers, but the representation of the elderly, children, women and other social groups are equally deserving of examination. We may also wish to compare the way television, radio and print media present the same news item – do they use similar or different words to describe what happened? Do they use emotive language in their description or is the language dry in its effort to be both informative and impartial? If the item is on the television news, are close-up shots used for emphasis? Is the representation of all parties fair or biased? How might this impact on the audience? The discourses of other groups such as politicians, religious leaders or pressure groups might infiltrate news discourse and become an accepted part of its structure. Investigation of such intertextuality, whereby genres and discourses can inform, influence or become embedded in an existing text, can produce some interesting insights. One example is media coverage of incidents of racist manifestations and hate propaganda. Cohen-Almagor (2001) argues the media should report such activities responsibly and not merely be a 'loudspeaker' for racial inciters.

Frameworks for analyzing news

As the focus of this chapter turns to news (or media) discourse it is intended to first view text as the 'outward manifestation of a communication event' (Garrett and Bell, 1998: 3) and second, for discourse to encompass two aspects: the social interaction of people mainly through language, and the social construction of reality (Fairclough, 1995: 18). A number of different frameworks for analyzing news discourse have developed over the years enabling media researchers to tailor investigations in specific directions depending on the text and what they are looking for. The following illustrate some examples which can be adopted or adapted.

Van Dijk's work on media discourse (1985, 1988a, 1988b, 1991) proposes an analytical framework for the structures of news discourse by bringing together production and interpretation of discourse as well as its textual analysis. Thematic analysis goes beyond micro-analysis of language and concentrates on the arrangement of themes in news reports, such as narrative patterns which create dramatic tension in a story, or the non-chronological description of events influenced by its news value or relevance. Van Dijk parallels this broad semantic structure with a syntactic structure termed 'schemata' – the conventions and rules that organize content and the complexity of news themes. This includes categories such as the headline, lead paragraph, previous events (what happened before), background and the main event, which can be analyzed and their interrelationships investigated.

Bell (1998) offers a step-by-step guide to analysis, which is used to determine the event structure in a news story and establish what a story actually *says* happened. Analysis of events, actors, times and places in a story 'shows up inconsistencies, incoherence, gaps and ambiguities within the story, conflicting forces during the story's production by journalist and copy-editor, and implications for readers' comprehension' (Garrett and Bell, 1998: 9). In *The Language of News Media* (1991), Bell focuses on three themes: the processes which produce media language; the notion of the news story; and the role of the media audience. By analyzing news discourse through a framework that draws on analysis of personal narrative and van Dijk's structural approach, Bell emphasizes the concept of the 'story' as being central to the news.

Fairclough's (1995) framework for critical discourse analysis of communicative events involves the three overlapping dimensions of text, discourse practice and sociocultural practice. Each area can be dealt with separately but the interrelationship of all three is integral to the framework. Analyzing text involves areas such as structure, vocabulary or representation of actors through image, language or sound. Discourse practice relates to processes of text production and consumption which Fairclough divides into two threads – institutional routines such as journalistic practices of news selection, and discourse practices

Japan may use 'military' on Greenpeace

Tokyo considers asking Australia to protect its whalers from Southern Ocean protesters

by Ainsley Thomson
political reporter

Japan has warned it may send armed aircraft to defend its whaling ships in the Southern Ocean if violent clashes with protest boats escalate.

The strongly pro-whaling nation also says it may ask the Australian Government to take action against Greenpeace protesters.

The increasingly tense conflict prompted a Green Party call last night for New Zealand to send a frigate to Antarctica in a monitoring role — an option the Government has quickly ruled out.

The protesters' confrontation with the whalers intensified yesterday, with an extreme conservation group, Sea Shepherd, threatening to ram and disable the Japanese whaling fleet.

The group's ship, Farley Mowat, is equipped with a blade device — known as the "can opener" — mounted on its side and designed to rip open a ship's hull.

Sea Shepherd's threat came as Japan's Fisheries Agency said it was considering asking its Maritime Police Agency to send armed aircraft to defend the whaling ships if the protest action worsened.

The Melbourne *Age*, which reported the proposal, described it as using "quasi-military aircraft under the guise of the police to quell a civilian protest".

The newspaper also reported that the agency might ask the Australian Government to act against Greenpeace — a separate organisation from Sea Shepherd — to "normalise the situation".

Two New Zealanders are among the Greenpeace protesters in vessels chasing the whalers.

New Zealand and Australia share strong anti-whaling views. Japan says the whaling is necessary for research.

Greens leader Jeanette Fitzsimons urged the New Zealand Government to send a frigate to monitor events in the Southern Ocean.

"New Zealand has taken a strong position against the resumption of commercial whaling, but now it is

ANTARCTIC STANDOFF

Japanese whaling ship Nisshin Maru collided with Greenpeace's Arctic Sunrise on Sunday, smashing a huge dent in the protest boat's hull. Each side blamed the other for the incident.

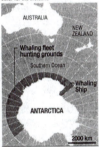

Source: Greenpeace, REUTERS/HERALD GRAPHIC

SEA DRAMA: A Greenpeace inflatable tries to block the transfer of a whale on to the Nisshin Maru factory ship.

time to stand up and be counted the way we did when we sent the frigate to Mururoa Atoll in 1973.

"New Zealand had the courage to take action then and it should do the same now."

But Conservation Minister Chris Carter said a frigate would be unlikely

to help the situation and instead urged the whalers and the protesters to act responsibly.

"Show restraint and act responsibly because this is a very dangerous part of the world and it would be very difficult to effect a rescue if people got into danger down there."

Duty minister Phil Goff also said there would be no role for a Navy ship.

"We have no legal authority over either party. Sending a frigate down there would serve no purpose because we would have no authority to act as intermediaries between the protesters and the whalers."

The Greens have also joined the Australian Green Party in calling for their respective Governments to stop Japanese whalers, military and police using New Zealand and Australia's ports and airports.

"Japan is flouting international agreements and public opinion by escalating its slaughter of whales, especially when everyone knows their claims of scientific research are just an excuse to get fresh whale meat on to Japanese dinner plates," said Ms Fitzsimons.

Greenpeace has had two ships, Esperanza and Arctic Sunrise, chasing the Japanese fleet across the Southern Ocean Whale Sanctuary since December 21 in an attempt to stop Japan killing the minke and fin whales.

Greenpeace claims Arctic Sunrise was rammed by the Japanese ship Nisshin Maru on Sunday, leaving it with a huge dent in its hull and a bent mast.

Sea Shepherd captain Paul Watson said his ship had side-swiped and damaged a Japanese ship to "get our point across".

"The whalers have assaulted whale defenders with water cannons and wooden poles. The whalers have rammed two Greenpeace ships and attempted to ram the Farley Mowat.

Sea Shepherd has been battling whalers since 1979 and in that time has sunk nine illegal whaling ships without causing injury.

Mr Watson said he would not try to sink a whaling vessel at sea because it would be "far too dangerous".

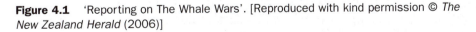

Figure 4.1   'Reporting on The Whale Wars'. [Reproduced with kind permission © *The New Zealand Herald* (2006)]

whereby texts can pass through a series of transformations. An example of this would be the text originating as an interview, which is then written up by a journalist, passes through the hands of a sub-editor, is published and then interpreted by the reader. Sociocultural practice requires consideration of outside influences or powers that affect the construction and production of a text, for example, politics, the economy or societal attitudes. Fairclough points out that users of this CDA framework might choose to emphasize one dimension more than the other, but maintaining a broad orientation to all three dimensions of a communicative event is still important.

The remainder of this chapter is dedicated to a case study of one newspaper story describing conflict in the Southern Ocean over whaling. In exemplifying the discourse analysis of news through an examination of the article's structure, the social, cultural and political discourses embedded within the text are brought to light, presenting a much clearer picture of what is really going on.

Case study: The Whale Wars

The article displayed as Figure 4.1 appeared as the lead story on the front page of the daily newspaper The New Zealand Herald on 11 January 2006. It was the most recent of several articles that had appeared over the previous three weeks documenting a conflict over whaling in the Southern Ocean near Antarctica. A Japanese whaling ship was pursued by protestors in boats from two conservation groups – Greenpeace and the Sea Shepherd Conservation Society. Both groups aimed to impede attempts by the Japanese to harpoon and capture whales for so-called 'scientific' purposes. The protestors held that the whaling ship was simply a factory ship harvesting whale meat for the Japanese market. New Zealanders had an interest in this story for several reasons: New Zealand is a firm supporter of the International Whaling Commission's moratorium on the killing of whales for commercial reasons, introduced in 1986; two New Zealanders were part of the Greenpeace protest; and New Zealand territory neighbours the whale sanctuary in the Southern Ocean.

A first impression is that this article presents a story about drama, heroism and conflict at sea. We are told of a dangerous journey to the cold and isolation of the Southern Ocean to save the lives of whales, of the ramming of ships, and of high emotions. It is a story that involves politicking between nations with threats of 'military' intervention and calls for countries to take action. The story has all the marks of a good movie, but it appears as a daily 'news' story, which stresses factuality and asks to be read with care. Analyzing the news discourse in this front page lead article enables us to take a closer look at what has happened here, to see the way the story has been constructed and what the mix of discourses is, embedded in its telling.

A full close analysis of the macro and micro levels of language and discourse in this story would consume a lot of time and space. We therefore concentrate on specific areas in applying discourse analysis to delve deep into the article and tease out a number of different layers to ascertain exactly what has occurred in this communicative event. These areas are:

1. The structure and coherence of the story.
2. Intertextuality.
3. The nature of the story's sources.
4. The positioning of the various parties involved, particularly through lexical choice.
5. The news practice behind the story.

Structure and coherence

Coherence relates to the flow of a news story, how information is structured and how well its various sections hold together. We examine the order of events assessing their chronology and newsworthiness, and how the story-line develops in relation to the actual news event.

News stories begin with a headline (although from the viewpoint of news practice, it is the last piece of the news text to be written). Here the eye is immediately drawn by the bold headline announcing **JAPAN MAY USE 'MILITARY' ON GREENPEACE**. This immediately puts Japan in the role of a potential aggressor, although – unusually for a headline – the nature of the force contemplated is mitigated by the scare quotes around 'military' (deriving from the description 'quasi-military' in the body of the story). It is also partly counterpointed by the 'standfirst' (the line of text after the headline that gives more information about the article) which announces: **Tokyo considers asking Australia to protect its whalers from Southern Ocean protesters.** This standfirst casts the whalers as being in need of protection and positions Japan as asking another nation to take some responsibility for the conflict. The metonym 'Tokyo' is used to indicate the Japanese government as the source of the request, although it appears from the body of the story that it is a state agency rather than the Government that has involved itself. The linking of headline and standfirst suggests a potential threat from Japan that unless Australia takes some action to intervene, Japan may take a more aggressive role. Japan is represented as taking a determinedly militaristic role in this 'war' against the anti-whaling protesters. By contrast, the very names of the protest organizations – 'green', 'peace', 'shepherd' – represent them as being concerned with the peaceful protection of the environment.

Moving into the main body of the story, we can number its paragraphs and identify their topics and how they relate to each other. The first three paragraphs cover the most recent round in the verbal conflict between Japan and its opponents, each side suggesting more aggressive intervention through the possible use of Japanese 'armed aircraft' and a New Zealand 'frigate'. The who, what, when, where and how of the story are immediately presented here at the start of the story. However paragraphs 4–5 divert from the present story to highlight the intensification of the conflict by jumping back in time to the events of the day before. This is in fact introducing a different set of events, although related as an explanation of the latest war of words. At this stage, although Greenpeace features in the headline, the dramatic actions of Sea Shepherd draw the most attention. Paragraphs 6–8 introduce the interplay of Japanese, Australian and conservation-group interests in the situation.

The next two paragraphs (9 and 10) background New Zealand's interest in the story, establishing that two New Zealanders are part of the Greenpeace protest, and align Australia and New Zealand as anti-whaling nations, in contrast with Japan's claim that whaling is 'necessary for research'. Paragraphs 11–19 function to relate the story to the New Zealand political and international scene by introducing comment from New Zealand politicians. The Green Party leader, Jeanette Fitzsimons, appeals to nationalism by referring to New Zealand's past involvement in maritime protests, such as against the 1973 French nuclear testing in the Pacific, and demanding that the Government should take similar action now by sending out a frigate. Two Government ministers introduce some of the typical vocabulary of diplomatic discourse. Both are quoted directly in ruling out the use of naval ships and distancing New Zealand from responsibility for the situation, with the repeated phrasing that the country has 'no authority' to intervene. Carter, the Conservation minister, implies some heroism on the part of the protestors in putting their lives at risk in 'a very dangerous part of the world'.

The story then adds chronological background (paragraphs 20 and 21) concerning the activities of the protestors and whaling fleet in the Southern Ocean and the collision of the Japanese and Greenpeace boats. The final four paragraphs (22 onwards) return to the story of the previous day's events, and include historical background on Sea Shepherd's activities and comment on their tactics.

Intertextuality

The discourses of different parties are introduced through direct quote and by being embedded in the reporter's words. The report drawn from the *Melbourne*

Age gives the New Zealand journalist the opportunity to introduce a military discourse into the story. Japan is associated with the word 'military', which leads on to other words of conflict such as *warn, armed* and *defend*. 'Military' is put into quotation marks in the headline to dissociate the newspaper from this reference, although the only actual evidence in the story that there is anything military involved is the quoted description from the *Melbourne Age* of 'quasi-military aircraft', which is not necessarily the same as outright 'military'. Discursive practice is also a factor here: news headlines are written by sub-editors who are working under tight space restrictions as they choose their words to attract buyers to the newspaper.

Jeanette Fitzsimons gets a further opportunity to promote her party's discourse in this area in a direct quote which challenges Japanese credibility. She characterizes Japan as being irresponsible in 'flouting' international agreements and public opinion and 'escalating' its slaughter of whales. She critiques Japan's discourse of science as a cover for whaling – 'everyone knows their claims of scientific research are just an excuse to get fresh whale meat on to Japanese dinner plates', appealing to readers' commonsense that they could not possibly believe otherwise.

Sources

Reading on, we discover that the source of the story about Japan looking to use 'military' action is actually embedded a third of the way through the article in paragraphs 6–8. What is reported from The *Melbourne Age* is the source and core of the story on which the rest of the article is built. First, we are told that the Japanese Fisheries Agency (not in fact the Japanese Government as implied in the headline and introduction to the story) was *considering* asking the Maritime Police to get involved. Second, we learn that this proposal was not sourced first hand by the New Zealand reporter but came from an article in the Australian newspaper the *Melbourne Age*. There is, however, no indication of what the source of the *Age*'s story is or when it was published. The *Age* is quoted directly as describing the Japanese proposal as being 'quasi-military aircraft under the guise of the police to quell a civilian protest'. This quote contains opinion and it is not clear whether the words come from another party, are taken from an editorial, or are possibly a reporter's comment. Third, it states that the newspaper 'reported' that the agency might ask the Australian Government to act against Greenpeace. As we close in on the gist of this story, we discover that its core becomes softer. The heart of this front page news article is based on what another newspaper said that the Agency said that it 'might' do or would 'consider' doing. Here we can see the reasoning behind the bolded headline and standfirst using the hedging verbs of 'may' and 'considers', because although the implications are threatening, the article is relying on evidence from another newspaper and can only allude to the action that may be taken, or considered, by Japan.

In addition to the main body of the story the article also features visual material – a map and a photograph. These are located below the headline and centrally, with the body of the story around them. They serve to focus the story and to frame it, especially since there is a headline above the map, 'Antarctic Standoff', which emphasizes the polarization of the parties. The map shows the location of the conflict, with Australia and New Zealand being the countries of closest proximity, therefore legitimizing their concerns. The map bears its own headline and features a short story, partly summarized from paragraph 21 of the main story, describing the collision of the Japanese whaling ship and Greenpeace's ship *Arctic Sunrise*. Although the article states that both sides blamed each other for the incident, the text already allocates responsibility to Japan by saying its ship collided with the *Arctic Sunrise* rather than vice versa, or by using an even-handed wording such as 'the boats collided'. Greenpeace is listed as the source of the map, and may also be the source of the photograph below it. The photograph is captioned 'Sea drama', and implies a David and Goliath battle as the side of the whaling ship looms over a small Greenpeace inflatable, while crew members direct a high-powered water canon down at the protesters on board. The use of visuals originating from one of the parties in such a polarized situation is a thorny one for journalistic practice, and may illustrate the extent to which the *New Zealand Herald* and its readers are anticipated to align with the protesters rather than the whalers.

Labelling

The article is based on a dichotomy of good versus bad, probably the essence of most narratives involving drama. There is obvious demarcation of two sides – those who are anti-whaling (New Zealanders, Australians, and the Greenpeace and Sea Shepherd protestors) and the 'other' side (the pro-whalers, the Japanese, the Japanese Fisheries Agency, the Japanese Maritime Police and the *Nisshin Maru* whaling ship). While the anti-whalers are a cross section of groups – Governments, Green parties and protestors – and the article includes comments from three New Zealand politicians and one protestor, the Japanese are represented by official groups only and with no direct quotes from a single Japanese spokesperson. The positioning of good versus bad is seen in how the groups are represented, on three levels – self-labelling, description by others, and the media's own representation.

Self-labelling: The self-labelling of groups such as the Green Parties, Greenpeace and Sea Shepherd, carries connotations of caring for the environment. Even the Greenpeace boats promulgate a discourse of enlightened caring through their names *Arctic Sunrise* and *Esperanza* (Spanish for 'hope').[1] In another example of self-labelling, Sea Shepherd captain Paul Watson refers to whale 'defenders' rather than 'protestors' in paragraph 23. Such labelling also contrasts markedly in this article with the Japanese groups which are tied in with officialdom and authority (police, maritime, agency) and industry (fisheries). There is no opportunity for the Japanese groups to self-label other than by their official names.

Description by others: Description by others can be used to promote or denounce other groups in a text. Jeanette Fitzsimmons has three paragraphs of reported speech where she juxtaposes New Zealand's courage against Japan's deceptiveness. Using words to invoke national pride in paragraphs 12 and 13, she seeks support for Government intervention in the conflict and in clichéd political discourse she says 'Now it is time to stand up and be counted…' Later, in paragraph 19, she discredits Japan saying it was 'flouting international agreements' in an attempt to 'get fresh whale meat on to Japanese dinner plates'.

Further suggestion of Japanese deceit is conveyed through a quotation from the *Melbourne Age* implying that the Japanese Maritime Police have a secretive militaristic agenda in using 'quasi-military aircraft under the guise of the police to quell a civilian protest'. While this last quotation does not appear until the 7th paragraph in the article, it is solely this comment that is the source for the use of the word 'military' used in the heading.

Media descriptors: Apart from direct quotations from the politicians and the Sea Shepherd captain, the way the parties are represented is the newspaper's doing. Japan is described as a 'strongly pro-whaling nation', and New Zealand and Australia 'share strong anti-whaling views', the conflict polarized and reified in the hyphenated descriptors. The use of the word strong further separates Japan from Australia and New Zealand and reinforces the conflict. Australia and New Zealand are positioned as cooperative with each other, for example, in their respective Green parties joining in the call for Government intervention.

Most of what 'happens' in this story is talk – on-the-ground action occurred yesterday, but today's story is largely an exchange of words. The talk verbs in the story include *warn, rule out, urge, called for, consider, may ask, may use.* The first two verbs – *warn* and *rule out* – can be viewed as authoritative, while *urge* and *called for* are more restrained, suggesting a politically responsible and tolerant attitude is being taken to the conflict in a diplomatic sense. The verbs *consider, may ask* and *may use* relate to the article's reporting of another newspaper's comments, which restricts the paper from using any other words which might alter the meaning.

The other most noticeable feature of the story's vocabulary is the range of conflict terms. The introductory paragraph has a concentration of these – *warned, armed, defend, violent, clashes, protest,* and *escalate.* Throughout the article other conflict words recur, such as *confrontation, intensified, extreme, threatening, ram, disable, rip open,* and *chasing.*

As can be seen, this analysis uncovers a great deal more going on within this article which might bypass readers as they flick through their morning paper. This case study is not intended as a criticism of this particular newspaper, journalist or story, or an attempt to side with any of the parties. Rather it illustrates that news discourse is something we take very much for granted in our daily lives. We have come to expect and accept news articles to be written a certain way and it is that acceptability which often hides our true understanding of a communicative event.

Conclusion

It seems somewhat ironic to point out that this present chapter, like DA itself, is built on academic discourse. This is something we cannot escape from but can be sensitive to (Phillips and Hardy, 2002). It also reinforces the concept that it is virtually impossible for a text *not* to have at least one discourse embedded within it. To highlight some of the debate surrounding discourse analysis as we know it today, we felt it important to show the roots of discourse analysis as a precursor to understanding the direction it is taking as a popular form of textual analysis. At the same time we have indicated DA's diverse use amongst varying disciplines, which has led to scholars' concerns over its blurring of boundaries and inconsistencies in its methodological application. A call for harmonization is apparent from many quarters.

In learning about DA as it continues to evolve, taking an objective viewpoint is essential. While this subject continues to be discussed at length, wide reading of appropriate books, journals and papers is called for to get a good sense of the ways it is used, and to critically evaluate whether it is done convincingly. Building confidence in making judgements when using DA, being aware of making too many assumptions, or realizing that analysis requires strong evidence to support interpretation are necessary at any level of scholarship. In the words of Hall:

The best way to 'settle' such contested readings is to look again at the concrete example and try to justify one's reading in detail in relation to the actual practices and forms of signification used, and what meanings they seem to you to be producing. (1997: 9)

The purpose of our *Whale Wars* case study as an example of news discourse was to demonstrate the different discourses that contribute to the construction of a single text and the inequalities or challenges of power that are inherent in it. Blommaert (2005) refers to the stratified layering of discourses in text, created by influences operating simultaneously but not necessarily equally. Using DA we were able to identify such layers in this article. The scholar's ability to uncover such stratification through DA by taking a multi-faceted approach looking at not just linguistic features, but also context, discursive practice, and historical, social and cultural aspects, encourages a much deeper understanding of ideologies at work. There is much to be gained through DA and with new patterns of communication surfacing through globalisation (Blommaert, 2005) there is certainly no lack of text – spoken, written and visual – to work from.

Summary

- DA is an emerging methodology which has grown from an examination of spoken or written language to include sound and image.
- Through DA we are able to question, analyze and interpret beyond the preferred reading of a text to assess what is really being said, and to question and understand social reality.
- A burgeoning of text types accompanied by a wide range of approaches to DA, often relating to the discipline of the researcher, has resulted in a call from academics for a synthesis in its application.
- The news has its own discourse, which is shaped by variables such as journalistic practice and media ownership.
- A number of different frameworks for analyzing news can be applied, including the micro-analysis of language, examination of event structure, text production and consumption and the influence of outside powers.
- Other discourses, such as those relating to social, cultural and political texts, can also be found embedded in the news.

GOING FURTHER

Bell, A. and Garrett, P. (eds) (1998) *Approaches to Media Discourse.* Oxford, UK and Malden, Massachusetts: Blackwell Publishers Ltd.
Includes chapters from various academics on their presentations and exemplifications of the main approaches to news discourse, a summary of frameworks and illustrative analysis to show how they work. See in particular Bell's chapter on 'The Discourse Structure of News Stories' pp. 64–104 for an example of an analytical framework applied in deconstructing a news story.

Lee, A. and Poynton, C. (eds) (2000) 'Culture and Text: Discourse and Methodology' *in Social Research and Cultural Studies.* St. Leonards, N.S.W. : Allen & Unwin.
Lee and Poynton discuss the use of discourse analysis as a research method in a range of cultural and social contexts

Matheson, D. (2005) *Media Discourses – Analysing Media Texts.* Maidenhead: Open University Press.
Seeks to clarify the term 'discourse' through the common ground of a variety of theoretical approaches, as well as providing an overview of the range of ideas, concepts and frameworks that can be applied.

Phillips, N. and Hardy, C. (2002) *Discourse Analysis: Investigating Processes of Social Construction.* London: Sage Publications.
Demonstrates the use of DA within critical management studies through research into refugee systems, the Canadian whale-watching industry, HIV/AIDS, an aid organisation in the Middle East and employment service organizations.

Wetherell, M., Taylor, S., and Yates, S. (2001) *Discourse as Data: A Guide for Analysis.* London: Sage Publications.
This book provides examples of the wide application of DA. It covers research topics such as psychic practitioners, New Labour discourse, and the construction of the disease M.E.

There are also a number of useful journals to consult including *Discourse and Society, Discourse and Communication*, and *Discourse Studies: An interdisciplinary journal for the study of text and talk* – all edited by T. A. van Dijk; the on-line journals *Critical Discourse Studies* (http://www.cds-web.net/) edited by Norman Fairclough, Phil Graham, Jay Lemke and Ruth Wodak, and *Discourse Analysis Online* (http://extra.shu.ac.uk/daol/) with an editorial management team consisting of Simeon J. Yates, Kathy Doherty, and Noel Williams.

STUDENT ACTIVITY 4.1

1. Choose a newspaper article that catches your eye.
2. Read it initially as you would normally when browsing through a newspaper and then jot down a few notes about what you think the article is about. Do not refer back to the article while doing this but keep these notes to one side.
3. Now do a more detailed analysis of the article by writing down notes relating to the following: First of all look at its placing on the page. Is it a lead story or buried amongst other articles? Why do you think the sub-editor placed it there? How many headlines are there? Do they relate directly to each other or do they relate to two different aspects of the story? How big is the typeface? Does the article include photographs or diagrams and are they directly related to what the article is about? What is their source?
4. Number each paragraph and then look to see if the order of events follows chronologically or not. List the paragraphs in their chronological order to compare with the article. How has the ordering of events affected the reader's interpretation of the story? What is the time frame of the story?
5. Looking carefully at the language used, what other discourses can you detect are embedded within the story? This may be shown in direct quotes or reported speech. Also assess whether the journalist has taken on board certain words that may suggest a certain viewpoint. What sort of language is used? Is it emotive? Is it trying to entertain, inform or persuade?
6. If possible see if you can find other texts which are related to this article. Does it stem from a news release or another document? Compare the language and see if their discourses are within the news text.
7. Finally, compare the notes from your first reading with your detailed analysis. What was your first impression on reading and is this still the same now that you have deconstructed the article? How has news discourse influenced the view of the reader?

References

Antaki, C., Billig, M., Edwards, D., and Potter, J. (2002) 'Discourse Analysis Means Doing Analysis: A Critique Of Six Analytic Shortcomings', *Discourse Analysis Online.* Accessed 6 October, 2005 http://extra.shu.ac.uk/daol/articles/v1/n1/a1/antaki2002002.html.

Bell, A. (1991) *The Language of News Media.* Oxford: Basil Blackwell.

Bell, A. (1995) 'Language and the media', *Annual Review of Applied Linguistics*, 15: 23–41.

Bell, A. (1998) 'The discourse structure of news stories' in A. Bell and P. Garrett (eds), *Approaches to Media Discourse*. Oxford, UK and Malden, Massachussetts: Blackwell Publishers Ltd. pp. 64–104.

Bell, A. and Garrett, P. (eds) (1998) *Approaches to Media Discourse*. Oxford, UK and Malden, Massachusetts: Blackwell Publishers Ltd.

Blommaert, J. (2005) *Discourse: A Critical Introduction*. New York: Cambridge University Press.

Burton, G. (2005) *Media and Society: Critical Perspectives*. Maidenhead: Open University Press.

Cohen-Almagor, R. (2001) 'Ethical Considerations in Media Coverage of Hate Speech in Canada', *Review of Constitutional Studies*. V1(1): 79–100.

Devereux, E. (2003) *Understanding the Media*. London: Sage Publications.

van Dijk, T.A. (1985) 'Structures of News in the Press' in T.A. van Dijk (ed.), *Discourse and Communication*. Berlin: De Gruyter. pp. 69–93.

van Dijk, T.A. (1988a) *News as Discourse*. Hillsdale, New Jersey: Lawrence Erlbaum Associates.

van Dijk, T.A. (1988b) *News Analysis: Case Studies of International and National News in the Press*. Hillsdale, New Jersey: Lawrence Erlbaum Associates.

van Dijk, T.A., (1990) 'Discourse & Society: a new journal for a new research focus', *Discourse and Society,* 1: 5–16.

van Dijk, T.A. (1991) *Racism and the Press*. London and New York: Routledge.

van Dijk, T.A. (1993) 'Principles of critical discourse analysis', *Discourse and Society,* 4(2): 249–83.

Fairclough, N. (1989) *Language and Power*. London: Longman.

Fairclough, N. (1992) *Discourse and Social Change*. Cambridge: Polity Press.

Fairclough, N. (1995) *Critical Discourse Analysis: The Critical Study of Language*. London: Longman Group.

Fairclough, N. (2001) 'The Discourse of New Labour: Critical Discourse Analysis' in M. Wetherell, S. Taylor and S. Yates (eds), *Discourse as Data: A Guide for Analysis*. London: Sage. pp. 229–66.

Fairclough, N. (1995) *Media Discourse*. London: Edward Arnold.

Fairclough, N. (1996) 'A Reply to Henry Widdowson's "Discourse Analysis: A Critical View"', *Language and Literature* (1): 49–56.

Fairclough, N. (2001). *Language and Power*. Harlow: Longman.

Fairclough, N., Graham, P., Lemke, J. and Wodak, R. (2004) 'Introduction', *Critical Discourse Studies,* 1(1): 1–7.

Fowler, R., Hodge, B., Kress, G. and Trew, T. (1979) *Language and Control*. London: Routledge and Kegan Paul.

Garrett, P. and Bell, A. (eds) (1998) 'Media and Discourse: A Critical Overview' in *Approaches to Media Discourse*. Oxford, UK and Malden, Massachusetts: Blackwell Publishers Ltd. pp. 1–20

Georgakopoulou, A. and Goutsos, D. (1997) *Discourse Analysis: An Introduction.* Edinburgh: Edinburgh University Press.

Hall, S. (1980) 'Encoding/Decoding' in S. Hall, D. Hobson, A. Lowe and P. Willis (eds), *Culture, Media, Language.* London: Hutchinson. pp. 128–38.

Hall, S. (1997) 'Introduction' in S. Hall (ed.) *Representation: Cultural Representations and Signifying Practice.* London: Sage. pp. 13–74.

Halliday, M. A. K. (1976) *Halliday: System and Function in Language: Selected Papers.* (G. R. Kress ed.) London : Oxford University Press.

Halliday, M.A.K. (1978) *Language as Social Semiotic: The Social Interpretation of Language and Meaning.* Baltimore: University Park Press.

Halliday, M. A. K. (1985). *An Introduction to Functional Grammar.* London: Edward Arnold.

Hammersley, M. (1997) 'On the foundations of critical discourse analysis', *Language and Communication,* 17(3): 237–48.

Hartley, J. (1982) *Understanding News.* London: Routledge.

Health NZ (2005) 'Chronology of Tobacco Control in New Zealand', http://www.healthnz.co.nz/smochronol.htm Accessed 19 January 2006.

Hodge, R. and Kress, G. (1988) *Social Semiotics.* Cambridge: Polity Press.

Lee, A. (2005) 'When is a text?', paper presented at the *International Conference on Critical Discourse Analysis: Theory into Research,* University of Tasmania, Australia.

Lee, A. and Poynton, C. (eds) (2000) *Culture and Text: Discourse and Methodology in Social Research and Cultural Studies.* St. Leonards, N.S.W.: Allen & Unwin.

Matheson, D. (2005) *Media Discourses – Analysing Media Texts.* Maidenhead: Open University Press.

Paltridge, B. (2000) *Making Sense of Discourse Analysis.* Gold Coast, Queensland: Antipodean Educational Enterprises Publishing.

Phillips, N. and Hardy, C. (2002) *Discourse Analysis: Investigating Processes of Social Construction.* London: Sage Publications.

Propp, V. (1970) *Morphology of the Folktale* (translated by Laurence Scott). Austin: University of Texas Press.

Silverstone, R. (1981) *The Message of Television Myth and Narrative in Contemporary Culture.* London: Heinemann Educational Books.

Stubbe, M., Lane, C., Hilder, J., Vine, E., Vine, B., Marra, M., Holmes, J. and Weatherall, A. (2003) 'Multiple discourse analyses of a workplace interaction', *Discourse Studies,* 5(3): 351–89.

Taylor, S. (2001) 'Locating and Constructing Discourse Analytic Research' in M. Wetherell, S. Taylor and S. J. Yates, *Discourse as Data: A Guide for Analysis.* London: Sage Publications. pp. 5–48.

Toolan, M. (1997). 'What is Critical Discourse Analysis And Why are People Saying Such Terrible Things About It?', *Language and Literature,* 6(2): 83–103.

Wetherell, M., Taylor, S. and Yates, S. (2001) *Discourse as Data: A Guide for Analysis*. London: Sage Publications.

Widdowson, H.G. (1995) 'Discourse Analysis: A Critical View', *Language and Literature,* 4(3): 157–72.

Willig, C. (1999) 'Introduction: Making a Difference' in C. Willig (ed.) *Applied Discourse Analysis: Social and Psychological Interventions.* Philadelphia: Open University Press. pp. 1–21.

Wodak, R. (2001) 'What CDA is about – a summary of its history, important concepts and its developments' in R. Wodak and M. Meyer (eds) *Methods of Critical Discourse Analysis.* London: Sage Publications. pp. 2–3.

Note

1 Most New Zealand readers of the article would be unaware that Sea Shepherd's boat Farley Mowat is named after a famous Canadian novelist who was also an activist against American cruise missile testing in Canada in the 1980s. However, the example still serves to show that groups have input in creating the discourse that surrounds them.

News Content Studies, Media Group Methods and Discourse Analysis: A Comparison of Approaches

Greg Philo

DEFINITIONS

Ideology: is used by the Glasgow University Media Group to mean an interest linked perspective, i.e., a way of explaining or describing the world which legitimizes the interests of a social group.

Discourse: can be used in varying ways, sometimes abstractly to mean statements in general or to refer to a particular group or type of statements (as in 'a discourse', Fairclough, 2003). Where these are ideological, it has been defined as a language or system of representation that has developed socially in order to make and circulate a coherent set of meanings, which serve the interests of a section of society (Fiske, 1987: 14).

Introduction

The work of the Glasgow University Media Group (GUMG) has essentially been directed at analyzing the construction of public knowledge and the role of the media within this. A major focus has been news programmes, since they are the key source of information for a majority of the public. But the Group has also examined the influence of other genres such as soap operas, documentaries and TV dramas in relation to public understanding of issues such as health, politics and international conflict. This chapter outlines the methods developed by the Group and compares them to other approaches to studying the content of texts. It begins by looking at traditional methods in content studies and then moves onto discourse analysis. As the previous chapter by Smith and Bell has demonstrated, there is now a very extensive literature on discourse analysis with many different theoretical strands. I will focus on the work of two theorists, namely Fairclough and van Dijk, since they are prominent in the area and their studies provide useful points of similarity and difference with the methods which we employ.[1] The main issue I will raise is that their text-based studies are limited in the conclusions which can be drawn, since their approach does not include the study of key factors in the production of a text or the analysis of audience understanding. Finally I will show through a case study how it is possible to study simultaneously the three processes of production, content and reception of news messages.

Content analysis

Traditional approaches to content analysis have often involved attempts to measure bias in, for instance, election coverage or to study the negative representation of various ethnic groups as in the racist descriptions of ethnic minorities. The methods employed usually involved the 'breaking up' of texts so that frequency counts could be made of specific words that were used or where the amount of newspaper coverage or air-time given to a specific issue could be calculated. Conclusions could then be drawn about the amount of time given to different candidates or the number of occasions on which certain pejorative words were used about one side rather than another. The problem with such an approach is that when texts are broken up in this way, the context in which words are used becomes blurred and their actual meaning and the manner in which they are being employed can be obscured. The 'meaning' of the measurements that are made tends to be added by the investigator. So, for example, if one candidate receives more media coverage than another in an election, it might be concluded that this is beneficial. But supposing that coverage included images of the candidate falling over or mistakes being made when making speeches, then it becomes less clear which 'box' the coverage should be put into. A much more sophisticated analysis is required of how meanings are established and how audiences receive and understand them.

We can see this by looking at what was actually a very developed approach to content analysis by Cumberbatch. He took the view that the number of times an issue appeared on television news could be seen as an indicator of the priority given to it by broadcasters. He then compared his counts of various issues with public attitudes towards their importance. When he found a disjunction between these, he concluded that the TV news 'did not set the agenda of important issues for the public' (Cumberbatch et al., 1986). His evidence came from a very extensive study into TV news coverage of the miners strike in Britain in 1984/5. In his list of issues which appeared on the news, the subject of 'talks and negotiations' between the strikers and management was at the forefront of coverage. But opinion polls showed that it was not seen as 'the most important' for the public. The difficulty for this conclusion is that it neglects what was actually said about these negotiations by journalists. This strike was a very long and bitter struggle, stretching over a full year. The journalists had to cover the negotiations in case a settlement was reached. But they actually had very little hope that each set of negotiations would produce a conclusion to the strike and they came very close to saying that the meetings were a waste of time. The BBC reported that:

> Agreement remained as far away as ever – the TUC insisted on talks, once again they went badly. (BBC1, late news, 3 March 1985)

And ITV News noted that:

> [They] took just under one hour to fall out again today. (ITV, late news, 23 May 1984)

So it is perfectly possible for a subject to be covered very extensively on the news, while journalists might also 'cue' the audience into seeing it as not very significant. So in this sense journalists are intervening and re-negotiating the significance of the event to reduce its importance. To reveal this requires a qualitative analysis of the text. By qualitative, I mean an approach which is adequate at the level of meaning – in the sense that it accounts properly for how an actual meaning is conveyed. Once this textual analysis has been accomplished, there is no reason why the meanings within a text cannot be counted. In fact, a quantitative dimension to such analysis is actually very important, for example, in demonstrating the dominance of some explanations in news accounts. But to do this requires data with a high level of qualitative integrity.[2] The problem with traditional content analysis was that it tended to count words rather than meanings and sometimes to bundle data up into the boxes or a priori categories which were thought up by the investigator. One response to this has been a greater focus on the qualitative description of text, notably in areas such as discourse analysis.

Van Dijk and Fairclough: discourse and ideology

Van Dijk is well known for his work in analyzing racism in news accounts. He points to the differences between traditional content studies in this area and between that of his discourse analysis which focuses on a systematic description of semantic and syntactic features of text:

> Traditional approaches to the role of the media in the reproduction of racism were largely content analytical: quantitative studies of stereotypical words or images representing minorities ... Discourse analytical approaches, systematically describe the various structures and strategies of text or talk, and relate these to the social or political context. For instance, they may focus on overall topics, or more local meanings (such as coherence or implications) in a 'semantic' analysis. But also the 'syntactic' form of sentences, or the overall 'organisation' of a news report may be examined in detail. (2000: 35)

There are many different theoretical strands in discourse analysis and the word discourse is used in varying ways. It is used abstractly to mean statements in general or to refer to a particular group or type of statements (as in 'a discourse'). Fiske refers to it as a language or system of representation that has developed socially in order to make and circulate a coherent set of meanings, which serve the interests of a section of society (1987: 14). The important point here is that for critical discourse analysts, such as van Dijk and Fairclough, discourse is linked to power and social interests. From such relationships, there emerge different perspectives on the world. As Fairclough writes:

> I see discourses as ways of representing aspects of the world – the processes, relations and structures of the material world, the 'mental world' of thoughts, feelings, beliefs and so forth and, the social world ... different discourses are different perspectives on the world, and they are associated with the different relations people have to the world. (2003: 124)

Fairclough and van Dijk are particularly concerned with ideological effects of discourse. As Fairclough notes:

> One of the causal effects of texts which has been of major concern for critical discourse analysis is ideological effects ... ideologies are representations of aspects of the world which can be shown to contribute to establishing, maintaining and changing social relations of power, domination and exploitation. (2003: 9)

Van Dijk notes that a key function of ideologies is to promote and coordinate the interests of a group and comments that dominated groups also need ideologies as a basis for resistance. That said, he reaches the conclusion that:

> It is of course true that many ideologies develop precisely in order to sustain, legitimate or manage group conflicts, as well as relationships of power and dominance. (1998: 24)

The intellectual origins of these approaches to ideology are in structuralism – in left/Marxist variants such as in Althusser's work (1969) for whom ideology was ultimately a function of class power in capitalism, to the development of it by Foucault, who shifted the source of power to language itself. In Foucault's work, discourse is a social force which has a central role in what is constructed as 'real' and therefore what is possible. So, for example, if homosexuality is defined in a medical discourse as an 'illness', then this is a definition of what is real, which constructs how people can think about how they can live and what will be their possible futures. Such constructions determine how the world can be seen and what can be known and done within it. Discourse is thus crucial in explaining how the social subject is positioned and limited. A key question which he highlights is: 'how are we constituted as subjects who exercise or submit to power relations?' (Foucault 1994: 318).

What emerges from these theoretical developments is a concern with how language embodies systems of thought which structure what can be understood. For example, in the earliest work of the GUMG we showed how news language was organized around very limited ways of understanding economic and political activity. In the 1970s, trade unions and their wage claims were blamed for economic problems such as inflation. There was alternative evidence to suggest other causes but the government view dominated the news. As we wrote:

> What there is here is an illusion of balance, whereby reports are included from what appear as different sides. But the reported views have a totally different status, legitimacy and meaning in the text. In a very real way, only one set of statements makes 'sense' in that we are systematically given the information necessary to understand the explanations and policies which they represent. (Philo et al., 1977: 13)

In our conclusion to *More Bad News*, we were critical of broadcasters claims to objectivity and impartiality when the news was actually reproducing the assumptions of the powerful about what was necessary and possible in our society:

> The bland assertion of objectivity and impartiality ... serves only to obfuscate what is in fact the reproduction of the dominant assumptions about our society – the assumptions of the powerful about what is important, necessary and possible within it. (Glasgow University Media Group, 1980: 115)

In his recent work on textual analysis, Fairclough writes on ideology in terms which have some resonance with this:

A particular discourse includes assumptions about what there is, what is the case, what is possible, what is necessary, what will be the case, and so forth. In some instances, one might argue that such assumptions, and indeed the discourses they are associated with, are ideological. (2003: 58)

In illustrating what is seen to be 'necessary', Fairclough takes the example of global economic change. He notes that this may be presented as an inevitable process, without human agency, and comments on a text published by the European Union:

It is similar to many other contemporary texts in representing global economic change as a process without human agents ... a process in a general and ill-defined present and without a history (it is just what 'is') which is universal (or, precisely, 'global') in terms of place, and an inevitable process which must be responded to in particular ways – an 'is' which imposes an 'ought', or rather a 'must'. (Fairclough, 2003: 45)

We offered a similar analysis in our *Really Bad News*, and noted how the harmful effects of movements in the world economy were likely to be treated on the television news as a form of natural disaster, rather than as the result of human decisions:

Recession, inflation and unemployment, if they are not being blamed on wage claims, were in the period of our study most likely to be treated as natural disasters. The world economy is presented as an omnipresent force, and movements in it ... are the problem, but these movements are rarely explained for what they actually are ... a multinational firm may be reported as regrettably being forced to close a factory in the north of England because it is uneconomic, but will not usually be spoken of as having made a *decision* to move its capital somewhere else because it can make more money there. (Glasgow University Media Group, 1982: 130)

Ideology and the manner in which some perspectives are legitimized and achieve dominance remains a central issue in textual analysis. The methods which are employed are the focus of the next section.

Three methods in textual analysis

I will look first at the thematic analysis developed by the GUMG, then at Fairclough's work on the semantic and grammatical features of texts and finally at van Dijk's use of what he terms the ideological square. The GUMG's work (which I was involved in) began with studies of television news. We focused on major thematic areas such as industrial struggles or international conflicts and then examined the explanatory frameworks or perspectives which underpinned the descriptions which were given. In any contentious area there will be competing ways of describing events and their history. Ideas are linked to interests and these competing interests will seek to explain the world in ways which justify their own position. So ideology (which we defined as an interest-linked perspective) and the struggle for legitimacy go hand-in-hand. Much of our work focused on the role of the media in these ideological struggles and how the reporting of events can embody different ways of understanding. We were interested in how language was linked to wider social processes and how individual meanings and communications related to conflict and divisions within the society as a whole. The language and definitions used were at one level the battleground for competing groups. The issue then was not to look simply at the descriptions which were offered of the world in a specific text, but to look at the social relations which underpinned the generation of these descriptions. Thus in our recent work on television and the Israeli-Palestinian conflict we gave an extended historical account of the dispute and showed how each phase in it had generated competing histories of what had occurred (Philo and Berry, 2004). When the conflict is reported in media on a daily basis, both sides struggle to assert the validity of their own accounts. This is so for each event in terms of descriptions about what has happened and 'who is to blame'. But it also relates to the more general frameworks of understanding and interpretation which underpin the public relations of each side. For example, when we analyzed news reports of the intifada between 2000–2, we were puzzled as to why the Israelis were not at that time stressing the issue of anti-semitism as part of making their case. There was evidence of anti-semitism in the speeches of some Muslim clerics, so we asked experts in public relations why there had not been a great emphasis on this. Nachman Shai had been chief spokesperson for the IDF (Israeli Army) and he described the decision to focus on the 'war on terror' rather than anti-semitism:

> We selected the first (war on terror) instead of the second (anti-semitism) because we are part of the Western world. We very much played the first argument. It worked better with governments, they gave us more support. It's like if you've run out of arguments, you're stuck with anti-semitism. The first one is based on common interests. (Interview with Nachman Shai, Philo and Berry, 2004: 249)

It is also the case that for Israel to present itself as part of the general 'war on terror' against those who dislike Western values also has the advantage of drawing attention away from specific actions by Israel which have contributed to the origins and development of the Middle East conflict. The Palestinians would, for their part, see the Israelis as state terrorists and would point to what they see as Israeli violations of international law in imposing a military occupation in the Palestinian territories.

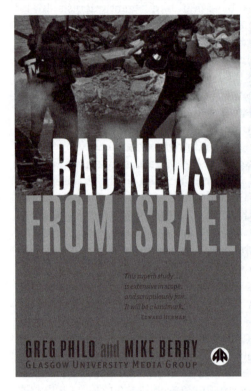 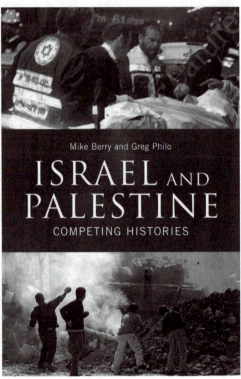

Plate 5:1   Using a combination of research methods, including the innovative News Game research exercise, the Glasgow University Media have consistently focused on the Mass Media's ideological role in Britain and beyond. Images reproduced by kind permission of Pluto Press, London. ©

The important theoretical point is that the interests behind an ideology may remain the same, but its immediate content does not. The parties in a conflict deploy different arguments in relation to constantly changing circumstances. To understand this process necessarily involves going beyond the immediate text. Our approach thus began from the assumption that different ways of explaining the world emerged from such conflicts and from other social divisions such as those between classes and sub-groups within these, from interests based on gender or from competing institutions. Such an approach necessarily involved us in the detailed analysis of public debate and its origins in political and social conflict.

This analysis was undertaken before work could begin on examining specific news texts to show how various perspectives were represented (or not) within them.

So an important first step in our method was to identify the range of arguments which existed on an issue. This showed what was available for journalists to choose from, as well as which arguments 'belonged' to different interests. It also made it possible to explore the conditions under which they were deployed. In the GUMG's work on TV news coverage of industry and the economy, they examined the public debate which existed at that time about the failings of the British economy (Glasgow University Media Group, 1980). In the 1970s and 80s, this was a matter of great concern as Britain was perceived to be falling behind the rest of the world's economies. In this public controversy the trade unions pointed to management mistakes in the organization of industry and to low levels of investment which meant that machines often broke down and production was much less efficient than that of competitors in other countries. In contrast, right-wing commentators (including the Conservative party) preferred to point to the actions of the workforce and blamed strikes for the failings of the economy. This became a favourite theme of the Conservatives in the 1980s, in the early years of Margaret Thatcher's government (see Philo et al., 1995). We were interested in how the TV news reported such arguments and the potential influence on public belief. We began by noting each of the explanations and ways of understanding which were put forward in public debate and the range of available evidence which could underpin different positions. We identified these from public materials such as books, reports, the press and TV and any other relevant sources. From these we constructed what was, in effect, a conceptual map of the different beliefs which were available in the political and economic debate of that time. Using this, we could then analyze how different parts of the debate were featured in the news. A key issue was the absence or presence of explanations and the manner in which some accounts were highlighted or 'preferred' in the text. We distinguished between statements that were simply reported by journalists as being from a specific source and those which they directly endorsed. This can be seen in the difference between a reported statement such as 'the government says that strikes are a major problem' as compared with a 'direct' statement as in this example:

> It's the kind of strike that has contributed significantly to the dire economic problems. (ITV, main news, 4 January 1975, cited in Philo et al., 1982: 29)

If Fairclough was analyzing these types of statement, he would refer to them as indicating differences in modality in as much as they relate to differences in 'commitments', 'stances', and therefore 'identification' (2003: 166). We did not always use the categories of formal linguistics and developed our own descriptions of what was occurring.[3] But it is clear that there are some parallels between these semantic and syntactical features of text which we examined and the later work developed by Fairclough. For example, he uses the concepts of hyponymy and synonymy to mean a pre-supposed semantic relationship. The first implies an inclusion and the second an identity between words. For example in the case of hyponymy, a neo-liberal might treat 'globalisation' and 'economic progress' as hyponyms. The point is to make such a relationship favour a particular perspective. In hyponymy one word is strengthened by its suggested closeness with the other. An even stronger relationship is in synonymy, where words are treated as being so close that they are interchangeable. We illustrated such a use of language in our study of strikes in the industry. We had shown how the lack of investment in new plants meant that machines broke down very often and that much production was lost. This, however, was ignored on the news and when destruction of output occurred it was related very largely to strikes. So when the strike ended, the plant was referred to as returning to 'full' production, even though such 'normal' periods included a loss of output which was greater than that caused by strikes in the factory. For example, a journalist commented that:

> With the engine tuners back at work … the plant was also back in full production.
> (ITV, lunch-time news, 7 January 1975)

We noted in our commentary on this that 'normal production and full production are treated as synonymous and are equated with being strike free' (Philo et al., 1982: 36).

Fairclough also uses the concept of 'collocation'. This means a regular or habitual pattern of co-occurrence between words. He gives the example of 'poor old' (as in 'poor old man') as being a more habitual combination than 'poor young' (2003: 213). We showed this process in our account of the treatment of wage claims in the news in the 1970s. At the time, inflation was high and was routinely linked in reporting to wage 'demands' by trade unions. We noted at the time that there were many other causes of inflation, such as speculation on property or increasing oil prices. The point about focusing on wages was that the government believed it could reduce inflation by forcing down wages and controlling wage claims. The view that wages had actually caused inflation was contested, but the TV news nonetheless very extensively featured the government view, as in these examples:

> [The Chancellor] has warned again of *excessive wage increases* as the miners start negotiating. (BBC1, main news, 11 February 1975, italics added, cited in Philo et al., 1982: 61)
> [The Chancellor's] warnings about wage-led inflation and *pay rises well in excess* of the cost of living. (BBC1, main news, 16 April 1975, italics added, cited in Glasgow University Media Group, 1980: 46)

So 'excessive' occurs in collocation with 'wage increases'. The link became routinized as the news monitored each new wage claim and commented on its potential effect on inflation. We developed this conception of how meaning was established by noting that such a relationship could become routinized to the point that journalists might actually dispense with the emotive word 'excessive'. As we wrote:

> When this economic view is pursued, the logic of who is to blame is inescapable. It seems perfectly natural to monitor wage claims ... this becomes so routine that journalists could dispense with apparently emotive terms such as 'excessive'. They have only to say 'and tonight another wage claim', for everyone to know what they mean and at whom the finger is being pointed. (Philo et al., 1982: 60)

We also developed at this time the concept of the explanatory theme. This is an assumed explanation which gives a pattern or structure to an area of coverage. For example, the explanatory theme that strikes were to blame underpinned whole processes of news reporting. This might include going to a factory, interviewing workers, asking them about strikes and crucially *not* asking the management about investment policies or their own mistakes, and then perhaps listing in the bulletin other strikes which had occurred that week. The crucial point is that the pattern of coverage and the subjects that it highlights can assume the explanation even without it being directly stated. Not all news is as closed as this suggests. There are a range of factors which can influence news output, some of which produce texts which are organized very tightly around such explanatory themes. But other factors can generate a greater diversity of explanation. To analyze these requires an approach which necessarily goes beyond the content of specific news texts and looks more broadly at the processes which underpin their production. I will suggest later that the absence of 'production studies' in the work of Fairclough and van Dijk means that the conclusions which they can draw are limited and sometimes problematic. Part of our work focuses exactly on this link between production and content. We can look briefly at this now and the issues which it raises for the development of appropriate methods.

Production processes and the analysis of news texts

The first issue to consider in studying production processes is the professional ideology of journalists and the institutions which they represent. Some news is dominated by specific explanations and ways of understanding but such assumptions are overlaid by other beliefs and practices. They include the need to feature some form of apparent balance between views – if only at the level of interviewing opposing sides. The credibility of television news and the legitimacy which it seeks for itself depends upon its claim to be even-handed and 'fair' in controversial areas. Our research suggests that it is skewed in favour of the powerful, but the broadcasting institutions are intensely reluctant to be seen as simply the mouthpiece of the state or other major interests. There is sometimes a real substance to their claims to be featuring a range of views. How 'balanced' they can be depends in part on the area of news. On issues where the state is very sensitive, such as the coverage of Northern Ireland in the period of the 'troubles', the news could become almost one-dimensional – alternatives were reduced to fragments or disappeared altogether (see Miller, 1994). But even in such a 'closed' area, there are still cases where journalists have jeopardized their own careers and become involved in intense controversies in order to release information and produce stories which they thought should be told. This is done from a sense of personal and professional commitment. In 1985, BBC journalists went on strike to protest about the banning of a *Real Lives* programme featuring elected representatives from Northern Ireland. The government had asked that the program be not shown and the Board of Governors of the BBC had concurred with this (for other examples from Northern Ireland, see Glasgow University Media Group, 1982: 140–3). We also encountered instances where journalists had deliberately undermined what they saw as the official 'line' of their own news organization. For example, during the Falklands War, the British military had ordered the bombing of the air-field at Port Stanley, the capital of the Falklands, which was occupied and being used by Argentine forces. The British Ministry of Defence claimed initially that this attack was successful and that the air-field could not be used. There was, however, evidence that it was still in use, including film of it in operation which was being flown out by the Argentines. But the TV news stayed with the official government view that it was out of action. The MoD was then forced to make a concession, so it issued a statement that the air-field could be used by 'light air craft'. An ITN journalist told us that when he received this, he deliberately went to find pictures of a very large Hercules transport plane going along the runway. He then placed these as the visual background to the MoD statement. We noticed this in our analysis as a contradiction in the text between the images and his report that:

> The MoD now concede that light aircraft can now use the runway. (ITV, main news, 14 May 1982, cited in Glasgow University Media Group, 1985: 86)

The point is that textual analysis alone could not reveal what had occurred and we had no way of understanding this until we spoke with the journalist.

There are other factors which should be considered in the news production process including the use of sources, the organization and logistics of news gathering and market pressures. The relation to outside sources is crucial and we have studied the manner in which external interests such as governments, corporations, NGOs and other lobby groups seek to promote their own perspectives. The state has some absolute powers in that it can impose censorship, though it rarely acts in such an overt fashion. Perhaps more importantly it is the key supplier of routine information to media institutions in areas such as employment or health or in relation to new policy development. Journalists depend on the access granted to them, and this becomes particularly acute in circumstances such as war or conflict where only a limited number may be allowed in to the key zones for reporting. Politicians in power are in a strong position to insist that their views are featured – especially in the publicly-regulated media. We describe the media in our work as a contested space. Not all of those in the contest are of equal power and journalists are subject to intense pressures which can effect the climate in which they work. In *Bad News from Israel*, myself and Mike Berry noted a number of key factors which influenced broadcast output including the political link between Britain and the US and the strong support in America for Israel, plus well organized lobbying and public relations, together with the intense criticism of journalists who were seen to be putting out negative reports on Israel. As we concluded:

> The pressures of organised public relations, lobbying and systematic criticism together with the privileging of Israeli perspectives by political and public figures, can effect the climate within which journalists operate. There is no total control and there are areas of the media where the debate is relatively open. But these factors go some way to explaining why journalists sometimes have difficulty in giving a clear account of the Palestinian perspective, while they can apparently more easily facilitate that of the Israelis. (Philo and Berry, 2004: 256)

Overall, the extent to which media are 'open' to alternatives and may feature many contesting views is likely to vary in relation to conjunctions of political, economic and institutional factors – including differences between publicly-regulated and privately-owned sectors.[4] We might expect a more open expression of varied perspectives when there is no clear account emerging from the most powerful groups or when they are divided. The divisions in the Conservative party over Europe in the 1990s would be an example of this or the controversy in the Labour party in the latter stages of Tony Blair's leadership.

The privately-owned media have often been used to promote political views, which has a limiting effect on the range of arguments and information which is featured within them. We noted this as a factor in the representation of the Israeli-Palestinian conflict (see Philo and Berry, 2004: 252–6). The economic interests of the media have strong effects on their political preferences. Not surprisingly, the right-wing press in Britain has normally supported the Conservative party. But the Murdoch organization has also a tradition of reaching agreements with various political parties in order to gain commercial advantage. In Britain, the Murdoch press had for many years supported the Conservatives and Margaret Thatcher, but in 1997 they switched support to New Labour, following a meeting and an unspecified agreement between Tony Blair and Rupert Murdoch. As Michael White commented in *The Guardian* newspaper:

> In every country in which Mr. Murdoch operates (and minimizes his tax bill) he is a power-broker, speaking power, not truth, unto power through his diverse media outlets. The Blairites have ... made a Faustian bargain with Rupert. They think they have a good bargain. (30 January 1998, cited in Philo, 1999: xi)

Most of the media in the UK are commercial institutions in their own right, so the need for market share – to gain viewers and readers – is a paramount concern. We have shown how this can override potential links to government or 'public' interests. For example, media coverage of mental health in the 1990s went largely against government policies of reducing long-term institutional care in special hospitals. The policy of 'community care' was attacked as the media focused on audience-grabbing stories of the dangers posed by the mentally ill – what has been referred to as the 'mad axe murderer syndrome' (Philo, 1996). In this area, the desire for market share was crucial and 'news values' which place a priority on fear, drama or spectacular events became central in the choice of stories and the angle taken.

The key theoretical point is that all these pressures exert major influences on the content of texts. For example, where there is an intense and controversial debate, as in the Israeli/Palestinian conflict, journalists might simply seek to avoid giving explanations because whatever they might say will draw criticism from one side or the other. There is also a limit to the amount of time that they will spend giving an account of the views of each side. As Lindsey Hilsum from Channel 4 News commented to us:

> With a conflict like this, nearly every single fact is disputed ... I think, 'Oh God, the Palestinians say this and the Israelis say that' ... I have to say what both sides think and I think that sometimes stops us from giving the background we should be giving because I think 'Well bloody hell I've only 3 minutes to do this piece in it and I'm going to spend a minute going through the arguments.' (cited in Philo and Berry, 2004: 245)

The history of the conflict and explanations of its causes are intensely controversial. We noted how rarely they were referred to in news programmes. It was also the case that when journalists did include references to them, they sometimes spoke in a form of short hand or code which noted an issue but was very inexplicit.

Thus an ITV journalist commented, 'The basic raw disagreements remain – the future, for example of this city Jerusalem' (ITV, early evening news, 16 October 2001, cited in Philo and Berry, 2004: 110). Some viewers would already have an understanding of the historical events which gives significance to this comment, for example that Jerusalem is sacred to both Muslims and Jews and East Jerusalem has been occupied (illegally, in the eyes of most countries) by Israel since 1967. But as we showed in our audience research, most of the population simply do not have this knowledge. So the journalist's comment has little meaning, in terms of the potential to understand what the 'disagreement' is about. The meaning cannot always simply be assumed using the cultural knowledge of the investigator. It also requires some knowledge of the audience.

The key conclusions in terms of methods which we drew, was that it was not possible to analyze individual texts in isolation from the study of the wider systems of ideologies which informed them and the production processes which structured their representation. It was also necessary to simultaneously study processes of audience reception before making judgements about social meaning and the potential impacts of texts on public understanding. This became the basis of our methodological approach and with this in mind I will now go on to consider the methods of text analysis employed by Fairclough and van Dijk.

Fairclough's critical discourse analysis

As we have seen, Fairclough is centrally concerned with issues of power and legitimacy and the '"common sense" assumptions which are implicit in the conventions according to which people interact linguistically' (2001: 2). He terms his approach critical discourse analysis and he challenges social theorists and researchers to show the effects of language in contemporary social life. As he writes, these effects include 'making the socio-economic transformations of new capitalism and the policies of governments to facilitate them seem inevitable' (Fairclough, 2003: 204). Drawing on Bourdieu and Wacquant, he notes that what is at issue is the process of classification, by which 'naturalised pre-constructions' generate a particular 'vision' of the world (Fairclough, 2003: 130, Bourdieu and Wacquant, 2001). Thus he notes that discourses can be differentiated

> in terms of semantic relations (synonymy, hyponymy, antonymy) between words – how they classify parts of the world – as well as collocations, assumptions, and various grammatical features. (2003: 133)

I have discussed collocations, synonymy and hyponymy above (antonymy is the opposite of hyponymy).[5] My own view is that the master category here has to be 'assumptions', since these underlie the deployment of the various textual strategies – as in treating economic progress as a hyponym of globalisation. Put another way, the textual strategies are used to 'frame' a description in accordance with the underlying assumption. Fairclough also analyses other dimensions of the rhetoric and 'promotional messages' of politicians such as Tony Blair. In a close analysis of political speeches, he shows how 'desires' are typically represented by Blair as actually 'existing'. For example, globalisation is spoken of 'as a fact' and at the same time as a project or plan (2003: 114). He also shows how Blair positions himself with his own audience in terms of what Fairclough refers to as the process of 'conversationalisation'. Blair presents himself as speaking as an individual, saying for example 'I realise why people protest against globalisation' (2003: 76). This simulates person-to-person conversation, thus reducing distance and explicit hierarchies (rather than saying for example, 'the government believes that ...'). This is an interesting account of rhetorical strategies but there are difficulties with Fairclough's approach in as much as it remains text-based. Fairclough does note the limits of textual analysis and the need to 'link the 'micro' analysis of texts to the 'macro' analysis of how power relations work across networks of practices and structures' (2003: 16). But my own view is that text analysis cannot be simply bolted on to other work. There are problems in that it is difficult to explain the construction and meaning of a text without simultaneously examining other factors such as production and reception processes.

In essence, I have suggested that discourse analysis which remains text-based encounters a series of problems specifically in its ability to show:

1) the origins of competing discourses and how they relate to different social interests
2) the diversity of social accounts compared to what is present (and absent) in a specific text
3) the impact of external factors such as professional ideologies on the manner in which the discourses are represented and
4) what the text actually means to different parts of the audience.

There are three other problems for what we might call 'text only' analyses to which I want to draw attention. The first is the issue of the accuracy of representations and the need to go beyond the text to check these. The second is the question of the significance of the text to our own audience (i.e. the readers of our critical work) and the third is what I will term 'Whose rhetoric is it anyway?' We can look first at the issue of the accuracy of representations. A key function of texts is to represent other entities – such as ideas, beliefs or actions (Fairclough, 2003: 27). A news text often represents these in terms of the reported statements of whoever is being featured. Fairclough seeks to criticize such representations by showing how they are sometimes 'framed' to give a favourable view of one side rather than another. We would do the same thing, but we would first examine the external context from which the statements were derived. An example from Fairclough's work would be his comments on a BBC Radio news report of September 1993 on the extradition of two Libyans accused of responsibility for the Lockerbie bombing in 1988. He points to the manner in which the UN Secretary General is reported as taking a tough line with Libya and is said to be using the word 'demand':

> Part of the framing here is the choice of 'demand' as the reporting verb – it is highly improbable that the Secretary-General said 'I demand that ...', so 'demand' rather than, for example, 'ask' would seem to be a framing conducive to an interpretation which casts the Libyans in an unfavourable light. (Fairclough, 2003: 53)

The question we would put is did he say it or didn't he? The research would be stronger without the guess about what the Secretary-General 'probably' said. But to find out requires going beyond the immediate text, to examine the original speech and to assess the significance of what it actually included.

The second issue is what gives power to critical analysis for our own readers. By this I mean, what makes people sit up and take notice? It might not come as much of a surprise to know that politicians exaggerate, that they use rhetoric, or that they speak of things they want to happen as if they are already happening. A critique is given more force by conveying a sense of what is excluded – of what we are not being told. This is especially so when it is possible to show that the excluded accounts have a strong evidential base. In our work, when we indicated that trade unions were blamed on television news for industrial failures, we were able to give more credence to alternative accounts by quoting from figures produced by management in the car industry. These revealed the role of their own mistakes in lost production which had not been featured in television news. We also quoted from other 'authentic' sources beyond the immediate news texts. We included the following report from the *Financial Times* which very clearly stated the trade union view:

> Shop stewards tell hair-raising stories about managerial failings, and point at the moment to constant assembly-track hold-ups caused by non-availability of supplier component parts. (6 January 1975)

Critical discourse analysis would be more powerful if it routinely included a developed account of alternatives.

The final point is what I have called 'Whose rhetoric?' and also relates to the need for an account of the social and political structures which underpin the content of texts. Fairclough does sometimes go beyond the immediate text in order, for example, to contrast the claims of neo-liberalism with its actual effects. In this, he shows a concern with the gap between rhetoric and reality and between what people say and what they do. In his *New Labour, New Language?* he also contrasts Blair's 'relaxed and inclusive style against evidence of "control freakery"' (2000: 156). But much of Fairclough's work is text-based in the sense that it focuses on texts to show how dominant perspectives are legitimized through various strategies in the use of language. There is another dimension to the issue of the difference between what politicians say and what they do which can create problems for such textual analysis. The point is that politicians sometimes speak in favour of policies in which they do not actually believe and which they have no interest in pursuing. The rhetorical strategies employed would not therefore be seriously intended to win support for the policy but may exist simply to gain personal support for the speaker. For example, in September 2002, Tony Blair made a speech about the need to 'continue to redistribute wealth':

> It must be a Britain in which we continue to redistribute power, wealth and opportunity to the many, not the few. (Tony Blair, 17 September 2002)

It was an unusual statement since the government's own figures on the distribution of wealth show that Britain has one of the most extreme divisions between rich and poor in Europe. Blair and New Labour have rejected any suggestion of increasing income or property taxes to dent the wealth of the super rich. On the TV news, the speech was attributed to the need for Blair to gather support in his own party for the coming war with Iraq. As this journalist comments:

> He [Tony Blair] has spent the past few weeks preaching a message about war and backing America that makes many Labour members nervous and some positively sick at the soul. So ahead of the party conference [Blair is making] promises more to their taste. He even used an old socialist word, one banned from the New Labour lexicon. (BBC1, early evening news, 17 September 2002)

So Blair's use of the old socialist word 'redistribution' might be seen as rhetoric designed simply to increase his support in the Labour party. This implies the existence of different types of rhetoric. One which we have seen earlier is designed to legitimate and develop a new economic order for the benefit of the powerful, and the other which might be called 'mere rhetoric' is designed for more limited personal or political advantage. There are gaps between rhetoric and reality in both types – between, for example, the claims made for the new order and what it actually delivers. But this is a different order of gap from when a politician is merely stealing the clothes of another group and is not seeking to legitimize fundamental changes. It also raises the question of whether there is much point in analyzing the textual strategies of a political speech in such a case as if it represents a fundamental commitment to an ideological programme, when by other (external) criteria we would know that it does not. In considering types of rhetoric, another possibility is of course that Tony Blair and New Labour do actually believe some of the progressive comments which they make, for example, on the need to abolish child poverty or debt in the developing world. So to distinguish these from 'mere rhetoric' and the legitimizing of economic power in neo-liberal speech requires a detailed exposition of current political debate, the perspectives within it and their relation to policy and real change. A discourse analysis which focuses on political rhetoric as legitimizing a new economic order and analyzes texts on this basis would miss such differences in political meaning and potential impact. Crucially, if the analysis remains 'within the text' it is not possible to explain the social relationships which underpin the presentation of the descriptions and accounts which appear. If we look, for example, at an analysis by Fairclough of another speech by Blair, we can see this more clearly. This speech was about the 'war on terror' and globalization. Fairclough shows how the structure of the speech 'dramatically constructs' a dialogue with imagined opponents (as in: 'people say we should do this, we have tried it, it didn't work, so now we must do our policy'). The point, which Fairclough's discourse analysis research reveals, is that in these parts of the speech Blair constructs the supposed opposition in such a way as to affirm the correctness of his own decisions. But in another part of the speech, which Fairclough doesn't discuss, Blair actually endorses the views of his opponents. He states:

> The demonstrators are right to say there is injustice, poverty, environmental degradation.
> (Tony Blair, 13 October 2001, cited in Fairclough, 2003: 47 and 238)

The problem is that when Blair does this, his opinions do not sound much different from those of Fairclough's. So if we stay 'within the text', it is not immediately clear what critical discourse analysis is being critical of. At such a point, it would be helpful to consider the political relationships which led to the use of such rhetoric and also to have a detailed account of the potential gap between it and the reality of what New Labour is actually doing, on, for example, the environment.

The key point is that to distinguish between types of rhetoric necessitates an analysis of political structures, purposes and strategies. It requires an account of the social and political system and conflicting interest within it, beyond what can be seen from an immediate text. Without this we cannot comment on the difference between rhetoric and reality in terms of the intentions of the speaker, the validity of representations and the relation between accounts that are featured and alternative versions of truth. Textual analysis should extend its methods to include the study of the structures and relationships which shape the content of texts. We will see this again in considering the work of van Dijk.

Van Dijk and the ideological square

As we have seen, van Dijk is also concerned with questions of ideology and particularly with the issue of the reproduction of racism in discourse. He notes that traditional studies of ideology and language have focused on 'lexical items', i.e. individual words which may imply a value judgement (for example, 'terrorist' or 'racist'). He suggests that a discourse analytical approach should go beyond this. He notes that opinions and the assumptions which they contain may be expressed in many complex ways in text and talk, in, for example:

> Headlines, story structures, arguments, graphical arrangements, syntactic structures, semantic structures of coherence, overall topics and so on. (1998: 31)

Some of his work parallels our analysis of texts. He highlights, for example, the importance of 'agency, responsibility and blame for actions' and 'the perspective from which events are described and evaluated' (1998: 44). Thus in *Bad News from Israel*, myself and Mike Berry showed how the Palestinians were often represented on the news as initiating conflict in the sense that they 'started' a problem by attacking the Israelis, who then 'retaliated' or 'responded' – as in this example:

> Five Palestinians have been killed when the Israeli army launched new attacks on the Gaza strip *in retaliation for recent acts of terrorism*.
> (Radio 4, 7.30 a.m., 6 March 2002)

So the agency and responsibility for initiating the violence is presented as being with the Palestinians. We showed in our reception studies how audience members could infer blame from such accounts. As one young woman commented in a focus group:

> You always think of the Palestinians as being really aggressive because of the stories you hear on the news. I always put the blame on them in my own head ... I always think the Israelis are fighting back against the bombings that have been done to them. (cited in Philo and Berry, 2004: 222)

The Palestinians do not see the conflict in this way. From their perspective, its origins lie in the loss of their homes and land when Israel was established, which made them refugees and in their situation as living under Israeli military occupation since 1967. A senior journalist from the BBC commented to us on the absence of this perspective on the news. What was missing, he said, was the view that this was an uneven war and that:

> It is a war of national liberation – a periodic guerrilla war, sometimes using violent means, in which a population is trying to throw off an occupying force. (Interview, with Paul Adams, cited in Philo and Berry, 2004: 260)

We also noted how the Israeli perspective, which, as we have seen, focused on the 'war on terror', was sometimes endorsed by journalists in their commentaries – as in this description of an Israeli action:

> The [Palestinian] attack only reinforced Israeli determination to drive further into the towns and camps where Palestinians live – *ripping up roads around Bethlehem as part of the ongoing fight against terror*. (ITV, early evening news, italics added 8 March 2002, cited in Philo and Berry, 2004: 187–188).

Another dimension of method which van Dijk notes is the value of quantitative demonstrations. These are important to establish whether 'overall strategies' exist in establishing differential descriptions of social groups. In our study, we used quantitative analysis to show the relative prominence of casual linkages explaining action and motive. For example, we showed in a major sample of news content that Israelis were said to be 'responding' or 'retaliating' to something that had been done to them about six times as often as the Palestinians (Philo and Berry, 2004: 160).

In his own work, van Dijk develops the concept of the ideological square which is intended to highlight key 'functional moves' in developing an ideological strategy. For van Dijk, the heart of this strategy is a polarization between 'us' and 'them', which involves positive in-group description and negative out-group description (1998: 33). So an ideological account would:

1. Emphasize our good properties/actions.
2. Emphasize their bad properties/actions.
3. Mitigate our bad properties/actions.
4. Mitigate their good properties/actions.
    (van Dijk, 1998: 33)

Using this theoretical model, van Dijk analyzes media texts, notably of British tabloids such as *The Sun*. He concludes that 'various levels of discourse may be involved in the enactment, expression or inculcation of negative beliefs about immigrants or minorities' (2000: 42). Myself and L. Beattie certainly found in our work that media coverage could stigmatize out-groups having the effect, as we wrote, of re-enforcing '*our* identity and *their* exclusion' (Philo and Beattie, 1999).

We did not, however, use a concept such as the 'ideological square'. The reason is that the four points of a square can easily become four boxes into which language is fitted (especially so in the hands of students who usually make it go in one way or another). My own view is that it is better to avoid such *a priori* categories when beginning the analysis of a text. Van Dijk is certainly right that there are many elements of media accounts which correspond to his schema. The difficult is that some do not, so the question is raised: How can we develop a method which can explain contradictions and variations? We can pursue this by looking at the case of *The Sun* newspaper. This has a differentiated readership and a complex marketing strategy which produces variations in its news coverage, editorials and features. The following editorial is on a woman who has built a 'mud hut' in her garden and would fit without difficulty into the ideological square:

> Mrs Desiree Ntolo's 20-ton mud hut is being demolished.
>
> She built it in the back garden of her council house in Dagenham, Essex because she was homesick for Cameroon.
>
> Just a thought: why doesn't she build the next monstrosity in the African home-land she's pining for?
>
> *The neighbours would no doubt club together to pay her airfare.*
>
> (*The Sun*, 26 September 1992 cited in van Dijk, 2000)

In van Dijk's words, this would 'favour the in-group and derogate or prob-lematize the out-group' (2000: 42), with the neighbours being the in-group who would pay the airfare for the 'out-group' African woman to go. But there are other cases of some news and editorial coverage which clearly contradict the model. How do we account for a commentary which appeared in *The Sun* crit-icizing 'the abuse hurled by some supporters' at black football players? It had the headline 'Racist Morons Ruin the Game'(1 September 1990). In another edi-torial *The Sun* explicitly attacked the sacking of a black chambermaid:

> *Jennifer Millington's job as a chambermaid lasted one day.*
>
> She was sacked, according to the owners of [a hotel] in Newquay, Cornwall, for one reason.
>
> She was black and some of the guests objected to her.
>
> We hope this disgraceful story has one certain result.
>
> *Any decent person going to Newquay will stay in any hotel but [this one].*
>
> (*The Sun*, 2 September 1991)

Here, the out-group are clearly the management and the guests but the story is described as 'disgraceful' and there are no mitigating factors given for their behav-iour. *The Sun* would defend itself against criticisms of being racist by pointing to such stories and also by noting its large number of black readers. This offers some potential insight into these apparent contradictions. *The Sun* has always been faced with the issue of selling to diverse readerships and with potential variations between its content and the views of those who buy it. It has a history of being a right-wing populist newspaper which sells to a predominantly working-class audience, many of whom vote Labour. When it supported Margaret Thatcher at the beginning of the 1980s, one of its targets was the left-wing head of the Greater London Council, Ken Livingstone. By the end of the 1980s, when the Thatcher government was in serious decline, *The Sun* actually gave a regular column to Ken Livingstone under the title 'A View from Labour'. He then used it to attack other columnists in the same paper for being too right-wing. *The Sun*'s approach to issues with 'racial' overtones, shows a similar concern to appeal to a diverse readership and specifically not to offend key minority groups. For example, in 2006 there was a major controversy over the publication by European newspapers of cartoons featuring the Prophet Muhammad. *The Sun* did not publish these. In an editorial, it stated that:

> The cartoons are intended to insult Muslims, and *The Sun* can see no justification for causing deliberate offence to our much-valued Muslim readers. (*The Sun*, 3 February 2006)

We spoke to a *Sun* journalist who dealt with 'race' issues. He expressed the view that his paper had deliberately avoided being in any way anti-Muslim in dealing with stories such as the Abu Hamza case, where a cleric was arrested and tried for inciting violence:

> I think we handled the Abu Hamza story well – concentrated just on what he was, it didn't spill over into being anti-Muslim. Being cynical I could say its because a lot of *Sun* readers are from ethnic minorities. (Interview, 21 June 2006)

To explain the apparent contradictions in *The Sun's* coverage really requires a production study and an analysis of the conflicting pressures which affect content. Van Dijk's method does not include this and when confronted by such variations, he can simply pass over them. Consider, for example, his commentary on newspaper coverage of the views of Enoch Powell, a right-wing politician who called for the repatriation of migrants:

> Despite its formal rejection of Powell's ideas, the conservative Press seldom misses the opportunity to publicize his racist views, so that millions of readers will know them. *The Times* even publishes another recent diatribe of Powell against immigrants, thereby legitimating his racist views as part of the public debate, even when it distances itself from such views. A 'reassuring' *Sun* poll shows that the majority of the British people do not support Powell's 'astonishing "blacks go home"' call. That white public opinion

(or the methods by which it is assessed) is fickle, is shown a few weeks later, after the Brixton and Tottenham disturbances, when the *Mail* reports that most white Britons want to stop further immigration and favour repatriation. (van Dijk, 1991: 97)

My own view is that when *The Sun* refers to Powell's opinion as an 'astonishing "blacks go home"' call and publicizes a study showing that most people disagree with him, then this is a significant variation from the hypothesis that *The Sun* is explicitly or implicitly racist. It really needs to be explained. But in this case, van Dijk simply passes over it and moves on to comment on the 'fickle' character of white public opinion, which is a different issue altogether. To explain the position of *The Sun* and other media requires a study of production and a method which includes analyzing the practices of journalists as well as newspaper marketing strategies. I am also not sure about van Dijk's claim that for the media to present views while criticizing them has a legitimating effect. There is a good deal of media coverage of Osama bin Laden and his video tapes when they are released but this does not legitimize his actions or those associated with him in British public opinion.[6] The impact of specific media messages really has to be assessed using audience studies.

In his more recent work, van Dijk analyses *The Sun*'s coverage of illegal migrants. He shows how in a report, they are presented as 'invading' Britain and he indicates the extremely negative quality of much of what is written. The text from *The Sun* is as follows:

> Britain is being swamped by a tide of illegal immigrants so desperate for a job that they will work for a pittance in our restaurants, cafés and nightclubs.
> Immigration officers are being overwhelmed by work. Last year **2191** 'illegals' were nabbed and sent back home. But there are tens of thousands more, slaving behind bars, cleaning hotel rooms, and working in kitchens. (*The Sun*, cited in van Dijk, 2000: 44)

But once again he is confronted by the issue of variations in the coverage, where as he notes, there is 'an element of empathy creeping into the article' when the journalists describe the immigrants as 'slaving' at their work (2000: 45). This relates to the poor conditions and salaries which the immigrant workers receive.

So there is an ambivalence in *The Sun* report between the implied violence and threat of an 'invasion' and the potential sympathy which might be invoked for the 'slave' workers. To explain this requires, as before, an investigation which goes beyond the text. When we interviewed television journalists, we found some who were intensely critical of media attacks on asylum seekers and migrants. One very senior editor from ITN told us that he believed some sections of the press should be prosecuted for their role in the promotion of violence against these groups.[7] He and others with whom we spoke had attempted to produce news items which went against the dominant flow. One focus of these 'alternatives' was the exploitation and poverty of migrant workers. We can see this in the following headline from ITN, which is from a special extended report in a news programme:

> They came in search of a better life – what they find is squalor and slavery. (ITV, late news, 22 May 2006)

In the case of *The Sun* report, it might be that the newspaper is attempting to appease different audiences as I noted above, or that the journalists are trying to introduce alternative ideas. Van Dijk's approach is first to acknowledge the contradiction in the report and then to attempt to resolve it by reinterpreting the text. He notes that when the journalists describe the immigrants as slaving: 'This totally converts (and subverts) the earlier characterisation of the immigrants as active and evil, and not as victims'. (van Dijk, 2000: 45) He then attempts to find potential meanings which could put the text back into his ideological square. He goes on to say:

> On the other hand, the use of 'slave' presupposes 'slave holders', and instead of mere empathy, this may suggestion accusation of restaurant owners who exploit their 'illegal' workers. (2000: 46)

I don't see how a connotation of 'slave holders' could reduce sympathy for the slaves in this context. The difficulty is that because van Dijk's methods remain text-based, there is no way in which it is possible to explain such contradictions other than by speculating on further potential meanings which can be derived from the text.

Without the analysis of production and reception processes, discourse analysis is limited in the conclusions that it can draw. There is a need to develop methods which can trace the communication of messages from their inception in contested perspectives, through the structures by which they are supplied to and processed by the media, then to their eventual appearance as text and finally to their reception by audiences. There follows a brief example from our own work to show how this might be done.

Production, content and reception of a message

This is a practical example based on news coverage of the Israeli-Palestinian conflict and specifically on reports about the shooting early in the intifada of a young Palestinian boy, Mohammed al-Durrah. The images of him and his father crouched against a wall were widely shown and became a potent symbol of the Palestinian intifada. The circumstances of this killing were highly contested and became the focus of an extensive propaganda struggle. We have seen earlier in this chapter how Israeli public relations focused on the 'war on terror' and sought to present Israel as threatened and essentially 'responding' to attacks. This provided an overall framework, but each new event in a conflict requires a specific public relations response. In the case of Mohammed al-Durrah, the Israelis issued a statement saying that the boy's death was unintentional. This was reported on TV news as follows:

> Israel says the boy was *caught unintentionally in crossfire.* (ITV, lunch-time news, italics added, 2 October 2000)

The Palestinians rejected this account and stated that the targeting was deliberate. This view appears on the news in an interview from hospital with the boy's father, who is reported as follows:

> Miraculously his father survived but his body is punctured with eight bullet holes. 'They shot at us until they hit us', he told me, and 'I saw the man who did it – the Israeli soldier'. (BBC1, main news, 1 October 2000)

The two accounts of the events are therefore opposed, but it is the Israeli view that became dominant on the news. Most significantly, it is endorsed by journalists as the 'normal' account of events. It is referenced not simply as a viewpoint in the sense that 'the Israelis say that he was caught in crossfire', but rather as a direct statement, as in 'the boy was caught in the crossfire'. There are a series of examples of this:

> Newscaster: Palestinians have been mourning the death of a 12-year-old boy killed in the crossfire.
> Journalist: The Palestinian death toll is rising steadily, among them a 12-year-old boy, Mohammed al-Durrah, who with his father *got caught in the crossfire.* (ITV, early evening news, italics added, 1 October 2000)
> Journalist: Nearby I met the mother of 12-year-old Mohammed al-Durrah, the Palestinian boy killed on Saturday *in the middle of a ferocious gun battle.* (BBC1, main news, italics added 3 October 2000)
> Journalist: The worst clashes have been in Jerusalem, the Gaza Strip, and the West Bank, where a 12-year-old boy was *killed in the crossfire.* (ITV, main news, italics added, 1 October 2000)

It is clear that the journalists are sympathetic and do say that it was the Israelis who killed the boy, but it is the Israeli explanation of this event which is most frequently referenced (for a full account see Philo and Berry, 2004: 148–50 and 225–31).

Box 5.1   The news writing exercise

This exercise (*aka* the 'news game') is an important element of the methods developed by the GUMG. It consists of giving small groups of people a set of photographs taken from actual news programmes. They are then asked to imagine that they are journalists and to write a short news item using the pictures as a stimulus. They can work as a group of three or four people (in which case it is useful to record their discussion) or as individuals (which gives a better measure of what each person knows and remembers from watching the news). The method developed from classroom work with students and was intended simply as a 'game' to initiate discussion. But it became apparent that those taking part could very closely replicate news headlines, as well as the text and structure of bulletins. So it was then decided to formalize the procedure as a research technique using carefully sampled groups and criteria such as age, gender and class. Its first use was in a study of beliefs and attitudes to the 1984/5 miners strike (see Philo, 1990). The power of it as a research tool was that it resolved a traditional problem in 'effects' studies. These had often involved showing audience groups material taken from television, such as political broadcasts, then asking questions about possible 'effects' on attitudes. The difficulty was the artificial nature of the exercise, in that many of the subjects might never normally even watch such programmes. So much of the material in the consciousness of the subjects came from the nature of the exercise rather than the 'normal' behaviour of the participants. The news writing exercise avoided this by asking people what they knew, in a sense, before the investigators arrived. The exercise is followed by asking group members a set of questions about the source of the information which they have used (to check whether it does actually come from TV or the press or some other origin such as personal experience). The questions also examine whether the audience members actually believe what they have written in their 'news items'. This is because the exercise could operate either as a projective test (i.e. reproducing the beliefs of group members) or as a re-enactment test (i.e. representing what they believed the television account would be). In later work the exercise was used to examine audience responses to other areas of media output such as TV soap operas and the portrayal of issues such as mental illness and child abuse (Philo, 1996; Kitzinger, 2004). In our studies, the questions asked to group members were often followed by a focus group discussion. With this combination of methods it was possible to demonstrate clearly what audience members had taken from television and to trace actual influences on beliefs and attitudes.

In our audience studies, we were then able to show how news accounts of these events had a measurable influence on the understanding and memory of them amongst viewers. For this work we brought together members of the public in focus groups. We also invited journalists to attend these and they took an active part in the research, asking questions about specific responses to coverage in which they had been involved. They were given 16 photographs which were taken from TV news footage of the conflict and asked to use these as a stimulus. They were not constrained to focus on these pictures but in practice could write anything they wished. As a method this was designed to show what audiences have retained from news programmes. We found that many participants had a remarkable ability to reproduce both the content and structure of news bulletins. One of the pictures in this exercise showed Mohammed al-Durrah with his father, others included the aftermath of a suicide bombing and the body of an Israeli solider being thrown from a window after he had been captured and later killed. There was no prior discussion of these and no attention was drawn to these or any of the pictures. These events were, however, referred to in some of the 'news stories' written by the audience group members. In the case of Mohammed al-Durrah, there was no reference made to the Palestinian view that he had been deliberately killed. Some group members did, however, reproduce the language of the original Israeli statement:

> A young boy was *caught in the crossfire* as Israeli troops opened fire in the West Bank. (middle class female, London – italics added)
> Israeli soldiers return fire and a father and son are *caught in the crossfire* – the boy is fatally wounded. (middle class male, Glasgow – italics added)
> The American flag has been publicly burned by the Palestinians following the death of a young child who had been *cornered in the crossfire* between the Jewish soldiers and Palestinians in Jerusalem. (middle class female, Paisley – italics added)

There was another very significant feature to the stories written by some members of the audience groups. They also reproduced the structure and sequence of accounts as they had most frequently occurred on TV news. This, as I noted above, included the presentation of Palestinian action as initiating a violent event, while the Israelis were then shown as 'responding'. In the case of Mohammed al-Durrah, this is an unlikely scenario since his death was at the very beginning of the intifada. But in order to retain what became the 'normal' sequence of action, some group members took events which had occurred *after* Mohammed al-Durrah's death and wrote about them as producing the Israeli 'response' in which the child was killed. This historical reversal occurs as in the following examples:

An Israeli soldier was taken hostage and thrown to his death by Palestinians on the rampage. The scene was witnessed live on TV by a shocked nation who took to the streets to protest ... the Israeli people vowed to revenge this act and in the fighting that followed a 10-year-old Palestinian boy was shot dead in his father's arms. (female teacher, Paisley)

A young boy was killed as his father helplessly tried to shield him from Israeli bullets. The Israeli onslaught came as a direct retaliation to a newly-wed Israeli couple being killed by a Palestinian suicide bomber in the latest Palestinian terrorist attack. (middle class female, London)

In this approach we can begin to show how TV news can shape not only the language which we use in ascribing meaning to events, but also the way in which we group and organize our memories.

Conclusion

We developed our methods with the intention of investigating mass communications as a totality in which meanings were circulated through the key dimensions of production, content and reception. The concept of circulation is crucial since it allows for the possibility of interaction between elements of the process and does not imply a single 'one-way flow' from the top to the bottom of the system (i.e. from production to reception). Those who supply information to the media certainly intend it to have an impact, but they are still aware of the contexts within which their messages will be received, So what is supplied will itself be shaped by an anticipation of the reception process, as well as by an understanding of the likely response of different elements of the media. We have shown how messages can have powerful influences on audience beliefs and understanding but our work also demonstrates how some audience members critique and reject what they see and hear in media accounts. The growth of new technology and the Internet has also, to some extent, increased the potential of ordinary citizens to develop their own systems of communication and has added to the interactive possibilities of traditional media. In terms of methodology, the key point is that all these elements must be understood and studied as part of a total system – rather than in isolation as with studies which remain focused on texts. Analyzing the processes of production, content, reception and circulation simultaneously is a complex task but it is the way forward if we are to come to terms adequately with the generation and reproduction of social meanings.

Summary

- To avoid the problem of positivism and the violation of 'actors meanings' requires a qualitative analysis of texts.
- This textual analysis also requires the study of the social structures from which competing ideological explanations develop.
- A 'discourse analysis' which remains text-based has problems in its ability to show:

  1. the origins of competing discourses and how they relate to different social interests
  2. the diversity of social accounts compared to what is present (and absent) in a specific text
  3. the impact of external factors such as professional ideologies on the manner in which the discourses are represented, and
  4. what the text actually means to different parts of the audience.

- There are other problems with 'text only' analyses in relation to; the accuracy of representations; the significance of texts to our own audience; and the question of how rhetoric 'belongs to' or is used by different social interests.
- To overcome these problems requires a method which analyzes processes of production, content, reception and circulation of social meaning simultaneously.

GOING FURTHER

Student readers will find the following websites useful in to learn about the debates that are taking place on the concepts of discourse and ideology:

http://www.gla.ac.uk/centres/mediagroup/

http://www.prwatch.org/

http://www.spinwatch.org/

http://www.mediachannel.org/

http://www.zmag.org/weluser.htm

http://www.chomsky.info/

http://www.discourses.org/

http://www.ling.lancs.ac.uk/staff/norman/norman.htm

STUDENT ACTIVITY 5:1

Try this variation on the 'news game' for a class of approximately 20 students. Divide the class into four groups of five. Before the class begins, collect five newspaper items on a prominent event, for example, the Israeli/Palestinian conflict. They can be selected from different newspapers giving varying accounts of events or aspects of the dispute. Then give copies of the five items to each group, so that each student has one item. They can then read it for a few minutes and after this a discussion begins with each student telling the others in the group the content of the one item they have read.

The task of each group is then to produce a short piece of TV news, using the press cuttings as source material. This is presented as a live performance by each group – one student as the news 'anchor', others as reporters, interviewees, etc. It can be on one day's events or a retrospective item, looking back over a period. They can supplement the press cuttings with any other knowledge they may have and can be told in advance to brief themselves on the subject using the Internet or other sources. The students can also be specifically instructed to produce a 'balanced' item giving the views of both 'sides', and also to include as much explanation and context as possible. After the presentations, a general discussion can be held exploring, for example, the concept of 'balance' and/or asking how it might be possible for news programmes to inform audiences and to go beyond 'event-based' news.

References

Althusser, L. (1969) *For Marx*, London: Penguin.

Bourdieu, P. and Wacquant, L. (2001) 'New-Liberal Speak: notes on the new planetary vulgate', *Radical Philosophy*, 105: 2–5.

Cumberbatch, G., McGregor, R., Brown, J. and Morrison, D. (1986) *Television and the Miners Strike*. London: BFI Broadcasting Research Unit.

van Dijk, T. (1991) *Racism and the Press*. London: Routledge.

van Dijk, T. (1998) 'Opinions and Ideologies in the Press' in A. Bell and P. Garrett (eds) *Approaches to Media Discourse*. Oxford: Blackwell.

van Dijk, T. (2000) 'New(s) Racism: A Discourse Analytical Approach' in S. Cottle (ed.) *Ethnic Minorities and the Media: Changing Cultural Boundaries*. Buckingham: Open University Press.

Fairclough N. (2000) *New Labour, New Language?* London: Routledge.

Fairclough N. (2001) *Language and Power* 2nd edn. London: Pearson Longman.

Fairclough, N. (2003) *Analyzing Discourse*. London: Routledge.

Fiske, J. (1987) *Television Culture*. London: Methuen.

Foucault, M. (1994) 'What is Enlightenment?', in P. Rabinow (ed.) *Michel Foucault, Essential Works Volume 1 (Ethics)*. England: Harmondsworth.

Glasgow University Media Group (1980) *More Bad News*. London: Routledge.

Glasgow University Media Group (1982) *Really Bad News*. London: Writers and Readers.

Glasgow University Media Group (1985) *War and Peace News*. Milton Keynes: Open University Press.

Kitzinger, J. (2004) *Framing Abuse*. London: Pluto.

Miller, D. (1994) *Don't Mention the War: Northern Ireland, Propaganda and the Media*. London: Pluto.

Philo, G. (1995) 'Television, Politics and the Rise of the New Right', in G. Philo (ed.) *Glasgow Media Group Reader: Industry, Economy, War and Politics*, Vol. 2. London: Routledge.

Philo, G. (1996) *Media and Mental Distress*. London: Longman.

Philo, G. (1999) (ed.) *Message Received, Glasgow Media Group Research 1993–1998*. London: Longman.

Philo, G. and Beattie, L. (1999) 'Migration in Media' in G. Philo (ed.) *Message Received*. London: Pearson Longman.

Philo, G., Beharrell, P. and Hewitt, J. (1977) 'One Dimensional News – Television and the Control of Explanation' in P. Beharrell and G. Philo (ed.) *Trade Unions and the Media*. London: Macmillan.

Philo, G., Hewitt, J. and Beharrell, P. (1982) 'Industrial News' in *Really Bad News*. London: Writersand Readers.

Philo, G. and Berry, M. (2004) *Bad News From Israel*. London: Pluto.

Philo, G., Hewitt, J. and Beharrell, P. (1995) 'And Now They're Out Again: Industrial News' in G. Philo (ed.) *Glasgow Media Group Reader: Industry, Economy, War and Politics*, Vol. 2. London: Routledge.

Philo, G. (1990) Seeing and Believing. London: Routledge.

Philo, G. and Miller, D. (2001) 'Cultural Compliance' in G. Philo and D. Miller (eds) *Market Killing*. London: Pearson/Longman.

Notes

1 Another reason for using their work is that they stand in a tradition of critical analysis, in which they are concerned to study the consequences of the use of language in its ideological forms – in other words it's effect in developing or reproducing social relations of power and exploitation. We share this concern with consequences in the real world of social relations and structures of power. Other approaches in discourse theory avoid such issues by 'bracketing off' what is real or true. Reality is seen as a product of discourse and of representation and is therefore indefinitely negotiable. This produces an inability to comment on the relationships of our society and is a form of intellectual quiescence. For a more extended critique of this see Philo and Miller (2001).

2 There is sometimes a false dichotomy suggested between quantitative studies which are (wrongly) termed as 'positivist' and 'scientific' at one end of research while 'interpretative' studies are presented as being at the other. But 'positivism' is not the same as using quantitative methods and it is certainly not 'scientific'. The problem with it is that it involves the incorrect application of the methods of natural science to social science and the neglect of the capacity of social actors to negotiate meaning. So it is inadequate at the level of actor's meanings. Once the meanings of a text or actions have been properly

understood by the investigator, they can be quantitatively assessed. The only other objection to this would come from constructivists who might argue that all meaning is indefinitely negotiated – that 'meaning is engendered in the encounter between the reader and the text' – and that this applies also to the investigator's attempts to hold meanings constant. If 'reality' is continually re-negotiated through language, they would say, then there is no fixed reality to be counted. But if this is seriously believed, then no research is possible, or indeed any form of social life. For a critique of this position see Philo and Miller (2001).

3 I think the principal reason for this was that it seemed to us that there were an indefinite number of ways in which characteristics of language in use could be described. Rather than attempt to label all these, we focused on the specific textual features which were the heaviest carriers of meaning – which we could establish through a combination of textual analysis and our work with audience groups. We then analyzed how these elements of the text worked to establish explanations – for example, through descriptions of sequences of action which implied cause or responsibility and reflected on the legitimacy of different parties (see, for example, Philo and Berry, 2004: 160–5).

4 For a fuller discussion of this and the impact of the release of the free market on broadcasting in Britain see Philo, 1995.

5 Where hyponymy implies inclusion in a group of words, antonymy would suggest exclusion from the group. 'Social cohesion' and 'organic community' would be hyponyms, with antonyms as 'polarization', or 'fragmentation'.

6 See for example forthcoming research by Sarah Oates and Mike Berry of Glasgow University on public attitudes to terrorism (ESRC New Security Challenges Programme) – *The Framing of Terrorist Threat in British Elections*, ESRC RES 228-25-0048.

7 The interviews were conducted in 2001–2 as part of our study of news coverage of the Israeli/Palestinian conflict. Since the issues of migrants and asylum seekers were very prominent at the time, several journalists made additional comments on coverage of these.

Framing and Frame Analysis

Jenny Kitzinger

DEFINITIONS

Framing refers to the process whereby we organize reality - categorizing events in particular ways, paying attention to some aspects rather than others, deciding what an experience or event means or how it came about. The term is used to refer to how we interpret our everyday encounters with the world around us. It is also used to refer to how a picture 'frames' a scene, and how a newspaper 'frames' a story.

Any representation of reality involves framing. If you take a photograph you are literally 'framing' the scene - freezing an image of a moment in time, from a particular perspective. Through the view-finder you select your focus, decide what to foreground and what to leave in the background, and exclude some aspects of the scene from the frame altogether. The resulting photograph does not show the whole of the landscape, it necessarily 'frames' a particular view.

Similarly a newspaper report cannot tell the reader everything. Journalists frame a story by selecting the 'relevant' facts and placing an event in what they consider to be the appropriate context. They tell the story in ways which highlight particular ideas about the nature of the event. They decide who they should interview and what questions they should ask. They portray key players in the drama in particular ways (the victims, the perpetrators or the policy-makers and politicians implicated in the crisis). They also present implicit and explicit ideas about the causes, and the solutions, to the problem.

Within media and communication studies, **frame analysis** is thus the term used when researchers try to unpick the processes through which a frame is presented. Frame analysts ask: How have journalists told the story and why did they tell the story in this way? What alternative frames could have been used? How might the problem, and the key players involved, have been presented differently? What alternative ideas about the causes and the solutions might have been considered? Analysts may also ask: What are the *consequences* of presenting events 'framed' in one way rather than another? How does the dominant framing of this issue impact on public understandings?

The basic idea of framing is thus, on one level, very straightforward – and is an extremely useful way of approaching critical analysis of the media (and, indeed, the social construction of reality more broadly). However, the concept is rather fluid, and can be a little difficult to get to grips with and use in a practical research project. This chapter starts by outlining some of the shifting, and sometimes confusing, ways in which the term 'frame' appears in a wide range of literature. It then goes on to give a much more practical introduction to various forms of frame analysis within media and communication studies.

Introduction

Terms such as 'frames', 'frameworks' and 'frame analysis' are used in a variety of overlapping ways in diverse disciplines ranging from sociology, politics and linguistics to psychology and fine arts. Any search for literature about 'framing' thus reveals a bewildering array of approaches. This chapter will focus on the way the concept is used within communication/media studies. In this introduction, however, I touch on the ways in which it appears in other disciplines too. I do this so that readers are not disconcerted when they read the term in other contexts. By understanding the range of ways in which the concept is used you may also be able to reflect on how communication/media studies connects with other disciplines.

Goffman (1974) is often credited with first popularizing the concept of the 'frame'. He used the term in describing social interaction and everyday cognitive structures. Goffman's concept of 'frame' refers to systems of classification that allow us to 'locate, perceive, identify and label' the diverse phenomena we encounter through the course of our lives (Goffman, 1974: 21). Other authors have defined frames as 'tacit theories about what exists, what happens, and what matters. [...] We frame reality in order to negotiate it, manage it, comprehend it, and choose appropriate repertoires of cognition and action' (Gitlin, 1980: 6). Frames have also been described as 'cognitive windows' through which stories are 'seen' (Pan and Kosicki, 1993: 59) or 'maps' helping us to navigate through a forest of multiple realities (Gamson, 1992: 117). From a media and communication perspective:

> To frame is to select some aspects of a perceived reality and make them more salient in a communicating text in such a way as to promote a particular problem definition, causal interpretation, moral evaluation, and/or treatment recommendations. (Entman, 1993: 52)

Frames operate in the conversation we have, the media we consume, the questionnaire we fill in. The way in which information is presented *to us* (the frame used in that act of communication) may prime us to respond in particular ways.[2] This has been researched by cognitive psychologists who demonstrate that subtle changes in the phrasing of survey questions create dramatic variations in measured opinion. For example, the percentage of respondents favouring more generous government financial assistance is higher where recipients are described as 'poor people' rather than 'people on welfare'. Framing is thus a key concept for questionnaire design, assessment of public opinion surveys and, indeed, for those concerned with improving communication (for example, between doctors and patients) (Kahneman and Tverskty, 1984).

Framing is also a concept used in the study of social movements: examining, for example, the strategies adopted by environmentalists, feminists, and campaigners for nuclear disarmament, workers' rights or lesbian and gay equality (see Benford and Snow, 2000). The interest here is how those questioning the status quo are able to negotiate shared understandings of some problem, articulate an alternative approach and urge others to join them. Any social movement has to 'reframe' issues – challenging, for example, ideas that nuclear arms are necessary and justified for protection, or that homosexuality is unnatural and sinful. Indeed, any campaign, from whatever political perspective is fruitful territory for the study of framing because they make visible 'the struggle over the production or mobilizing and countermobilizing of ideas and meanings' (Benford and Snow, 2000: 3). For example, in the US, wealthy families have funded a campaign to abolish estate/inheritance tax. The adverts present the tax as a plot to 'destroy family businesses' and have successfully re-branded it 'the death tax' – 'a ghoulish phrase that invokes images of vulture-like tax inspectors hovering over the beds of the dying' (Cohen, 2006: 11). Protest groups also sometimes deliberately produce hard-hitting visuals in an effort to dislodge taken-for-granted frames and replace them with the campaigners' preferred perspective on reality. One controversial TV ad, for example, showed a terrified little girl trapped in a cramped cage. The over-voice intones 'A chimp has the mental and emotional age of a four-year-old child.' The advert (which was banned in the UK as 'political') clearly seeks to challenge 'specie-ist' views (in which other species do not deserve the same consideration as our own). The advert is designed to encourage people to reframe their perceptions to adopt an animal liberation perspective (Cohen, 2006).

The study of social movements, campaign strategies and advertisements obviously overlaps with the study of the mass media. Many researchers into 'framing' have been interested in how campaigning groups present their cause and are portrayed themselves, or how mainstream or alternative views are represented in the mass media (for example, Gitlin, 1980). The concept of 'framing' has also readily been taken up within media studies because it offers insight into how messages are produced. As many media sociologists have pointed out, journalists are consummate 'framers' of reality – as are the professional PR workers who help control and shape the supply of information to the media. When journalists report an event (or when PR sources talk to journalists) they are doing more than being a mere conduit of information. (See also John Corner's treatment of 'Spin' in Chapter 9 of this textbook). They are selecting highlights and directing attention to some aspects and not others.

Crucially, it is important to note that a report is 'framed' even if it is 'balanced'. Indeed, a frame can happily incorporate controversy – and may even be more robust because of it (Gamson and Modigliani, 1989: 3). The journalist's frame still sets the agenda and the terms of the debate – guiding not only who should be interviewed, but also what questions they are asked, how they are introduced and edited. The words journalists use, the way they structure the narrative, the facts they select to include or exclude, and the people they choose to quote, all help to shape the story in particular ways.

The concept of 'framing' builds on, but involves much more than, the traditional notion of agenda-setting. It goes beyond commenting on the *extent* or *degree* of media attention, focusing instead on the *nature* of that attention and the aspects that are highlighted as *salient*. The notion of framing is also far more radical than the idea of bias because it acknowledges that *any* account involves a framing of reality. The notion of 'bias' suggests that there is an objective and factual way of reporting an issue 'correctly', but that some reports distort this. The notion of 'framing', by contrast, suggests that all accounts of reality are shaped in some way or other. Indeed, without the ability to frame, the world would be a confusing morass of sensations – we would be lost with no sense of meaning and significance.

From the above introduction it can be seen that framing theory applies to all levels of the circuit of mass communication:

- Frame analysis can be used to examine the *production* of media coverage: how journalists and their sources operate , and how this can affect the way a story is told.

- It can also be used to analyze *content*: how an issue is represented in the newspaper, on television or, indeed, on a website.
- It also has implications for *audiences*: frame analysis either makes assumptions about, or actually empirically explores, how frames influence people's reactions.

These are also all interlinked through the fact that frames may be deeply anchored in a culture shared by journalists, their sources, and their audiences alike. In the following discussion I will address each of these areas in turn.

First, however, a brief word of warning: even within communication/media studies, there is no single agreed definition of framing beyond those outlined above. People work with the concept in very different ways and often disagree. For some the word 'frame' is nothing more than a metaphor (Brosius and Eps, 1995); for others it is a central organizing structure, which can be systematically and empirically tested. The one thing writers seem to agree on is the vagueness of the term. Framing research is a 'scattered conceptualization' or a 'fractured paradigm' (Entman, 1993: 51). This need not necessarily limit its usefulness – while some writers urge the establishment of a united paradigm of framing research, others argue that the concept can usefully be employed in very diverse ways (D'Angelo, 2002). Here I will certainly not attempt to impose uniformity on the wide range of framing research. Rather, my aim is to guide readers through some of the litera-ture in order to give them a sense of how to critically read such work. I also hope this summary might provide readers with a starting point for their own research.

Analyzing media production

The first strand to consider in framing research is the issue of how media repre-sentations are produced. The key question here is: 'Where do frames come from?' How do social institutions, power structures, professional practices and values impact on the selection and shaping of accounts of reality? Research methods to explore such questions could include examination of press releases, the study of funding and regulatory structures, observation in newsrooms, and interviews with journalists and their sources. Ironically it is this fundamental aspect of framing which is perhaps the least explored – at least in projects explicitly identified as 'framing research'. As Carragee and Roefs complain, researchers have often focused on content and effects almost to the exclusion of attention to 'frame sponsorship' and the wider political and social contexts which shape 'framing contests' (Carragee and Roefs, 2004). Harking back to Tuchman's study in the 1970s, they argue that the origin of framing research in media sociology directly linked the framing process to the distribution of social and political power but that much contemporary research has ignored this scholarship. While I agree with Carragee and Roefs, that work focused on media frames rarely trace such frames back into media production processes, it is possible to draw on other work (not explicitly labelled 'framing research') to inform our understanding of such processes. In particular a great deal of relevant enquiry has been pursued under the political economy model and the sociology of journalism. One recent example of an interesting investigation of production processes from within a framing paradigm is Entman's research into how 9/11 was reported. He examines how the WhiteHouse presented the terrorist assaults as acts of war committed by an evil enemy – and called for the country to unite behind the invasion of Afghanistan. He contrasts this with the framing challenge offered by two journalists who attempted to shift the focus onto Saudi Arabia (Entman, 2003). A good overview is also provided by books such as Johnson-Cartee's (2005) *News Narratives and News Framing*, which pulls together some of the sociology of journalism with framing theory.

Analyzing media content: What do frames look like? How can they be detected?

The second, and by far the most popular, level of framing analysis applies to media content. Researchers have examined, for example, how the media represent poor people, left-wing activists, feminists, and people with mental illness, or how they tackle broad issues such as 'The War on Terror', affirmative action, poverty reduction strategies, health care or economic conflict.

Framing researchers are often concerned with at least four key questions: How is the problem defined? How are key players portrayed? Who is presented as responsible? What solutions are proposed? They also usually work with a sense of *opposing* or *alternative* frames. For example:

- The shooting down of an airliner can be framed as an unwarranted act of war or an unfortunate accident (Entman, 1991).
- The enlargement of the European Union can be presented in terms of risk or opportunity (Schuck and de Vrees, 2006).
- The normal working of the capitalist economic system can be made invisible or problematized (Glasgow University Media Group, 1980).

Although a great deal of framing research is concerned with specific substantive issues (such as those outlined above), another strand of framing research addresses overarching or generic frames. These writers are concerned with patterns that cross-cut the media coverage of diverse stories. Scholars have explored how journalists rely on archetypal narratives (for example, a 'Rags to Riches' storyline) and highlighted deeply embedded assumptions that inform reporting such as 'individualism' or 'ethnocentrism'. Alternatively, researchers may examine particular styles or genre of reporting. From this perspective the interest is in how a story may be written up through, for example, a 'human interest' or 'conflict' frame or researchers may examine whether a news report adopts an 'episodic' frame (depicting concrete events) or a 'thematic' approach (presenting collective or general evidence) (Iyengar, 1991).

How researchers analyse frames in texts

Framing researchers use the full range of techniques found in content and discourse analysis to identify the type of frames that, they believe, are being promoted. For some people, framing analysis is achieved through systematic, quantitative content analysis. For others, however, framing analysis is just another word for discourse analysis. Whichever approach they use (and some scholars employ both quantitative and qualitative methods) researchers often start by immersing themselves in the media coverage. They may complement this by looking at the material produced by relevant campaigning groups, or talking to key stakeholders and 'everyday folk' about the issue. A particular set of frames are then identified.

My review of existing literature suggests that this task may be carried out with varying degrees of methodological rigour, sophistication or sensitivity. Researchers may quickly identify the major frames that they think are in circulation, and then focus on how these frames may be identified in diverse texts. Alternatively, they may give more attention to deriving and testing the range of frames that might exist and exploring the ways in which they overlap and diverge. (Frames rarely, in any case, exist in their 'pure' form – see below for a fuller discussion and suggestions about how to reflect on identified frames.)

The next step is to identify key discursive cues associated with the different frames. Particular attention is given to how an event is categorized – this is a crucial moment in the development and application of a frame. This is true in any process – whether we are talking about journalists or, for example, the police. Consider, for instance, what happens if police officers make the assumption that a murder is a consequence of a 'gang feud' or is a 'random attack'. This will lead them in a different direction than if they consider that it might be a 'racist murder'. Such categorization reflects, and influences ideas about motive, it will impact on who police will interview and where they will look for evidence, and indeed, may lead to the 'framing' of different suspects. The same is true for how journalists categorize an event and begin to define the problem and propose policy solutions.

In addition to examining how an event is categorized, framing researchers look out for words and images with powerful cultural resonances – which seem to be highly-charged and memorable. The underlying idea here is that frames have 'condensing symbols ... making it possible to display the package as a whole with a deft metaphor, catchphrase or other symbolic device' (Gamson and Modigliani, 1989: 3). The point is that the whole frame does not have to be spelt out in every detail in order to invite readers/viewers to recognize and place the issue within that frame.

Significant cues may be identified through traditional discourse analysis and/or through systematically tracing and testing patterns of association within texts. Specific elements of a text may be seen as particularly significant sites for framing, for example, headlines and opening and closing paragraphs. The placement within the newspaper may also be important (for example, the 'frame' implied by locating an item on 'The Women's Page'). Over and above this, analysis will include examining various aspects of language, image and narrative (see Box 6.1). In some cases frames may also be explicated through exploring how people recall media accounts – focus group discussions will then inform the researcher's framing analysis of media texts.

Box 6.1   Aspects of a text which might be examined to identify key 'cues'

- Images used
- Type of language used
- Labels and definitions employed
- Explanations offered
- Responsibility assigned
- Solutions proposed
- Narrative structure
- Contextualization and links
- Historical associations invoked
- Similes and metaphors

(Continued)

- Emotional appeals
- Who is invited to comment
- How different speakers are introduced
- How different characters, groups, social movements or entities are described.

The need for different degrees of sophistication may depend on the topic under study or the level of framing being explored. The researcher may be interested in very broad frames, or in very finely calibrated distinctions. Thus some researchers highlight a few key terms, such as the different frames implied by the use of the term 'terrorist' or 'freedom fighter', others create complex matrices of key concepts and phrases. Gamson, for example, lists about 30 key statements associated with each of his frames about the Arab-Israeli conflict. He assigns key statements to different frames such as the 'Feuding neighbours' frame, the 'Arab intransigence' and the 'Israeli expansionism' frame (Gamson, 1992: 243–5).

Once particular frames and associated discursive cues have been identified then researchers can map how particular frames dominate the representation of an issue. They may also chose to explore how different frames *compete*, or compare how frames shift across key variables. You can, for example, ask questions such as:

- How are diverse frames applied to ostensibly similar events? (See Entman, 1991)
- How do frames shift over time? (for example, how was nuclear power discussed in the 1970s, and how is it discussed now?)
- How might frames vary across diverse media? (for example, blog sites versus mainstream news.)

Some examples of framing analysis of media texts

Perhaps the best way of helping readers to grasp framing analysis is to outline a couple of straightforward examples in detail. My first example is drawn from a study examining the representation of the human embryo. My second example examines the representation of asylum seekers.

Example 1: Framing the embryo

The rights and wrongs of abortion are a key area of social contest – several studies have examined how the framing of abortion has shifted over time, varies across cultures, or how 'framing contests' have been fought out between 'pro-choice' and 'anti-abortion' campaigners (for example, Ball-Rokeach et al., 1990; Ferree et al., 2002). Recent advances in scientific research add a new dimension to this conflict because embryos are now seen, by some people, as invaluable scientific resources for experiments in human cloning and stem cell research. This is a cutting edge biotechnology, often heralded as the future of medicine, offering hope for those with diseases such as diabetes, cancer, Parkinson's and Alzheimer's. However, using human embryos in such experiments has led to international controversy and very different regulations have been adopted by different countries across the world. In the US, for example, the funding of such work is very restricted. In the UK, however, legislation (introduced in 2001) allows research to be carried out on embryos up until they are 14 days old.

The way in which the cloning and stem cell debate played out in the UK (leading up to the 2001 legislation) is a useful case study of how competing frames are mobilized at a key moment in a conflict over politics, science and morality. Tracking of the words, images and metaphors used in the media reporting identified clusters of competing rhetorical techniques. Those who wanted to promote embryonic stem cell research emphasized that such research would only be conducted on the *pre-14 day old* embryo, a cell mass sometimes technically called a 'blastocyst' (proponents sometimes used this word in preference to the term embryo). This was, they explained, a very tiny ball of cells and they invited readers to imagine its size by, for example, stating that it was 'almost invisible to the naked eye' or 'no bigger than this full-stop'. Magnified images of the microscopic cell cluster (sometimes dyed green) were displayed to show that it looked alien, and certainly nothing like a foetus (See Fig 3). Proponents of embryonic stem cell research also emphasized that the embryo used in such research was usually the by-product of fertility treatment – surplus, 'waste' material that would otherwise be thrown away.

By contrast, the opposing frame presented in the UK media came from those who saw embryonic stem cell research as immoral. These speakers highlighted the embryo's humanity and were outraged that it would be 'dismembered' or 'killed' during the research process. If they mentioned its size at all, they did so to emphazise its vulnerability as a 'tiny human being'. These 'pro-life' campaigners invited people to consider embryos as persons embedded in family networks with parents and siblings, and the focus was on the *embryo's* potential, rather than the potential of stem cell research. They also focused on the fact that research might be carried out on *cloned* embryos, deliberately created for research purposes (and implied that this might lead to full reproductive human cloning). Box 6.3 presents the matrix of framing devices displayed in the media coverage of this debate.

Box 6.2 Newspaper cutting. Picture of magnified ball of cells 16 August 2000

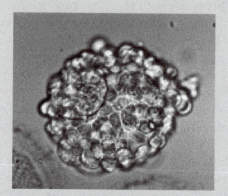

Plate 6:1 Photographs of magnified ball of cells often featured in the press coverage of stem cell research. These images help to 'frame' the debate in particular ways. The image above appeared in the *Daily Telegraph*, under the headline: 'This is what the human cloning row is about' (August 16th 2000). Reproduced by kind permission of The Stem Research Group, University of Edinburgh © 2000.

Box 6.3 Framing the embryo in stem cell research – devices displayed in the UK media coverage of the embryonic stem cell debate

	Pro-embryonic stem cell research: Embryo = invaluable material for developing therapies	Anti-embryonic stem cell research: Embryo = precious human life
Metaphors which 'humanize' or 'dehumanize'	'florescent frogspawn'	'very young human being'
References to the *size* of the embryo	Frequent references to 'microscopic' size or 'smaller than this full-stop'	Size not mentioned – or only to emphasise vulnerability, for example 'tiny, vulnerable being'

Use of photographs Images of cells	Frequent photographs of the pre-14 day old embryo and descriptions 'showing' it is not a human being	Ignore appearance (or show an embryo/foetus several months old)
Language about cells	'Blastocyst'	'human embryo' (pre-fix 'human' used three times as often)
Origins of embryo	'left over' or 'surplus' (from fertility treatment)	'Deliberately created to be destroyed' (by cloning techniques)
… and destinies	'destined to be discarded'	'a new entity which, *if left alone*, will flower into a human being'
Words to describe outcome	'Dismantling'	'Dismembering'
Personification	Of patients. (Introduce those with disease as identifiable individuals who urgently need help)	Of embryo. (Present pre-14 day old embryo as having gender, family relationships, character)
What or whose 'potential'?	The word 'potential' applied to the potential of the research to lead to medical advance.	The word 'potential' applied to embryo's potential to become human being.

For full discussion of how the embryo is framed in the debate, see Williams et al., 2003.

It is important here to note how framing strategies are not linked to positions and they change over time. A 'right-to-life' campaigner against abortion will highlight the appearance of the embryo, with tiny fingers and toes, whereas this does not work in the stem cell debate where the appearance of the 'blob of cells' is more useful to those who wish to promote the use of embryos in research. It is also important to note how individual concepts such as 'potential' or even specific words, such as 'tiny', vary depending on the *context* in which they are placed. Yes, size matters – however the meaning of being 'tiny' depends on the way it is linked to other concepts (for example, insignificance on the one hand, or vulnerability on the other).

Example 2: Framing asylum seekers

My second example is drawn from a study of the coverage of asylum seekers. Van Gorp (2005) examined the framing of asylum seekers as innocent victims or intruders. He developed a detailed matrix which included coding the type of asylum seeker portrayed in the story, how the problem was defined, what was seen to cause it and who was responsible for solving it. He also examined metaphors, emotional appeals and visuals. For example, one story might focus on a refugee family in fear for their lives, frame the problem as one of how to best welcome victims of persecution and appeal to compassion and justice. By contrast another story might: describe a 'flood' of individuals seeking to abuse asylum rights; present the asylum-seeker as a threat to 'our' culture; focus on the problem of lax asylum policy; and appeal to xenophobia (Van Gorp, 2005: 461).

Using the matrix outlined in Box 6.4, Van Gorp systematically coded, and then statistically examined, the clustering of such faming devices. This confirmed that news reports do indeed contain clusters of framing devices and that the victim-frame was present in its pure form in 21% and the intruder-frame in 26% of the articles. Van Gorp's analysis also revealed differences in framing over time – the 'innocent victim' frame becoming more prevalent during the Christmas period. It seems as if the 'season of goodwill', celebrating the birth of Jesus (who was, after all, himself a refugee), impacts on which news frames come to the fore. Van Gorp's systematic approach also showed that some indices of the frame were more pertinent than others. He notes, in particular, that some words, which he had thought would be associated with particular frames were less indicative than predicted. The terms 'asylum-seekers', 'refugee' and 'illegal immigrant' were used inter-changeably and he notes, therefore, that 'linguistic orientated framing devices did not seem to be the most powerful indicators to determine to what extent the eight newspapers used the two frames' (Van Gorp, 2005: 496). (See below for further reflection on this point.)

Box 6.4   Framing the asylum seeker*

	Victim-frame	Intruder-frame
Type of asylum seeker	Refugee	Would-be asylum-seeker who abuses the right to seek asylum
Role of asylum seeker	Passive	Active/adventurer or criminal
Problem definition	How to receive refugees who are victims of persecution	Threat to 'our' culture
Problem source	Violence, persecution, poverty	Lax asylum and deportation policy
Responsibility	Borne by democratic countries (for example, on basis of the Geneva Convention)	Policy-makers and asylum-seekers
Policy solution	A humane and a flexibly cautious and effectively applied asylum policy	Deportation and discouragement
Moral and emotional basis	The moral duty to help people in affliction. Compassion	Protect the interests of native people. Emotion: xenophobia, distrust of strangers
Metaphors/ stereotype	Shelter, Europe Helpless, Anxious victim	Flood, Garbage, The dangerous stranger
Lexical choices	'returning home' = death	'The degeneration of the neighbourhood'
Visuals	Families with children; pictures that represent distress, fear and misery	A batch of asylum seekers, especially single

*This is a simplified version of the grid reproduced (with permission) from Van Gorp 2005.

Some clarifications for developing frame analysis and a call for reflective research

In the above discussion I have explored framing analysis through examples of how people have used it. It may be equally useful to say a little about what is *not* a frame. The first point to re-emphasize is that frames depend on *clusters* and *patterns*. A frame is about the organization and inter-relation of ideas. The significance of particular words and labels, facts and statistics therefore have to be considered in context.

Reflecting on the significance of words and labels

Although the use of a term such as 'freedom fighter' or 'martyr' rather than 'suicide bomber' or 'terrorist' is strongly associated with a particular frame this is not true of all labels.

- Neoconservatives may have to use the phrase 'affirmative action' even if they would prefer to talk of 'reverse discrimination' simply because 'affirmative action' has become the official label.
- Equal rights campaigners may compromise and campaign for 'gay marriage' rather than 'equal marriage rights' even though the latter is a better phrase from their political perspective.
- It is not just a question of which terms have become common currency. Sometimes a slippage between terms from diverse frames can serve insidious political ends – a seamless shifting between the term 'illegal immigrant' and 'refugee', for example, seeks to tar one group with the stigma of another and deliberately conflate the issues.

Media production processes and values also intervene in the type of labels used in reporting. In the above analysis I highlighted how the term 'embryo' is a heavily laden symbol, and proponents of embryonic stem cell research sometimes, therefore, preferred to use the term 'blastocyst'. However, efforts to promote such 'technically correct' scientific terminology failed. Even science correspondents who were supportive of developing embryonic stem cell research still referred to the 'embryo' rather than the 'blastocyst'. This was because they thought their readers would relate to the former term more easily.

Reflecting on the significance of facts and statistics

The presentation (or withholding) of particular information is an important part of the framing process. Highlighting that a vandal comes from a broken home, that a murderer has schizophrenia or that a rapist is black, for example, can imply ideas about causation or typical characteristics.

- Although references to such information may be factually accurate, this does not mean that they are neutral. Is such information really relevant? A physical description of a rapist, for example, may well be relevant if he is on-the-run, but should otherwise not be salient to the story.
- Information also needs to be considered in context. Perhaps the mental illness was relevant to this particular murder, but what other images of people with schizophrenia are represented in the media coverage in general – is mental illness disproportionately associated with violence in the coverage overall? (Philo, 1996).
- It is also worth considering whether particular information is highlighted in a symmetrical way? If some reports highlight that a criminal is black, it is worth asking whether reports are equally likely to mention that the perpetrator is male or white. There is often an asymmetry in the use of such signifiers. In one study, for example, 50 newspaper articles in one year identified sexual assaults on children as 'homosexual', not a single assault or assailant was labelled as 'heterosexual'. This was in spite of the fact that the majority of the attacks reported involved men assaulting girls. The consequences of such reporting can be to reinforce homophobia and create a misleading conflation between paedophilia and homosexuality (Kitzinger, 2004: 127).

Facts do not speak for themselves. Just as specific words and labels can not *a priori* be assumed to be indelibly associated with only one frame, the use of particular facts and statistics also can be multi-layered. Thus the focus on the oppression of women in Afghanistan, for example, suddenly becomes news in the context of justifying the 'War on Terror' (Stabile and Kuman, 2005). Clearly, displays of concerns for women's rights are not inherently progressive but can be framed in particular ways, at particular times, to support particular ideological goals.

Overlapping with the above point it is worth highlighting that bare statistics are less important than the way they are inscribed with meaning and contextualized by a frame. This has been amply demonstrated in work on the representation of risks: for example, the threat of nuclear accidents, global warming or the risks posed by GM crops. On one level, any risk can be represented as a simple formula involving the *likelihood* of occurrence and the extent of the *impact*. Once risk becomes framed as a story, however, much more important issues come into play, such as *who* is at risk from the threat, who controls it (and are they trustworthy) and who benefits. It is these framings rather than the statistics which influence media coverage and public debate and responses (Hughes et al., 2006).

Reflecting on the complexity of frames and their limitations

As the above discussion makes clear, identifying frames involves sensitive and detailed reading of the texts under investigation. Different frames will be identified from different perspectives. Researchers need to be open to testing their assumptions and expanding their understanding of the number and type of frames in operation. Some researchers try to categorize media frames as simply 'positive' or 'negative'. Such categorization may be useful to give a crude overall indicator of patterns of coverage, however, this approach is limited for various reasons. Most importantly, perhaps, because conflating a frame with a 'pro' or 'anti' position obscures rather than elucidates the actual framing process. For example, those opposing aspects of stem cell research may draw on a Catholic or feminist understandings of the world. A mainstream Catholic opposition is based on a commitment to the sanctity of life at every stage, and is allied to an anti-abortion position. Some feminists, by contrast, may be 'pro-choice' but be concerned about how the use of eggs and embryos in scientific research might impact on women. To reduce frames to issue positions neglects the really crucial concern – how issues are defined – and it is this, after all, which is the entire point of frame analysis (Carragee and Roefs, 2004). Frame analysts also often adopt a binary approach – identifying just two opposing frames. Although the media often do adopt this approach (indeed 'binary framing' is itself a generic frame), researchers should also be sensitive to the fact that most problems can be framed in more than two ways.

There are various techniques to help the researcher avoid prematurely foreclosing on the range of potential frames which might come into play. One such technique is that researchers should pay attention to statements that do not 'fit' with the frames they have identified so far. For example, an asylum seeker might be viewed with compassion as a 'victim' or with condemnation as an 'invader'. However, how would you classify a statement that immigrants were essential to the well-being of the host country – providing much needed labour as well as fuelling new business initiatives and supporting a vibrant culture and economy? Similarly most reporting of the embryo stem cell debate presented the embryo as either 'valuable research material' or 'precious human life' (see Box 6.3) – but there were exceptions to this binary representation. One newspaper column, written by a woman undergoing infertility treatment, described how, for her, each embryo is simultaneously both a potential child and useful research material she might donate to scientists. Noting such exceptions may not change your understanding of the dominant frames, but should certainly help to raise awareness of their limitations (Williams et al., 2003). If the media coverage does prioritize just two frames – excluding ambivalence or marginalizing a third perspective – this is, in itself, worthy of comment.

Thinking outside the box(es): sociological imagination and contextualizing frames

Finally, it is vital that researchers think 'outside the box' of the texts under consideration in the main analysis. Frames are often so implicit that they seem like common sense. In fact, the most powerful frame is perhaps the hardest to detect – because it comes across as a transparent description of reality. In the days before gay liberation, for example, the debate was simply whether homosexuality was a sickness or a sin, whether it should be punished, treated or tolerated. It took a social movement to challenge the underlying premise that homosexuality was an undesirable aberration. Anyone trying to analyze frames should thus try to step outside their common-sense understandings and reach beyond the limitations of their cultural and historical context. This is an almost impossible task – but can be helped by doing background research to locate the voices excluded from the debate. You could try looking at the websites of radical campaigning groups and also talking to 'everyday folk' or those with particular personal experiences. Historical and cross-cultural reflection can also be invaluable. In the debate about embryonic stem cell research, for example, one could go beyond the framing analysis outlined in Box 6.3 to ask: Why is the embryonic stem cell debate framed as being a *debate about the embryo* at all. The reasons for this may seem self-evident but are actually rooted in particular social, religious, organizational and historical conditions. A good frame analysis should include reflection on the different ways in which debate *could* be framed. For example, in the stem cell debate, you might ask:

- What happens if women's bodies (instead of the embryo) were positioned at the centre of the debate about the use of eggs and embryos in stem cell research?
- What if you take a particular *Buddhist* rather than Christian-oriented perspective on the circle of life or if the discussion were informed by Confucian ideas about the relationship between the individual and the collective?
- How would the debate play out if disability or suffering were not assumed to be eradicable evils?
- What if environmental causes rather than technical fixes were the focus of health research?
- What if questions of distributive justice were the key concern? (Williams et al., 2003; Haran et al., 2007)

Analyzing media impacts: testing the effect of 'frames' on audiences

The final strand in the circuit of mass communication which can be subject to a framing analysis relates to the audience. Indeed ideas about the audience are, at the very least implicit, in any framing analysis. This is because frame analysis assumes that frames carry some meaning, or have some impact on, or engagement with, the schemata inside people's heads or the ideas which circulate within our social networks. Once audiences are made the explicit subject of empirical investigation the key question shifts from 'How do the media frame this issue?' to 'What frames do people use in their thinking about this issue – and how do they relate to the frames presented in the media?' Research which examines how people actually engage with frames appears in two main forms: experimental/survey work and in-depth qualitative work often using focus group discussions.

Experimental audience research

Experiments involve techniques such as presenting different groups of people with 'doctored' news reports adopting opposing frames. People are then asked to respond to questionnaires about the issue in question. Any differences in response are then examined to highlight how diverse framings may impact on the point of view respondents adopt in response. There is a large body of work in this vein, often conducted by cognitive psychologists interested in how different frames might activate different group identities (for example, Richardson, 2005). This line of research is also pursued by political scientists interested in how news impacts on expressed public opinion, and hence on policy debates. Perhaps the best known experimental framing research, however, is the classic study by Iyengar. He was interested in how news reporting which is 'episodic' (depicting concrete events) might impact on people and compared this to reporting which was 'thematic' (presenting collective or general evidence). He showed some people episodic reporting about key political issues, and, showed others thematic reporting. He then examined how each group responded. His work is complex, and multi-layered, highlighting various subtleties about how frames operate and how audiences react. For example, Iyengar found that news reports about a poor black person or a criminal black person tended to elicit more *individualistic* attributions of responsibility than reports on a white person who was poor or a criminal (Iyengar, 1991: 3). The 'episodic' or 'thematic' framing is thus clearly cross-cut by other discursive cues. At the same time Iyengar was able to identify overall evidence for a 'framing effect'. He concludes:

> The studies reported in this book show that episodic news makes viewers less likely to hold public officials accountable for the existence of some problem and also less likely to hold them responsible for alleviating it. Since television news is heavily episodic, its effect is generally to induce attribution of responsibility to individual victims or perpetrators rather than to broad societal forces, and hence the ultimate political impact of framing is pro-establishment. (Iyengar, 1991: 18)

Qualitative audience research

Qualitative research exploring how people frame issues during discussion in focus groups adds another layer to understanding how frames might engage people. This approach takes framing research out of the laboratory and into an everyday context (Hertog and McLeod, 2001: 160). Gamson's classic study, *Talking Politics* is a fine example of such work. He conducted 37 focus group discussions around a range of political issues and presents an invaluable exploration of the complex process of opinion formation. A similar method was adopted in my own work on *Framing Abuse* (Kitzinger, 2004). This included 79 focus group discussions about child sexual abuse and sexual violence and explored the ways in which media representations resource such discussions and help frame people's understandings of the problem.

Transcripts from such group discussion can be analyzed rather like media texts. Researchers can examine the discursive cues and frames that people use – and see how such cues operate in practice in ordinary conversations. They can also pay close attention to the interactions within the focus groups – analyzing which ideas, phrases, and metaphors prompt agreement (or disagreement) and understanding (or confusion), and where it all leads. In fact this approach may alert researchers to the significance of particular discursive cues from the media reporting that they had previously overlooked. If you are thinking of doing a content-based analysis it may, therefore, be worth running a focus group discussion around that topic first, simply to help you refine your media analysis.

Combining production, content and reception studies of framing

In the above discussion I have distinguished between framing analysis focused on *production*, that focused on *content*, and that focused on *audience*. I pointed out that most framing studies have focused on media content – if only for practical reasons. Some studies have, however, adopted a broader approach by looking at audiences or production processes – and these tend to include some analysis of content as well. (After all, it would make little sense to look at audiences or journalists/sources in isolation without knowing what the media coverage looks like). Studies which address all three levels of the circuit of mass communication are uncommon – not least because they are very labour intensive. However, such multi-level research projects can be a very revealing way of conducting frame analysis too.

My analysis of the media coverage of child sexual abuse, for example, highlighted how the mass media framed the problem of child sexual abuse largely in terms of 'stranger-danger' and focused on the 'solution' of identifying convicted sex offenders (rather than other child protection strategies). This is in spite of the fact that very few sex offenders are ever convicted and most are ordinary and well-integrated members of their families and neighbourhoods.

Complementing the analysis of media coverage with *interviews with journalists and their sources* highlighted how the 'stranger danger' framing of the problem was supported by particular production structures. For example, few sponsors wanted their name associated with campaigns which addressed sexual abuse within the family or which highlighted how many unidentified sex abusers already lived in the community.

The *audience research* produced further insights. Discussions with 'ordinary members of the public' showed how the taken-for-granted label – 'the paedophile' – encouraged people to think about sexual abusers as if they were a distinct species of being (not friends and neighbours). This research also demonstrated how the 'stranger-danger' frame was underwritten by patterns of everyday talk and the 'social currency' of different personal experiences: the slightest hint of a threatening stranger was widely circulated public knowledge, attacks closer to home were often kept secret. In addition, the emphasis on convicted offenders being released into the community was also supported by the deep sense of disenfranchisement experienced by some local groups. For some people the housing of released sex offenders in their neighbourhoods had come to symbolize their own powerlessness and vulnerability in the face of an uncaring and incompetent bureaucracy.

Studies which track frames across production, content and reception can help to illuminate how frames are produced, circulated and sustained. Such work can also illuminate why some frames are so powerful, while others become marginalized. Multi-level framing research – addressing all aspects of the communication circuit – can also help to clarify the role of specific discursive cues. An example of this would be the 'template' framing device (Kitzinger, 2000; 2004). Media templates are historical analogies which come to be closely associated with new events as they unfold and can have profound implications for audience understandings. Let me summarize this part of my research very briefly. I examined media reports of 'The Orkney case': an emerging scandal where children had been taken into care because of suspicions of abuse. This case became a cause celebre, framed as an inappropriate intervention into innocent families by incompetent social workers. Content analysis highlighted how, from the very start, the Orkney case was repeatedly associated with a previous scandal called 'The Cleveland case'. Production analysis showed that such associations were vigorously promoted by parents' pressure groups. Such associations were also underwritten by journalists' own practices as they drew on memories of the former scandal to help shape their reports of unfolding events in Orkney.

The importance of such framing practices and devices became strikingly obvious in the focus group discussions. It emerged that research participants knew few details about events in Orkney and had not necessarily paid much attention to the coverage. However, they frequently reiterated the association between Orkney and Cleveland – and used this to underpin their judgements about what was going on in the Orkney case. The effect of the pervasive Cleveland analogy was to provide audiences with a sense of recognition and promote the frame: 'innocent families torn apart (yet again)' through the 'persistent incompetence' of social workers. Interestingly, however, this 'template', although very powerful, did not completely determine the framing of the problem for everyone. In fact, for a few people this framing device back-fired. These research participants responded to the Orkney–Cleveland anal-ogy in unexpected ways. They said that because the previous scandal in Cleveland had caused such outrage, social workers must have had very good reason to act as they did in Orkney, because they were forewarned of the likely backlash (Kitzinger, 2004: 65–6). (For discussion of how historical references such as 'datum events' and 'exemplary cases' inform journalistic practices or public understanding see also, Corner et al., 1990; Edy and Daradanova, 2006).

Conclusion

In its broadest sense 'framing' concerns how events are turned into news stories or social issues and how reality itself comes to be defined and under-stood. It can be a very broad concept, used in a wide variety of ways, researched via a diverse range of methods. In spite, or perhaps *because* of such diverse approaches, framing is a very useful way to think about how representations of the world are shaped. The above discussion has, I hope, helped readers to consider how to read framing research critically and how they might set about conducting such research themselves. This chapter has, of course, also itself been an exercise in framing. It has 'framed' the concept of framing – inviting a particular way of thinking about the theoretical and methodological issues, highlighting some aspects and excluding others. Readers would be well advised to look to alternative sources for different framings of frame analysis!

Summary

- Frames are ways of organizing reality. They invite (but do not necessarily determine) particular ways of understanding the world.
- Framing analysts ask questions such as: How is reality represented? How are key participants portrayed? How is the problem defined? Who is assigned responsibility for this issue? What solutions are presented?
- Frames can be analyzed at all levels of the circuit of mass communication, including: how frames are used by journalists or their sources; how media accounts promote particular frames; how people work with such frames (or employ different frames) in their everyday talk.
- Key 'discursive cues' which may be important in promoting particular frames include labels, images, metaphors and analogies or 'media templates'.
- Frame analysis benefits from close attention to detail and a reflective engagement with the data. Words, facts and statistics all have to be considered in context. Frame analysis can not be reduced to counting isolated individual units.
- The researchers also need to find imaginative ways of 'thinking outside the box' in order to identify the full range of frames in operation, and reflect on their limitations.
- Where possible, research on framing can usefully go beyond analyzing media texts, to include analysis of people's talk, campaigners' strategies and journalists' production practices. A broader engagement with the range of potential alternative perspectives – as well as the broader social and political context – is also important.

GOING FURTHER

For useful examples of framing analysis focused exclusively on content analysis, I recommend scanning the references below for discussions in your own area of interest. For particular texts, which explore how media frames relate to audience discussions, see the three books annotated below.

Gamson, W. (1992) *Talking Politics.* Cambridge: Cambridge University Press.
A detailed account of media framing and how people discuss a range of issues: nuclear power troubled industry, affirmative action and Arab-Israeli conflict. The study involved 37 focus groups. Particular attention is given to 'collective action frames' and how people become mobilized in social movements. The book includes a useful appendix describing coding categories.
Iyengar, S. (1991) *Is Anyone Responsible? How television frames political issues.* Chicago: The University of Chicago Press.

(Continued)

This book examines how 'episodic' and 'thematic' reporting frames political issues for the American public. The substantive topics included: crime, poverty, and racial inequality. Iynegar used content analysis of the media combined with surveys and experiments to explore how episodic and thematic frames might impact on audiences. The method is described in detail.

Kitzinger, J. (2004) *Framing Abuse: Media influence and public understandings of sexual violence against children.* London: Pluto Press.

This study involved media analysis combined with in-depth interviews and 79 focus group discussions. People were invited to discuss how they defined sexual abuse, talk about their views of perpetrators, reflect on what they thought caused the problem, and where the solution might lie. Particular attention is given to how media representations impact on understandings of events in our own lives as well as perceptions of social problems. The book also explores how people draw on their own experiences to amplify, resist or negotiate with the frames on offer. One chapter focuses on the role of analogies and media 'templates'. The research method is described in detail with examples of the materials used in the focus groups.

STUDENT ACTIVITY 6.1

Activity 1: Choose a high profile event (for example, a racist murder, a terrorist attack or crisis in international conflict). Examine the reporting of this event in different outlets which you think might adopt contrasting frames (for example, newspapers from different countries or from different political perspectives).

- Describe the different frames in operation within and across the diverse outlets.
- Identify the discursive devices being employed to evoke different frames.
- Can you imagine yet another way in which the event could have been framed? Try writing an account from a very different perspective.

Activity 2: Get together a group of friends or acquaintances. Ask them to discuss the event, addressing questions such as: What caused the problem, who is responsible, how should it be solved? Tape-record the discussion if possible. Then write up your analysis:

- What frames and discursive cues are they using?
- To what extent do these overlap with, or differ from, the frames and discursive cues you identified in the media outlets?

- Do individuals stick with one framing of the issue, or borrow from different frames? How do the discursive cues operate in the discussion? What assumptions are shared, when is consensus disrupted, and what seems to influence people to change their minds?

References

Ball-Rokeach, S. J., Power, G., Guthrie, K. and Waring. H. (1990) 'Value-framing abortion in the United States', *International Journal of Public Opinion Research*. 2(3): 249–73.

Benford, R. and Snow, D. (2000) 'Framing processes and social movements: an overview and assessment', *Annual Review of Sociology*. 26: 611–39.

Brosius, H. B. and Eps, P. (1995) 'Prototyping through key events: News selection in the case of violence against aliens and asylum seekers in Germany', *European Journal of Communcation*. 10: 391–412.

Carragee, K. and Roefs, W. (2004) 'The neglect of power in recent framing research', *International Communication Association*. 54(2): 214–33.

Cohen, N. (2006) 'Political advertising would be a step too far on British television', *Observer*, 30 July 2006: 11.

Corner, J., Richardson, K. and Fenton, N. (1990) *Nuclear Reactions: Format and Response in Public Issue Television*. London: John Libbey.

D'Angelo, P. (2002) 'News Framing as a Multiparadigmatic Research Program: A Response to Entman', *Journal of Communcation* 52 (4): 870–88.

Edy, J. A. and Daradanova, M. (2006) 'Reporting through the lens of the past: from Challenger to Columbia', *Journalism*. 7(2): 131–51.

Entman, R. (1991) 'Framing US coverage of international news', *Journal of Communication*. 41(4): 6–27.

Entman, R. (1993) 'Framing: towards clarification of a fractured paradigm', *Journal of Communication*. 43(4): 51–8.

Entman, R. M. (2003) 'Cascading activation: contesting the Whitehouse's frame after 9/11', *Political Communication*. 20: 415–32.

Ferere, M. Gamson, W., Gerhards, J. and Rucht, D. (2002) *Shaping Abortion Discourse: Democracy and the Public Sphere in Germany and the United States*. Cambridge: Cambridge University Press.

Gamson, W. (1992) *Talking Politics*. Cambridge: Cambridge University Press.

Gamson, W. and Modigliani, A. (1989) 'Media discourse and public opinion on nuclear power: a constructionist approach', *The American Journal of Sociology*. 95(1): 1–37.

Gitlin, T. (1980). *The Whole World is Watching: Mass Media in the Making and Unmaking of the New Left.* Berkeley, USA: University of California.

Glasgow University Media Group (1980) *More Bad News.* London: Routledge & Kegan Paul.

Goffman, E. (1974). *Frame Analysis: An Essay on the Organization of Experience.* New York: Harper & Row.

Haran, J., Kitzinger, J., McNeil, M., O'Riordan. K., (2007) *Human Cloning in the Media.* London: Routledge.

Hughes, E., Kitzinger, J. and Murdock, G. (2006) 'Risk and the Media' in P. Taylor-Gooby and J. Zinn (eds) *Risk in Social Science.* Oxford: Oxford University Press.

Iyengar, S. (1991) *Is Anyone Responsible? How television frames political issues.* Chicago: The University of Chicago Press.

Johnson-Cartee, K. (2005) *News Narratives and News Framing: Constructing Political Reality.* Lanhahm: Rowman and Littlefield Publishers.

Kahneman, D. and Tverskty, A. (1984) 'Choices, values, and frames', *American Psychologist.* 39: 341–50.

Kitzinger, J. (2000) 'Media templates: patterns of association and the (re)construction of meaning over time', *Media, Culture and Society.* 22(1): 64–84.

Kitzinger, J. (2004) *Framing Abuse: Media Influence and Public Understandings of Sexual Violence Against Children.* London: Pluto Press.

Kitzinger, J,. Williams, C., and Henderson, L. (2007) 'Science, media and society: the framing of bioethical debates around embryonicstem cell research between 2000 and 2005' in P. Glasner, P. Atkinson and H. Greenslade (eds) *New Genetics, New Social Formations.* Routledge: London. 204–31.

Pan, Z. and Kosicki, G. (1993) 'Framing Analysis: an Approach to News Discourse', *Political Communication.* 10(1): 55–75.

Philo, G. (ed.) (1996) *Media and Mental Distress.* London: Longman.

Reese, S., Gandy, O. G. and Hahwah, A. (eds) (2001) *Framing Public Life: Perspectives on media and our understanding of the social world.* New Jersey: Lawrence Erlbaum Associates.

Richardson, J. (2005) 'Switching social identities: the influence of editorial framing on reader attitudes toward affirmative action and African Americans', *Communication Research.* 32(4): 503–28.

Schuck, A. and de Vrees, C. (2006) 'Between Risk and Opportunity: News framing and its effects on public support for EU enlargement', *European Journal of Communication.* 21(1): 5–23.

Stabile, C. and Kumar, D. (2005) 'Unveiling imperialism: Media, gender and the war on Afghanistan', *Media, Culture and Society.* 26(5): 765–82.

Tuchman, G. (1978) *Making news: A study in the construction of reality.* New York: Free Press.

Van Gorp, B. (2005) 'Where is the frame? Victims and intruders in the Belgian press coverage of the asylum issue', *European Journal of Communication.* 20(4): 484–507.

Williams, C., Kitzinger J. and Henderson, L. (2003) 'Envisaging the embryo in stem cell Research: rhetorical strategies and media reporting of the ethical debates', *Sociology of Health and Illness.* 25(7): 793–814.

Notes

1 Acknowledgements: This chapter draws in part on work developed for a project on Media Framing and Discourses of Risk. Thanks are due to the ESRC, award no: RES-336–25–001. Thanks also to Claire Wardle for her useful comments on an earlier draft.

2 The theory is that 'frames' also exist inside our heads as repertoires of organized patterns of thought – these 'frames', or what are sometimes called 'schemata', are triggered by the framing devices presented in the media.

Mass Media Re-Presentations of the Social World: Ethnicity and 'Race'

7

Amanda Haynes

DEFINITIONS

Race: A means of categorizing people on the basis of physical characteristics like their skin colour and facial features. 'Race' is a social construct in that, given that there is no scientific basis for this categorization, it is an idea not a biological fact. People, not biology, place significance upon such characteristics and determine the boundaries and status of the groups they construct on this basis. The social divisions created by people acting on their beliefs in the significance of 'race' are, however, very real and the grouping into which one is categorized can have very real consequences for one's experience of privilege or disadvantage.

Ethnicity: Ethnicity signifies cultural identity. Members of a group are held to share a common ethnicity on the basis of their shared cultural characteristics and on the basis that both members and non-members recognize the distinctiveness of the group on this basis. Ethnic groups may also be racialized when their cultural characteristics are held to be biologically determined or immutable.

Introduction

People are multi-composite individuals. Their experiences and life chances are determined not just by their racial or ethnic identity, but also by their gender, sexuality and socio-economic class for example. Nonetheless, ethnicity and 'race' remain among the most powerful sources of social stratification. Ethnicity and racial categorization have and continue to be used to 'legitimize' invasion, colonization, slavery and genocide. In even the most equitable nations, ethnic minority status is closely tied to socio-economic disadvantage. Globally, Whiteness and advantage are contemporaneous experiences. As such, researchers retain a keen interest in 'race' as a potent determinant of power and privilege.

Many among those who study 'race' and ethnicity are interested in the mass media and its relationship to racist discourse. As social constructs, the power of 'race' and racialized ethnic identity are founded on their currency. The mass media, as a key institution for the transmission of culture, plays an important role in determining what kinds of discourses about ethnicity and ethnic identities are disseminated in the public sphere, and indeed whether racial thinking is reproduced, challenged or excluded.

In this chapter, we will examine some of the key issues regarding the relationship between the mass media and contemporary social understandings of ethnicity and 'race'. We will examine this relationship from a tripartite perspective, focusing not only on media content, but also on its producers and audience. We will begin by taking a closer look at the concepts of 'race' and ethnicity and the significance of the mass media to ethnic and racial relations, including debates regarding the impact of media content on the audience. Then we will examine the significance of under-representation, focusing also on the field of production. A critical overview of contemporary representations across a variety of media and genres follows, including a case study of casting decisions in the 2005 film *Hitch*. Finally, we will conclude by looking at the potential of minority media for positive change.

Plate 7:1 The 2005 movie Hitch is an interesting example of the limitations to the advances made in the representation of minority groups in the mass media. © 2005 Columbia Pictures Industries, Inc. All Rights Reserved Courtesy of Columbia Pictures.

Concepts of 'race' and ethnicity

Any consideration of the significance of 'race' and ethnicity in the mass media must begin with a critical review of the concepts of 'race' and ethnicity and an elaboration of the differences between academic and 'common sense' under-standings of these terms.

'Race'

The idea of 'race' is particularly problematic. 'Race' is a relatively recent concept, first used in English in the sixteenth century (Fulcher and Scott, 2003). The term 'race' refers to the means by which people are categorized into groups on the basis of physical characteristics like their skin colour and facial features (their phenotypical characteristics). 'Race' is understood alternately as a biological fact (a biological construct) or as something that is merely a product of society (a social construct). Where 'race' is understood as a biological fact, it signifies that group-ings who are categorized differently on the basis of skin colour and facial char-acteristics also differ in terms of their genetic make-up; such 'differences' are held to permit the hierarchical ranking of 'races' on the basis of relative superiority or inferiority and to determine behaviour and attributes. Understood in this way, people have used the idea of 'race' to 'legitimize' the oppression, exploitation, enslavement and genocide of those they define as lesser.

Scientists have proven such arguments to be unfounded and refuted the existence of any relationship between the racial groupings into which people are categorized and their genetic make-up. Biological scientists have found that there is often greater genetic divergence between members of the same 'race' than between members of different 'races' (Fulcher and Scott, 2007: 199–200). Moreover, social scientists generally reject the idea that people's behaviour and attributes are deter-mined by their ancestry, placing much greater significance on learned behaviours and the availability of opportunities (and resources) to maximize one's potential.

Researchers still use the term 'race', but not as a biological construct. They understand 'race' to be an exclusively social construct, i.e. the categorization of people into racial groupings and the very real social divisions that have devel-oped between people on this basis exist only because enough people in society choose to believe that this form of categorization has significance and act on that basis. It is in acting as if these groupings matter, that people give form to the idea of 'race'. Because of both past and current discrimination informed by the idea of 'race', racial categorization remains a major source of social stratification, i.e. impacting on people's access to authority, status, resources, opportunities and power within a society. It is to signify that they use the term 'race' with the understanding that it has no biological, only a social, reality that researchers and academics often place inverted commas around the word.

Ethnicity

The concept of ethnicity has gained increasing popularity in recent decades and is often seen as a favourable alternative to 'race'. Although both are social constructs, 'race' and ethnicity have significantly different meanings. Ethnicity describes a person's cultural identity. As such, ethnicity, like culture, is learned. Indeed, it is not absolutely necessary for one to be born into an ethnic group to be accepted by that group as one of its members. Acceptance is more dependent on the person's adoption of the group's cultural heritage. Markers of ethnicity are not physical, rather they relate to such things as a shared sense of history, dress, language and religion.

Culture is also not considered to determine a person's behaviour and attributes. Although our ethnic heritage provides us with a set of resources that we can deploy in our social interactions and which may shape our behaviour, like values, norms and customs, we are not confined to acting in accordance with that heritage. Indeed, depending on the situation in which we find ourselves, our gender identity, class identity or sexuality may be more significant to shaping our behaviour. We may also reject our ethnic identity, assimilate the ethnicity of a more dominant group, or self-identify with a hybrid identity, which is particularly common in immigrant societies, where people commonly have hyphenated ethnicities, for example, Irish-American, French-Algerian, French-Canadian. Ethnicity itself changes over time as groups alter their common understanding of what distinguishes them from other ethnicities, of what marks them out.

Nonetheless, although the academic understanding of ethnicity is of a fluid identity whose impact on our behaviour is continuously negotiated and flexible, the common sense use of this term may differ. The ambiguity of the concept of ethnicity lends itself to misinterpretation and there is evidence that sections of the general public may interpret ethnicity as determining immutable behaviour and attributes in the same way as the biological construct of 'race'. In the media, there is evidence that markers of ethnicity (and nationality, citizenship status and immigrant status) may be deployed merely as a signifier of 'race' perpetuating racist discourses through a more subtle use of language.

> In the New Racism, minorities are not biologically inferior, but different. They have a different culture, although in many respects there are 'deficiencies', such as single-parent families, drug abuse, lacking achievement values, and dependence on

welfare and affirmative action – 'pathologies' that need to be corrected of course … (van Dijk, 2000: 33–34)

The significance of the media to ethnic and racial relations

The media is a key social institution. Both in fictional and factual formats it is regarded as a major force for the transmission of culture, including cultural stereotypes. The media re-presents to us the social world within and beyond our own experience; a re-presentation which is necessarily mutated through perception, interpretation and reproduction. In selecting which aspects of the social world to portray and how to explain them to their audience, the media plays an important role in determining which topics gain status, in influencing which facts about those topics are perceived as most salient and in framing the audience's interpretation of those facts.

It is, of course, the case that the audience does not necessarily take the media's representation of the social world at face value. The 'hypodermic' or media-effects model of reception, which suggests that the audience is strongly and uniformly influenced by media content has largely been rejected in favour of a more agentic understanding of the audience.

The ongoing significance of the media is, however, highlighted by the factors that serve to limit the audience's potential for taking oppositional or negotiated readings of a text. Key issues here are whether the audience has access to alternative information about or framing of a topic and particularly whether the audience has some personal experience or knowledge of the topic through which they can mediate their interpretation of the dominant message. For example, the Glasgow University Media Group have found that audience members are most likely to accept the intended meaning of a media text where they do not have the opportunity to draw on such alternate sources (see Elridge, 1993 and Chapter 5 by Greg Philo in this textbook).

In relation to the representation of ethnic and racial minorities, the degree of social contact between minorities and the dominant group (and indeed among minorities) is therefore of significance to understanding the impact of dominant media messages on public understandings. A key issue here is that, even in ethnically diverse societies, group members' contact with each other may be limited. We tend to seek out and sustain connections with those that we perceive to be most similar to us, including on the basis of 'race' and ethnicity. This phenomenon, termed homophily:

... limits people's social worlds in a way that has powerful implications for the information they receive, the attitudes they form, and the interactions they experience. Homophily in race and ethnicity creates the strongest divides in our personal environments, with age, religion, education, occupation, and gender following in roughly that order. (McPherson et al., 2001: 415)

The limited reach of personal networks and direct experience, in comparison to the scope of media coverage and their key role in mediating messages from potential alternative sources such as political leaders and experts, all restrict the capacity of groups to negotiate media messages about other ethnic and 'racial' groups.

Of course, the media have the potential to disseminate a variety of messages about any group or topic, and supportive and positive representations of minorities are in evidence. Nonetheless, producers of media content are socialized into the same racial and ethnic prejudices that may affect their audience and may consciously or unconsciously operate through the lens of these prejudices. The limited representation of ethnic and racial minorities in media production (and among the 'experts' upon which the media draw in producing texts) and the often limited capacity of minority groups to challenge misrepresentations (van Dijk, 2000: 37), further support the hegemony of the dominant group's framing of minority groups. Nonetheless, it is essential to remember that in representing ethnic and 'racial' minorities, the media do no more than draw upon pre-existing constructions within society. Representations, positive or negative, are re-produced, not produced, by the media. Nor would representations which are limited, stereotypical or racist, continue to be re-produced if they did not find an audience.

Recent decades have seen significant improvements in mass media representations of ethnic and 'racial' minorities. Overtly racist discourses are unusual, though they still persist. As will be evidenced over the course of this chapter, stereotyping and racialization remain in evidence, but occur less frequently and in more subtle forms. Nonetheless, minority issues, experts, entertainers and producers alike continue to be under-represented in the mass media and, where included, are often drawn upon and lauded specifically as members of a minority group. At the core of this issue, lies the fact that Western-owned and produced (often globally distributed) mass media continue to assume the centrality and normality of Whiteness and White privilege. In comparison, ethnic and 'racial' minorities remain deviant, outside the norm, the standard of which is Whiteness. Even in the face of very real progress, the ongoing significance of ethnicity and 'race' in the mass media is evidenced by the invisibility of (first world, middle-class) Whites in analyses of and commentaries on ethnicity and 'race' in the media. Their invisibility is a function of the ubiquity of this racial identity – in news, in entertainment, across roles and genres, in production, among experts and owners. The apparent unremarkability of Whiteness, a measure of the power of this 'racial' category, remains remarkable. While Whiteness remains the standard of normality, 'race' and ethnicity remain significant to the mass media.

Analyzing 'race' and ethnicity in the mass media

The significance of 'race' and ethnicity is not confined to any particular aspect of the mass media. As sources of social stratification and aspects of identity, they are universally applicable concepts. In the following sections, I will present key understandings of the import of ethnicity and 'race' relating to such fundamental facets of the mass media as ownership, production, content and audience, and review some of the research that has informed their development.

This discussion will be organised into two sections, the first relating to issues of quantity, i.e. under-representation and the second relating to issues of quality, i.e. interrogating the content of representations. For those who are interested in the role of the media in mediating both self-perception and inter-group relations, both the visibility of ethnic and 'racial' groupings and the nature of their portrayal is significant.

Much of what follows focuses on the (under/mis) representation of people of colour. However, the reader should maintain an awareness of the overarching context of ubiquitous Whiteness.

Under-representation

For Whites, cultural invisibility is rarely, if ever, an issue. Given the globalized nature of Western media, wherever a White person travels, they can turn on the television, open a newspaper, or look at a billboard to see their own reflection. Through representation in the mass media, they experience themselves as citizens of the world – globally present, globally relevant.

For ethnic and 'racial' minorities, cultural invisibility is a much more salient issue. It is an experience shared with other marginalized groups like people with disabilities and gay, lesbian, bisexual and transgendered persons. Cultural invisibility means not seeing one's ethnic or racial identity, or the culture, lifestyle, experiences and needs associated with that identity, represented in the public sphere. It aggravates other linked forms of exclusion – economic and political – by denying an important platform for awareness raising and participation. It can generate a strong sense of social exclusion, of 'UnBelonging'.

In addition, exclusion from mainstream mass media productions may cause minorities to retreat from this forum for inter-group dialogue, restricting their media consumption to minority media products. While one should not underestimate the importance of minority-oriented media products and minority media as sites for enhanced visibility and positive self-construction, their impact on inter-group relations is limited.

The under-representation of ethnic and 'racial' minorities in mass media content reflects the cultural hegemony of Whiteness and the perpetuation of White self-interest. This invisibility has been facilitated by the under-representation of ethnic and 'racial' minorities among media producers and in producers' and owners' conceptualization of 'the audience'.

Production

Although minorities are more visible in mass media organizations, they are still significantly under-represented among owners and in production (van Dijk, 2000: 37), particularly in decision-making roles (Heider, 2000). Despite the existence of some positive-action training schemes and employment policies (Law, 2002), employment in the mass media is still highly unequal.

Box 7.1   Newsroom employment survey (American Society of Newspaper Editors, 2005)

A 2005 survey by the American Newspaper Editor Association found that minorities still account for only:

- 17.3% of photographers
- 14.6% of reporters
- 11.9% of copy/layout editors
- 10.8% of all newsroom supervisors

Data from the US census indicates that, by 2000, racial and ethnic minorities accounted for almost 23% of the population (US Department of Commerce, 2001).

Research suggests that minority employment may be a key factor in altering the under- and mis-representation of minorities in the media; progress in this area has already been linked to improvements in the coverage of 'race'-related news (see Ainley, 1998). While media ownership and production remain overwhelmingly in the control of the dominant culture, it is likely that so will the identities, understandings, interests and perspectives represented therein.

Homophily is equally as significant to understanding production as reception. As in all industries, we have a tendency to hire those whom we find most similar to ourselves, who share our characteristics, beliefs and values. Nonetheless, many media organizations are working to combat its effects on hiring practices by instituting policies which explicitly support the achievement of diversity through recruitment. By enhancing minority representation in media ownership and production, conventional media constructions of the audience may be altered and the need to adequately represent their heterogeneous identities and diverse cultures recognized. Law (2002: 148) notes that '... there may be "ripple effects" from personnel changes, ranging from better organisational understanding of diverse cultures to the creation of role models.'

Nonetheless, diversity in ownership and production does not guarantee diversity in content. Wider organizational and industry support is core to normalizing the progressive representation of minorities in media content.

Box 7.2   Inculcating new recruits

Wilson et al. (2003) cite socialization into the existing norms and values of an organization as a key factor in limiting the potential for the recruitment of minority members to impact upon media content. As an example, he relates Breed's (1955) description of the processes by which journalists are socialized into the existing policy orientation of a news organization. Breed (1955) described their socialization as proceeding through familiarization with the existing product and with the values and interests of executives; through consistently editing the journalists work to conform with existing values and norms and through reprimand when their work contradicts the policy orientation of the organization. Breed (1955) proposed that journalists tend to conform because if they do not they may be subject to sanctions, because they perceive non-conformity as an obstacle to advancement, because they esteem their superiors, because productivity is prioritized over objectivity, and because they may identify with those in the news organization more than with outside interest or groups. While these propositions were developed in relation to journalism, they describe a process of socialization which will be familiar to those working in diverse organizational contexts within and outside of the media industry.

Not wishing to detract from the potential of minority recruitment to effect change represented or the importance of advancing employment equality for its own sake, it is interesting to note that discourses which place responsibility for transformation on the shoulders of minority members serve to highlight another aspect of White privilege. Members of ethnic and 'racial' minorities, involved in media production or ownership are often expected to carry the burden of representation because of their minority status. However, as Hohman (2000), cited in Spencer (2006), points out, Whites are never asked to speak or act for their entire 'race'.

Imagining the audience

Like any industry, media organizations must imagine their audience in order to orient production to their markets. Key to understanding the persistence of under(/mis)representation, is the degree to which the mass media conceptualize their market in terms of the majority ethnic or 'racial' group. With the exception of products that specifically seek to cash in on 'the minority market' or fulfil 'diversity requirements', the majority of print and broadcast productions are oriented to the (global acceptability) of the dominant White culture. As the case study included in this section will demonstrate, the provision of a central place to ethic or 'racial' minority persons or interests in mainstream content may be constructed as a marketing risk – in stark contrast to the assumed universal market for content oriented around White persons and elite interests.

Box 7.3   The significance of organizational culture

Simon Cottle (1997) is one of the few researchers who have managed to access media organizations with the specific remit of exploring producers' perceptions of the issues involved in giving coverage to ethnic minorities. He found that, in the context of a highly competitive environment, they viewed minority issues as a marketing risk. Even for those organizations whose remit was 'diversity programming', content with wider-based appeal was held to be a safer investment of time and resources then that which was, as a result of focusing on a specific ethnic group, assumed to appeal only to a narrow audience.

Content: Minorities outside of the frame

Given the predominance of White producers and conceptualizations of the audience as White, it is unsurprising that minority issues have long been under-represented in mass media content, both fictional and factual.

The Kerner Commission (1968), reporting to the US government in the aftermath of 'racial' minority unrest, found that 'The media report and write from the standpoint of a white man's world'. In the twenty-first century, the same accusation might be justly made. The under-representation of ethnic and 'racial' minority perspectives in the news media continues, perpetuated by the prioritization of the (presumed) viewpoints of the affluent White market and the domination of editorial decision-making and agenda setting functions by White decision-makers (Wilson et al., 2003).

While it is more in evidence than in the past, 'enlightened and progressive reporting, however, still remains the exception' (Wilson et al., 2003: 124). Much news coverage of ethnic and 'racial' minorities is negative. With decades of experience in the analysis of new media discourse in the UK and Netherlands, van Dijk (2000: 38) notes that:

> ... most ethnic relations [are] represented in terms of problems and deviance if not as a threat as well, most typically so in news about crime, drugs and violence minorities are associated with. On the other hand, many topics that are also part of ethnic affairs occur much less in the news, such as migrants leaving the country, the contributions of immigrant workers to the economy, everyday life of minority communities, and especially also discrimination and racism against minorities.

The infrequency with which minority members are used as sources and experts in both television (Campbell, 1995) and print media news (van Dijk, 2000 and Wilson et al., 2003) contributes to the limited and frequently negative coverage of ethnic and minority groups.

Sources

Both as a consequences of the under-representation of minorities (who might reasonably be expected to have more extensive network ties with minority members) in production and the under-representation of minorities in positions of authority in society more generally, members of ethnic and 'racial' minorities are much less likely than members of the dominant ethnicity to be selected by producers as sources, experts and official commentators. This in turn limits the representation of minority perspectives in the mass media, supporting the hegemony of the dominant groups' viewpoints. It limits opportunities for self-representation, for directly challenging stereotypes and misrepresentations within content, and for the dominant ethnic groups' exposure to minority group members in the role of an authority. (van Dijk, 2000)

Campbell (1995: 57) notes that 'Even though the news is not entirely white, the infrequent presence of journalists of colour and minority news sources dictates an otherness that is compounded when the coverage that does exist perpetuates traditional racist notions about minority life'.

Change through market growth

The case of American television indicates however that not all minorities are equally under-represented in the mass media. While Latinos, Asians and Native Americans remain significantly under-represented in US television, Black Americans have gained ground in terms of their presence in this medium (Mastro and Robinson, 2000) to a point where in the US their televisual presence parallels their presence in the population (Greenburg and Brand, 2004, cited in Mastro and Robinson, 2000). Broadcasters include Black-oriented programmes in their schedules to cash in on this niche market as well as to enhance their own corporate image (Gray, 2000).

Box 7.4   Top Ten TV – Ethnic minority group representation on popular television

An analysis of the ten most viewed television programmes in the UK, over four weeks in late 2000 provides some interesting comparisons with US data. The study, produced for the Commission on Racial Equality, sampled a wide variety of programmes according to rating, including quiz and game shows, documentaries, soap operas, consumer programmes (for example, gardening and antiques shows) and police and detective shows. The programmes in the sample included both US (11.8%) and UK (6.9%) productions (US productions were more likely to include minority participants). In line with Mastro and Robinson's (2000) comment on the increased numbers of Black people on US television, UK

(Continued)

productions actually over-represented Black persons (3.7% of programme participants) compared to their representation in the population (2.1%), while other ethnic minorities continued to be significantly under-represented. Only 1% of programme participants were Asian, compared to 3.7% in the population. 'Other minorities', which included Chinese people, constituted only 0.2% of programme participants compared to 0.6% of the population (Cumberbatch et al., 2001: 2).

Parallels are found in research specific to advertising, 'the bread and butter of the media' (Wilson et al., 2003: 139). While some minorities remain largely invisible due to their smaller size, more populous groups have attracted significant attention from the advertising industry. The most populous minorities, i.e. Blacks and Latinos, have experienced the greatest increase in their representation in TV advertising in the US. The representation of Asians is also beginning to evidence an increase, in parallel with recent population growth. On the other hand, Native Americans have increasingly disappeared from advertising as the use of overt stereotypes of their group has been restricted (Wilson et al., 2003).

Qualitative research commissioned by the UK Government's Central Office of Information found a similar situation in the UK, where Asian people continued to feel that they were extremely under-represented in advertising (and that portrayals that did exist were commonly stereotypical) while Black people felt themselves to be better represented, although it was commonly held that the range of roles filled by Blacks in advertising was limited. It is a point of interest that the results of this qualitative study suggest that ethnic minority viewers are highly aware of the representation of their minority group in advertising, to the degree that their comments strongly reflect the findings of empirical research (Turnstone, 2003).

Overview

In summary, the issue of under-representation in the mass media remains salient for ethnic and 'racial' minorities. In print and broadcast media, among owners and producers, in fictional and factual content and in advertising, White interests remain hegemonic. While some minority groups have seen a quantitative improvement in the frequency of their representation, this appears to be more the consequence of favourable market forces than a deeply held commitment to prioritize equity (over profit).

Interrogating representations

In the last section we quantified the frequency of representation. In this section we will concentrate instead on the quality representation, and in particular on the issues of ghettoization, stereotyping and racial thinking.

Ghettoization

Ghettoization is a term which Downing and Husband (2005) have used to describe the restricted representation of ethnic and racial minorities, through identification with a limited range of genres and topics (and roles) for example. In discussing this process, I am less interested in the stereotypes with which the exact nature of the representation may be associated, than I am with the marginality of minority representations. Interrogating ghettoization highlights their peripheral nature in contrast to the centrality of Whiteness. In some cases, analyses suggest that even this peripheral presence exists to serve White interests, rather than minorities' desire for visibility, participation and adequate representation.

Gray (2000: 119) holds that Black-oriented productions and productions including Black leads remain 'confined largely to the genre of situation comedy and entertainment variety'. Moroever, he sees the genres in which Blacks are represented as signifying a televisual segregation – programmes situated in the public sphere (for example, *ER, Homicide, NYPD Blue*) are those which are most likely to represent Blacks as part of an integrated cast, while those that are located in the private sphere of relationships and domesticity are more likely to represent Blacks as part of an all-Black cast. Such segregated programming allows networks to cash in on the Black market niche while avoiding the risk of alienating the dominant culture by addressing integration in the private sphere.

Van Dijk (2000: 38) identifies the most common topics that are associated with news media coverage of ethnic minorities and immigrants as:

- New (illegal) immigrants are arriving.
- Political response to, polices about (new) immigration.
- Reception problems (housing, etc.)
- Social problems (employment, welfare, etc.)
- Response of the population (resentment etc.)
- Cultural characterization: How are they different?
- Complications and negative characterization: How are they deviant?
- Focus on threats: Violence, crime, drugs prostitution.
- Political response: Policies to stop immigration, expulsion, and so on.
- Integration conflicts.

We have previously noted that factual content relating to ethnic and 'racial' minorities often identifies them as problems (van Dijk, 2000: 38). These issues are defined as problems because of their assumed implications for Whites (and indeed for White privilege). These topics are in fact topics which are newsworthy because of their interest to the dominant ethnic group. The representation of minorities is incidental.

A well-known journalistic convention, called McLurg's law, states that '1 dead Briton is worth 5 dead Frenchmen, 20 dead Egyptians, 500 dead Indians and 1,000 dead Chinese.' Although originally the law was said to reflect the ever declining newsworthiness of an event the further away from London it occurred, the law similarly reflects the relationship between the newsworthiness of events and issues and the status of the group to which they relate. (See Chapter 10 by Shoemaker et al. on understandings of newsworthiness).

In previous sections we have discussed the under-representation of minorities as news sources. A variety of research has confirmed similar patterns of marginality across both fictional and factual coverage. Cumberbatch et al.'s (2001) study of television content in the UK found that minority members were much less likely to make a major contribution to the programme than Whites (only 5.7% of major roles), particularly in factual programmes (3%). They were most likely to appear as minor interviewees (66% of minority programme participants) and much more likely than White participants to contribute only sound bites or very brief interviews (21% compared to 4%) (Cumberbatch et al., 2001: 3–4).

Likewise, Entman and Rojecki's (2000) analysis of ethnic group representations in US television advertising found that even when calculated as a percentage of advertisements in which they actually appeared, White characters were twice as likely than Black characters to be shown speaking to the audience, instructing the audience, or in close-up, three times more likely to be shown in the prominent positions of first or last speaker and four times more likely to appear first on screen.

Stereotyping

Stereotyping is a key feature of racist discourse. A stereotype is an exaggerated and factually incorrect representation that is applied indiscriminately to all members of a group on the basis of their racial categorization or ethnic identity (Macionis and Plummer, 2005: 278). Stereotypes are the tools by which hierarchical rankings of ethnic and 'racial' groups are created and maintained. They are key to the racializing process, i.e. the process of creating racial categorizations. By constructing all members of a group as the same, the determining nature of 'race' or ethnicity is supported. Because 'racial' and ethnic stereotypes are used to construct inherent and immutable differences between 'racial' and ethnic groups, the process of stereotyping differentiates 'them' from 'us' and creates 'them' as 'other'.

Although they may be positive or negative, stereotypes used to other racial and ethnic minorities are commonly negative. They frequently construct the racial or ethnic other as a threat to the dominant group. In doing so they enable that group to 'legitimize' (in)action that limits minorities' access to power, resources, opportunity, status and authority. For the elite, stereotypes serve to maintain support for the status quo and the maintenance of privilege. For those among the dominant group who benefit least from this privilege and feel their position to be most at risk, stereotypes enable them to focus their fear away from structural factors that often seem immutable, the impact of which may also be represented to them as individual 'failures'.

> Symbolic boundaries are central to all culture. Marking 'difference' leads us, symbolically, to close ranks, shore up culture and to stigmatize and expel anything which is defined as impure or abnormal. (Hall, 1997: 237)

In communicating with audiences, producers of media content, socialized to be aware of stereotypes, may consciously or unconsciously use these ready-made images to transmit a desired image or message to their audiences. Stereotypes serve as mental shorthands which, because they are culturally transmitted, both the producer and the audience share access to. It is important, however, not to simply dismiss the dissemination of stereotypes through the media as merely the result of lazy thinking or even individual racism. Where ethnic and 'racial' stereotypes appear in media content, where they are not recognized, they evidence institutional racism. As Downing and Husband

(2005) eloquently point out, we are perfectly capable of thinking outside of stereotypes should we chose to do so.

The blatant application of racist stereotypes has decreased dramatically during the last 50 years, in part as a consequence of campaigning on the part of ethnic and 'racial' minorities. Nonetheless, research continues to evidence their continued, if less frequent, occurrence. For example, in their analysis of top rated UK televisual content, Cumberbatch et al. (2001) describe, among others, the reproduction of traditional racist stereotypes of criminality, aggression and Black male hypersexuality. They also report the reproduction of occupational stereotypes. For example, minority members, particularly Blacks, were more than twice as likely to be represented as sports persons than Whites, while Asians were five times more likely than other ethnicities to be represented as shopkeepers.

Box 7.5   The longevity of traditional stereotypes

2004 and 2005 saw a number of newspapers, across the UK and Ireland, draw on traditional stereotypes of African associations with 'black magic' to frame a number of separate, but particularly disfiguring, murders of individuals from ethnic and 'racial' minorities.

The following is a reproduction of an article entitled *Gardai* [Irish Police] *compare canal murder to London ritual killing* published in a respected Irish broadsheet on 17 April 2005:

> Detectives have examined the case files in London on a so-called ritual killing as part of Garda investigation into the headless body murder on the Royal Canal in Dublin.
>
> [The newspaper understands that] detectives travelled to London a week ago to liaise with officers who dealt with the bizarre death of a five-year-old boy, whose headless body was found in the Thames in 2001.
>
> Scotland Yard concluded that the boy was the victim of a religious cult killing. Garda sources confirmed this weekend that they were now actively examining the possibility of a similar gruesome scenario in Dublin.
>
> Detectives declined to discuss evidence that may point in the direction of a ritual murder. The man, believed to be a west African in his 20s, has still not been identified. (O'Kelly, 2005)

Anonymous official sources are employed to legitimize the connection drawn, while the use of the word 'cult' signifies the deviancy of the motivating religion.

While photographs are often used to provide the reader with the racial identity of the subject of discussion, the victim was at the time unidentified. Instead the victim's origin is provided, enabling the reader to draw on stereotypes of traditional African religions to determine what denomination might have been involved.

Two Irish women have since been convicted of murder and manslaughter respectively.

The construction of the racial and ethnic 'other' as a threat to the dominant group transcends all forms of mass media and is an international phenomenon. The particular stereotypical images of which that threat is constructed are manifold, but commonly relate to risks to the predominance of the majority culture, national and personal economic prosperity and privilege, and national and personal security, including personal safety and the security of private property. Drawing on stereotypical images that have also been used to 'legitimize' stratification on the basis of class, gender and sexuality for example, ethnic and racial minorities are stereotyped as a source of acculturation, an economic drain, criminal, a source of social conflict and hypersexual (Haynes, Devereux and Breen, 2006).

The application of such stereotypes not only perpetuates existing racial categorizations, it can also underlie a process of racialization, i.e. 'the extension of racial meaning to previous racially unclassified relationships, social practice or group ...' (Omi and Winant, 1986: 64, cited in Downing and Husband, 2005: 4). This process is evident in contemporary discourses regarding immigrants, particularly asylum seekers and refugees. The terms 'asylum seekers' and 'refugee' are conflated, both these statuses and the multitude of ethnic and national identities of their wearers are collapsed (Haynes, Devereux and Breen, 2006). It is this anonymized deindividuated asylum seeker mass that is re-presented, as a more digestible concept, to the mass media audience. Someone once said that the first causality of war is not truth, but complexity. Perhaps, given that asylum seekers and refugees have been portrayed by some sections of the media as 'the enemy without', it should be unsurprising that like ethnic and 'racial' minorities, asylum seekers' and refugees' diversity is lost in representation.

In addition to the deindividuation that is characteristic of stereotyping, portrayals of asylum seekers and refugees also evidences a process of racialization in drawing on notions of fixed characteristics and attributes, although these are linked to cultural rather than physical differences – the new racism which many authors have identified as a response to the public unacceptability of overt racism. Downing and Husband (2005: 76) note that 'The French National Front proclaims the right to cultural difference as one of the two justifications for its fiercely anti-immigrant propaganda ...'.

Nonetheless, it is the same stereotypes as those which were used in expressing traditional racism, that are employed to mark the boundaries between 'us' and 'them', to legitimize the maintenance of our privilege in the face of their claims for succour:

> For those who have studied the pathologising of people of colour, or the racialisation of the Irish ..., these motifs will be all too familiar. Categorisation as irredeemable (incapacity to integrate), as a cause of racial conflict, as underserving (illegitimate), as unproductive, as criminal, immoral and diseased were also integral to the discourses which racialised and othered these groups. (Haynes et al., 2006: 115)

Gale (2004: 323) is also clear that 'racial' politics are central to discourses about the superficially non-'racial' category of refugees and asylum seekers. Although they are not depicted as 'racially' inferior ' ... their cultures and values are commonly represented in media discourse as "alien" and a threat to whiteness, and western, core values or democracy itself'. The centrality of 'racial' thinking to such discourses about asylum seekers and refugees, lies as much in the construction of an homogeneous us as in the (intertwined) assumption that 'we' are culturally distinct from 'them' (Haynes, Devereux and Breen, 2006). In an example of media discourse centring on border controls, which although Australian in origin might be drawn from any number of (White) Western nations, Gale (2004: 334) holds that 'Refugees arriving ... are represented as the "illegal", non-western, non-Christian Other. Common representations include stereotypes of the uncivilized, "illegal", "queue jumping", if not barbaric Other.'

It is among immigrants that the overlaps between stereotyping on the basis of class and 'race' are also particularly evident, with stereotypes applied to both groups being used simultaneously.

Accommodating racism

Downing and Husband (2005) describe racial thinking as evidenced when we 'employ race as real' in our thinking. In this section, we will focus on some of the ways in which those involved in the production of mass media content accommodate (even if they personally reject) racial thinking, the basis of racism, for the purposes of profit. This process is evident in relation to casting-decisions wherein producers' selections not only assume, but purposefully accommodate, the racial thinking of the market.

In previous sections we have noted that many minorities are numerically under-represented in mass media content, and even when included, often play only minor or incidental roles.

Entman and Rojecki (2000) are quite clear that such patterns result not only from unconscious assumptions of the normalcy of Whiteness, but also from the conscious consideration of the racial 'sensitivities' of audience members. Those who produce mass media content continue to operate in a highly 'race'-conscious mode, for example, from the assumption that:

> ... Whites react negatively to commercials that have 'too many' Blacks. ... They frequently decide to represent Blacks on screen, but virtually always outnumbered by Whites, a pattern that reenacts racial categorization and preference. (Entman and Rojecki, 2000: 180)

Needless to say evidence indicates that this conscious accommodation of racial thinking is not confined to advertising. Downing and Husband (2005: 50) cite an article from the *New York Times* (Lyman, 2002: 1) relating that a Hollywood executive gave the following reasons for declining to cast Halle Berry, daughter of an African American father and a white English mother, in a movie:

> We love Halle, we just don't want to go Black with this part; ... milk is milk until you add a little Hershey ... It doesn't matter if you add a little Hershey or a lot.

Box 7.6   Race-conscious casting at the movies

The 2005 box office hit *Hitch* is a particularly interesting example of the limitations to the advances made in the representation of minority groups in the mass media.

Hitch stars Will Smith, an African American actor with a record of box office success. Smith's star status, in itself, represents progress in the position of ethnic and 'racial' minorities in the media industry.

(Continued)

Smith is regularly signed to lead roles in major mainstream movies, such as *Independence Day*. In recent years Smith has transcended co-star status and proved himself capable of carrying box office blockbusters based on his own popularity with the general movie-going public, as evidenced by the box office taking of movies such as *Hitch* and *I-Robot*. He is able to negotiate salaries equivalent to the top White male actors in Hollywood; reportedly receiving US$20,000,000 for *Hitch*.

That the number of African American actors that have achieved this status in Hollywood forms such a small elite demonstrates that while progress has been made, it also has its limits. However, statements that Smith has made regarding his experiences with the movie *Hitch* evidence that even his status has not fully protected him from the impacts of racial thinking.

Smith has been widely reported (MSNBC) as saying that possible public reaction to the racial categorization of his co-star was a key factor in producers' considerations regarding the choice of his leading lady. According to Smith, producers assumed that a White co-star, cast alongside an African American lead, would have offended the American market. On the other hand, he relates that they felt an entirely African American leading couple would have disinclined audiences globally. The final choice of leading lady was Eva Mendes, an American-born actress of Cuban heritage, who interestingly has twice previously played the love interest of Denzel Washington (*Training Day* and *Out of Time*).

> There's sort of an accepted myth that if you have two black actors, a male and a female, in the lead of a romantic comedy, that people around the world don't want to see it...We spend 50-something million dollars making this movie and the studio would think that was tough on their investment. So the idea of a black actor and a white actress comes up – that'll work around the world, but it's a problem in the US. (Jones, 2005: 3)

Entman and Rojecki (2000: 194) note that their analysis of the box office takings of top US films released in 1996 found that:

> once the number of Whites in the top category reaches 70%, the average box office gross nearly doubles; and with nearly all-White films (those with nine or ten Whites in the top ten), there is another jump up in revenues.

Such analyses suggest, unfortunately, that the segregation of racial categories in the media is not merely the product of anachronistic media production values, but continues to be bolstered by public support.

Nonetheless, this awareness of the on-going colour-consciousness of media producers permits more subtle analyses of the casting of media content. One of the revelations emanating from such analyses is that where minority members are cast in mainstream content, producers favour lighter-skinned individuals. Wilson et al. (2003) note, for example, that increases in the representation of minorities in advertisements have been supported in part by the finding that featuring lighter-skinned Blacks does not alienate White audiences. An analysis of the skin tone and features of participants in UK television also found evidence of '...a bias in favour of white idealisation of ethnic minorites (at least for women) who appear to be only reluctantly admitted to our screens' (cumerbatch et al. 2001: 5).

Compromises between the potential of the minority market and the assumed racism of the majority market, are also made by casting minorities in group situations and as a minority in such contexts, effectively 'diluting' their impact. Whites on the other hand are rarely depicted in the minority within integrated groups (Entman and Rojecki, 2000; Cumberbatch et al., 2001).

Although the American film industry abandoned the code which included a prohibition of 'miscegenation' in the late 1960s, for Hollywood inter-racial relationships remain at least highly controversial if not taboo. Certainly, both film and television producers, particularly outside of the US, are starting to breech this informal prohibition. But it remains usual for members of two different racial categorizations to be cast in a (heterosexual) relationship, unless the inter-'racial' nature of that relationship is dictated by the storyline. This remains particularly the case where the male in question is a person of colour. Relationships between White males and women of colour, in avoiding threats to White patriarchy, are far less threatening to White privilege.[1] For example, Feng Sun (2002: 658) notes that while Asian men are often depicted as asexual or conversely as potential rapists of White women, and intra-Asian romance is rarely portrayed on television or in film, Asian women (whether represented as passive or aggressive) are constructed as sexually available to White males. Such representations have their routes in colonial discourse, in the requirement for the 'exotic other' to be civilized by the White Western male.

But it is not only inter-'racial' contact that remains infrequent or inequitable in visual mass media content. The depiction of physical contact *among* members of minority groups is also less frequent than the depiction of contact among Whites. Research in both the US (Entman and Rojecki, 2000) and the UK (Cumberbatch et al., 2001: 39) found ethnic and 'racial' minorities to be significantly less likely to be depicted sharing affection than Whites. This includes affection expressed between parents and children.[2]

Overview

Clearly, improvements in the quantity of ethnic minority representations and reductions in the frequency of overt stereotyping is not evidence that the media industry holds the interests of minorities in parity to those of the dominant group. Entman and Rojecki (2000) suggest that improvements have been negotiated against the potential for 'offending' White audiences whose presumed disturbance by racial and ethnic difference is normalized, accepted and serviced. The examples that have been used above to illustrate this process, also evidence the manner in which accommodating racism supports its perpetuation by continuing the 'othering' of minorities. In an attempt to avoid 'offending' White audiences, minorities are depicted as less frequently engaged in the most basic humanizing acts of giving and receiving love, while the potential for love is depicted as racially segregated.

Conclusion

While this chapter has focused on the shortfalls in mass media representations of ethnic and 'racial' minorities, it is important to also acknowledge the strides that have been made, particularly as a result of the campaigning of minority groups and anti-racists. Minority members are better represented in production, particularly in the most visible roles. Minority-related content is more numerous and portrayals more varied. Most significantly the overt exercise or expression of racism, although it continues, is commonly regarded as unacceptable in contemporary content.

The mass media have also made some positive contributions to anti-racism. In some cases, they have challenged or subverted traditional racist stereotypes and provided a forum for the positive depiction of minorities' everyday lives. Broadcast media have increasingly included diversity programming. Some local print media have evidenced genuine efforts to cater to their minority populations. The film industry has shown itself capable of providing a global forum for anti-racist messages with the distribution of films like *Crash* (2005).

Nonetheless the qualitative and quantitative progress that has been made to date does not yet signify any real shift in the underlying order. Globalized mass media and the mass media organizations of much of the developed world, continue to operate through the lens of White privilege. Ethnic and 'racial' minorities have not achieved the ubiquitous presence across the range of genres, topics and roles that is a defining feature of Whiteness.

As the shortfalls in representation documented in this chapter continue, minorities turn to specialized ethnic media (Gray, 2000; Turnstone, 2003). Such media provide a key site for groups' positive self-construction, particularly in the context of negative or stereotypical mass media representations. It may be argued that such media, in maintaining strong intra-group ties (See Chapter 16 by Karim on Media and Diaspora), may also make assimilation more difficult. Downing and Husband (2005) are, nonetheless, positive about the impact of minority ethnic media, noting that they may rather be directed to provide precisely the tools required for 'dual cultural citizenship'.

Throw (1997) holds that minorities are increasingly likely to utilize ethnic media as their purchasing power grows, and media conglomerates are already taking advantage of this opportunity for diversification. Karim (see Chapter 16, Media and Diaspora) notes the growing absorption of ethnic media into existing conglomerates, potentially at the expense of their community-orientation. Ethnic minorities who cannot compete economically or numerically are likely to continue to rely on specialized media, if the market is to be the key driver of progress. But, for those ethnic groups whose market share prospects are bullish, corporate interest is likely to extend to them the African-American experience of (slow) progress towards a better quality and quantity of representation in the future.

Such developments are important, because while ethnic media are usually accessed only by the group in question, it is the mainstream mass media that provides the potential for inter-group communication and for affirmations of and challenges to our mutual self-imagining as a society. Arguably, the mainstream mass media provides *the key cultural site* for challenging hegemonic Whiteness. Progress is clearly evident in this respect, however, reliance on the aligned interests of equity and profit would offer a shaky foundation for the future, particularly for those groups who are less affluent and populous.

Summary

- 'Race' and ethnicity are both social constructions. Neither concept has any meaning beyond that which people assign to it.
- The media is significant as a key mechanism by which socially and geographically distant groups learn about each other and as a site for the reinforcement of society's values and norms (including those that support racism or anti-racism).

- Ethnic and 'racial' minorities have been numerically under-represented in the media.
- There is some evidence to show that as the purchasing power of minorities has increased, mass media organizations have made a greater effort at least to increase minorities numerical representations.
- Nonetheless, ethnic and 'racial' minorities continue to be represented in relation to a limited range of roles and topics, and often only to the degree that their inclusion pertains to, or will not offend or threaten, White interests.
- The use of traditional overtly racist stereotypes is significantly less evident than in the past, however, more subtle stereotypes relating to cultural difference continue to be employed.

GOING FURTHER

Broadly-based texts, which cover a variety of media and genres:
Cottle, S. (2000) (ed.) *Ethnic Minorities and the Media*. Buckingham: Open University Press. Populated by chapters from many of the leading authors in the field. Relevance to production, content and reception. Highly original contribution from Simon Cottle himself, regarding the production of ethnic minority television.

Wilson II, C.C., Gutiérrez, F. and Chao, L.M. (2003) *Racism, Sexism and the Media: The Rise of Class Communication in Multicultural America*, (3rd edn.) London: Sage.
Wide ranging, US-oriented text. Particularly useful chapters on the significance of the media, audience segmentation and achieving change. Includes material on the film industry, public relations, advertising, minority media and video games.
Texts which are particularly strong on theorizations of the relationship between the mass media, 'race' and ethnicity:

Downing, J. and Husband, C. (2005) *Representing 'Race': Racisms, Ethnicities and Media*. London: Sage.
Recommended for its rich, yet accessible, theorization. Comprehensive but comprehensible discussions of the concepts of 'race' and ethnicity. Concise overview of the key concepts employed in research on racism, ethnicity and the media. Case studies of the role of the media in key ethnic conflicts. Useful discussion of indigenous and minority media. Chapter on media monitoring and codes of practice.

Spencer, S. (2006) *Race and Ethnicity: Gender, Identity and Representation*. Abingdon, Oxon: Routledge.

Not specific to the media, but particularly recommended for its insightful discussions of otherness, Whiteness, the intersections between 'race' and class. Chapters on colonialism and theories of 'race' and ethnicity. Case studies include a discussion of the treatment of Aborigines by the Australian media.

Empirical research studies of particular interest:

Campbell, C. (1995) *Race, Myth and the News.* Thousand Oaks, CA.: Sage.
A useful example of a textual (i.e. qualitative) analysis of local television newscasts.

Cumberbatch, G., Gauntlett, S., Richards M. and Littlejohns, V. (2001) *Top Ten TV: Ethnic minority group representation on popular television.* London: Commission for Racial Equality.
   Commissioned by the UK's Commission for Racial Equality, this quantitative analysis of UK television is particularly interesting because its sampling strategy was based on viewership. Thus, while many studies are confined to a single genre, this research transcends genres and also includes both US as well as UK programmes.

Entman, R.M. and Rojecki, A. (2000). *The Black Image in the White Mind.* Chicago: University of Chicago Press.
An extremely comprehensive and well researched study of 'race' in the mass media. The research focuses on the US and specifically on African-Americans in the context of ubiquitous Whiteness. Examines a range of genres including network and local news, prime-time dramas and sitcoms as well as the film and advertising industries.

van Dijk, T. (1991) *Racism and the Press: Critical Studies in Racism and Migration.* London: Routledge.
A seminal text on racism in the press. An exemplar of theoretically informed, systematic and rigorous empirical research. Utilizes critical discourse and quantitative analyses.

STUDENT ACTIVITY 7.1

In this exercise you are going to investigate the representation of different ethnic and 'racial' groups on mainstream television.

   For each weekday (Monday to Friday), select a fictional television programme which is aired on a mainstream terrestrial or satellite television station between 8 and 9 pm. In many countries this is the period during which most viewers are tuned in and therefore the period during which producers are most likely to target what they regard to be their mainstream audience. In the case of each programme, make a record of the ethnic or 'racial' identity of any characters who have a speaking part (you may find it easier to avoid recoding information on all of the extras!). Try to answer the following questions about the actors on whom you have gathered data:

- Which actors are regular cast members, for example, those appearing in the opening credits?
- Which actors play a lead or a supporting role?
- What occupations do these actors' characters have?
- Are the core cast of characters represented as part of a multi-racial workplace, organization or community?
- Are the core cast of characters represented as part a multi-racial friendship group or intimate relationship?

Having recorded your findings, consider the following questions:

- Which ethnic or racial identities are most commonly represented (a) in your five programmes (b) among the programme's regular cast (c) in lead roles?
- Examine the occupations which the characters have. Do these occupations play to 'racial' or ethnic stereotypes? (See this chapter for examples.) Which groups are most likely to be represented in positions of authority?
- Are multi-racial groups commonly represented on screen? In what contexts are such representations most likely – the public sphere (for example, work) or the private sphere (for example, intimate relationships)?
- Are there any differences between the quantity or quality of the representation of different minority ethnicities?

Consider explanations for your findings, for example, by reference to the ethos of the station, the composition of the audience, the setting or scenario of the fictional programme, and the political or economic power of the group in question.

References

Ainley, B. (1998) *Black Journalists, White Media*. Stoke-on-Trent: Trentham.

American Society of Newspaper Editors (2005) *Newsroom Employment Census*. Available at http://www.asne.org/index.cfm?id=5650 [Accessed 2005].

Breed, W. (1995) 'Social Control in the Newsroom', *Social Forces*, 33: 326–35.

Campbell, C. (1995) *Race, Myth and the News*. Thousand Oaks, CA.: Sage.

Cottle, S. (1997) *Television and Ethnic Minorities: Producers' Perspectives*. Aldershot: Avebury.

Cumberbatch, G., Gauntlett, S., Richards, M. and Littlejohns, V. (2001) *Top Ten TV: Ethnic minority group representation on popular television*. London: Commission for Racial Equality.

van Dijk, T. (2000) 'New(s) Racism: A Discourse Analytical Approach' in S. Cottle (ed.) *Ethnic Minorities and the Media*. Buckingham: Open University Press. pp. 33–49.

Downing, J. and Husband, C. (2005) *Representing 'Race': Racisms, Ethnicities and Media*. London: Sage.

Eldridge, J. (ed.) (1993) *Getting the Message: News Truth and Power*. London: Rouledge.

Entman, R.M. and Rojecki, A. (2000) *The Black Image in the White Mind*. Chicago: University of Chicago Press.

Feng Sun, C. (2002) 'Ling Woo in Historical Context: The New Face of Asian American Stereotypes on Televsion' in G. Dines, and J.M. Humez (eds) *Gender, Race and Class in the Media: A text reader*. (2nd edn.) Thousand Oaks: Sage. pp. 656–64.

Fulcher, J. and Scott, J. (2003) *Sociology*. (2nd edn) Oxford: Oxford University Press.

Fulcher, J. and Scott, J. (2003) *Sociology* (3rd edn) Oxford: Oxford University Press.

Gale, P. (2004) 'The Refugee Crisis and Fear: Populist Politics and Media Discourse', *Journal of Sociology*, Vol. 40, No. 4, December, SAGE, pp. 321–40.

Gray, H. (2000) 'Black Representation in the Post Network, Post Civil Rights World of Global Media' in S. Cottle (ed.) *Ethnic Minorities and the Media*. Buckingham: Open University Press.

Greenberg, B. and Brand, B. (1994) 'Minorities in the mass media: 1970s to 1990s', in J. Bryant and D. Zillmann (eds) *Media Effects: Advances In Theory And Research*. Hillsdale, NJ: Lawrence Erlbaum. pp. 273–314.

Hall, S. (1997) 'The spectacle of the 'other' in S. Hall, (ed.) *Representation: cultural representations and signifying practices*. Milton Keynes: The Open University, 223–90.

Haynes, A., Devereux, E. and Breen, M.J. (2006) 'Fear, Framing and Foreignness', *International Journal of Critical Psychology*, Spring, 16. pp. 100–21.

Heider, D. (2000) *White News: Why Local News Programs Don't Cover People of Color*. Mahwah, New Jersey: Lawrence Erlbaum.

Hohman, K. (2000) 'Race relations: Whiteness studies. A look at White Privilege and Whiteness studies and how they pertain to race relations', http://recerelations.about.com/library/weekly/blwhiteprevillage.htm

Jones, A. (2005) 'Where there's a Will'. *Birmingham Post*. 23 February E1.

Kerner Commission (1968) *Report of the National Advisory Commission on Civil Disorders*. Washington: U.S. Government Printing Office.

Law, I. (2002) *Race in the News*. Basingstoke: Palgrave.

Lyman, R. (2002) 'Black actors: Still keeping their eyes on the prize', *The New York Times*, 27 February, E1.

Mastro, D.E. and Robinson, A.L. (2000) 'Cops and Crooks: Images of minorities on primetime television', *Journal of Criminal Justice*, 28: 385–96.

McPherson, M. Smith-Lovin, L. and Cook, J.M. (2001) 'Birds of a Feather: Homophily in social networks', *Annual Review of Sociology*, 27: 415–44.

Njeri, I. (1991) 'The Last Taboo: Does Wave of Interracial Movies Signal a Real Change?', *Ebony*, September. pp. 74–7.

O'Kelly, B. (2005) 'Gardai compare canal murder to London ritual killing', *Sunday Business Post*. 17 April.

Omi, M. and Winant, H. (1986) *Racial Formation in the United States*. New York: Routledge.

Spencer, S. (2006) *Race and Ethnicity: Gender, Identity and Representation*. Abingdon, Oxford: Routledge.

Throw, J. (1997) *Breaking Up America: Advertisers and the new media world*. Chicago: Chicago University Press.

Turnstone Research and Connect Research and Consultancy (2003) *Ethnic Minority Communities: Executive Summary*, Prepared by Turnstone Research and Connect Research and Consultancy. London: Central Office for Information.

US Department of Commerce (2001) *2000 Census of Population and Housing: Profile of General Demographic Characteristics*.

Wilson II, C.C., Gutiérrez, F. and Chao, L.M. (2003) *Racism, Sexism and the Media: The Rise of Class Communication in Multicultural America*. (3rd edn) London: Sage.

Notes

1 Notably, shows which have depicted inter-racial relationships have also received objections from Black audience members (Ebony, September 1991), evidencing that racism is by no means the exclusive remit of Whites and may be perpetuated even by its victims.

2 On the other hand, an analysis of the depictions of Blacks in movies released in 1996 (Entman and Rojecki, 2000), evidenced a greater tendency for them to be shown giving and receiving affection than Whites. However this should be taken in the context of their more frequent sexualization.

Media Representations of Social Structure: Gender

Joke Hermes

DEFINITION

Gender is the cultural significance given to biological difference of reproductive organs. It refers to men and women, as well as to appropriate and less appropriate ways to be a man or a woman (masculinity and femininity). Gender is closely related to sexuality and to difference more generally. Often gender is seen as the 'original' difference and as a universal divide in all human groups. This, however, is arguable. There are more than two biological categories. Gender does not assume the same cultural significance everywhere, and gender codes have changed significantly over time. The analytical importance in using gender as a concept is to denote how society is structured in terms of power relations. It points to the huge difference between social categories and the qualities we ascribe to groups. In turn, it is of vital importance to understand that categories never fully describe how actual individuals live their lives.

Introduction

This chapter will show why it is important to understand how the media represent gender. It will argue that constructions of femininity and masculinity are part of a dominant ideology that prescribes 'proper' behaviour for men and for women (Goffman, 1976; Macdonald, 1995). Central to such proper behaviour is to have the 'correct' sexuality. In the Western world dominant ideology, however, is not currently imposed on us dictatorially. There are varieties in proper and less proper ways of being a woman or a man. There is room for different sexualities. The media, in their capacity of informing us about the world and as entertainers, show us an immense range of possibilities and practices of 'doing gender'. The value attached to these varied possibilities is not equal, nor is it always possible for all of them to be shown. To be or become aware of the many ways in which gender can have meaning, and the weight attached to different forms in different contexts, is what we need to train in order to understand both the media and the societies in which they operate.

Why bother with gender in media studies? So much has changed in society since the Second World War. White middle-class women in the Western world are now aware that they have more options than to try and be a housewife and mother (with or without a part-time job). Non-White and working-class women are less punished for being ambitious beyond what used to be their social status (Skeggs, 1997). Men know how to change a diaper. Machines take care of cleaning dishes and clothes. This changed view of women's role and social position, in place since the nineteenth century for middle and upper-class households, is marked by Friedan's famous book *The Feminine Mystique* (1963). It shows how in the early 1960s to be a woman meant that you lived in a fake world. A husband, a home and children were supposed to provide instant gratification but did not. It left women wondering whether that was all there was to live for. The 'fakeness' of the world was mostly produced in and through the media. Women's magazines counselled readers that to be a mother was difficult but fulfilling. Romantic stories promised that heterosexual marriage was a state of bliss. News stories showed solely men who were politicians or important figures in the world of business. The genders were represented with a marked difference in the media.

Friedan and other feminist authors of the 'second wave', in Europe and the US, unleashed a powerful movement in the 1970s that redefined what it meant to be a woman. Instead of being ornaments in a man's life or responsible for their offspring, women had options and could have careers, provided that childcare and home arrangements were to change. In many regards, the women's movement was extraordinarily successful, if not in truly becoming a 'rainbow coalition' that brought together all kinds of women (hooks, 1994). Media representations did change in the wake of social change and became more diverse, although the systematic oppression of human beings based on their gender has remained an issue. Female circumcision is but one gruesome human rights example that we know of via documentary film and news stories. The fact that women all over the world, including the West, are paid systematically less than men for the same work, is another regularly repeated news item.

Box 8.1   Hearth and home

In a famous large-scale study in the early 1970s, Tuchman (1978) showed that women made up a significant part of the North-American work force. The media however, depicted them solely in domestic roles, in relation to men, their husbands, fathers, brothers. She suggested that women were 'symbolically annihilated' by the media. In turn, that would provide young women with an entirely skewed notion of what society needed from them when they grew up. It would not prepare them adequately. Underlying the symbolic annihilation-thesis is the idea that the media provide 'role models'. Given the right role models, girls would behave less 'girlishly' and stop under-achieving in order to do well in the marriage market. Gender, argued feminists such as Scheu, a German researcher, and de Beauvoir, a French philosopher and novelist, was not imprinted on one's genes. It was de Beauvoir who famously remarked: 'On ne naît pas femme: on le devient' (One is not born a woman, one becomes one) in *Le Deuxième Sexe* (1949). Scheu and many others echoed this observation in books that after 30 years are still in print, for example, Scheu's *Wir werden nicht als Mädchen geboren, wir werden dazu gemacht* [We Are Not Born Girls], first published in 1977. Although the role model theory is seen as somewhat less than adequate today, it is still an important political tool. It fits well enough with discussion today that suggests that gender is a social construction that is build and rebuild as it were, in different situations and contexts. This points to the need to understand the codes, conventions and rules that make up 'gender' in a specific time and place.

'Musculinity'

The lives of men and the representation of masculinity changed as much as the equivalent for women over the last half of the twentieth century. Former bread-winners and heads of the household, men found that their bodies too could be commercially exploited. Although the male suit remains today's chain mail, undressed male bodies are widely on public display. Going by popular television drama, the average actor has to spend considerable time in a gym to tone muscles and gain the required 'strong' look. Ridge Forrester, in the long-running American soap opera *The Bold and the Beautiful*, provides such an example. 'Musculinity' became the norm for such genres as the action film, according to Tasker (1993). First Hollywood and then the other world cinemas (from Bollywood to Asian film) reacted to the changes wrought in our perception of men and masculinity by the feminist critique of the 1960s through to the 1980s. For straight men, the new challenge was to be both caring and strong, and above all, to look good. The off-jokes that Bruce Willis's and Mel Gibson's characters make in the *Die Hard* and *Lethal Weapon* film series, attest to the exercise required in building a new masculine ideal of such widely disparate elements. The love lives of the characters they play moreover, attest to the quite spectacular lengths they have to go to, to find and live up to the standards set by the women they find attractive.

The twenty-first century is not a feminist Valhalla. It may be for some, but for most it is not. Gender, for both men and women, still consists of a complex set of rules, distinctions and ideals that are difficult to live up to. It requires extensive cultural knowledge to know what behaviour and dress style are appropriate under specific circumstances. The media guide us in this regard. They offer examples of what is 'done', and what not, of how to combine different types of gendered behaviour. They teach us how to enjoy both traditional and innovative ways of dealing with gender, and offer examples for us to discuss with others. In itself this is enough of an argument to bother with how the media represent gender. By informing us and entertaining us, the media implicitly teach us about proper gendered behaviour as much as how to resist and subvert gendered codes. Learning how to decode media messages about gender is enriching for any television viewer, women's magazine or newspaper reader. It is an especially good test case for young and up-and-coming media professionals to test and train their cultural awareness and sensitivity.

There is a second good argument to bother with gender, and with representation of gender in the media. Regardless of social change since second-wave feminism, and whether and how gender is a source of oppression, there is the systematization of the difference between femininity and masculinity that is embedded in media representations. A half-naked woman in a rap video offering herself for (symbolic) consumption is not necessarily in itself problematic. Bubbling in rap shows us impressive and powerful women. Nor is it a problem that women in positions of power in drama series are either bitches or mothers. Taken together, however, they point to how femininity is defined in terms of sexuality, rather than, say, professionalism. While this may not have direct consequences for real people, the implicit message is part of a wider system of codes that is hardly beneficial to the chances for half of the population if they want to be taken seriously as anything other than a sexual being: nun or whore; virgin, mother or slut.

Likewise with the representations of masculinity. What sex does for the representation of femininity, power does for masculinity. This works in a slightly different way. Masculinity, much more than femininity, is always invested with hierarchical difference. Whether it is the rapper versus the women around him, the detached professionalism of CTU agent Jack Bauer in *24* (Fox TV) which allows him to be far more violent than other agents, or the knowledgeable and experienced authority of the *chef de clinique* in hospital series, power is the key ingredient for successful masculinity. Just imagine what would have happened to a less powerful figure than the president of the US if you are a public official who is caught having seedy affairs and lying about them. It is generally not easy if, as a man, you do not belong to the top dogs. If you are too young, or too old, if you are gay or not White, your chances of being taken seriously, like those of women, are slimmer the more you divert from the White, heterosexual, male norm (Segal, 1990).

Of course, there are plenty of men who are lust objects (*America's Temptation Island*, or the yearly male pin-up calendars published by fire brigades for fundraising purposes are but two examples) and who are defined in sexual terms. Authoritative women can easily be found who have more balls than the guys around them (true of many a woman politician) (van Zoonen, 2005). Cultural logic does not define individual women or men in their entirety. Rather, all men and women are individually defined by pretty much unique mixes of masculine and feminine qualities. Individuality, the unique mix we partly orchestrate ourselves and partly find ourselves in, is pulled however, towards conventional criteria for our gender. However creative or innovative we are, or however little we intend to mean by the headscarf, the mini skirt, the suit or cowboy boots we wear, dominant frames of interpretation in a relentless either/or logic impose gendered identities on us.

In Western society, we like to set store by individualism and individual examples. To point to underlying cultural logics is easily disqualified as not doing justice to individuals and their solutions. Or it is seen as being overly politically correct. So be it. The point is not that femininity is the inescapable fate of any woman, or masculinity that of all men, rather, the point is that similar practices (wearing make-up, or a skirt, sporting a moustache) signify differently for women and for men. Moreover, as interpreting someone's 'look' is done by other persons who have their own cultural knowledge and experience, the make-up, the skirt, the facial hair, may be given different meanings or different weight. Last but not least, interpreting cultural codes always involves decoding sets of clues, that may well point in different directions or outright contradict one another. The shadow of a moustache on a dark-haired girl in a sexy dress is more easily overlooked than body hair in some parts of male gay subculture.

Therefore, acquiring a certain sensitivity to how gender is an important social structure to all of us, is not easy. It does matter. Differences that are made systematically are strong forces of inclusion and exclusion, and of (self) censorship. It matters secondly, because social and cultural differences are linked. Gender difference is often understood as an original distinction, drawing on such sources as the Bible. It would seem to be indisputable and natural, like the one between man and matter. But just as we are both objects and beings, it is questionable whether the original difference is the one between men and women. Not just because many hybrid forms exist (hermaphrodites, for example) but because it can be argued that all identities, including gender identities need to be *performed* to exist. Butler, a renowned queer theorist, uses the example of drag (cross-gender dressing) to make her case. Drag, she states, 'enacts the very structure of impersonation by which any gender is assumed' (Butler, 1991: 21). We do not go about stark naked, we dress ourselves. Because social contexts differ, we style how we dress as much as how we behave. We thus, mundanely, appropriate and theatricalize gender. 'If this is true', says Butler, 'it seems, there is no original or primary gender that drag imitates, but *gender is a kind of imitation for which there is no original* (1991: 21) (italics in original).

As this is part of an essay in which Butler explores what being a lesbian means, she goes on to discuss how 'the "reality" of heterosexual identity is performatively constituted. Heterosexuality, after all, needs gender difference more than other sexualities. As an imitation that has no original, heterosexuality is always in the business of living up to a fantasy of what it might be. It is, according to queer theory, a project that is bound to fail because people differ in their taste and preferences in their sex lives as much as in other regards. It is also quite difficult for men to perform to the standards set by the norm. Much to the angry regret of viewers of *Sex and the City,* neither of Carrie's two main love interests live up to it. 'When Big showed up looking all broken and pathetic at Aidan's country house to cry over that movie star lady, that was pretty much it for me. I've always looked at Big like Mr. Macho, cool as a cucumber, and that episode made him look about as cool as a wet noodle (www.jumpthe-shark.com, 2006).' Suggesting that heterosexuality is the one and only original sexuality is a doomed project. It works well however in creating the kind of distinction that nation-states have a vested interest in (Donzelot, 1979; Foucault, 1977). It privileges families and child birth (future citizens, child-bearers, soldiers, workers and consumers). It is important in regulating and disciplining populations (Foucault, 1979). Because it is such a useful fiction, it is repeated again and again, implying in its wake a much bigger difference between men and women than actually exists.

By understanding gender as the crucially important difference between men and women, heterosexuality maintains itself as absolute norm. Fortunately this is never an entirely successful project. We recognize many other sexualities, which in a range of contexts may be appreciated and legitimate. While masculinity in many ways is defined as how not to appear to be gay (a wimp or queer), a range of queer identities has nonetheless become available, starting with the new men of the early 1980s who wore make-up and flirted with both sexes. Bands such as Pet Shop Boys (Maus, 2001) and performers such as Boy George are key examples. Box 8.2 gives another type of example of how we understand the difference between men and women as fundamental and as the norm, but, at the same time, hugely enjoy the subversion of that norm. It is concerned with the ongoing attraction of presenting characters in drag in (mainstream) cinema.

Box 8.2   Why is drag sexy?

Film culture has given us a vast range of men in drag. Interestingly, these men are often more than comic figures, however awkwardly they move around in a dress, proving how difficult it is to perform femininity well. They charm us. They convince us, contradictorily, of their masculinity in a romantic scenario. In some cases they allow us to be moved by the drama of dichotomous identity: *Some Like it Hot* (dir. Billy Wilder, 1959); *Tootsie* (with Dustin Hoffman, dir. Sydney Pollack, 1982), *The Birdcage/La Cage aux Folles* (with Robin Williams, dir. Mike Nichols, 1996), *The Crying Game* (with Jaye Davidson, dir. Neil Jordan, 1992) are but the obvious examples.

Women too overstep and challenge boundaries, and are 'more than meets the eye', by pretending to be men. *Victor Victoria* (with Julie Andrews, dir. Blake Edwards, 1982) is an example; as is *Orlando* in Virginia Woolf's novel, or the two central characters in *Tipping the Velvet* (BBC television, 2002). The shifting of codes makes room for unlawful interpretations and possibilities; the usual prohibitions do not hold. A woman in a suit suggests she is playing hard to get, making the chase more exciting. Men in skirts make themselves more freely available for sexual fantasy than men 'protected' by pants, and certainly than those encapsulated in a suit and tie.

Gender and genre

The rules guiding representation of gender are complex. Take, for instance, a newsreader. Newsreaders need to have neutral faces, after all, news programmes are supposed to inform us and support processes of opinion formation. However, in competitive television environments news anchors may need more than a neutral face or to exude authority. They may need to be sexy as well. Or, if one of the competing partners is public broadcasting, yet another type of appeal may be called for. In the Netherlands, for example, a host of women newsreaders was hired in the 1980s, just before the Dutch broadcasting system was opened to commercial stations. These women, argues van Zoonen, were hardly chosen for being sexy. Rather, they provided another type of authority. They were busty maternal types, putting the nation to bed after a hectic day (van Zoonen, 1991, and see Holland, 1987).

Generally, genre codes prescribe gender expectations in the media. Genre does more of course. Neale (1980) has famously defined genre as the contract between audiences and producers. Having an idea of what you can expect makes it easier to fully enjoy a series, a documentary or a quiz. Knowing the rules is half the fun. Genre conventions regulate how a story is told, or how a quiz is to be played, or what constitutes valid evidence in a documentary. Included in those rules is who can be a hero, a contestant, a host or an expert. Experts, for instance, are often men. Think of Dr. Phil, formerly Oprah Winfrey's expert psychologist, now a show host in his own right. When the expert is a woman, dress code is important. Cleavage or bare leg tend to undermine the expert's credibility. Despite such old stereotypes as the fuzzy professor, we expect our experts to be sharp, able to deliver judgements and information in short sound bites and, most of all, not to distract our attention onto themselves. They need to disappear behind their expertize to be the disembodied voices of science and reason.

The nexus of gender and genre also produces specific pleasures for us as media audience members. As both gender and genre are complex constructions, the pleasures involved in making media content meaningful are layered and of different orders. There is, first of all, the simple pleasure of recognition, of understanding the logic of a programme, a game or a magazine. Second, there is the pleasure of understanding how any one cultural text itself will contain different storylines, for example, or be host to a set of conflicting norms and values, embedded in relationships between characters. Third, in reading a book or viewing a film, we are often aware of references to other texts, to historical events or persons in the 'real' world. Such intertextual references may add yet another kind of pleasure. In addition, all of these different kinds of recognizing what a film, game or book are all about, may point to one another and twist what at first sight may have appeared to be forthright definitions of gender or implementations of genre rules.

Although, as Johnson has argued in *Everything Bad is Good For You* (2006), we have become incredible smart audiences, our media literacy does not extend to the ability to discuss well what it is we like and what we think media texts are about. Johnson's examples are concerned with, amongst other things, games and television drama. By using simple graphics Johnson shows convincingly that popular television drama has become much more complex over a quarter century. Whereas series such as *Starsky and Hutch* only had a small number of storylines per episode, many a popular drama series after the millennium will have more than ten storylines going on in any one episode. The interesting thing of course is that day-time soap opera has a long pedigree of what Johnson calls 'multi-threading' (see also Modleski, 1982; Newcomb, 1974). The innovation, according to him, came with *Hill Street Blues*, a police series. 'Bochco's genius with Hill Street was to marry complex narrative structure with complex subject matter'(Johnson, 2005: 68). While *Dallas*, in Johnson's recapitulation, had shown that soap opera's interweaving of many storylines could survive week-long interruptions, and sit coms such as *All in the Family* had tackled difficult social issues, *Hill Street Blues* combined 'richly drawn characters confronting difficult social issues, and a narrative structure to match' (ibid).

Television, a key mass medium, has offered us more and more complex pleasures, which attests to a mostly unnoticed development amongst audiences. We have become much smarter in decoding difficult content. Unfortunately we have also been quite complacent about this. We manage to be smart viewers and stupid public debaters, who hold on to simplified notions about the mass media in general, witness discussion of children and media, and to simplified notions of social structures, be they gender, class, ethnicity or nationality. This is partly due to another article of faith; that you should not spoil your pleasures in entertainment by analysing them too closely. Partly it also has to with the dominance of what Hartley has called 'the knowledge class' (1999). Those of us who are or will be teachers, for example, benefit from hierarchical knowledge structures that appoint us as guardians of truth and insight. Television as well as other media compete for the attention of audiences.

But constructions of gender difference, of traditional femininity and masculinity do not either appear or disappear under closer scrutiny, they are there all the time. Nor does the pleasure in any kind of entertainment dissolve when one is able to analyze and discuss it. Arguably, even what are referred to as 'guilty pleasures' (I should be doing something more useful with my time) may gain legitimacy or prestige under conditions of public media literacy. To show the interlinked layers of understanding and enjoying media texts and how they construct gender roles, the following will offer two examples. The first concerns women characters in police series, and focuses on how women may be portrayed as professionals. Interesting work on women as victims in such genres, also exists.

Box 8.3   Women as heroes and as victims

The police series is an interesting and long-running television genre. It can be argued to be a domain of oppression for women. In *Rape on Prime Time*, Cuklanz (2000) shows that most of the victims in police series are women, while sexual crimes are one of the most important categories of misdoing. Police series are also a domain in which television has engaged with feminism by introducing women characters as police officers. Sometimes they suggest that women's emancipation is fully achieved and that women can be fully integrated and respected members of the force. There are, however, also examples of series that show how lonely and difficult is to be a woman in a male-dominated world. The BBC series *Prime Suspect* (1990–2006) was known for its exciting and provocative portrayal of detective Jane Tennison. She was ambitious and worked all hours, putting her work before her private life at all times. Although understandably hardened by her experience of being excluded by the guys, she came, at times, uncomfortably close to a stereotypical harridan.

While bearing in mind that it is hardly television's project to be a progressive social force, it is of interest to see how sheer industrial dynamics have forced the medium to continue innovating (cf. Caldwell, 1987). The police series example below will show how this includes the level of storylines and characterization. The second example deals with men's magazines. Although a long-existing (sub) genre in the magazine market, only recently men's magazines have come to be a gendered umbrella genre, which women's magazines have long been. The importance of such an example is in showing how highly traditionally gendered content, such as that offered by so-called 'lads' magazines' may, at the same time, show how masculinity is as much a gender as femininity, rather than an ungendered norm for all.

Gender and professionalism: the police series

Women have always had a strong presence in crime fiction. Although crime is related to violence, which is commonly associated with masculinity, women have always been authors of crime fiction (Agatha Christie, for example), and literary creations in it. Although outnumbered by men, women detectives have never been absent from the end of the nineteenth century onwards (Swanson and James, 1996), able to voice a wide range of perspectives. In television too, generally most law enforcers are men. But Pepper (in *Police Woman*, NBC, 1974–78) or *Charlie's Angels* (ABC, 1976–81) prove that too pessimistic a view of women's role as police officers and private investigators is not historically correct. From the spinster detective such as Miss Marple to Charlie's Angels women have both been cast within and against stereotype. Sometimes using the authority of the spinster, so reminiscent of the figure of the governess or the elderly teacher in charge of both Order and Truth; sometimes using the appeal of the tom boy, making use, at least partly, of the 'drag' factor. More recently, women characters took in feminist social criticism. *Prime Suspect*'s Jane Tennison (BBC, 1990–2006), for example, was a strong mix of sexy femininity (fired by actress Helen Mirren's status and reputation), feminist will to power and the tragedy of being a lone woman outsider in a male police force (Brunsdon, 1998).

Crime and action drama clearly shows the importance of recognizing the subtlety and context-relatedness of gender distinctions in specific genres, which shift with the different layers in the text. Gender distinctions unfold between three rather than two poles, to start with. Detectives are not just either man or woman; it matters also whether or not they are feminists. As a result we have characters who have feminine, masculine and feminist traits in different degrees. Generic rules, in addition, offer a range of possibilities taking us in different directions, be they action-adventure, police procedural or the psychological thriller. Suspense is important to all but in varying degrees and in different ways. Film is often more subtle than television. Some action is also part of most crime drama.

Politics, on the other hand, mark a quite sharp line of distinction. State politics are more to be found in film than television, and clearly have a masculine leaning. An example would be *Enemy of the State* (1996, Tony Scott, USA, starring Will Smith), or, on television, *24* (Fox, 2001 – present), starring Kiefer Sutherland as Jack Bauer. Local politics and social movement issues, on the other hand, have been mostly taken up by women authors and protagonists in novels rather than on the small or on the big screen. An example would be the feminist private investigators of the 1980s, such as journalist Lindsay Gordon (by author Val McDermid). The socialist-feminist backgrounds of these new women heroes for a long time kept them from becoming financially successful in their line of work. They had become sleuths after all because of their ideals and not for the money. Only in the 1990s did authors such as Marcia Muller allow her heroine to become an employer and managing director of a well-earning detective agency.

Women then may have a strong presence is a male field. Femininity is sometimes an asset to them. It is, however, always combined with a sharp intelligence, and often with effective fighting technique. What makes this example especially interesting is how gender distinctions (both as feminine versus masculine and as feminist or non-feminist) relate to and infuse professionalism. The mark of a strong professional in fiction is often that this is a figure who in many ways is beyond gender distinction. Often they are single – married, for better or worse, to the jobs that they are dedicated to. Inspector Morse, for example (Thomas, 1997) is mostly unlucky in love. His considerable powers of deduction are directed at work, rather than at such frivolities as dating or sex. Inspector Frost (*A Touch of Frost*) is a widower who never puts a girl before the job. Sam Ryan in *Silent Witness* (1997–2004) communicates more easily with the dead she lovingly examines than with living human beings. Dedication and a strong sense of justice mark professionalism in all kinds of crime drama. True dedication is a mix of motherly and fatherly care: it involves both a certain tenderness and feeling both for persons involved and for relations between human beings. But there is also cold logic, anger and unrelenting pressure on those suspected of not telling the truth or committing a crime. All in all, professionalism can be defined beyond gender, suggesting that contrary to deeply embedded ideological convictions, gender does not always matter. Gendered qualities can be shared between the sexes. Television allows us to see and understand it by layering in these different viewpoints in its narratives.

Box 8.4   *24 and fatherhood*

Gender is most directly marked by reference to femininity and masculinity and to sexual codes. Immediately after these, gender is marked by the difference between men and women as parents. The expectations we have of mothers have to do with warmth, comfort, softness and being there. Fathers on the other hand can be mostly absent. They can be authoritarian figures abiding by strict rules or they may use humour to prevent becoming too involved emotionally in genres such as the television comedy. In the action series *24* the main character Jack Bauer presents a new twist to how gendered codes and conventions are always under pressure to adapt, however slowly, to social change. From Season 2 onwards, Bauer is a single parent to his teenage daughter

Kim. We have gotten to know Kim as the quintessential silly girl. She takes up with the wrong friends endangering her entire family as well as herself. Hated by many a *24* fan, Kim Bauer takes stupidity to new heights in the second season. She meets with a mad hermit, a cougar, and is involved in a convenience store hold-up. Her father meanwhile is busy saving the US from a nuclear device. Only at the end of the season the two are to be united again. Although in later *24* series too, Kim proves to be a remarkable idiot and Jack an absentee father, there is a strong sense of connection between these two. For those interested in rethinking parenting, Jack Bauer as a character suggests that fatherly care might involve having your children learn by experience to deal with life itself, and making yourself available for sound advice by new mobile communication technologies. After all, in later seasons, Kim returns, to be an agent in the unit her father initially worked for. It bears thinking about whether she presents an argument in an ongoing debate about the status of children, whether and how they should be granted status as independent persons, and what care, ideally, they should receive. When conceived of as a layered text, *24* can be shown to offer arguments in favour and against such a thesis.

Men's magazines: gender as a contradictory system of rules

If women can have a strong presence in a male genre such as the police series, can men infiltrate in women's genres in the same way? Given historical power dynamics between masculinity and femininity, it would seem to be less likely for men to move into feminine, by definition, lower-status genres. After all, the dominance of masculinity over femininity was defined in terms of masculinity being 'the norm'. It needed no further definition. White, heterosexual, physically healthy and unemotional manhood set the standard for 'mankind'. A standard failed by all of those who deviated from it. They are called women, perverts, wimps, Chinks, Niggers. With amazing cruelty there was, and in many ways still is, little room for being 'different', whether that be more emotional, shorter or taller than what is deemed normal, to be gay, non-White or physically or mentally disabled.

Men's magazines mark an interesting exception to the rule that status governs what media products will have a chance with audiences. Commercial magazine publishing in the Netherlands did not, until the late 1990s, really recognise such a thing as 'men's magazines' apart from (semi) pornographic publications such as *Playboy* and *Penthouse*. There were 'family magazines' that catered quite clearly more to fathers than to mothers and included male sensationalist reporting and humour side-by-side. War and crime stories combined with sexist jokes and general interest articles that addressed business and social misdoing.

The 1990s saw the introduction of new man and lad magazines produced in the US and in the UK (Benwell, 2003). The logic of media production subsequently sees them franchised all over the world. The new man is inspired by feminism, he is softer and not afraid to show his emotions. Not only can men have feelings, but these feelings matter. The contrast here is with a broad understanding of manliness as providing society with its moral definition, based in public duty, morality, standards and moral restraint. The codes of journalism in quality newspapers still attest to these very norms.

Magazines such as *Arena* (UK, 1986–), *L'Uomo* (Italy), *Vogue Hommes* or the American restyled *GQ* (*Gentleman's Quarterly*), broke with an older understanding of masculinity and addressed the 'new man'. Although most often straight, they catered to men who were interested in (men's) fashion and cosmetics, who were 'into consumption', formerly an exclusively feminine domain. The mid-1990s saw the introduction of *Loaded*, again a men's lifestyle glossy but now full of an aggressively heterosexual, 'laddist' rhetoric. As glossy however, *Loaded* too took on board the changes wrought in how we think and practise gender inspired by feminism and the new man. Like its counterpart *FHM* (*For Him Magazine*) it suggests that masculinity, far from hiding in anonymity as the 'norm' for all human beings, is asserting itself in its own, not always very pleasant right. They show that how one is to be a 'man', is as dependent on historical period and circumstance as is practising femininity. And even more interestingly, they show how an older patriarchal logic that defined masculinity as all things non-feminine (neither weak, nor emotional, nor over involved or too taken with appearances) is no longer in place. Real men do not only eat quiche, they use moisturizers and anti-wrinkle cream while discussing women's physical attributes.

In the end the laddist lifestyle magazines differ considerably from women's magazines. They mostly do so by their insistent use of irony and humorous insult. Moreover, on the letter's pages, and in the advice given by the magazines, little private or personal knowledge is exchanged. Benwell argues that '(m)agazines in general may be seen to fulfil this function of private

Plate 8:1   Cover of the Dutch celebrity glossy *Gullit*, a single and special edition of Linda. Reproduced with kind permission © Mood for Magazines June–July 2006

communication within the public sphere; but in men's lifestyle magazines the denial of the private sphere is marked' (2001: 22). They contain none of the real-life drama or the incitement to empathy and emotional learning that characterize women's magazines. The letters' pages of *Loaded,* for example, are marked, notes Benwell, by swearing and expletives. The end result of this exercise is the reinforcement of traditional masculinity. Women and gay men are kept at a distance, all reference to the possibility of homosexual desire is disavowed. Swearing references strength and rebellion. But while rebelling against feminism, traditional masculinity has allowed itself to be lured into 'the open'. Nowhere else is it as clear that to understand media representations of gender, we must recognize how media texts are layered and always part of broader historical-discursive systems. The result is that *Loaded* and *FHM*, or *Gullit*, a Dutch, celebrity-branded copycat laddist lifestyle magazine, are in some regards extremely funny and a strong force against self-righteous political correctness, while in other regards they are insulting and frequently disgusting. The editors of the new lad magazines will doubtlessly be delighted with this evaluation.

Conclusion

The media representation of gender consists of a complex system of codes, conventions and rules. Together they produce a version of what societies are about. Tellingly, in quantitative research, it is still the case that the media go with the powerful and give us two times more men and male bodies than women (*Monitor Diversiteit,* 2002) despite soaps, despite women's magazines, comedy series or new types of populist news or civic journalism. There is now far more room for individual women to be portrayed differently and in their own right. The same goes for gay women and men, although homosexuality is still ruled by what was called symbolic annihilation in the 1970s and 1980s.

It is as if the representation of gender follows the logic of playing an accordion. As easily as it unfolds, it will fold again to the tune of dominant ideologies. This entails that as media scholars we need to understand generic rules in relation to specific contexts. We need to unearth what gender meanings are embedded in both fiction and non-fiction media content to recognize when and where they may be actualized and where they remain dormant. Second, we need to understand how, for audiences, it is dependent on their (local) knowledges, what meanings and layers in a media text are 'activated' and what meaning they are given.

Recently, a rerun of the witty American sit-com *Will and Grace*, featuring two gay men and two straight women in Manhattan, New York as its central characters, followed right on the heels of a news item about a gay pride rally in Moscow. The march had been banned because it was claimed by the authorities that it could trigger violence. A courageous group took to the streets nonetheless where they were met by nationalist and Orthodox Christian groups chanting anti-gay slogans and shouting abuse. The naked hatred in the faces of these bystanders was echoed in the words of the Moscow mayor who said he believed homosexuality was not natural and that a gay pride event would cause outrage in society. (http://news.bbc.co.uk, 27 May 2006 'Banned Moscow gay rally broken up').

History teaches us that the reactionary response in Moscow against gay people is as easily marshalled against women claiming individual rights. As a Western viewer I am in a privileged position to be able to 'read' both *Will and Grace* and the news item about this rally. It is unlikely that this would be true for the Russian anti-gay protesters. What is needed therefore is the ability to decode media texts and sensitivity to its layeredness. These may well present any number of contradictory 'messages'. In addition we need to understand how media representations are not only in themselves constructions of particular realities but that they are decoded by others in other ways than we would.

Summary

- Gender is about femininity, masculinity, sexuality and power.
- We understand gender via media representations through our (implicit) knowledge of codes and conventions.
- The Western world allows for an amazing range of definitions and practices, all with their own codes and conventions.
- Under pressure, and in other places, neither this range nor the individual freedom that comes with it may be available.
- The media have been, and can again be, part of an authoritative and totalitarian gender regime.

GOING FURTHER

Journals that are of interest by presenting contemporary case study examples:

• Media and cultural studies journals generally

As well as:

• *Feminist Media Studies*
• *European Journal of Women's studies*
• *Journal of Popular Culture*

Many monographs exist that deal with the representation of gender in media genres. On soap opera, for example, there is Ien Ang's study of *Dallas* (1985), and Christine Geragthy's (1991) overview of both American and British soaps. Men's magazines too are a rich field with studies that focus on history and content (*Masculinity and Men's Lifestyle Magazines*, 2003 by Benwell); content and reception practices (*Making Sense of Men's Magazines*, 2001 by Jackson et al.); and on production (*Representing Men: Cultural Production and Producers in the Men's Magazine Market*, 2004, by Crewe).

For other further reading the following texts may be of use

Hermes, J. (2005) *Rereading Popular Culture*. Oxford: Blackwell.
This book is somewhat exceptional in that it combines diverse reception case studies with discussion of media representation of gender.
MacDonald, M. (1995) *Representing Women*. London: Arnold.
One of the most accessible introductions and overviews of discussion.
van Zoonen, L. (1994) *Classic Feminist Media Studies*. London: Sage.
This classic text situates questions of images and representation of gender in a broader context including media production and feminist media theory.

References

Ang, I. (1985) *Watching Dallas. Soap opera and the melodramatic imagination*. London: Methuen.
Beauvoir, Simone de (1949) *La deuxieme sexe*. Paris: Gallimard.
Benwell, B. (2001) 'Male gossip and language play in the letters pages of men's lifestyle magazines', *Journal of Popular Culture*, 34(4): 19–33.
Benwell, B. (ed.) (2003) *Masculinity and Men's Lifestyle Magazines* Oxford: Blackwell/ Sociological Review.

Brunsdon, C. (1998) 'Structure of Anxiety: Recent Britain Television Crime Fiction', *Screen*, 39(3): 223–43.

Butler, J. (1991) 'Imitation and Gender Insubordination' in D. Fuss, (ed.) *Inside/Out: Lesbian Theories, Gay Theories.* New York: Routledge, pp. 13–31.

Caldwell, J.T. (1987) *Televisuality: Style, Crisis and Authority in American Television.* New York: Rutgers University Press.

Crewe B. (2004) *Representing Men: Cultural Production and Producers in the Men's Magazine Market.* London: Berg.

Cuklanz, L. (2000) *Rape on Prime Time: Television, masculinity and sexual violence.* Philadelphia: University of Pennsylvania Press

Donzelot, J. (1979) *The Policing of Families.* New York: Random House.

Foucault, M. (1977) *The History of Sexuality. Vol I: The Will to Knowledge.* New York: Random House.

Foucault, M. (1979) *Discipline and Punish.* New York: Random House.

Friedan, B. (1963) *The Feminine Mystique.* New York: Dell Publishers.

Goffman, E. (1976) *Gender Advertisements.* New York: Harper & Row.

Hartley, J. (1999) *Uses of Television.* London: Routledge.

Holland, P. (1987) 'When a Woman Reads the News' in H. Baehr and G. Dyer (eds) *Boxed In: Women and Television.* London: Pandora Press, pp. 133–50.

hooks, b. (1994) *Outlaw Culture: Resisting Representations.* London: Routledge.

Jackson, P., Stevenson, N. and Brooks, K. (eds) (2001) *Making Sense of Men's Magazines.* Cambridge: Polity Press.

Johnson, S. (2006) *Everything Bad is Good For You.* London: Penguin.

Macdonald, M. (1995) *Representing Women, Myths of Femininity in the Popular Media.* London: Arnold.

Maus, F. (2001) 'Glamour and Evasion: The Fabulous Ambivalence of the Pet Shop Boys', *Popular Music* 20(3).

Modleski, T. (1982) *Loving with a Vengeance: Mass-Produced Fantasies for Women.* London: Methuen.

Monitor Diversiteit (2002) Hilversum: Publieke Omroep Nederland.

Neale, S. (1980) *Genre.* London: Bfi.

Newcomb, H. (1974) *TV: The Most Popular Art.* Garden City NY: Anchor Books.

Scheu, U. (1977) *Wir werden nicht als Mädchen geboren, wir werden dazu gemacht,* Frankfurt: Fischer.

Segal, L. (1990) *Slow Motion: Changing Masculinities, Changing Men.* London: Virago.

Swanson, J. and James, D. (eds) (1996) *By a Woman's Hand* (2nd edn.) New York: Berkley Prime Crime.

Skeggs, B. (1997) *Formations of Class and Gender: Becoming Respectable.* London: Sage.

Tasker, Y. (1993) *Spectacular Bodies: Gender, Genre and The Action Cinema.* London: Routledge.

Thomas, L. (1997) 'In love with Inspector Morse' in C. Brunsdon et al. *Feminist Media Criticism*. Oxford: Oxford University Press, pp. 184–204.

Tuchman, G. with A. Kaplan Daniels and James Walker Benet (eds) (1978) *Hearth and Home: Images of Women in the Mass Media*. New York: Oxford University Press.

van Zoonen, L. (1991) 'A tyranny of intimacy: women, femininity and television news' in C. Sparks and P. Dahlgren (eds) *Communication and Citizenship: Journalism and the Public Sphere in the New Media Age*. London: Routledge, pp. 217–36.

van Zoonen, L. (2004) *Feminist Media Studies*. London: Sage.

van Zoonen, L. (2005) *Entertaining the Citizen: When Politics and Popular Culture Converge*. Boulder, CO: Rowman and Littlefield.

Media, Power and Political Culture

John Corner

DEFINITIONS

Mediated democracy: a condition reached when the involvement of media representations not only in popular knowledge about politics but in the conduct of politics becomes a factor of primary systemic significance.

Power: the economic or cultural capacity to exert influence over public affairs, whether by open strategies to win advantage or by less obvious or hidden means.

Citizenship: the normative relationship of individuals to the state in a democracy, involving rights and responsibilities and assuming both levels of knowledge about politics and attitudes towards political engagement.

Propaganda and spin: forms of 'bad communication' in which deliberate distortion of knowledge is undertaken, directly or through the media, in a way that supports 'bad politics'.

Introduction

In this chapter I want to place a focus on the relationship, important and often sensitive, between media systems and political systems. It is now hard to imagine a political perspective within which the media do not figure as an important agency. This is even if formal theories of politics still often either exclude or marginalize the media in their accounts, relating back to a core literature of political philosophy produced at a time when media (then only weekly newspapers) were seen essentially as agents of information relay and debate – important but not a priority for political analysis and debate (see Scammell and Semetko, 2000 for a discussion of this 'oversight'). Within accounts of 'democracy' that do mention the media, they are variously tasked with the job of providing the informational base and the forum for discussion and deliberation upon which citizenship can be grounded, and with scrutinizing the activities of the state (and in a broader view, the corporate sector too) for abuses of power (Street, 2001, provides a comprehensive review of the principal ideas). How well they perform these tasks has provided a long-running and heated point of dispute in public life and in academic inquiry. Totalitarian regimes (for instance, the USSR, many Fascist regimes of Latin America, North Korea and, with changes in approach, China) have often openly employed media systems as highly coordinated means for sustaining popular support for government, while various levels and forms of less explicit and indeed clandestine attempts to secure favourable media coverage have been a factor in the political history of most democracies. State success in achieving positive media outcomes and media success in shaping a dominant 'public opinion' has varied and the situation has become at least a little more precarious with the arrival of international television channels and the Internet.

With the intensification of media activity introduced by the steady growth of television services (including 24 hour news channels such as CNN and BBC World), the application of new communications technologies and the development of a global media market, the idea that politics is 'mediated', that insofar as we live in democracies, these can be described as 'mediated democracies', would find a good level of agreement. This does not mean to say that *all* political processes have significant media linkage, nor does it ignore the fact that, certainly since the development of the newspaper press, most political systems have had an important media component – one capable of supporting change as well as reinforcing state positions. However, the positioning of the media as key agencies for the circulation of political knowledge, the framing of political address and comment, the formation and then the measuring of public opinion, the identification of disagreement, and the formulation of challenges all seems to suggest that the fact of mediation is now a defining rather than ancillary aspect of the political sphere.

Although the European origins of media-political relations are strongly informed by *hope* – by the eighteenth century Enlightenment belief in the spread of rationality and the organization of public affairs through the circulation of knowledge and argument in part encouraged by newspapers (Keane, 1991 provides a condensed history) – it is fair to say that much current thinking about media and politics turns on *fears*, on anxieties about distortion and deception. Perhaps the most influential concept in international discussion of media-political relations points in both directions; Habermas's idea of the 'public sphere' as the necessary space for the circulation of knowledge and deliberation (Habermas, 1992 is the principal, influential text here). (For an elaboration, see Chapter 15 of this textbook, by Kevin Howley and Chapter 3 by Michael J. Breen.) It looks back to Enlightenment values and the sense of emancipatory *possibilities*. It also attempts to project these possibilities against a critique of current tendencies towards the denial of sustained critical engagement, towards a thinning out of civic culture. Of course, to see the real early history of the media as a movement towards an ever-increasing circulation of knowledge in the interests of democratic political development would be a gross misreading of a complex and varied record, one in which both press and then later broadcasting have played their part in the sustaining of inequality and the suppression of dissent. But why is it that so much emphasis is now placed, by international media research, on the negative dynamics of the media-political connection? What lies behind the gloom about relations of power?

I want to explore this question by attempting to tackle it at two levels. First of all, I want to suggest something of what is actually going on in media-political relations – how they are changing and why. This is the *descriptive* aspect of the chapter. Second, I want to look at some of the values, established and emerging, which are implicated in these changes. This is the *normative* aspect of what I want to say. The structure I shall follow will involve looking at some of the key areas of change, examining something of their context and their interconnection. I shall then identify what I think are principal points of focus for future debate and inquiry.

This is an interesting time to be studying questions of media and politics, not only because of the significant shifts in the character of politics and the operations of the media that many countries have seen in the last decade or so but because there are clear indications that political studies, internationally, are becoming more interested in questions concerning media structure and operation and that media research is adopting a more focused approach to the study of political processes. The turbulence of global politics is one reason for this, while the growth of political marketing and debates about 'propaganda' and 'spin' (see Box 9.1) have made questions of media-political linkage hard to ignore. The work of scholars such as, Schudson and Bennett in the US, and Street, van Zoonen, Dahlgren and Esser in Britain and Europe have brought new energies and ideas to the exploration of these issues. (This is to pick just a few examples from a growing body of writers. See the references and the 'Going further' reading list at the end of this chapter for relevant citations.)

The idea of 'power' is central to my theme, simply because the degree of influence that political systems can exert over the media, and the degree of influence that media systems can variously have over political affairs, are always factors right at the core of dispute about how the media work politically and how they might be different. To signal aspects of this power, words like 'propaganda' and, more recently, 'spin' have been used, mostly within strongly negative assessments. I want to give these terms some attention in this chapter, because it seems to me that quite a lot of inadequate thinking about media and politics today stems, in part, from the conceptual laziness that they tend to encourage.

Box 9.1   'Propaganda' and 'spin'

As the main text suggests, these two terms are not precisely interchangeable but they share the same idea of communication, that in order to persuade will not only exaggerate but resort to deliberate deceit ('misinformation' is another term often used).

'Propaganda' is a term with extensive application throughout the twentieth century, particularly in relation to wartime (Nazi propaganda being a defining instance), although criteria are often loose and contradictory. Some writers allow for the idea of 'virtuous propaganda' (for instance, anti-smoking publicity and drink driving campaigns) making it a matter of ends rather than means, but others work with a firmly negative definition, sometimes grounding this in the level of emotional and subconscious appeal that propaganda often seeks to generate. It is still possible to find groups who self-describe their own publicity as 'propaganda' but this has become a questionable thing to do in the face of so much negative usage.

'Spin' is altogether more recent, applied mostly to political publicity and, although seen as anti-democratic, is not generally viewed with the degree of seriousness and alarm which has prompted many commentators to condemn propaganda. This is one reason why popular culture has been able to pick up on it as essentially a comic practice (as in the television series The West Wing (NBC, 1999–2006) and In the Thick of It (BBC, 2005–present).

An excellent account of the issues surrounding the idea of propaganda is to be found in Walton (1997) and a review of different approaches to its analysis is put forward in O'Shaughnessy (2004). See also Corner (2006). A recent, excellent commentary on the history and character of 'Spin' is Andrews (2006), which cites all the main studies to date, including Gaber (2000).

In discussing media power, I shall be working with the widely-accepted idea that the media are central channels of popular information and knowledge and that, as such, they necessarily exert a degree of defining power over the character and the terminology of popular political understanding. The precise measuring of this power is a matter for audience studies and poses a methodological challenge (see, for instance, Chapters 5, 13 and 14, in this text). However, in broad terms the power/influence character of the media's 'knowledge effect' seems to me to be something that we can bring in to our analysis straight away, even if particular instances always need care (for example, the media power levels achieved in shaping public understanding of a shift in economic policy might be different from those achieved in respect of, say, a food scare). Political power works through meanings, of course, but it also works through direct legislative constraints, involving various forms of penalty, including fines and imprisonment. Power of this kind is exerted on the media system of most countries to some degree, through the general framework of the law and the specific framework of media regulation.

With a measure of simplification, it is possible to see two conflicting tendencies at work in current thinking about the way in which politics and media interact as spheres of activity. In one view, politics is still the dominant partner, even if this is not always visible, and media activities are framed by political factors that severely reduce the scope and independent agency of the media system. In other accounts, however, 'media logic', with its strong ties to market values, has had a transforming impact upon the political sphere, driving changes here rather than being a subordinate partner. National histories and political and media systems vary considerably, of course, and this will effect the way the power relationships between the two spheres is debated, and their perceived level of interpenetration or fusion. Whether the emphasis is finally given to the political or media side, however, no one doubts the central importance of *economic* factors – of how the media get their revenue. Media economics necessarily raises questions of media regulation or the lack of it. Many debates about media power end up being debates, if only by implication, about forms of regulation.

Another term I want to bring in is that of 'political culture'. By this, I mean to indicate the broader context of meanings and values, hopes and anxieties, within which the more formal business of politics is conducted. Political culture is the setting within which the apparatus of politics works and within which we think, feel and act as citizens in relation to the self-presentations and claims of politicians and the accounts of political journalists. It is easy to leave 'political culture' out of the picture when studying politics, seeing it perhaps as a 'soft' and un-measurable extra. However, if the growth of cultural studies has taught us anything, it is the importance of attending to systems of meaning and value underlying surface structures and behaviours, whatever the analytic challenge this brings with it. Certainly, when we look at some of the changes that have shown themselves in the media-political relations of many countries in recent years, then engagement with the cultural becomes a requirement. This is because, in large part, we are talking about matters of *political subjectivity*, about the way people experience politics, consciously and unconsciously, in their everyday lives.

Four factors of change

Change, its direction and consequences, is clearly right at the centre of debate about media and politics. I want to highlight four areas where significant change has occurred.

1. The changing character of political publicity and news management (the word 'spin' has been widely used in the UK in respect of the latter).
2. The changing profile and tone of political journalism within a changed media economy ('spin' has had its impact here too, along with an intensified focus on political celebrity and political gossip and scandal).
3. Shifts in the nature of 'citizenship', in the way that people relate to their rights and obligations within the political system and use the media in this relation (the impact of 'consumerism' has to be considered here).
4. The consequences of new communications technology (the Internet has implications for all the previous points, having both private, professional and public applications within the political and media spheres, but the attention it has received warrants separate discussion).

*1. The changing character of political publicity
and news management*

This is right at the centre of this chapter's concerns and I will therefore give it greater attention than the other three factors, each of which needs to be understood in the context it provides. There have been significant shifts in the way that the component agencies of many national political systems go about the business of producing political publicity (on behalf of the government, political parties and various kinds of special interest lobbying organizations, including 'protest' groups). It is important to note here that when, in many countries, television replaced the press as the primary medium for popular political knowledge, it introduced new vocal, visual and dramatic elements into the mix. Newspapers had worked primarily through the written reports of political events produced by journalists, with politicians' own words featuring at points but always necessarily at second-hand. Radio systems introduced a strong and novel element of politicians' making their own direct appeals, through talk formats and interviews. This reproduced some aspects of that traditional mode of political address – the public meeting – but it not only vastly increased the size of the audience, it also allowed new techniques of speaking to develop. Most notable here were ways of addressing audience members as individuals in their own homes, getting a new level of intimacy and individuality into the political relationship. Contemporary television systems have added visual performance to this development, making television, in some respects, a 'theatre of political performance', which is not only a 'theatre of voices' but also one of faces, bodies and actions.

The daily alignment between the political world and the everyday world which television now provides within its routine news frame (its regular window on the constructs of 'nation' and 'world') turns on the projection and analysis of these performances within political news-making. Politicians and their aides work to get their actions and their views into the news frame in the most positive possible way and to limit the impact of opposing views or the damage that follows from the reporting of 'bad events' that reflect negatively upon their policies and decisions. Political contest has not transferred itself totally to television, much is still done behind closed doors or within Parliament, but television has become a crucial space within which aspects of that contest become visible and heard (in the case of leaks, 'overheard') by the general public.

A whole range of publicity strategies are open to those seeking to win political space on television and also in the press. However, governments and their departments of state clearly are elite players in the contest for publicity, both as a result of their status as sources for news and as a result of the resources and the experience they can bring to the task of achieving good publicity outcomes (see Wolsfeld, 1997, for a useful schematic account).

A great deal of recent writing on political publicity, including that in the UK, has variously examined the phenomenon of 'spin' (see Box 9.1). 'Spin' is a word taken initially from American baseball usage, literally referring to an angle put on the flight of a ball by careful delivery. Applied to publicity, it means a statement or comment that is 'angled' to produce a positive effect, a matter of exaggeration or careful concealment but always a kind of trick, a device of deception. Of course, politicians have nearly always been committed to the production of publicity that selectively emphasizes the positive. The term 'propaganda' (see Box 9.1) is widely used to describe this tendency as well as the complementary one of being selectively negative about political opponents and issues around which they wish to generate anxiety. 'Propaganda' is perhaps seen most openly in its commercial application, in product advertising. However, product advertising is widely regarded as a kind of licensed, acceptable exaggeration in many modern societies and many might see 'propaganda' and certainly 'spin' as the wrong words to use here, *when we all know what advertising is trying to do* and there is usually no concealment of the motive to persuade. On the other hand, there is a degree of uncertainty and uneasiness about precisely what kinds of 'rules' *should* be followed by political publicity and that is why critical terms continue to have regular use in assessing it. It is widely agreed that attempted deception through serious omission or, worse, lying, is unacceptable in any kind of communication by politicians (most countries have rules to limit acts of lying in commercial advertising). At the same time, and against this ethical standard, both omission and various modes of lying are seen to be so commonly practised that they have become almost defining of political speech itself. To complicate things further, it is also recognized, or half-recognized, by many people that political communication is *necessarily* 'strategic communication' and that it will frequently involve departures from the principles of directness, frankness and honesty on difficult points that one might expect in other spoken or written contexts. I shall return to this crucial, and I believe, insufficiently explored, point later.

One of the key questions concerning political publicity, perhaps particularly that issued from governments and government departments, is how far is it uncritically accepted by political journalists? Is there a direct 'propaganda' effect, in which the media broadly reproduce official accounts and interpretations, or is there a degree of scepticism and challenge to what comes down from above. National histories vary in what they show here, including in some cases the direct and open control of the media by governments, and in others a vigorous critical opposition to government policies. In the UK, following the election of a New Labour Government in 1997, 'spin' started to become the major running story not only about government communications but about the government in general, as a new, tougher and more strategic approach to winning positive coverage was adopted by those in power. The journalists who wrote regularly and critically about 'spin' were often involved in a degree of self-contradiction. For the new approach to be the serious threat it was made out to be, it would really have had to show itself as effective in persuading journalists to accept it. Yet the very fact that journalists wrote about it as a kind of 'running scandal' of government clearly indicated that many of them saw it as a target for attack and for derision rather than something to be accepted and used uncritically in writing political stories. One might say that a significant consequence of 'spin' was unintentionally positive – to create more general awareness about the processes of media management. Strongest initially in the US, and then perceived as a radical change to media relations in the UK, 'spin' has variously been picked up as a term of analysis and critique in other countries (see Esser et al., 2000 for an account of some European comparisons here).

It is clear that in many countries the news media depend on good relations with government sources to sustain strong, competitive political news coverage. It is equally clear that politicians also need the publicity 'reach' of the media to project their claims and their denials. This means that even in those many countries where direct 'management' of the news agenda is impossible, there will be a range of 'trade-off' deals that can be made with individual editors and reporters to get publicity value into items of coverage. Many media professionals will, however, be acutely aware of the commercial risk, as well as the loss of esteem, that would follow from seeming to be a 'government mouthpiece'. They will also be aware of the disadvantages of concealing information that might otherwise have provided news material of high commodity value and which, in any case, might well be carried by their competitors, perhaps at a later date.

A final point to note here is the way in which, during periods of cross-party convergence on major ideological issues and when loyalty to political parties is weak (both conditions can be said to be true of the UK at the time of writing), the dependency of political claims-making on strong media performances increases. Moreover, in these situations, political claims-making is likely to focus increasingly on the personal qualities of leaders and upon managerial capacities within a relatively stable policy agenda. One has to be careful here, since both leadership and perceived capacity to manage are almost always elements in political publicity. However, as electoral support becomes more a matter of 'permanent campaigning' in a context of uncertainty and where differences over matters of broad policy directions reduce, then the 'branding' of political alternatives inevitably puts emphasis on these two factors. Securing popular support starts to require a more subtle, demographically aware and culturally smart, 'pitch'. The language of politics itself starts to change, becoming even more demotic and informal, attempting thereby to reduce the divisions between the political class and the citizen.

2. The changing profile and tone of political journalism within a changed media economy

Here, once again, national variations abound. However, an interest in reporting not just on politics but on political publicity itself has become apparent in much media commentary. As I noted, political attempts to 'spin' become a focus in journalists' political story-telling, including by anticipation (for example, what *will be* the publicity moves made by political actors in response to an upcoming event or challenge?). As there is increased emphasis on political personality, there is also increased scope for stories of scandal and, at a lower level, for a regular flow of political gossip comparable to that which now surrounds other spheres of celebrity, particularly the entertainment industry and sport. The overall character of the political knowledge in circulation thus changes, if very differently in relation to different kinds of outlet and their intended audiences and readerships. Combinations of traditional 'hard' and new 'soft' stories appear. Sometimes transformations from one mode to the other occur (for example, what appeared to be a strong item of political news then trailing away in weak follow-ups which downgrade it; conversely, what looked like idle gossip becoming a big and confirmed news lead). The extensive use of Internet-based sources, together with email linkage, greatly increases the number of informal routes through which a story can develop, including as a result of leaks that follow either from carelessness or strategic design (Thompson, 2000, provides a detailed account of the changing character of political scandal).

All these changes, which nevertheless may still leave space for serious political commentary, may well take place (as they do in the UK) in the context of a media system that is being defined more sharply in terms of market competition. What people will actually want to listen to, watch or read about in a setting of increased 'choice' becomes important in the allocation of resources to political reporting and in the kind of reporting that gets done.

Although I have identified this as the second factor in my list, some would see a case for making it the first. They would argue that changes in the media system have actually brought about the changes in political publicity described earlier and they would certainly contest the idea that shifts in political journalism can be seen essentially as reactions to what has happened in the political sphere. There is strength to this view. I have chosen to start with political publicity because that has been the most frequent point of focus in debate but it is clear that broader shifts in the nature of the media have encouraged many of the changes that have occurred in political self-presentation and discourse. Moreover, in what is then a second and 'return' phase of the process, there is little doubt that journalists have adopted some of their present tactics and modes of coverage as a response to these changes. So it is best to see the relationship between publicity and journalism as a closely interactive one, involving a degree of uncertainty and, often, degrees of struggle in the play-off of factors contributing to relative power, benefit and concession. As I indicated above, with national variations this is likely to be true more generally of the relationship between political system and media system.

3.   Shifts in the nature of citizenship

In many democratic countries, the relationship of ordinary people to the official political process has changed as a consequence both of economic development and shifts in social structure and popular culture. These changes have a strong national specificity, but across the variations it is possible to see some common tendencies. Amongst these, an increasing emphasis on consumer identity in the context of an expansion of the areas of everyday life affected by consumer relationships is perhaps the most significant. Crucially, the relationships not only follow from the purchase of *goods* and leisure products (including holidays) but also of *services*, including those such as health and education which in many countries have been, until recently, provided largely outside the market framework. It has been widely observed that the 'citizen' role and the 'consumer' role have been brought into new kinds of alignment or convergence as a result of underlying changes in the economic character of everyday life. This process has frequently been seen as an uneasy one, most often involving the domination of consumer identity over the citizenship role or, indeed, the virtual elimination of the latter. The dualities of 'citizen-consumer' or 'consumer-citizen' have been widely used, not only in the academic literature but also in the accounts of public bodies (such as at the UK national communications regulator, Ofcom), with debate about the consequences of such pairings.

The assessment of change in this area has not always been made negatively however. The idea that a shift towards a stronger emphasis on consumer identity could bring a strengthening of democratic process, rather than a weakening of it, has also been advanced. This is not surprising given the way in which many societies have encouraged a 'consumer ideology' in which the advantages of choice, indirect involvement in product improvement, and legal protection against faulty or otherwise unacceptable goods and services have been given extensive publicity. It has been suggested that the 'consumer' role, far from being an imposed identity, pressing people into convenient forms of consciousness for capitalist development and carrying only a displaced residue of traditional citizenship, is actually a form of empowerment undercutting the privilege and deference which traditional modes of social and political organization involved. As other chapters in the present volume will variously show, this question is one of the most central, underlying themes in international media and cultural research. The tensions which it carries surface in a number of ways around issues of popular taste, popular consciousness, the quality of media output and media regulation in relation to market structures.

Insofar as citizenship has become modified by consumer identity, regardless of the evaluation finally made of this, the relationship both to politicians and to political media is shifted as a consequence. Politicians are perceived more as 'service providers', performing a managerial role in relation to national policies with greater or lesser efficiency. In seeking the acquiescence of citizens, they are carried further towards the kinds of 'branding', product differentiation and publicity strategies that I discussed under the first heading above. Versions of 'political marketing' become more intensive and developed, partly in response to an emerging pattern in which degrees of indifference and cynicism are important constitutive elements. The media inevitably act as a cultural resource for this changed context of political relationships at the same time as they also take their cue from the reconfigured profile of concerns and points of anxiety (foci of political 'choice') it produces. This reinforces the tendencies in coverage I have already discussed. Themes of aspiration and hope may also figure too, but a politics of anxiety (for example, the threat of terrorism, ecological disaster, economic downturn and its consequences for areas such as employment, prices and pensions, and decline in the standard of central services) is likely for wider reasons to eclipse a politics of positive vision. This will be reflected in the agenda and priorities of political mediation.

4. The consequences of new communications technology

As many other parts of this book will demonstrate, the implications of new technology for media economics, organization and format are huge. When applied to the television industry, it has led to multi-channel systems and a much more intensive, and frequently 'deregulated' pattern of competitive provision in many countries, with output framed more directly by market dynamics. However, it is the rapid rise of the Internet that has rightly attracted most attention from those interested in how the media relate to power and to politics. While the reconfiguration of the television industry has often been viewed critically as a further assault on resources for 'public' knowledge by the commodity market in 'private' entertainment, the rapid development of Internet access in many countries encouraged hopes in some commentators of a reinvigorated citizenship. It was claimed that this would allow a bypassing of the degraded central systems of mediation in favour of a more independent, varied and critical range of resources for political knowledge, including those situated well outside the established limits. It would also permit interaction and assist the development of group level political formations. It seemed to be the ideal means by which a 'public sphere' could be created that was not almost entirely reliant on the performance of the institutionalized media system and that was free of at least some of the primary modes of direct state control and commercial dependence.

There is no doubt that the impact of the web upon international politics has been significant and is growing with the increase (sometimes fast, sometimes very slow) in the conditions of national access and use. A whole range of 'unofficial' voices, working across national boundaries and sometimes working past the previous bounds of 'official' national acceptability, has gained an input into the international knowledge system. However, as many writers have pointed out, information is not by itself a sufficient condition for political engagement even though it is a necessary one (see Street, 2001 and Brimber, 2003, for examples). The web has worked best politically for those who have come to it with political uses in mind, uses derived from their non-web experiences. The emerging profile suggests that the web will not become an agent of some kind of 'electronic democracy' simply by its availability, although generational variations here and an awareness of a broadened notion of politics, in which local issues and single-issue concerns are given stronger emphasis, has lead some commentators to continue to be optimistic (as in Dahlgren, 2003).

Perhaps the most significant general influence of the web upon politics to date has been through its use by journalists, who have not only publicized various sites and bloggers for wider independent use but have taken a whole new range of information and commentary into their story-building activities. Without overstating the scale of the shift this has produced so far, it can be seen to have altered the character of much political journalism, both at international and national levels, providing a richer and often more critical range of sources and adding a new dimension to the established practices of 'leaking' and trading in speculative gossip.

Having outlined these four broad factors of change, I want to give brief attention to two topics which cut across them in different ways and which seem to me to deserve more consideration than they often get.

Promotional ethics and political culture:
Two areas for further inquiry

1. Promotional ethics: I have suggested that there is a lack of clarity regarding the expectations made of political discourse and the norms or ethics by which it can be judged. We might work with the idea that politicians should simply tell the truth to the best of their ability, whether their communications are intended for each other, for specific elite groups or for the public at large (via the media or directly). However, this principle would fail to recognize what is widely accepted – that politicians are *by the very nature of politics itself* involved in forms of promotional speech, in which there is a strong element of strategic design.[1] This is intended to present the speaker and their political group in the best possible light across a range of listener perspectives and to reduce the visibility of negative factors. Under scrutiny from media interviewers, evasion will be practised on difficult points, using a variety of devices to achieve this. Admission of serious error will be rare and achievements will be played up, even if this requires strenuous attempts at repetition and reworking of the terms of questioning.

How do terms like 'propaganda' and 'spin' aid us in judgements on the intensive 'theatre of voices' that I have suggested describes modern political mediation? My view is that they fatally lack the clarity to be of real use. 'Propaganda' might be used descriptively of the essential, routine character of much political discourse, or it could be used only to identify an unacceptable level of resort to lies and deception such as that which surrounded the involvement of the UK in the 2003 invasion of Iraq. To say politicians are extensively involved in propaganda might therefore be a common sense observation or a shocking condemnation, depending on definition. 'Spin' lacks the sinister overtones of 'propaganda' (see Box 9.1) but all it tells us is that a particular political statement (probably addressed to journalists rather than to the public directly) is angled to promote and/or conceal and that it needs careful scrutiny as a basis for knowledge. It will really be questions of *scale and significance* that are of concern rather than the existence of 'spin' itself.

Questions are prompted about the kinds of political structure and political culture, including media practices, that might reduce the extent to which politician's have to resort to strategic promotional discourse outside the context of electoral contest (which is explicitly promotional as part of its very nature). However, we know that strategies of appeal in political communication have a very long history. We also know how (ironically) many of its present forms are closely connected with the rise of popular democracy – with the growing need to sustain a continuous campaign for popular support in the face of competitive claims-making and critical challenges from opponents and media commentators (see McNair, 1998, for a provocatively positive reading of some aspects of this history, and Davis, 2002, for a broader account of the expansion of 'public relations' activity).

More study of present practices and their history, together with a scrutiny of the standards used by the public and by journalists in assessing political accounts, would help to assemble a clearer picture of the realities of political promotionalism and the forms of democratic deficit that it encourages. It would also help to get sharper focus into debate about ethical reform and the preconditions for changed practice. We need to ask more questions about the consequences of the presentational styles currently in use and the kind of changes that would have to precede as well as follow a reduction in their employment. The promotional character of political discourse obviously has consequences for the performance of political journalism, as I noted earlier. It also relates importantly to the idea of political culture.

2. Political Culture: An engagement with the wider contexts of meaning and value within which politics occurs, including the emotional, is now required both in media research and political studies. I observed how this brings into focus questions about political subjectivity – about how the political becomes an *experience*. A number of recent studies have shown what is to be gained by way of improved understanding here (for example, Corner and Pels, 2003; van Zoonen, 2004). In a suggestive overview of comparative work on political communication, Gurevitch and Blumler (2004) note how the idea of political culture provides a multi-dimensional approach to the study of what can too often become a list of discrete topics. For instance, it allows an analytic connection of the value systems of the political class to those of the professional culture of journalism and then to the complex range of cultural factors that underpin and inform the idea of 'politics' for many citizens. As well as allowing for the emotional and sentimental elements that have always been a factor in political engagement, it opens out on to what we can see as the *aesthetics* of politics – the concern with pleasing and stimulating imagery, language and bodily self-presentation, the alignment of political leaders and policies with particular kinds of *style* (see Corner and Pels, 2003 for an exploration of the idea of political style).

The recent election of David Cameron as leader of the Conservative Party in the UK shows, like the progress of Tony Blair some ten years earlier, the impact of a given political style within, and upon, a given political culture. It shows how certain words, looks, images and personal characteristics align with a set of fears and of hopes, markers of suspicion and of trust, ideas of the probable, the possible and the desirable. This all occurs within a strategic perception of the inevitability of change and the need to revise and reconfigure (the term 're-branding' has been applied here) the terms in which positive political identity is secured through publicity. Research able to push forward its exploration of these kinds of interconnections will make a major contribution to our understanding of the present dynamics of political mediation and power.

Conclusion

I have described a situation in which many things are changing, including the promotional behaviour of politicians, the practices of journalism and the expectations of citizens. Drawing attention to four different factors of these shifts, I have discussed their implications for our understanding of media, power and politics. Finally, I have focussed on two topics that I think have key significance for the future.

Plate 9:1   Putting on the Style: The Leader of the Conservative Party, David Cameron, on the front of *GQ Magazine*, June 2006. Reproduced by kind permission of Condé Nast UK ©

Summary

- The practices of political publicity within a promotional culture need continued attention, even though we may judge that to exert persuasive power through strategies of communication is endemic to the conduct of politics. This is not usefully analyzed by depending on terms like 'propaganda' or 'spin'. A more detailed focus on the pragmatics and ethics of political communication is needed.
- Political mediation, including that through journalism, is reflecting some of the broader changes in the media industry, as it becomes more market-driven, competitive and linked to the provision of entertainment. This has implications for the media's performance as political knowledge providers, including for its modes and forms.
- Citizenship itself is changing and one factor here is the shift towards stronger consumer identity. This displaces established roles, relationships and attitudes in ways that can be empowering but can also undercut civic values.
- The broad idea of 'political culture' is a useful one for relating different elements in the complex politics-media-people pattern. It gives emphasis to questions of value and meaning and to the *baselines of popular experience* that the activities of politics and of the media help form but from which they also take their cues and fashion their appeals.

GOING FURTHER

Street, J. (2001) *Mass Media, Politics and Democracy.* London: Palgrave.
A clear and constantly engaging guide to the broad and disputed area of media-political relations. The links made between political science approaches and those of media and communication studies make this an excellent textbook for students in both fields.

Corner J. and Pels, D. (2003) *Media and the Restyling of Politics.* London: Sage.
A collection of essays on political celebrity, political marketing and change in political culture. Introduces questions about the 'aesthetics' of politics and the idea of politics as involving different kinds of performance.

van Zoonen, L. (2005) *Entertaining the Citizen.* Lanham, Maryland: Rowman and Littlefield.
A provocative account of the relationship between politics and popular culture, focusing on ideas of entertainment in relation to political knowledge. Develops the argument that forms of entertainment have the potential to revive citizenship rather than further undermine it.

STUDENT ACTIVITY 9.1

Take a full range of national newspapers on a given day and explore some of the factors at work in contemporary political culture by answering the following:

1. What politicians (domestic and foreign) are photographed and in what settings?
2. How many stories lead with issues about policy?
3. How do the stories show their 'independence' from government sources?
4. In what ways is a sense of dispute or conflict introduced into coverage? (for example, different articles, quotations from different sources, editorial stance-taking on an issue.)
5. How is political judgement managed (what range of words is employed to show clear approval or disapproval of specific political activity)?
6. How much reporting concerns the strategies of political publicity?

References

Andrews, L. (2006) 'Spin: from tactic to tabloid', *Journal of Public Affairs* 6(1) 31–45.

Bennett, L. (2005) 'News as Reality TV: Election Coverage and the Democratization of Truth', *Critical Studies in Media Communication* 22: 171–7.

Brimber, B. (2003) *Information and American Democracy*. Cambridge: Cambridge University Press.

Corner, J. and Pels, D. (eds) (2003) *Media and the Restyling of Politics*. London: Sage.

Corner, J. (2006) 'Simply Propaganda?' in *Flow* 4(4), online magazine of University of Texas at Austin (online archive available at http://jot.communication.utexas.edu/flow/about.php).

Dahlgren, P. (2003) 'Reconfiguring civic culture in the new media milieu' in J. Corner and D. Pels (eds) *Media and the Restyling of Politics*. London: Sage.

Davis, A. (2002) *Public Relations Democracy*. Manchester: Manchester University Press.

Esser, F., Reinemann, C. and Fan, D. (2000) 'Spin-doctors in the US, Great Britain and Germany', *Press and Politics* 6(1): 16–45.

Gaber, I. (2000) 'Government by spin: an analysis of the process', *Media, Culture and Society* 22(4): 507–18.

Gurevitch, M. and Blumler, J. (2004) 'State of the Art of Comparative Political Communication Research' in F. Esser and B. Pfetsch (eds) *Comparing Political Communication*. Cambridge: Cambridge University Press, pp. 325–43.

Habermas, J (1992) *The Structural Transformation of the Public Sphere*. Cambridge: Polity.

Keane, J. (1991) *The Media and Democracy*. Cambridge: Polity.

McNair, B. (1998) 'Journalism, politics and public relations: an ethical appraisal' in M. Kiernan (ed.) *Media Ethics*. London: Routledge, pp. 49–65.

O'Shaughnessy, N. (2004) *Politics and Propaganda: Weapons of Mass Seduction*. Manchester: Manchester University Press.

Rawnsley, G. (2005) *Political Communication and Democracy*. Basingstoke: Palgrave.

Scammell, M. and Semetko, H. (2000) 'Introduction: media and democracy: democracy and media' in M. Scammell and H. Semetko (eds) *Journalism and Democracy*. Aldershot: Ashgate pp. xi–xlix.

Schudson, M. (1998) *The Good Citizen: A History of American Civic Life*. New York: Simon and Schuster.

Street, J. (2001) *Mass Media, Politics and Democracy*. Basingstoke: Palgrave.

Thompson, J.B. (2000) *Political Scandal: Power and Visibility in the Media Age*. Cambridge: Polity.

van Zoonen, L. (2004) *Entertaining the Citizen: When Politics and Popular Culture Converge*. Lanham MD: Rowman and Littlefield.

Walton, D. (1997) 'What is propaganda, and what exactly is wrong with it?', *Public Affairs Quarterly* 11(4): 383–413.

Wolsfeld, G. (1997) *Media and Political Conflict: News From the Middle East*. Cambridge: Cambridge University Press.

Note

1 Strategic design in political communication and its implications for political decision-making were issues raised both by Plato and by Aristotle, within different frameworks of judgement. See the discussion of the classical debate in relation to the modern one in Rawnsley, 2005.

Proximity and Scope as News Values

Pamela J. Shoemaker, Jong Hyuk Lee, Gang (Kevin) Han and Akiba A. Cohen

DEFINITIONS

Proximity refers to the geographic distance between an event and a media organization's newsrooms and/or its audiences.

Scope addresses psychological judgements about which domains the event reaches and how wide the implications of the event are.

Newsworthiness is a cognitive assessment of (a) how deviant or socially significant an event is and (b) how complex the event is.

Deviance is a characteristic of people, ideas or events that sets them aside as different. Dimensions of deviance include statistical (unusual or odd); normative (breaking laws or norms), or social change (challenging the status quo).

Social significance is a characteristic of people, ideas or events that makes them important or interesting. Dimensions of social significance include the political, economic, cultural and public well-being.

Introduction

Among the most commonly accepted determinants of news coverage is the news value *proximity*, both for domestic (Buckalew, 1979; Martin, 1988; Morton and Warren, 1992) and international news stories (Chang and Lee, 1992; Chang et al., 1987; DeFleur and Dennis, 1998; Gans, 1979; Galtung and Ruge, 1965; Han and Zhang, 2000; Hargrove and Stempel, 2002; Hester, 1971, 1974; Rosengren, 1974, 1977; Shoemaker and Reese, 1996). Stevenson and Cole (1984) state that proximity is a universal news value, with journalists selecting news more from their immediate region than from other parts of the world.

In the simplest sense, proximity is the physical distance between an event[1] and a media organization's offices. This definition ties proximity to an objective referent – the physical spot, site, setting or surrounding in which an event occurs or the coverage area of the newspaper and television or radio news (Bridges & Bridges, 1997). The assumption is that physical closeness makes an event more newsworthy.

But just how important is proximity? How powerfully can proximity predict whether an event will become news and how prominent the news coverage will be? If physical closeness is a powerful predictor of news coverage, then we might expect the news media to mostly cover events in their local geographic area, with state or province, national, and finally international news being lower in priority. If this were the case for all media, across all cultures, then news everywhere would be primarily local, and international news would be rare. In fact, this does not happen, causing us to doubt the power of proximity. Many scholars have shown that there is a geographic imbalance in news coverage of international news coverage, with some parts of the world being more likely to appear in news items and others only rarely (for example, Gerbner and Marvanyi, 1977; Golding and Philip, 1979; MacBride, 1980; Masmoudi, 1979; Mowlana, 1985, 1993; Sreberny-Mohammadi, 1984; Stevenson & Shaw, 1984).

Proximity does not always lead to news coverage (Luttbeg, 1983). In the US, for example, news items about events outside of the country rarely come from South America or Africa but more frequently come from Europe or Asia. This suggests that physical distance is not by itself a good predictor of event coverage, at least in international news (Chang et al., 1987). There is also uncertainty about whether geographic closeness can predict which local events become news. In some studies, proximity predicts not only which events become news, but also the extent and type of coverage (Gans, 1979; Rubin, 1979; Shapiro and Williams, 1984; Shapiro and Schofield, 1986). But Kiernan (2003) maintains that the event's topic may be more important than geographic closeness. In his study of newspaper coverage of science and medicine, proximity was not important, possibly because scientific findings and health care events are relevant to audiences, no matter where they occur.

We believe that the use of proximity can help predict whether an event will become news, but we agree with scholars who suggest that proximity is a multi-dimensional construct, and not tied to physical distance alone (Adams, 1986; Hicks and Gordon, 1974). On the one hand, Morton and Warren (1992: 1023) argue that it is necessary to distinguish between two components of proximity – geographic distance and localization.

Localization is the extent to which an event has meaning for the community in which a news organization exists. For example, a war on the other side of the world has a local 'angle' if the mayor's son was killed or if a community's family doctor, a member of her country's army reserve force, is given orders to report for active duty in the war zone country. Localization can overcome the negative force of long physical distance that would otherwise make events unlikely to become news. In this regard, this study conceptualizes scope as a characteristic of news events, given by journalists. The scope includes not only localization but also regional, national or international spin.

This is consistent with the *gatekeeping* processss, in which each gate (or decision point) in the news process is surrounded by *forces* that facilitate (positive forces) or constrain (negative forces) the likelihood that an event will become news (Lewin, 1947a, 1947b, 1951; Shoemaker, 1991; White, 1950). Although physical distance is a negative force, keeping most international events out of the news, a local angle to a faraway war could be a positive force that pushes information about the war's events along the news channel, past many gatekeepers.

On the other hand, some scholars have conceptualized proximity as the strength of cultural, political or economic ties between nations, with 'connected' nations being more likely to appear in one another's news (for example, Adams, 1986). Therefore one would expect countries that have many business ties to cover each other's events more often than those in countries with which there is little commerce.

Berkowitz and Beach (1993) and Martin (1988) show that newspapers are more responsive to news that most affects and interests their local readers, even when they chose international news (for example, Hester, 1971; Hicks and Gordon, 1974; Riffe, 1996; Sparks and Winter, 1980). Hargrove and Stempel (2002) found that in the US, reader interest is highest for stories from the Middle East, then from neighbouring countries (Canada and Mexico), then from Africa and Western Europe and last from South East Asia. In an earlier study, Maclean and Pinna (1958) noticed the same strong correlation between geographic proximity and news interest among Italian newspaper readers.

This may be similar to the psychological context of proximity that Cohen et al. (1990) refer to in their study of social conflict and television news. They point out that individual subjective reality is organized by 'zones of relevance, which differ on the basis of their proximity from the here and now of the individual's immediate environment' (1990: 36). Individuals interact with social actors or elements within either 'close' or 'remote' zones of relevance. Close zones of relevance are generally direct contacts, whereas remote zones of relevance involve a more abstract and indirect experience. The selection of zones of relevance may lead to which scope is used: close zones of relevance make a news story presented with a narrow scope, while remote zones of relevance lead to a story with a broad scope.

Cohen and his colleagues suggest that proximity has a psychological component, that people perceive patterns of conflict among social systems, with geographic proximity partitioning a person's schematic pattern into international, national and local levels. In this study, we separate the physical and psychological aspects of proximity into one measure of geographic closeness and another that addresses the psychological space through which the event operates. Unlike geographic closeness, which is immutable, journalists can enhance an event's psychological closeness by emphasizing the local, state, national or international angle of the event, regardless of its physical closeness.

Theory

Both journalists and scholars have assumed that the audience is more interested in things close to home than in those far away. In the literature, the term *proximity* is defined as both physical and psychological closeness. Following Cohen and his colleagues (1990), we would rather separate these types of closeness and propose that psychological closeness be termed *scope*.

By making this distinction, we can use the concept of *congruence* to compare the proximity and scope of an event. In general, we believe that, if physical and psychological assessments of an event's closeness have the same level, for example, both are local, then the event is more likely to pass through news gates and more likely to be transmitted to the audience.

Finally, we tie the congruence of proximity and scope to the event's deviance and social significance (Shoemaker, 1996; Shoemaker and Cohen, 2006).

Proximity

Why is proximity a standard news value? It implies that people are most interested in things close to home, which makes sense if we assume that local events impact people more than those farther away. Yet even the idea of physical closeness is not such a simple concept. When journalists use proximity as a news value, what referents do they use in geographic space? We suggest above that proximity is most often a comparison of the physical locations of the event and of the news organization. But what about the audience?

Historically, a news medium covered events in its local community, because information about events farther away was difficult to come by. The news medium's office and its audience were in the same community and equally close to events. But today it is easy to transmit messages both in and out of the local community (for example, first by using the telegraph, then cables, and now satellites). Many news organizations have offices around the globe, and can choose to distribute their messages to specific geographic locations or to worldwide audiences. This makes physical closeness of the event to the news organization's offices much less important. This is surely the case when we consider news on the World Wide Web, where addresses are digital identifiers from the virtual community of the Internet, and physical geography has little or no role.

Therefore, we suggest that defining proximity in terms of physical closeness should include the closeness of the event to the audience. Such a definition complicates as much as it clarifies, however, because there are many audiences in many physical locations. With so many actual and accidental[2] audiences, to whom are journalists writing? Within the same news organization, one journalist may write to an international audience, while another writes to those in the local community. An event that is close to one journalist's audience can be far from another's. Journalists who work for satellite-transmitted cable news television networks know that their messages are technically available to people on certain continents or even worldwide, but this does not tell them how physically close they are to the audiences who actually watch their news programmes.

This approach is in stark contrast to operationalizing proximity as the exact distance – perhaps in miles or kilometers – between the event and the news organization. Like audiences, today's news organizations are here, there and everywhere. Still, journalists do work for organizations with home offices somewhere, and people in those offices hire the journalists to write stories, and those stories are meant to be for someone, whether close by, within a certain region, within a country, or for many countries. Therefore, we assume that journalists have in mind an intended audience, whether nearby or across the world. We also assume that journalists judge how physically close an event is to their audiences, and that journalists give events close to their audiences a higher likelihood of becoming news (other things being equal) than those farther away.

Scope

Of course, all other things are never equal, and there are multiple causes for all events, especially in the gatekeeping process. Psychological closeness is a cognitive assessment of how wide the implications of the event may be for the news medium's audience. Although events take place in a specific location or locations, the impact or effects of the event can expand beyond the immediate locale of the event (Cohen et al., 1990). For example, once an event is selected to become news, editors and producers may issue instructions for the journalist to create a story that emphasizes the event's local implications, regardless of how physically close the event is to the audience.

Although proximity is a characteristic of an event and not controllable by the news organization, scope is a characteristic of how the news organization covers the event. Journalists cannot control whether an event is close or far away, but they may decide (or be given instructions) to give an event a local, regional or international spin. A local event can be the trigger for a story of national scope, whereas an international (distant) event might have a focus that reveals the event's local scope.

Scope addresses the domains that the event reaches or the implications that the event has. But implications for whom? Journalists consider an event and decide (or are assigned) to create a news item about the event's interest to all or part of the audience. Such mental judgements are not limited to journalists, of course, although the judgements of journalists and their sources have a direct impact on the scope an event is given in the news. News organizations are not blind to the interests of their audiences (and perhaps their advertisers), and so decisions about an event's scope may also be influenced by market forces.

Physical distance may ultimately be less important than psychological distance once the event has passed through many news gates. For example, if a community's mayor is murdered, this is a local event in terms of physical distance, because the mayor and the news organization are from the same community. Whether this event has scope beyond the community depends on a more subjective judgement: To what extent does this murder affect or interest the state or province, the country, or the world? If the town is small, the murder will have local and perhaps state interest, but probably will not be of interest to national and international audiences. But if mayors all over the country are being murdered, then the local news organization would probably cover the local angle (perpetrator, survivors, and so on) plus the national angle – making a pattern of murders across the country psychologically close to the audience. A local event may have only local interest or it may reach beyond the local audience to have implications for nations. The wider the scope, the more likely an event is to become news.

The congruence of proximity and scope

Cohen et al. (1990) say that journalists can manipulate scope by changing the dominant angle given the event. For example, while the main topic of a news story might be the murder of a high school student, which is a local issue to the local media, the story angle might be high school murder statistics of the country, and so the scope of the article becomes nationwide. Although the proximity of an event is physically determined, and the scope of an event is a cognitive assessment, we can compare whether an event is covered on similar or different levels, from local to international. If proximity and scope are both at the same level, for example, an event with local proximity and a news item with local scope, then proximity and scope are *congruent*. If they are on different levels, proximity and scope are *incongruent*.

Considering the congruence of scope and proximity may provide journalists with an easy first assessment of an event's newsworthiness: a reporter for a small-town newspaper is told to cover events of interest and relevance to the local community. If she learns that the biggest grocery store in town is going out of business, then she instantly understands that she should write a story about it from the local angle. Similarly, if a foreign correspondent who covers the Middle East for a cable news network discovers that one country has declared war on the other, then it is obvious that she should cover it as international news. In both examples, the level of proximity is the same as, or congruent with, the level of scope. When journalists judge events as having obviously congruent proximity and scope, the event is more likely to become news.

On the other hand, if proximity and scope are incongruent, journalists' decisions may require more thought: consider a small-town reporter who is assigned to write stories about government in the capital city. Through his capital sources, he hears about a scandal involving the mayor of his small town. The event is local in terms of physical closeness to his audience, but his job is to write about events that occur further away, and to give them a local angle. The event presents an ambiguous situation and requires more thought. The journalist is uncertain about whether this event fits the parameters of his job. If the journalist perceives that scope and proximity are incongruent, then more cognitive effort will be used to decide whether to cover the event, and other news values will be given more weight.

This is not to say that all events judged to be congruent become news; obviously they cannot. Other news values are always considered, but if the journalist interprets an event as having congruent scope and proximity, then it automatically passes through the first gate and is in the pool of events that might become news that day. Incongruent events are more difficult to categorize. The journalist needs more information.

Deviance and social significance

News values provide information that the journalist can use to make decisions about events. Do they involve conflict or controversy? Is there something odd or unusual? Is the event important or interesting to the audience? Shoemaker and her colleagues (Shoemaker, 1996; Shoemaker et al., 1991) propose that such news values are operational indicators of the theoretical constructs, *deviance* and *social significance*. Deviance is a characteristic of people, ideas or events that sets them aside as different from others in their region, community, neighborhood, family and so on (Shoemaker and Cohen, 2006). When events are deviant, journalists may apply the operational indicators novelty, oddity or unusualness; conflict, controversy or sensationalism to the events. Shoemaker (1996) suggests that *deviance* has three dimensions: (1) *normative* deviance, which refers to the breaking of norms and laws; (2) *social change* deviance, which identifies ideas, people or events that challenge the status quo of the social system, whether large or small; and (3) *statistical* deviance, which judges an idea, person or event to be very different from the average – being odd, unusual or novel.

Social significance has four dimensions. An event's *political* significance is the extent to which the event has potential or actual impact on the relationship between people and government or between governments. The *economic* significance of an event refers to the event's potential or actual impact on the exchange of goods and services, including the monetary system, business, tariffs, labour, transportation, job markets, resources and infrastructure. *Cultural* significance compares the event to a social system's traditions, institutions, and norms, such as religion, ethnicity or the arts. Last is *public* significance, the enhancements or threats an event has for the public's well-being.

When journalists judge events to have incongruent proximity and scope, the deviance and social significance of the event have more influence on whether the event passes through the news gates.

Hypotheses

Following the above, we propose that the congruence of scope and proximity influence whether events are covered and how much deviance and social significance the covered events have.

Hypothesis 1: The scope and proximity of news items are more likely to be congruent than non-congruent. Congruent events pass through the first news gate most easily, because it takes less cognitive effort for journalists to categorize congruent events as 'possibly newsworthy'. Therefore, there should be more congruent news items.

Hypothesis 2: Incongruent news items have a higher level of deviance than congruent items.

Hypothesis 3: Incongruent news items have a higher level of social significance than congruent items.

To justify covering a local story with national scope or a national story with local scope, the journalist must pay more attention to other news values. Shoemaker et al. (1987) argue that deviance and social significance underlie many of the indicators affecting newsworthiness. If an event cannot automatically be put in the 'possibly news' category because proximity and scope are congruent, then journalists must pay close attention to attributes such as deviance and social significance.

Methods

Our study uses data collected as part of an international research project, which was conducted in the beginning of 2000.[3] The study examined news media coverage of two cities – large and small – in each of ten countries: Australia, Chile, China, Germany, India, Israel, Jordan, Russia, South Africa and the US. Research teams in each country coded news items from three media – newspaper, television, and radio – and two different cities, using one constructed week as the sampling design. One mass communication scholar in each country was responsible for its data collection. The news item is the unit of analysis.

Four concepts were used in this study: the proximity, scope, deviance and social significance of each of the more than 30,000 news items that were studied.[4] Proximity was operationally defined to have four levels: local (the event occurs in the same community that the news medium is in); regional (the event

occurs in the region surrounding the community that the news medium is in);
national (the event occurs in the country that the news medium is in); and international (the event occurs in or involves a country other than the one the news
medium is in). Scope was also measured on four levels: local scope indicates
that the event is treated on a local level, events of regional scope are treated on
a regional level, national events are those treated on a national level, and international events treated on that level.

The deviance of the news items was operationalized as three dimensions:
statistical deviance, social change deviance, and normative deviance. Each dimension was coded on a four-point scale, where one indicates no deviance and four
indicates extreme deviance. A deviance index was created by averaging scores
across the three dimensions. Social significance was measured as its four
dimensions: political significance, economic significance, cultural significance,
and public significance. The scores across four dimensions were averaged into
an index. The two indexes are used in the following analyses.[5]

Results

A total of 30,742 news items were examined as to their proximity, scope, three
types of deviance, and four types of social significance. As Table 10.1 indicates,
most news items were of local or national proximity and of national scope. The
most common kind of deviance was statistical and the most common type of
social significance was of public importance (Table 10.2). After the deviance
and social significance indexes were created, the average level of deviance was
low, but as Shoemaker and Cohen report (2006: 50, 66), about two-thirds of
news items were coded as having some amount of deviance and eight out of ten
were coded as having social significance.

Supporting hypothesis one, 60% or more of news items were of congruent
proximity and scope. In Table 10.3, the cells on the diagonal represent congruence, with the ones above and below the diagonal representing incongruence.

A series of one-way ANOVAs[6] compare the deviance of four cells including
one congruent and three incongruent cells. In addition, *Scheffé* post hoc tests
compare each of the incontruent cells with the congruent cells. Six of the twelve
incongruent cells in Table 10.4 are more deviant than their congruent referents,
therefore Hypothesis 2 is partially supported.

The same sort of analysis is shown in Table 10.5. Within each value of proximity (columns), there is an overall statistically significant difference in the
social significance of congruent and non-congruent news items. *Scheffé* post hoc

Table 10.1 Percentages for values of the proximity and scope of events that become news items

Variables	%
Proximity	
Local	33.6
Regional	12.4
National	31.5
International	22.5
	100%
	(N = 29,227)
Scope	
Local	23.5
Regional	10.9
National	40.6
International	25.0
	100%
	(N = 30,699)

Table 10.2 Mean deviance and social significance of events that became news items, N = 30,742

Deviance & Social Significance Variables*	Mean	SD
Statistical deviance	1.88	.87
Social change deviance	1.37	.71
Normative deviance	1.38	.77
Political significance	1.53	.87
Economic significance	1.46	.79
Cultural significance	1.44	.73
Public significance	1.74	.85

*1 to 4 scale, where 4 = most of the concept

Table 10.3 Crosstabulation of scope by proximity (N = 29,215)

	Proximity			
Scope	Local	Regional	National	International
Local	60.2	10.3	5.3	4.0
Regional	6.2	65.1	2.6	1.3
National	25.2	20.1	82.5	12.7
International	8.4	4.4	9.6	82.1
Total	100.0%	100.0%	100.0%	100.0%
N	(9,823)	(3,619)	(9,190)	(6,583)

Grey cells indicate that proximity and scope are congruent.
Chi square = 36,304.94, Cramer's V = .644, df = 9, p < .001

Table 10.4 Columns represent four one-way analyses of variance of scope on the deviance* of news items, within each level of proximity. Scheffé post hoc tests show that deviance is often higher when scope and proximity are incongruent, especially when proximity is local

Scope of events	Proximity of events			
	Local	Regional	National	International
Local	1.40	1.52	1.60	1.72
	(.49)	(.54)	(.59)	(.70)
Regional	1.54[a]	1.49	1.72[a]	1.74
	(.48)	(.53)	(.64)	(.63)
National	1.59[a]	1.54	1.53	1.90[a]
	(.57)	(.55)	(.57)	(.74)
International	1.49[a]	1.61[b]	1.61	1.73
	(.55)	(.52)	(.60)	(.69)
F	80.61	4.58	14.41	13.24
df	3, 9819	3, 3615	3, 9186	3, 6579
Sig.	$p < .001$	$p < .01$	$p < .001$	$p < .001$

Grey cells indicate that proximity and scope are congruent.
* The deviance index = statistical deviance + social change deviance + normative deviance, then divided by 3, resulting in a 1 to 4 scale, where 4 indicates the most deviance.
[a] $p < .001$
[b] $p < .01$
[c] $p < .05$

tests show that seven of the twelve incongruent cells have more social significance than their accompanying congruent cells. Of the remaining five incongruent cells, two have less social significance than their referent cell. Hypothesis 3 is also partially supported.

Conclusion

Our chapter investigates an old news value, proximity, and introduces a new one, scope. As for proximity, we question whether it should be operationalized as physical closeness to the news organization's offices or to its audience or audiences. With many news organizations having satellite offices in multiple locations and audiences as large as the entire world, deciding how to measure physical closeness is more complicated than it once was. Scope addresses the psychological closeness of the event for the audience. One event may be covered in multiple stories, each with a different scope. Therefore scope is controlled by the news media, to the extent that news personnel judge an event to

Table 10.5 Columns represent four one-way analyses of variance of event scope on the social significance* of news items, within each level of proximity. Scheffé post hoc tests show that social significance is usually higher when scope and proximity are incongruent

Scope of events	Proximity of events			
	Local	Regional	National	International
Local	1.40	1.46	1.43[c]	1.41[c]
	(.47)	(.52)	(.60)	(.55)
Regional	1.73[a]	1.49	1.72[a]	1.55
	(.62)	(.53)	(.70)	(.60)
National	1.73[a]	1.67[a]	1.59	1.83
	(.64)	(.60)	(.60)	(.72)
International	1.61[a]	1.70[a]	1.69[a]	1.69
	(.56)	(.62)	(.62)	(.66)
F	260.39	27.79	23.34	28.92
Df	3,9773	3,3615	3,9202	3,6594
Sig.	p < .001	p < .001	p < .001	p < .001

Grey cells indicate that proximity and scope are congruent.
* Social significance index = political significance + economic significance + cultural significance + public significance, then divided by 4, resulting in a 1 to 4 scale, where 4 indicates the most social significance
[a] p < .001
[b] p < .01
[c] p < .05

have importance for the audience locally, within the province or state, regionally, or between nations. Although proximity is a characteristic of an event and tied to physical referents, scope is a cognitive variable that represents journalists' judgement of the event's psychological closeness to the audience and the subsequent spin that they give news items about the event.

As news values, proximity and scope combine to produce another construct – congruence. We found that the majority of news items have the same level of each variable, that is, scope and proximity are usually congruent. However, one quarter of local events were covered with national rather than local scope. In other words, the scope of the events was *broadened* in the news items. Conversely, 10% of events having regional proximity were given local scope in their news items. The scope of the events was *narrowed* in these news items.

When scope is either broadened or narrowed, we hypothesized that the events would have to be of higher deviance and social significance (Shoemaker and Cohen, 2006) to make it through all of the news gates and finally become news. There was some support for this idea. For example, if a four-year-old child drives a car and causes an accident in his community, this local event may be given national scope in some news items, because the event is statistically and normatively deviant. Conversely, if the newly elected president of a country takes action to radically change tax laws, this is an example of social change deviance and economic significance. Although this is a national event, some news items may give local or regional scope, because journalists want people to know how the change will affect their local industry and schools.

These hypotheses were partially supported. In other words, it is often observed that broadened scope and narrowed scope are associated with increased deviance and social significance. This was more true for broadened scope than narrowed scope. News items have more deviance and social significance when scope is broadened, rather than when narrowed. Having more deviance and/or social significance justifies giving a local event national scope.

Summary

- Proximity is a characteristic of an event and tied to physical referents, whereas scope is a cognitive variable that represents journalists' judgement of the event's psychological closeness to the audience and the subsequent spin that they give news items about the event.
- One event may be covered in multiple stories, each with a different scope. Scope is controlled by the news media.
- By combining values of proximity and scope, we can determine whether they are congruent (for example, local proximity with local scope) or incongruent (for example, national proximity with international scope).
- Scope and proximity are congruent in the majority of news items.
- News items have more deviance and social significance when scope is broadened, rather than when narrowed.
- Having more deviance and/or social significance can justify giving a local event national scope.

GOING FURTHER

Gans, H.J. (1979) *Deciding What's News: A Study of CBS Evening News, NBC Nightly News, Newsweek and Time*. New York: Pantheon.
One of the classic books in media sociology discussing the determinants of news coverage, a participant observation of the news process at four US mass media.

Galtung, J., and Ruge, M.H. (1965) 'The structure of foreign news: The presentation of the Congo, Cuba and Cyprus crises in four Norwegian newspapers', *Journal of Peace Research*, 2(1): 64–91.

Another classic study in the determinants of news. The article proposes a system of twelve factors describing events that together are used as a definition of 'newsworthiness'.

Shoemaker, P.J. (1991). *Gatekeeping* (Communication Concepts 3). Newbury Park, CA: Sage.

An explication of the gatekeeping concept, beginning with Lewin's model of the 1950s and ending with a new gatekeeping model that takes into account gatekeeping processes on five levels of analysis. Gatekeeping is shown to include not only selection of events to become news, but also of how the events are covered.

Shoemaker, P.J. (1996) 'Hardwired for news: Using biological and cultural evolution to explain the surveillance function', *Journal of Communications*, 46: 32–47.

The author proposes that standard indicators of newsworthiness used by journalists represent two theoretical constructs – deviance and social significance – and that these are the result of the processes of biological and cultural evolution.

Shoemaker, P.J. and Cohen, A.A. (2006). *News Around the World: Practitioners,Content and the Public*. New York: Routledge.

This study of newspaper, television and radio news in ten countries shows the relationship between the deviance and social significance of events and their prominence in the news media. A distinction is made between news (a social artifact) and newsworthiness (a mental judgement), and the complexity of an event is proposed to enhance newsworthiness.

Shoemaker, P.J. and Reese, S.D. (1996) *Mediating the Message: Theories of influences on mass media content*. White Plains, NY: Longman.

As one of the 'significant journalism and communication books of the 20th century' named by *Journalism and Mass Communication Quarterly*, this is a must read for students of mass communication who are interested in how mass media content is shaped and filtered by influences on five levels of analysis.

STUDENT ACTIVITY 10.1

Select stories from various pages in your capital city's newspaper. Evaluate the proximity and scope of each event and whether they are congruent or incongruent. Are the incongruent stories about events with more deviance? With more social significance? What other differences are there between stories about congruent and incongruent events?

References

Adams, W.C. (1986) 'Whose lives count? TV coverage of natural disasters', *Journal of Communication,* 36 (Spring): 113–22.

Berkowitz, D. and Beach, D.W. (1993) 'News sources and news context: The effect of routine news, conflict and proximity', *Journalism and Mass Communication Quarterly,* 70(1): 4–12.

Bridges, J.A. and Bridges, L.W. (1997) 'Changes in news use on the front pages of the American daily newspaper, 1986–1993', *Journalism & Mass Communication Quarterly,* 74(4): 826–38.

Buckalew, J.K. (1979) 'The local radio news editor as gatekeeper', *Journal of Broadcasting,* 18: 211–21.

Chang, T.K. and Lee, J.W. (1992) 'Factors affecting gatekeepers' selection of foreign news: A national survey of newspaper editors', *Journalism Quarterly,* 69(3): 554–61.

Chang, T.K., Shoemaker P. J. and Brendlinger, N. (1987) 'Determinants of international news coverage in the U.S. media', *Communication Research,* 14(4): 396–414.

Cohen, A.A., Adoni, H., and Bantz, C.R. (1990) *Social Conflict and Television News.* Thousand Oaks, CA: Sage.

DeFleur, M.L. and Dennis, E. E. (1998) *Understanding Mass Communication: A liberal arts perspective.* Boston: Houghton Mifflin Company.

Galtung, J. and Ruge, M.H. (1965). 'The structure of foreign news: The presentation of the Congo, Cuba and Cyprus crises in four Norwegian newspapers', *Journal of Peace Research,* 2(1): 64–91.

Gans, H.J. (1979). *Deciding What's News: A Study of CBS Evening News, NBC Nightly News, Newsweek and Time.* New York: Pantheon.

Gerbner, G. and Marvanyi, G. (1977). 'The many worlds of the world's press', *Journal of Communication,* 27(1): 52–66.

Golding, P, and Elliot, P. (1979). *Making the News.* New York: Longman.

Han, G. and Zhang, G. (2000) 'A comparative study on international coverage in China and Japan: From *People's Daily* to *Asahi Shimbun* [in Chinese]', *Journalistic Studies Quarterly (Xin Wen Da Xue),* Spring: 33–39.

Hargrove, T. and Stempel, G. H. (2002) 'Exploring reader interest in international news', *Newspaper Research Journal,* 23(4): 46–51.

Hester, A.L. (1971) 'An analysis of news from developed and developing nations', *Gazette,* 7: 30–40.

Hester, A.L. (1974) 'The news from Latin America via a world news agency', *Gazette,* 20(2): 82–98.

Hicks, R.G. and Gordon, A. (1974) 'Foreign news content in Israel and US newspapers', *Journalism Quarterly,* 51: 639–44.

Kiernan V. (2003) 'Embargoes and science news', *Journalism & Mass Communication Quarterly,* 80(4): 903–20.

Lewin, K. (1947a) 'Frontiers in group dynamics: Concept, method and reality in science; social equilibria and social change', *Human Relations*, 1: 5–41.

Lewin, K. (1947b). 'Frontiers in group dynamics II: Channels of group life; social planning and action research', *Human Relations*, 1: 143–153.

Lewin, K. (1951). *Field theory in social science: Selected theoretical papers.* New York: Harper.

Luttbeg, N.R. (1983) 'Proximity does not assure newsworthiness', *Journalism Quarterly,* 60: 731–2.

MacBride, S. (1980) *Many Voices, One World: Communication and society, today and tomorrow.* Paris: UNESCO.

MacLean, M.S. and Pinna, L. (1958) 'Distance and news interest: Scarperia, Italy', *Journalism Quarterly*, 35(Spring): 36–48.

Martin, S.R. (1988) 'Proximity of event as factor in selection of news sources', *Journalism Quarterly*, 65(Winter): 986–9.

Masmoudi, M. (1979) 'The new world information order', *Journal of Communication*, 29(2): 172–85.

Morton, L.P. and Warren J. (1992) 'Proximity: Localization vs. distance in PR news releases', *Journalism Quarterly,* 69(4): 1023–8.

Mowlana, H. (1985) '*International Flow of Information: A global report and analysis.* Paris, France: UNESCO; New York: UNIPUB [distributor].

Mowlana, H. (1993) '*The Global Media Debate: Its rise, fall, and renewal.* Norwood, NJ: Ablex.

Riffe, D. (1996) 'Linking international news to US interests: A content analysis', *International Communication Bulletin,* 31: 14–18.

Rosengren, K.E. (1974) 'International news: Methods, data and theory', *Journal of Peace Research*, 11(2): 145–156.

Rosengren, K.E. (1977) 'Four types of tables', *Journal of Communication*, 27(1): 67–75.

Rubin, B. (1979) 'International news and the American media' in D.B. Fascell (ed.) *International News: Freedom under attack.* Beverly Hills: Sage. p. 188.

Shapiro, M.E. and Schofield, L.B. (1986) 'How proximity, circulation and geographical distribution influenced coverage of Miami's overtown disturbance', *Newspaper Research Journal.* 7(4): 55–61

Shapiro, M.E., and Williams, W. (1984) 'Civil disturbance in Miami: Proximity and conflict in newspaper coverage' *Newspaper Research Journal,* 5(3): 61–69.

Shoemaker, P.J. (1991) *Gatekeeping,* (Communication Concepts 3). Newbury Park, CA: Sage.

Shoemaker, P.J. (1996) 'Hardwired for news: Using biological and cultural evolution to explain the surveillance function', *Journal of Communications,* 46: 32–47.

Shoemaker, P.J., Chang, T., and Brendlinger, N. (1987) 'Deviance as a predictor of newsworthiness: Coverage of international events in the US media' in M.L. McLaughlin (ed.). *Communication Yearbook* 10 Newbury Park, CA: Sage. pp. 348–65.

Shoemaker, P.J., and Cohen, A.A. (2006) *News Around the World: Practitioners, content and the public.* New York: Routledge.

Shoemaker, P.J., Danielian, L.H. and Brendlinger, N. (1991) 'Deviant acts, risky business and US interests: The newsworthiness of world events', *Journalism Quarterly,* 68: 781–95.

Shoemaker, P.J., and Reese, S.D. (1996) *Mediating the Message: Theories of influences on mass media content.* White Plains, NY: Longman.

Sparks, V. and Winter, J.P. (1980) 'Reader interest in foreign news', *ANPA News Research Report,* No. 28, Sept. 15.

Sreberny-Mohammadi, A. (1984) 'The world of news', *Journal of Communication,* 34: 121–34.

Stevenson, R. L. and Cole, R. (1984) 'Patterns of foreign news' in R.L. Stevenson and D.L. Shaw (eds) *Foreign News and the New World Information Order.* Ames: The Iowa State University Press. pp. 37–62.

Stevenson, R.L. and Shaw, D.L. (eds) (1984) *Foreign News and the New World Information Order.* Ames: The Iowa State University Press.

White. D.M. (1950) 'The gatekeeper: A case study in the selection of news', *Journalism Quarterly,* 27: 383–90.

Notes

1 Although much news is tied to events, news may also revolve around people, organizations, social institutions, or ideas. We use the term *event* here to represent 'things' that occur in the world and that may or may not become news.

2 By using the term *accidental audience*, we include the distribution of messages beyond the journalist's intended audience. For example, some people share newspapers and magazines intentionally or by merely leaving them in public places for use by someone else.

3 This study uses data collected for the *News Around the World* study, by Shoemaker and Cohen (2006), although the variables *proximity* and *scope* are not discussed in the book.

4 In the original study, there are more than 32,000 news items. News items that were visual only, for example, maps, figures or solitary photos, were not included in these analyses.

5 The research team from each country conducted their own intercoder reliability tests. Scott's pi coefficients are reported in Shoemaker and Cohen (2006). Although India, Jordan and Russia did not report reliability estimates, those from other countries were mostly higher than .80.

6 ANOVA is an acronym for ANalysis Of VAriance, a statistical procedure that tests for differences between observed means. If the conclusion is that the means are somehow different, then *Scheffé* post hoc tests tell us which pairs of means are most responsible for the difference. For example, in Table 10.5, there are four ANOVAs, one for each column (level of proximity). The F statistic produced by ANOVA for the column 'local proximity' tells us that the deviance of events observed *among* the four cells in each column differ from each other, but we do not know which cell or cells contribute most to the difference. In the local proximity column, the *Scheffé* post hoc tests compare the deviance *between* the four levels of scope and tell us which combinations are most different on the concept *deviance.*

Text and Textual Analysis

Peter Hughes

DEFINITIONS

Text

The word 'text' has a number of meanings, such as:

1. An organized collection of words (the most 'everyday' sense of the term).
2. A literary object such as a poem, play or novel (a sense from literary theory).
3. An organized collection of signs (such as words, images or sounds) by which potential meanings are produced in a convention based system which can be apprehended by analysis (a semiotic understanding of the term, and the definition most relevant to this chapter).

The literary conception of 'text' tends to emphasize words above other elements, and frequently assumes a hierarchy of value in which certain forms of 'text' are valued over others. Media outputs such as newspapers, television programmes, billboard advertisements and web pages are examples of texts which are both produced and understood by means of conventions. In this 'semiotic' understanding of 'text' no hierarchy of value is intended.

Textual analysis

Textual analysis is a general term applied to a variety of means by which researchers and students may analyse how texts produce potential meanings and what those potential meanings are.
This chapter argues that there are two main traditions of textual analysis: those that understand texts as 'reflections' of the world; and those that understand texts as culturally produced and interpreted 'constructions'.

Introduction

Early chapters in this book dealt with the media in their social, cultural, economic and organizational contexts, before the focus shifted to the outputs of the media: the representations the media produce. This chapter will take that focus even closer. Representations are produced in the media by 'texts': films, television programmes, newspaper articles, websites and pop songs, for example.

The detailed examination of media texts is usually given the overall name 'textual analysis', but there is no single methodology of textual analysis. Indeed, the term is understood differently in different contexts. Some people understand the output of the media as discrete messages independent of receivers, including the analyst, which can be scientifically studied as phenomena, much like those in the 'natural world' which have an existence separate, and prior to, the process of analysis. For such students of media the method known as content analysis is appropriate. For others, however, (including me) media outputs are 'texts' which cannot be separated from their social and cultural contexts. As we have already seen in earlier chapters, media texts are both produced within powerful institutions and are themselves sites of power and contesting debates. For analysts seeking to grasp the complexity of 'textuality', to grasp the ways texts produce potential meanings, and the ways these meanings are circulated, exchanged, and incorporated into people's lives (including that of the analyst), content analysis is insufficient to the task, although it may provide much useful material during early stages of an analysis.

This chapter will present one possible approach to the study of texts, an approach which seeks to be systematic, yet not to make claims to 'scientific detachment'. It will recognize the role of quantitative methods such as content analysis, but will draw mainly on 'constructivist' and 'structuralist' approaches to media outputs which understand media texts as complex constructions, produced, circulated and made sense of in complex social and cultural contexts. It will also seek to provide some guidance on how to go about textual analysis – something often missing from other discussions.

I use one text as my example: a half hour natural history documentary, produced and screened as a sequel to the series *Walking with Dinosaurs*. I have chosen *The Ballad of Big Al* for the following reasons:

- It is relatively brief. The programme was paired with another documentary about the 'science of *Big Al*', but was just under 30 minutes long.
- It uses digital imaging technologies to a more sophisticated level than any previous documentary programme, and in a manner that raises some interesting questions about the relationship between the television image and 'reality'.

- It is a hybrid form: while it is clearly a form of documentary on one level, it has a strong narrative which might be understood as similar to fiction, and it also demonstrates elements of parody. Hybridity is one of the dominant features of television programming in the first decade of the twenty-first century (Bondebjerg, 1996; Roscoe, 2001; Wood, 2004).

In performing this analysis I am interested in how *Big Al* produces potential meanings and what some of those meanings might be.

This chapter will cover the following topics:

- The background to the programme being analyzed: the context of the text.
- The analysis of the text.
- A discussion of some of the issues which arise from this analysis.

You will find, in common with other chapters in this book, a set of suggested readings, a list of student activities, and some boxes on 'how to do' textual analysis.

Finally, you might ask, 'Why bother with such a textual analysis?' I offer several reasons, drawing on the work of other writers. In various sources about the impact of digital imaging techniques, a number of writers have argued that audiences need to learn to 'read' images, and that this is especially true of non-fiction images such as documentaries (Battye, 1996; Hoffman, 1998; Mitchell, 1998; Winston, 1995). In the case of *Big Al*, audience members presumably 'know' that they cannot actually be watching footage of live dinosaurs – but they 'know' this from evidence beyond the programme, not from the text itself. While it is known that the images are 'false', all the textual cues work to assert the opposite. The claim that is being made is not so much 'these are real dinosaurs' but rather 'this is what real dinosaurs would have been like'.

Mitchell makes the point that the truth of photos is contextual, not inherent (actually in the photos). In the case of this documentary, the digital images it uses are complex animations – more analogous to paintings than live footage (Hughes, 2006). Animations are more clearly constructed than photos are, but this documentary works to efface this constructedness.

From a perspective in which media outputs are seen as 'messages' (a 'positivist' perspective), images simply represent aspects of the world (natural or social) and can be assessed in terms of the degree to which they 'accurately' reflect the world. A structuralist (such as a semiotician) would argue that an image can function in a number of ways, one of which is as an index: the image provides 'evidence' for the event, person or place in the image because the camera and the event, person or place had to be co-present at some stage. It is from this perspective that an image taken by a security camera might be tendered in court as evidence. However, digital imaging (such as that used in the production of *Big Al*) challenges this indexical relationship and requires that audiences regard images as constructions. If individual images are constructions then complex texts constructed from a series of images, sounds and words (spoken, or as graphics on screen) are even more so.

Fairclough (1995) has suggested four reasons why textual analysis needs to be utilized in the social sciences:

- *Theoretical:* language has often been 'misperceived' as transparent (the 'realist' perspective), but texts are a form of social action (the 'constructivist' perspective).
- *Methodological:* texts are a major source of evidence for the social scientist.
- *Historical:* texts can be seen as 'barometers of social processes'.
- *Political:* texts are sites of social control and domination (or ideology).

The force of each of these arguments is that media texts provide evidence for social scientists, but cannot simply be seen as a reflection of social processes, but rather as social practices in their own right. They need to be 'read' or 'interpreted' in this light drawing on the techniques of textual analysis.

Media debates need evidence to support the claims being made, and textual analysis provides the evidence from media texts. Each of these arguments, however, suggests that media texts are valuable as evidence of social phenomena, but do have value in their own right. This view underestimates the importance of media texts, which are also sites of considerable pleasure to audiences (think of the loyal fan base for such programmes as *Buffy the Vampire Slayer*, or *The OC*), and any form of textual analysis needs to attend to the text itself, not merely to 'see through it' to some social phenomenon beyond.

Any understanding of an individual text begins with some understanding of its context(s) of production, reception and analysis.

Context

1. Natural history programming on television

The Ballad of Big Al: Natural history, or wildlife, programming has long been a staple of television non-fiction, with a number of well-known 'blue chip' programs regularly receiving large audiences; and several channels on pay or cable TV being devoted to natural history documentaries (Aldridge and Dingwall, 2003; Cottle, 2004; Kilborn, 2006). Measured in terms of audience, one of the most successful series in the last decade has been *Walking with Dinosaurs,* a six part television series co-produced by the BBC with a number of international media organizations, and first screened in the UK in October 1999 (Darley, 2003; Kilborn, 2006; Richards, 2001; Scott and White, 2003). A major marketing feature of this series was its reliance on 'cutting-edge computer graphics and animatronics effects' in the creation of most of what is seen on screen (British Broadcasting Corporation, 2006) 'employed to help fabricate the illusion of wildlife film footage' from the time of the dinosaurs (Darley, 2003: 228). This was equally true of the *'Walking with Dinosaurs* special', *The Ballad of Big Al* (UK, 2001). One of the concerns of this analysis is understanding how this illusion of wildlife film footage is constructed.

The programme tells the story of an Allosaurus fragilis which lived in the Late Jurassic period, 145 million years ago, the bones of which were found in Wyoming, USA. Nicknamed *Big Al,* the program constructs a narrative of 'how Al may have lived and died' (Freeman, n.d), beginning with his emergence from an egg and ending with his death in a dry river bed, during a drought.

The special has been screened in a number of markets around the world including, at least, the UK and Australia, North America (where it was known as *Allosaurus: A Walking With Dinosaurs' Special* and was 'revoiced' by Avery Brooks), France (where it was revoiced by Andre Dussolier) and Finland. This episode and the series as a whole are examples of a globalized media text, an area of increasing interest to media researchers.[1] Not the least issue here are different 'performances' by each of the narrators and how audiences in different locations might interpret these.

Like the original series, the 'special' raises a number of questions about the natural history documentary, and about discourses on science in the media, one of which is the impact of digitization on the status of the image. There is a growing literature on the contemporary natural history programme on TV. While some of these authors concentrate on the specific case of the *Walking with Dinosaurs* phenomenon (Benton, 2001; Darley, 2003; Richards, 2001; Scott and White, 2003), a number of others have canvassed larger issues to do with the broad context of natural history programming (Aldridge and Dingwall, 2003; Bousâe, 2000; Cottle, 2004; Delofski, 1995; Kilborn, 2006; Philo and Henderson, 1998).

Kilborn (2006) makes the point that 'all observers are agreed that the wildlife TV landscape has changed dramatically over the last decade or so' with programme-makers under pressure to develop new styles and approaches to engage audiences. This chapter will examine *The Ballad of Big Al* to identify some of these approaches, with a view to understanding how these approaches produce potential meanings, and to understanding what some of these potential meanings are. While agreeing with Cottle's (2004) important argument for more attention to the 'encompassing' discursive and institutional constraints within which natural history programming is produced, this chapter will, nevertheless concentrate on the analysis of a single text. In doing so I am performing a 'reading' of the text, and not making any claim to finding a single, unified 'truth' of the text.

Frameworks for textual analysis

All research is undertaken within intellectual frameworks, by which researchers make sense of the world, including the research process itself. In understanding media output one such framework is based upon understanding the world as having an existence beyond and separate from the observer. In this positivist (or 'realist') view the output of the media can consistently be seen as messages about the world, in which already existing information ('content') is passed from one person or group to others via a means of communication (including the 'mass media'). The means of communication may be more or less inhibiting on the clarity of the message, but generally the message has a separate existence from the means of its communication. In such a view it would be reasonable to assume that the role of the analyst was to uncover the 'message(s)' being transmitted. This view of media is based on a 'transmission model' such as that developed in the late 1940s by Shannon and Weaver (Shannon and Weaver, 1949. For one critique of the underlying assumptions of this 'linear model' of communication see Hall, 1984). There is an element of this model of text in the assumption often made by students that the purpose of textual analysis is to find the 'hidden meanings' in the text, a view that assumes the text is like a 'vessel' containing messages, or meanings, which a well trained analyst is able to find and extract.

Content analysis is one methodology, based on this view of the process of communication, which seeks to study the message(s) in media output. Content analysis makes some claims to being a 'scientific' method of textual analysis and seeks generally to reduce messages to quantifiable elements – elements that can be clearly delineated in media output and then counted or measured. Often this is to enable a comparison between one text or series of texts and another, or perhaps to make a comparison between 'messages' and reality, and it is often the case that the research seeks to find the 'truth' – the true meaning of the text.

Alternative ways of understanding texts draw on constructivist or structuralist understandings of communication and assume that there is no single 'message' encoded into media outputs but that communication is one of the ways human beings seek to make sense of the world, and that texts construct meaning rather than carry meaning. In this view, meaning is produced by the interaction of texts and their readers through pre-existing structures. One purpose of textual analysis is to uncover the structures (the rules that govern the system of communication) that produce texts. Going further, the purpose of textual analysis might then be to uncover the potential meanings produced by an individual text. From this perspective meanings are always potential, to be negotiated between the text and the reader of the text.

Sometimes the analyst is interested in the operations of ideology (Fairclough's fourth argument for textual analysis above) and, assuming that texts produce and reproduce ideology, is seeking to analyze the text to understand the operation of ideology, a position that may come close to seeking the 'truth' of the text, or to seeing texts as producing 'misleading messages'. One objection which can be made to some of these approaches is that they tend to look through the text to something beyond – and in doing so lose sight of the fact that people interact with texts because they derive pleasure from doing so. Pleasure is seen as being suspect and so little attention is paid to the pleasurable aspects of the text (O'Connor and Klaus, 2000).

In the view of textual analysis being developed by this chapter there is no single meaning in the text and the goal of textual analysis is not finding the 'correct meaning' of the text but 'finding out likely interpretations' (McKee, 2003).

My approach is broadly 'hermeneutic' in the sense of being 'interpretive'; however, consistent with the approach being taken throughout this volume my approach is eclectic, that is, I am using a number of strategies of textual analysis rather than attempting to be purist in approach. I draw on content analysis and formalism to get a clear sense of what is 'on the screen'; from semiotics I draw the sense that what is on the screen are signs, which function in a relational fashion (syntagmatically and paradigmatically); from narratology I draw a method for understanding the larger structures of this text. From discourse analysis I draw the concept that the sign functions in terms of larger structures – including those beyond the text itself. From hermeneutics itself I draw a method of operation (known as the hermeneutic circle), in which the reader examines the text in some detail, makes some 'hunches' about how it produces meanings, then goes both to the wider contexts in which the text is located and back to the text itself to find the necessary evidence to check these 'hunches'.

Textual analysis is a social practice producing an argument about that text, so it needs to provide evidence for that argument. This is why it needs to be systematic. However, I do not want to argue that being systematic will produce results which are replicable and verifiable. This is the chimera of positivism. One way to think about the attempt to be systematic is that it is like the requirement in mathematics to 'show your working out' – how you got the answer.[2]

The social context of documentary

This book places an emphasis on the mass media in their social context: the variety of contexts within which they are produced; and those in which they are received, made sense of and incorporated into people's daily lives. Textual analysis as a social practice always occurs within a social/cultural context; texts cannot be divorced from their contexts. In this case there are a number of relevant contexts. The first is institutional: *The Ballad of Big Al* was produced by an independent production house for the BBC, the original broadcaster, a public service broadcaster with a privileged social and cultural position worldwide (even if its economic position is less privileged!) It was repeated on various other networks worldwide. It was later released as a DVD, available for purchase in a two part set (the second part being 'a scientific detective story to trace the evidence of *Big Al*' (ABC Shop, 2006). As the programme is accessed via TV screen its reception is most frequently a domestic context (although it may be seen in a course at school or university, where its reception will be different depending on whether it is seen within a course on paleontology, or on media studies).

In semiotics (a theory and methodology of texts on which much of this chapter will draw), a 'text' is 'an assemblage of signs (such as words, images, sounds and/or gestures) constructed (and interpreted) with reference to the conventions associated with a genre and in a particular medium of communication' (Chandler, 2003). Initially then, a semiotician must determine what counts as a 'text'. In this case I would designate *Big Al* as a text because:

- it has a title suggesting a degree of autonomy from other texts;
- institutionally, it is marked off from other texts in the broadcasting schedule by a discrete time slot; and it is marked off by a range of publicity and promotional materials (including a number of websites which still exist several years after its broadcast);

- textually, by markers such as the title sequence near the beginning and the credit sequence at the end;
- and physically, it is now available for purchase as a physical object – a DVD.

Another context is the 'discursive' context: *The Ballad of Big Al* has been described as a documentary (Benton, 2001). Documentary is a form of discourse, in the sense that it is a sense-making social practice with orderly features, whose purpose is to generate knowledges about the social, or natural world. Documentary has a privileged place in the culture and in the TV schedule (for example, on free-to-air TV there are special 'timeslots', and on cable TV there are whole channels dedicated to documentaries – and especially to natural history documentaries such as this). This privileged place provides documentary with its 'discursive power'. While there was considerable debate about the degree to which *Walking with Dinosaurs* can be seen as science (Answers in Genesis, 2000; Benton, 2001) I do not wish to enter into this debate, I am concerned not at the 'scientific accuracy' but rather how the programme seeks to produce knowledges about the world – how it works as discourse.

Winston (1995) has pointed to the historical role of documentary as scientific discourse, a feature of the documentary which was reinforced by an important movement which occurred in the 1960s – the so called 'fly on the wall' perspective of observational cinema. Observational forms of documentary have been particularly influential on television, not least in the area of natural history, where a common trend is to observe the behaviour of animals in the wild from a supposedly neutral, scientific perspective (although sometimes mediated by a presenter such as Sir David Attenborough or the late Steve Irwin). One paradox of *Big Al* is its apparent use of observational techniques, but of creatures which died out millions of years before cameras were invented – an illusion central to its structure and argument. Although it is constructed very much with digital imaging technologies, an examination of this documentary can reveal the conventions of documentary in general and of 'natural history' documentary in particular, along with the arguments about the natural world being constructed by the text. In this case arguments about dinosaurs and arguments about the nature of scientific investigation.

This discursive context will have a bearing on the context of reception. We can expect this programme to be understood differently by a Christian believer who understands the Bible to be the literal story of the creation of life (Answers in Genesis, 2000) than by an individual who has been schooled in, and accepts contemporary scientific discourses on the origins of life (Benton, 2001).

The Text

Semiotics

One of the methodologies on which this textual analysis draws is semiotics. (For some good background on semiotics see Bignell 2002; Butler 2002; Gripsrud 2002; Seiter 1994). Semiotics (which can be traced back to the work of linguist Ferdinand de Saussure and philosopher Charles Sanders Peirce) seeks to study the relationships of one element in a system to another. Examples of 'systems of signification' which can be studied include word based systems such as sentences, and image based systems such as photography, film and television. A text such as *Big Al* is produced by the operation of a number of systems.

For semioticians, all elements in a text function as 'signs', and signs produce potential meanings, not through their relationship to 'the real world' (the referent) but to other signs. Any given sign can be located at the intersection of two axes called the syntagm and the paradigm. These concepts are useful from the smallest units of analysis to the largest – texts themselves function in a similar system of differences: *Big Al* can be located at the intersection of these two axes. So, what are these 'axes'?

One way to understand a syntagm is as all the elements that are present, while a paradigm is all those elements that could be present. So a syntagm is about presence, a paradigm is about absence, potential, and choice (Bertrand and Hughes, 2005). To give a simple example: a sentence made up of words in sequence is a syntagm ('The military said at the time that it killed only four people in the raid, which is said to have targeted an insurgent linked to al-Qaeda'). However, in this sentence any word in the sequence could be replaced by one or more other words which exist on the paradigmatic axis: the word 'killed' could be replaced by 'murdered' or 'eliminated', to take two possibilities. The word 'only' could be replaced by 'as few as' or 'as many as', 'up to' and so on. Each of these constructs a particular way of understanding the event being spoken about by the military spokesperson. A syntagmatic structure may exist in a verbal system or a visual system, and may be as small as a phrase or a single photo, or a novel, a feature film or television series.

Big Al exists on a syntagm of television programmes within the weekly schedule of programming on the station on which it was broadcast (or did so in the week in which it was screened). Paradigmatically it is one documentary among the thousands of documentaries which could, potentially, have filled that slot in the schedule. Indeed, at the point on the schedule at which it was screened it would have been possible for the network to have screened some other form of TV programme, so natural history documentary itself is one choice among a paradigm of potential programming choices. The differences between one natural history documentary and another arise from choices made on the paradigmatic axis. Much of the critical response to *The Ballad of Big Al* is focusing, without saying so, on paradigmatic choices made in production between different potential approaches to the subject matter.

So we can place this individual text as one of a series of programmes screened on television on a particular night, and as one of a series of possible programmes that could have been screened on that night. All the alternatives that were foregone in screening this programme, provide some of its privileged status.

As a text, *The Ballad of Big Al* is a syntagm of shots arranged in a particular order (they have a serial relationship to one another), each of which consists of sound and image (often the visuals are made up of dense layers of image superimposed at the post production stage), and has a running time of approximately 28 minutes (including final credits). Any one shot can be understood, syntagmatically, in terms of its relationship to other shots in a sequence, or in the text as a whole. In addition, any individual shot can be understood, syntagmatically, in terms of the various relations within the shot (composition, lighting, colour, sound/image relations).

Semiotics is an attempt to provide a means of systematically analyzing how meanings are produced by texts, going beyond subjective and intuitive means of analysis. Clearly it would be a huge task to analyze a text of hundreds of shots lasting approximately 28 minutes systematically, and this is usually the case with any media text. For this reason semiotics frequently takes a small section of a work (ranging from a single shot to a sequence) and uses that as the basis for analysis. Later in this analysis I take as an example the title sequence and the 'framing narrative' which follows it.

In a positivist framework, such as that of content analysis, an attempt would be made to obtain a sample 'representative' of the whole. In the case of a single work, such as a documentary, this might work at several levels. The choice of text might be made on the basis of some assumption that it was representative of the category of works to which it belonged (such as natural history programming); at a finer level it might seek to find a sequence which was representative of the whole (to use a term from semiotics, it might seek to find a metonym of the work – a part that can stand in for the whole).

A semiotician does not normally make any claim that any section under analysis is a 'representative sample'. How can a short sequence from a film or

TV programme act as a 'representative sample' of it? To extract a single item from a textual continuum the semiotic researcher may just use common sense (Bertrand and Hughes, 2005: 206). In this case I selected *The Ballad of Big Al* purely because I thought it raised some interesting issues to do with the nature of documentary, to do with changes in the media brought about by digital imaging technologies, and because it raised interesting questions about how humans respond to and imagine nature. All these reasons seem to me to be valid, but they are all subjective decisions. As it then turned out, when I did some reading, the original series also interested a number of other writers.

Case study: the process of analysis

I began my analysis of *Big Al* by watching the documentary several times. In doing so I was looking for what seemed to be patterns in the documentary – whether they were patterns of images, sounds, or 'themes'. Semiotics, like all 'structuralist' endeavours searches for underlying structural patterns – in texts, systems or cultures. To assist me in this process I also read:

1. A number of journal articles about natural history documentary (Aldridge and Dingwall, 2003; Cottle 2004; Delofski 1995; Kilborn 2006) and *Walking with Dinosaurs* (Benton 2001; Darley 2003; Richards 2001);
2. Some of the websites and other publicity materials produced about the documentary (ABC Shop, 2006; Answers in Genesis, 2000; British Broadcasting Corporation, 2006);
3. A large number of books and articles on documentary film theory.

In other words I had conducted a survey of the literature relevant to this text (Bertrand and Hughes, 2005: 206). This provided me with a number of issues to explore in relation to *Big Al*, including debates about its representation of science and its use of digital imaging technologies.

Semiotics makes the assumption that everything in a text is meaningful. This is not an assumption, however, that what we find in a text is evidence of the intention of the 'author' of the text. So I am looking for patterns in the text to understand how it produces meanings, not to prove something about the author's intentions.

For semiotics, a text is a rule based system – a system of signification. Looking for patterns in the text is a way of looking for the 'rules' which underlie the text. Here the researcher needs to begin by carefully noting all the elements of text: all those things which appear visually on screen and on the soundtrack. These are part of what some semioticians refer to as the 'denotative level' of the sign system.

The following is a list of what potentially may exist at the 'denotative' level in the documentary, one way is to think about the following areas:

- What can be seen
- What can be heard
- How the material is organized

Another way to think of this is to draw on discourse analysis. While there are a variety of approaches to discourse analysis, one tradition emphasizes the systematic verbal features of discourse (Kress, 2001). This comment assumes a verbal text under analysis, as does so much 'discourse analysis', but to attend closely to the 'textual features' of an audio-visual text it is important to know what those textual features are. I have tried to list such textual features in a systematic fashion in Box 11.1.

Box 11.1   Textual features of documentary

All the elements of a film or TV programme function as signs – that is they produce potential meanings through a system of differences. So it is useful in trying to approach a text systematically to think about all the elements which are potentially available within any text as signs. I have argued that any reading of a text begins with a question being asked of the text, in which case it is perfectly acceptable to discuss only those elements of the text which are most relevant to answering that question. This checklist might help you.

What can be seen

Begin by trying to systematically understand just what it is that you are looking at and listening to.

What type of image is this:

- What type of text is this (film/TV/CD ROM/Web page – one aspect of the context of the work)
- Genre (for example, is it (broadly) fiction or non-fiction?)

(Continued)

A television text may well use some or many of the following:

- Moving footage
- Still image
- Photographic
- Non-photographic
- Drawing
- Painting
- Lithograph
- Computer graphic

(Note that each of these are generally alternatives to one another – although all may be present in the text, they are not usually present in the same place at the same time in the text – so they are alternatives on the paradigmatic axis.) In relation to each of the categories above the following choices may also exist:

- Colour
- Black and white
- Specially shot
- Obtained from an archive or family collection
- Professional
- Newsreel
- Ethnographic and 'scientific' footage
- Advertising
- Home movie/video
- Letters
- Official documents
- Personal documents
- Photos
- Paintings, drawings, lithographs
- Objects
- People

(Again each of these is an alternative on the paradigmatic axis. The text will consist of a syntagmatic arrangement of elements from this list, each item on the list being a paradigmatic choice. Every point in the text is at the intersection of the resulting sequence, and a choice which has been made over alternative means of representation. At any point, part of the 'meaning' of any individual shot, is the alternative which has been foregone. It is in this sense that the paradigmatic axis is also about absence.)

What form does the image take?

- Drama
- Interviews
- Is the interviewer seen/identified?
- Are the questions heard, or cut out?
- Graphic elements
- Titles
- Intertitles
- Subtitles
- Animation
- Transition effects (wipes, dissolves, etc.)

(Syntagmatically the text can use several of these elements at once – for example, a title can be superimposed upon a still photograph, or a moving image.

Because an image is organized spatially (in space), in this case the syntagm is about spatial arrangement of elements in the resulting image, as well as about the sequential arrangement of images one after the other (a form of temporal organization). Every televisual text is organized both spatially and temporally. The choice to use titles or not to use titles, and to use one font rather than another in titles, are both choices made on the paradigmatic axis. In doing textual analysis these choices are 'meaningful' – all the elements in the image are signs).

Formal qualities of the image:

- Film
- Film stock (different film stocks have different properties, which produce differences in the resulting image. These differences are meaningful – they produce potential meanings. For example, an image might seem 'warmer' or 'colder', might seem 'old fashioned', 'impersonal' or 'personal' depending on the stock used.
- Video
- Lighting
- Composition/camera angle
- Use of colour, line, shape
- Texture

What can be heard?

- Speech
  - Dialogue
  - Voice-over
  - By a character from the narrative (diegetic)
  - By a voice from beyond the narrative (non-diegetic)
  - Is this voice identified?
  - Is it a 'voice of god' (never identified)?
- Music
  - From within the action (diegetic)
  - Non-diegetic
- Sound effects
  - Diegetic
  - Non-diegetic

How is it all organized?

- What is the relationship of sound to image?
- What is the relationship of image to image?
- Look for patterns in the text
- Narrative events
- Sound elements
- Pace and rhythm (created through editing)

(Continued)

- Repetition and variation
- Shots and motifs (key repeated images and sounds)
- Sequences
- Narrative events
- Sound elements
- Comparison and contrast
- Shots and motifs (key repeated images)
- Sequences

- Elements of unity and disunity/ coherence and incoherence
- Structural choices
- Narrative organization
- Linear?
- Use of flashback
- Closure
- Changes of perspective/ voice/addressee
- How is the text structured?/ What are the main structuring devices? for example, narrative/argument.

How do all these elements:

- Create point of view?
- Position the audience/create a mode of audience address?
- What is the effect of all these elements?
- Identification and involvement.
- Distancing.

All of the elements detailed in Box 11.1 (which an indicative, not an exhaustive, list) can be used to do a close analysis of a small segment of the programme, or to search for patterns throughout the programme. You will not seek to do a complete listing of all elements, but will choose from this list to attend to those elements which suit your purpose; those which will assist you in answering the question you have asked about the programme. If you wish to examine larger structures in the text there are a number of ways you can proceed.

Narrative structure: All of the elements in Box 11.1 can be seen to operate in a particular documentary at the intersection of the syntagmatic and paradigmatic axes. The various signs which make up a television programme can be organized in a number of ways. Two possibilities are argument and narrative. Documentaries construct arguments about the world. They may do so explicitly using a series of claims which are supported by various forms of evidence, or they may do so more implicitly using narrative (as does *Big Al*). Frequently the argument moves along by means of a narrative. A narrative and/or an argument will be built up using a combination, in sequence, of shots and sounds. The audience is invited to 'read' each event shown by comparing it to other events as the narrative progresses – and narrative is a form of syntagm.

Content analysis often uses detailed 'coding sheets' on which instances of categories being counted are listed, but I do not know of a standard way of 'coding' a text in qualitative approaches to textual analysis. However, one way of trying to record notes for a semiotic analysis is by means of a shot list, (Bertrand and Hughes, 2005: 206) using a layout similar to that used in post-production scripts, as outlined in Box 11.2. Such a (tran)script is one way of visualizing the syntagmatic structure, but in doing so I am constructing a different 'text', different in significant ways from the TV programme I am studying.

Box 11.2   Shotlist for *Big AL*

I have been arguing throughout this chapter that several methods of textual analysis (including semiotics, discourse analysis and narratology) all seek out the patterns evident in the text. The purpose, and benefit, of this shotlist is that it makes it possible to see patterns that might otherwise escape the attention of the textual analyst. The result is something close to a 'post-production' script which is often used in the post-production and marketing stages of documentary production.

The layout of the script makes it easier to see the relationships between:

- image;
- sound;
- music; and
- narration.

All of which have a syntagmatic relationship to one another. It you are able to do so you can supplement this with a 'story board' (like a comic strip) which might remind you of the image on screen at any given moment. All of these elements can assist you in 'freezing' the text long enough for some analysis, but it should be remembered that in creating this shotlist and story board you are constructing another text, and in doing so you are already involved in processes of interpretation.

To create the shotlist I used a DVD version of the program, playing on my computer. Using the DVD player software on the computer I was able to pause the DVD, step backwards and forwards or scan at slow speed backwards and forwards. I entered my notes into a spreadsheet which I then printed off and was able to scribble notes onto.

(Continued)

Shotlist – *The Ballad of Big Al*					
Time codes	Visuals	Music	Sound effects	Voice	Comments
0.00	horizon, sun begins to rise, caption centre screen just below mid point} 'BBC' (overall colour cast: red/orange)	music begins			Series of shots containing 'ghostly' images of various types of dinosaurs
0.03	dissolve to longer shot of sun, framed by pine trees, swirling mists (red/orange)				
0.06	super of stegosaurus spine walking screen right to left (red/orange)	drum roll			
0.08	dissolve swimming dinosaur swims toward camera then toward top left of screen (overall colour cast: blue)	rising			
0.10	Spikey tail structure walking R to L against forest. Tail spans frame parallel to horizon (green)				
0.13	Forest, large tree in centre frame backlit by strong light, dinosaur enters frame head in foreground, walks L to R (yellow)				

Shotlist – The ballad of *Big Al* (Continued)

Time codes	Visuals	Music	Sound effects	Voice	Comments
0.16	Forest, horizon slopes L to R dinos flying toward camera, L to R slightly (blue)	rising urgency			
0.18	Head of dino rises into frame centre from below frame, moves to upper screen L (blue)				
0.19	screen roughly split mainly black with large yellow area on right. Dino flies from yellow into black				
0.20	purple sky for about one third of screen. Left hand black. Clouds moving quickly L to R. Lightning in sky				
0.21	'ghost' image of dino enters frame from right, fills one third of frame, snarls	continues to rise			
0.23	Supered title: Walking with / DINOSAURS Dino head pulls back out of screen R	Crescendo			Oblique = line break in caption
0.25	Word SPECIAL added to super title. Background fades to black. Sky stormy		thunder rolls		on third line

Shotlist – The ballad of *Big Al* (Continued)

Time codes	Visuals	Music	Sound effects	Voice	Comments
0. 28	Background image dissolves to interior of museum. Title begins to fade. Night. Dino skeleton diagonally across frame R to L with head in lower LH corner		thunder fades		
0.32	Caption gone. Movement at centre screen – lit office in museum	fades out			
0.33	Cut to head of skeleton framed from below. Lightning flashes light interior at night				
0.34	Camera slowly tracks right along skeleton from approx human head level	quiet back ground music		All that we have left today of the mighty dinosaurs are their long dead bones.	
0.40	Tracking continues			It is easy to forget that these were once living animals.	
0.43	Lightning flash on cut to shot of underside of belly of large dinosaur walking R to L, approx ten frames. Ends with flash		crash of lightning, dino roars		(Shots from later in the program of hunting sequence)
0.44	Track along skeleton in museum continues			Surviving in a world of unimaginable violence	

Shotlist – The ballad of *Big Al* (Continued)

Time codes	Visuals	Music	Sound effects	Voice	Comments
0.48	Flash. Cut to dino in 'flight' from predator screen R to L. approx ten frames, flash				
0.52	Tracking camera picks up speed, past head of one dino. (Flash cut: Dino hunting) Tail of second appears in frame. Tracks along skeleton			But if you know what you're looking for the signs of life are clear, as in this remarkable allosaurus skeleton, nicknamed 'Big	
1.00	Camera rests on head of dino on word 'Al'.	music reaches crescendo, fades		Al'	
1.02	Flash. Cut to 'alive' version of head in close up		growl		
1.03	Cut to skeleton head. Lightning flashes continue as if storm outside		sound effects of storm		
1.04	Cut to close up of rib cage of skeleton. Rack focus				
	Something moving beyond rib cage in background of shot			In fact there is just enough evidence	

Shotlist – The ballad of *Big Al* (Continued)					
Time codes	Visuals	Music	Sound effects	Voice	Comments
1.06	Cut to interior shot of museum. On screen left table with something on it lit. On screen right dino skeleton. Mid third of frame empty	music enters		to raise the	
1.16	'Ghost' of Al walks in to fill empty space	music swells		ghost of Big Al from his ancient grave.	
	Cut to different angle. Table screen L now in foreground				
1.19	'Al' walks out of frame to right			Bit by bit a story of how he might have lived can be pieced together.	
1.24	Cut to CU of items on table (rocks, moulds?)				
1.26	Slight shift in focus	music begins to fade		It's a story that started, like all dinosaurs	
1.30	Dissolve to egg. Fade up title: The Ballad of / Big Al			with an egg	Oblique = line break in caption
1.31	Camera begins to track left. Begin dissolve to shot of eggs as camera continues to track left	music out	croak		

On my copy of the script I make notes about what choices were actually made, and what appears on the screen, looking for patterns of repetition and difference. Are there visual patterns which are repeated? Are any narrative patterns established – events which are repeated? If so, any difference in the presentation of the event becomes significant. In making a choice, from a range of possibilities, about what image will follow an previous image, a director is making a choice on the paradigmatic axis. In *Big Al* the choices made are based on narrative conventions. In terms of narrative structure, *Big Al* is structured just like a fiction film (such as *Jurassic Park* (Spielberg, USA, 1993) to which the series *Walking with Dinosaurs* has been compared (Darley, 2003). Every choice is meaningful. This is not to say that we can know from the text itself what the director's intention was, although there is some assumption, when a claim is made that a documentary produces an argument about the world, that some form of agency is involved.

When beginning to examine the narrative structure of *Big Al*, the following structure emerges:

1. Title sequence
2. Framing narrative – the 'museum sequence'
3. The short life of *Big Al*
4. Return to framing narrative
5. End titles

It would be quite possible to make section three the whole program – the framing device could conceivably be eliminated, so the choice to include it is significant. The audience is invited to read the main narrative in the context of this framing narrative. So what potential meanings is the framing narrative setting up? These are to do with the nature of scientific discovery and scientific argument – in other words to do with scientific discourse. Several articles about the original series deal specifically with the issue of the representation of scientific discourse (Benton, 2001; Darley, 2003; Richards, 2001; Scott and White, 2003). I am suggesting that an analysis of this type makes it possible to sustain such arguments with textual evidence.

By far the longest section is section three. This can be further divided into sections, each of which is preceded by a title which introduces the next part of the narrative:

- The Ballad of Big Al
- Wyoming – 145 million years ago
- Al's second year
- Al's fifth year
- Al's sixth year

In making these comments my method is to compare an individual section of the overall syntagm of the documentary to other moments in the syntagm. I look for moments which seem similar and moments which are different. The existence of such repetitions means that any variations become significant, not because they have an inherent meaning, but because they are part of a system of similarities and difference.

Having found such a pattern I look to some very specific instances in the documentary to see if, at a detailed level, the pattern holds up. One way to do this is to examine a single shot in the documentary. An assumption being made here is the semiotic assumption that the text is a unified whole (a point challenged by poststructuralism, but that comes later in time and in theory).

Conclusion

The field of textual analysis is broad and encompasses a range of methodologies, each of which is, in turn, based upon a particular intellectual framework by which the nature of the world itself is understood and by which ways of knowing about the world are also understood. Definitions of what constitutes a text, and methodologies for analyzing texts are highly controversial. Some fields of study consider empirically-based methods to be more reliable (or perhaps the only reliable methods) and favour quantitative approaches which seek to produce numerical data about texts. Other fields of study, such as cultural studies, place emphasis on qualitative methods of analysis drawing on structuralist or constructivist conceptions of the processes of meaning-making. While this view of textuality is dominant in media and cultural studies, in some areas of the social sciences (particularly in behavioural science) this view of text is still anathema. Within media and cultural studies, debates are still ongoing about the extent to which meaning can be determined by texts, and the extent to which individual texts can be seen as autonomous, as opposed to being embedded within networks of intertextuality.

There are a number of areas not covered in this discussion, perhaps the most pressing of which is this concept of intertextuality, an issue in poststructuralist approaches to text and to discourse.

One of the main concerns in the material in this chapter has been to find some way of understanding the text which does not merely reduce it to verbal discourse, but which takes proper note of all the textual features of an audio visual text.

I have tried to detail some approaches to textual analysis, but it is up to you to develop an argument about the individual text under study and to use appropriate methods of analysis to develop a sound understanding of the text and to support your argument.

Summary

It would take a lot more space than is available in this chapter do complete a detailed analysis of *The Ballad of Big Al*, and there are a number of articles which provide analysis of the original series to which this is a sequel. Instead, this chapter has tried to:

- provide an argument for the use of constructivist and structuralist approaches to textual analysis in social science studies of the media;
- provide an argument for detailed attention to the text itself in undertaking such an analysis; and
- provide some indication of methods that a student could use to undertake a detailed analysis of the text.

GOING FURTHER

Aldridge, M. and R. Dingwall (2003) 'Teleology on Television: Implicit Models of Evolution in Broadcast Wildlife and Nature Programmes', *European Journal of Communication*. 18(4): 435-53.

A growing literature examines the social contexts of scientific discourse, and the place of natural history programming in such discourse. This article argues that natural history programming often uses language which implicitly supports an argument for a notion of design behind evolution.

Barthes, R. (1974) *S/Z*. New York: Hill and Wang.

Barthes, R. and S. Heath (1977) *Image, Music, Text*. Fontana communications series. London: Fontana.

Barthes' work has been very influential in media semiotics and narratology. His concept of 'anchoring' has been useful in understanding the relationship between, for example, captions and photography. Any serious student of textual analysis should read Barthes's work.

Battye, G. (1996) 'The Death Of Photography Revisited'. *Metro* 105: 43-50.

Battye argues that a common theme in critical writing about photography for over 100 years has been a claim that the death of photography is imminent. Digital imaging technologies have sparked similar claims, which although unfounded, do point to the need to read photographs as discourse.

Bertrand, I. and Hughes, P. (2005) *Media Research Methods: Institutions, Texts, Audiences*. Basingstoke, New York: Palgrave.

A textbook on various methods of media research. Roughly one third of the book examines ways of researching media texts, providing an introduction to the historical use of each methodology, the philosophical underpinnings of each philosophy, and practical suggestions on undertaking your own research.

Bignell, J. (2002). *Media Semiotics: An Introduction*. (2nd edn.) Manchester: Manchester University Press.

A very useful introduction to the theory of semiotics and the practical application of semiotics to media analysis. Includes useful work on television news.

Bousâe, D. (2000) *Wildlife Films*. Philadelphia: University of Pennsylvania Press.

A key recent text in the discussion of wildlife, or natural history, programming.

British Broadcasting Corporation (2006) 'Walking with Dinosaurs', *Science and Nature: Prehistoric Life*. Available from: http://www.bbc.co.uk/sn/prehistoric_life/tv_radio/wwdinosaurs/. [Accessed 6 February 2006].

It is becoming common practice to provide a website to accompany television programming, as a means of developing audience, engaging particular demographic segments, and constructing particular viewing positions from which to understand individual documentaries. Such sites become an important aspect of the 'discursive ecology' of individual texts. For the researcher they can provide useful background information on the production itself and provide clues about how potential ways of understanding the text are being suggested. This site is one such example, interesting for what it both does, and does not, say about the series that preceded *Big Al*. One aspect of the intertextuality of *Big Al*.

Chandler, D. (2003) *Semiotics: The Basics*. London: Routledge.

Chandler has a website which students find very useful, containing some very detailed work on semiotics. This book developed from that website and provides a very comprehensive introduction to semiotics, based on years of refining teaching materials in the field.

Cottle, S. (2004) 'Producing Nature(s): On The Changing Production Ecology Of Natural History TV', *Media, Culture and Society*. 26(1): 81-101.

One of the many articles in recent years that has examined natural history, or wildlife, programming on television. Cottle is particularly interested in the political economy or institutional functions of such programming.

Darley, A. (2003) 'Simulating Natural History: Walking With Dinosaurs As Hyper-Real Entertainment', *Science as Culture*. 12(2).

Darley argues that the work on simulation of Jean Baudrillard, and Fredrick Jameson's work on pastiche, provide a useful way of understanding the series as a simulation of wildlife documentary.

Delofski, M. (1995) 'Beastly Stories' *Metro* 104: 14-19.

Through the discussion of one example *(Kangaroos: Faces in the* Mob (Aldenhoven and Carruthers, Australia, 1994), Delovski examines the anthropomorphism and sexual politics of one natural history documentary. It is possible to undertake a reading of *Big Al* also in terms of its sexual politics and anthropomorphism (tendency to understand animals as if they were humans).

Fairclough, N. (1995) *Critical Discourse Analysis : The Critical Study Of Language*, Language in social life series. London & New York: Longman.

Fairclough is one of the most important theorists in the field of Critical Discourse Analysis.

Freeman, A. (n.d.) 'The Ballad of *Big Al*', *Science and Nature: Prehistoric Life*. Available from: http://www.bbc.co.uk/sn/prehistoric_life/tv_radio/big_al/big_al1.shtml. [Accessed 6 February 2006].

Another part of the BBC's contextual website. Most of this material was also 'repurposed' for use in Australia by the Australian Broadcasting Corporation.

Hall, S. (1984) 'Encoding/decoding' in S. Hall, D. Hobson, A. Lowe and P. Willis (eds), *Culture, Media, Language*. London: Hutchinson/Centre for Contemporary Cultural Studies. (Republished in S. During (ed.) (2003) *The Cultural Studies Reader*. London: Routledge. pp. 508-17).

An important essay, available in a variety of sources, which introduced the notion of 'preferred readings' of texts and alternative ways of reading texts. Hall begins his discussion with a some useful comments on the linear model of communication.

Hoffman, K. (1998) '"I see, if I believe it" — Documentary And The Digital', in T. Elsaesser and K. Hoffman (eds), *Cinema Futures: Cain, Abel or Cable?* Amsterdam: Amsterdam University Press. pp. 159-166.

One of a number of useful introductions to some of the issues for cinema and media students by digital imaging technologies.

Hughes, P. (1998) 'Putting The Audience In Its Place'. in J. Doyle, B. van der Heide and S. Cowan (eds) *Our Selection On: Writings On Cinemas' Histories* Campbell. ACT: NFSA/ADFA. pp. 119-32.

An examination of different strategies by which broadcasters seek to shape and constrain audience responses to television texts.

Hughes, P. (2006) '*AFTER MABO*' in G. Mayer and K. Beattie (eds) *24 Frames: The Cinema of Australia*. London: Wallflower.

Argues that, in relation to John Hughes' documentary *After Mabo,* painting is an appropriate metaphor which opens up a reading of the documentary as a critique of processes of media representation.

Kilborn, R. (2006) 'A Walk On The Wild Side: The Changing Face Of TV Wildlife Documentary', *Jump Cut* 48. Available from: http://www.ejumpcutorg/currentissue/AnimalTV/text.html [Accessed 15 March 2006].

A useful survey of debates around natural history programming, particularly in the context of current trends in 'Reality TV' programming.

Kress, G. (2001) 'From Saussure to Critical Sociolinguistics: the Turn Towards a Social View of Language' in M. Wetherell, S. Taylor and S. J. Yates (eds) *Discourse Theory and Practice*. London: Sage. pp. 29-38.

Although more advanced than some of the other texts on this list, this is a theoretically informed introduction to discourse analysis.

McKee, A. (2003) *Textual Analysis: A Beginner's Guide*. London: Sage.

A clear argument about poststructuralist approaches to textual analysis. It does lack detail, however, on how to actually undertake such analysis.

Mitchell, W.J. (1998) *The Reconfigured Eye: Visual Truth In The Post Photographic Era*. London: MIT Press.

A key text on digital imaging and its impact on culture.

O'Connor, B. and Klaus, E. (2000) 'Pleasure and Meaningful Discourse: An Overview Of Research Issues', *International Journal Of Cultural Studies*. 3(3) 369-87.

A bibliographic essay on debates around the merits of approaches to media which focus on ideology, or on the role of pleasure.

Philo, G. and Henderson, L. (1998) *What The Audience Thinks: Focus Group Research Into The Likes and Dislikes Of UK Wildlife Viewers*. A report by the Glasgow media group, commissioned by Wildscreen.

An empirical study of audience responses to wildlife programming.

Rankin, Aubree (n.d.) 'Reality TV: Race To The Bottom. A Content Analysis Of Prime Time Broadcast Reality Series', *Parents Television Council*. Available from: http://www.parentstv.org/ptc/publications/reports/realitytv2/main.asp [Accessed 7 December 2004].

An example of content analysis being used for polemical purposes. Only cited as an example of a case where content analysis is used when the researcher has a strong dislike or objection to a text or series of texts. The site makes a claim to be using 'scientific methods' of textual analysis to prove its case that 'Reality TV' shows are offensive and have a negative influence on young members of the audience.

Richards, M. (2001) 'Digitising Dinosaurs', *Media International Australia (incorporating Culture and Society)* 100: 65-79.

Scott, K. D. and White, A. M. (2003) 'Unnatural history? Deconstructing the Walking with Dinosaurs phenomenon', *Media Culture and Society*. 25: 315-32.

Like the previous citation this article examines the role of digital imaging and media in scientific discourses.

Seiter, E. (1994) 'Semiotics, Structuralism, And Television' in R. C. Allen (ed.) *Channels of Discourse, Reassembled*. London: Routledge. pp. 31-66.

Another introduction to key concepts in semiotics as applied to the study of television - in this case television drama.

Shannon, C. and Weaver, W. (1949) *A Mathematical Theory of Communication*. Urbana: University of Illinois Press.

Has historical importance as an early, key text in communication studies. Proposes a linear model of communication in which it is assumed that communication transmits pre-existing information from encoder to decoder through media (a realist framework). Although considerably modified over the years, it has been used as the philosophical framework for much media effects research.

Wood, B. (2004) 'A world in retreat: the reconfiguration of hybridity in 20th-century New Zealand television', *Media Culture and Society*. 26(1): 45-62.

A useful discussion of the role of hybrid forms of non-fiction in contemporary television. The argument deals specifically with the New Zealand situation and is supported by a content analysis, but some of the general comments are applicable in many other locations.

Winston, B. (1995) *Claiming the Real*. London: BFI.

Winston is one of the more important writers on documentary and this book examines many of the claims that have been made about documentary, including claims to be able to observe the world from a 'scientific' perspective.

STUDENT ACTIVITIES 11.1

The following are some suggestions for work that students, in groups or individually, could undertake to extend their understanding of ideas being developed in this chapter.

1. As indicated above, it is common practice to take a small section of a text and do a detailed analysis of that section to enlighten an understanding of the text as a whole. This might be a section as small as one shot, or a short sequence.

   Take a single shot of a program (you can freeze frame it on the VCR/DVD player or capture it on a computer) and undertake a detailed analysis of it. You can begin with Box 11.1 and make detailed notes on all that is in the shot and the relations (syntagmatic and paradigmatic) between various elements in the shot. Develop a 'hunch' about what you think the program is about and then use this analysis of a single frame to test this hunch. Does your analysis provide support for your reading of the text as a whole?

   Alternatively, or as an extension to this, you can then undertake an analysis of a sequence of the programme. Find a sequence which seems likely to provide evidence to test your claims about the programme. Do a semiotic analysis of the sequence examining the syntagmatic structure of the sequence and then consider the paradigmatic choices that were made. Then look at larger structures. Does the sequence have a narrative structure? How is this developed? Who are the main players in the narrative? What are the main elements in the narrative? How does the narrative fit into the overall structure of the programme?

2. A syntagmatic relationship exists between the visuals in a TV programme and the audio elements – narration, dialogue, sound effects and music. Sometimes these elements work to support one another, in which case they may work to 'anchor' meaning (to use a concept developed by Roland Barthes), sometimes they may work to challenge the image in some way. Your task here is to do a detailed study of the music in *Big Al*. What type of music is used? When is music used and when is it not used? What patterns seem to emerge here? How can you systematically study the music in a program such as this?

3. Continuing with the study of 'anchoring' in the text, examine the use of narration in *Big Al* (make sure you understand the difference between narration and the larger concept of narrative). The narration can be examined from several points of view: it is a verbal text so you can undertake a linguistic analysis of it.

   How does it serve as an 'anchor' for the images, suggesting certain ways of understanding them ('preferred readings'). Note the fact that most of the narration is in the present tense, suggesting an imperative rather than conditional understanding of the on-screen events ('This is what happened' rather than 'scientists, on the basis of the following evidence, speculate that this may be what happened').

You can also analyze the narration as a performance (by famous actor Kenneth Branagh). How might the performance support your linguistic analysis of the narration, or challenge it?

Do linguistic or performance features of the narration work to establish a sense of familiarity, possibly of anthropomorphism (the tendency to understand animal behaviour as if it were human behaviour)? What evidence can you provide, using a systematic analysis of the text, for your claim?

4. This chapter has concentrated on the text itself. A more extensive analysis might examine its intertextual relations. Intertextuality can be understood in two related ways – sometimes texts are embedded in relations with other texts. This can happen, for example, when a programme makes a deliberate reference to another. 'Collateral texts' (such as publicity materials, including websites) and 'contiguous texts' (such as those 'adjacent' to the text in the broadcast schedule (Hughes, 1998)) may influence audience readings, which raises the second major understanding of intertexuality in which the audience makes connections between one text and others and understands it in terms of such connections. It is possible, for example, to read the *Walking with Dinosaurs* series in intertextual relationship with a range of other wildlife documentaries on the one hand, or with fiction on the other, such as *Jurassic Park*.

(In Australia in 2006 there was a TV ad campaign for red meat, starring Sam Neil, which can be read as a parody of a David Attenborough performance, but has a degree of menace which might link it to *Jurassic Park*.)

To undertake such an analysis you will need to do careful and systematic analysis of each text to be able to justify your claims, and you will need to be very careful not to make claims about audience behaviour, as such claims cannot be supported by textual analysis, but must be supported by audience research.

Your task here is to map some possible intertextual relations between *Big Al* and other texts.

References

ABC Shop, (2006) *Walking with Dinosaurs – Ballad of Big Al*. Available from: http://shop.abc.net.au/browse/product.asp?productid=714212 [Accessed 2 February 2006].

Aldridge, M. and R. Dingwall (2003) 'Teleology on Television: Implicit Models of Evolution in Broadcast Wildlife and Nature Programmes', *European Journal of Communication*. 18(4): 435–53.

Answers in Genesis, (16 April 2000) 'Walking with … untruths!' *Answers in Genesis*. Available from: http://www.answersingenesis.org/docs2/4276news4-15-2000.asp [Accessed 6 February 2006].

Barthes, R. (1974) *S/Z*. New York: Hill and Wang.

Barthes, R. and S. Heath (1977) *Image, Music, Text*. Fontana communications series. London: Fontana.

Battye, G. (1996) 'The Death Of Photography Revisited', *Metro* 105: 43–50.

Benton, M. J. (2001) 'The Science of 'Walking with Dinosaurs', *Teaching Earth Sciences*. Available from: http://paleo.gly.bris.ac.uk/Essays/WWD/default.html.

Bertrand, I. and P. Hughes (2005) *Media Research Methods: Institutions, Texts, Audiences*. Basingstoke, New York: Palgrave.

Bignell, J. (2002) *Media Semiotics: An Introduction*. (2nd edn.) Manchester: Manchester University Press.

Bondebjerg, I. (1996) 'Public discourse/private fascination: hybridization in "true-life-story" genres', *Media, Culture and Society*. 18: 27–45.

Bousâe, D. (2000) *Wildlife Films*. Philadelphia: University of Pennsylvania Press.

British Broadcasting Corporation (2006) 'Walking with Dinosaurs', *Science and Nature: Prehistoric Life*. Available from: http://www.bbc.co.uk/sn/prehistoric_life/tv_radio/wwdinosaurs/. [Accessed 6 February 2006].

Butler, J. G. (2002) *Television: Critical Methods And Applications*. (2nd edn.) LEA's communication series. Mahwah, N.J.: Lawrence Erlbaum Associates.

Chandler, D. (2003) *Semiotics: The Basics*. London: Routledge.

Chris, C. (2006) *Watching Wildlife*. Minneapolis: University of Minnesota Press.

Cottle, S. (2004) 'Producing Nature(s): On The Changing Production Ecology Of Natural History TV', *Media, Culture and Society*. 26(1): 81–101.

Darley, A. (2003) 'Simulating Natural History: Walking With Dinosaurs As Hyper-Real Entertainment', *Science as Culture*. 12(2).

Delofski, M. (1995) 'Beastly Stories', *Metro* 104: 14–19.

Fairclough, N. (1995) *Critical Discourse Analysis: The Critical Study Of Language*. Language in social life series. London & New York: Longman.

Freeman, A. (n.d.) 'The Ballad of Big Al', *Science and Nature: Prehistoric Life*. Available from: http://www.bbc.co.uk/sn/prehistoric_life/tv_radio/big_al/big_al1.shtml. [Accessed 6 February 2006].

Gripsrud, J. (2002) 'Semiotics: Signs, Codes and Cultures' in J. Gripsrud (ed.) *Understanding Media Culture*. London: Edward Arnold. pp. 99–127.

Hall, S. (1984) 'Encoding/decoding' in S. Hall, D. Hobson, A. Lowe and P. Willis (eds), *Culture, Media, Language*. London: Hutchinson/Centre for Contemporary Cultural Studies. (Republished in S. During (ed.) (2003) *The Cultural Studies Reader*. London: Routledge. pp. 508–17).

Hoffman, K. (1998) "'I see, if I believe it'', — Documentary And The Digital', in T. Elsaesser and K. Hoffman (eds) *Cinema Futures: Cain, Abel or Cable?* Amsterdam: Amsterdam University Press. pp. 159–166.

Hughes, P. (1998) 'Putting The Audience In Its Place'. in J. Doyle, B. van der Heide and S. Cowan (eds) *Our Selection On: Writings On Cinemas' Histories.* Campbell, ACT: NFSA/ADFA. pp. 119–32.

Hughes, P. (2006) '*AFTER MABO*' in G. Mayer and K. Beattie (eds) *24 Frames: The Cinema of Australia.* London: Wallflower.

Kilborn, R. (20060 'A Walk On The Wild Side: The Changing Face Of TV Wildlife Documentary', *Jump Cut* 48. Available from: http://www.ejumpcutorg/currentissue/AnimalTV/text.html [Accessed 15 March 2006].

Kress, G. (2001) 'From Saussure to Critical Sociolinguistics: the Turn Towards a Social View of Language' in M. Wetherell, S. Taylor and S. J. Yates (eds) *Discourse Theory and Practice.* London: Sage. pp. 29–38.

Lewontin, R. C. (2005) 'The Wars Over Evolution', *The New York Review of Books*, 52(16). Online version available from: http://www.nybooks.com/articles/18363 [Accessed 25 October 2005].

Philo, G. and Henderson, L. (1998) *What The Audience Thinks: Focus Group Research Into The Likes and Dislikes Of UK Wildlife Viewers.* A report by the Glasgow media group, commissioned by Wildscreen.

McKee, A. (2003) *Textual Analysis: A Beginner's Guide.* London: Sage.

Mitchell, W.J. (1998) *The Reconfigured Eye: Visual Truth In The Post Photographic Era.* London: MIT Press.

O'Connor, B. and Klaus, E. (2000) 'Pleasure and Meaningful Discourse: An Overview Of Research Issues', *International Journal Of Cultural Studies.* 3(3) 369–87.

Rankin, Aubree need date 'Reality TV: Race To The Bottom. A Content Analysis Of Prime Time Broadcast Reality Series', *Parents Television Council.* Available from: http://www.parentstv.org/ptc/publications/reports/realitytv2/main.asp [Accessed 7 December 2004].

Richards, M. (2001) 'Digitising Dinosaurs', *Media International Australia (incorporating Culture and Society).* 100: 65–79.

Roscoe, J. 2001. 'Real Entertainment: New Factual Hybrid Television in New Television Formats', *Media International Australia.* 100: 9–20.

Scott, K. D. and A.M. White (2003) 'Unnatural history? Deconstructing the Walking with Dinosaurs phenomenon', *Media Culture and Society.* 25: 315–32.

Seiter, E. (1994) 'Semiotics, Structuralism, And Television' in R. C. Allen (ed.) *Channels of Discourse, Reassembled.* London: Routledge. pp. 31–66.

Shannon, C. and W. Weaver (1949) *A Mathematical Theory of Communication.* Urbana: University of Illinois Press.

Wood, B. (2004) 'A world in retreat: the reconfiguration of hybridity in 20th-century New Zealand television', *Media Culture and Society*. 26(1): 45–62.

Winston, B. (1995) *Claiming the Real*. London: BFI.

Notes

1 An example of this might be research begun in 2004 by an international group headed by Martin Barker from the University of Aberystwyth which examines audience responses to the final film in the *Lord of the Rings* series.

2 For the 'working out' metaphor I am grateful to my colleague, Dinah Partridge.

Analyzing Fictional Television Genres

12

Kim Akass and Janet McCabe

DEFINITIONS

Genre: is a French word meaning 'type' or 'kind'.

Structuralism: a method of deconstructing the text to understand how its underlying structures work to convey meaning.

Poststructuralism: a means of identifying ambiguity and multiple interpretations produced by the text, to suggest that no definitive meaning is possible.

Introduction

Genre has long been used in literary and later film criticism before its adoption in television studies in the 1970s (Newcombe, 1976). Analyzing generic forms proved one of the earliest methods used to identify texts possessing shared properties and norms, from visual features and narrative tropes to setting and character, as well as differences between groupings. Of such a theoretical endeavour, Feuer describes, 'Genre theory has the task both of making ... divisions and of justifying the classifications once they have been made' (1992: 138). But genre is more than rhetorical categories notes Neale: it instead involves coherent 'systems of orientations, expectations, and conventions that circulate between industry, text and the subject' (1980: 20). Any one genre is a system based on perceived similarities and differences and on a set of expectations and assumptions shared by the reader/viewer.

When talking about TV genre, what emerges is a notoriously contentious and hard to define concept. Turner outlines key problems involved in studying genre and television as 'conditioned not just by the formats and forms of television itself but also by the history of genre as a concept, the uses to which it has been put, and the other art and media forms to which it has been applied' (Creeber, 2003: 3). 'Radio, film, written fiction, theatre, journalism, music and other art and media forms have all played an important part in television and its history' (Creeber, 2003: 3), and for Turner these influences are further complicated by the 'ways in which genre has figured in these forms, and in the theories and debates that have surrounded them, [which] has had an important effect on theories and debates about genre and television itself' (Creeber, 2001: 3).

A key issue is that of definition: How do we define genre? What in fact counts as a genre within a media aimed at the broadest constituency possible? How do we begin to apply generic groupings to programmes increasingly seen as examples of postmodern hybridisation? And how exactly does the television industry account for and use generic categories? Taking our examples from contemporary American television, this chapter identifies various theorizations of genre in television, focusing on major trends, approaches and critical methodologies as we attempt to address the question: How useful is it to study television in terms of genre?

Genre: origins and developments

Before looking at television genre – what it is and how it is used, it is important to first trace genre's intellectual and historical roots to give a sense of why and how particular methods are used, and to situate such thinking within broader intellectual traditions. Put simply, it is important to grasp how the different theories and approaches to genre used today not only evolved from previous work, belonging to much longer histories, but also must be situated within changing intellectual and industrial contexts.

The intellectual roots of genre can be traced back to 300BC and the Greek philosopher Aristotle, who identified some basic principles for understanding dramatic forms like comedy and tragedy. Literary theory owes an enormous debt to Aristotle's thinking, as it concentrated in the beginning on producing defining characteristics for particular genres based on historic usage. It took a structuralist approach, deconstructing the structural elements to find patterns and repeated motifs in how stories are told. Offering at least a provisional notion of what constitutes a genre, literary criticism provided the new field of television studies with an established approach to analyzing a text; but in adopting methodologies from a more reputable discipline, television studies enhanced its credibility in its bid for academic legitimacy.

Despite its initial usefulness, Feuer identifies a problem with how literary criticism defines certain generic forms as ideal, implying that meaning never changes but instead remains somehow static, timeless and universal. For a start, such an approach is blighted by the problem of justifying 'aesthetic and cultural *value*' (1992: 138) rather than merely applying theoretical and objective modes of classifying a text. She claims that taking generic category names from literature's 'ideal types' are far too broad to be successfully applied to television, insisting instead on the historically transitional and culturally ephemeral nature of the medium (1992: 139). To this end, she suggests that we need to search for more apposite ways of classifying television forms and formats, as in her view 'attempts to measure the ... forms of mass media against the norms of drama are doomed to failure' (1992: 140).

What can be concluded from these attempts to categorize a particular genre is the role played by the critic or theoretician. Feuer aptly summarizes the difficulties involved in such theoretical endeavours. 'The methodology that the analyst brings to bear upon the texts determines the way in which that analyst will construct the genre. Genres are made, not born. The coherence is provided in the process of construction, and a genre is ultimately an abstract concept rather than something that exists empirically in the world' (1992: 144).

Genre and the audience

Box 12.1   British cultural studies

British cultural studies is rooted in thinking developed at the Centre for Contemporary Cultural Studies at the University of Birmingham (established in 1964). Growing out of poststructuralist approaches to theorizing ideology (Althusserian Marxism, Lacanian psychoanalysis, Barthes and semiotics, Lévi-Strauss and myth), and combining theory with the political, cultural studies found new ways of thinking about how ideology produced meaning in, and constituted individuals as subjects within, cultural institutions, texts and practices.

(Continued)

Textual analysis combined with an acute awareness of the specific historical and socio-cultural context defines this inter-disciplinary methodology.

Anthropologist, Lévi-Strauss worked to understand rules governing kinship relationships as well as the function of myth within traditional (or 'primitive') societies. Stripping away the surface layer of myth led him to expose the contradictions at work in any given social structure.

Neale (2003) points out that generic norms and conventions may be recognized and mutually understood by the academy, but they are also familiar to and generally accepted by audiences, readers and viewers. Hans Jauss (1982) focuses on the 'horizons of expectation' aroused through genre; while Altman talks about the 'generic audience' as a way of defining those 'sufficiently familiar with the genre to participate in a fully genre-based viewing' (1996: 280). Genre frames audience expectations, whereby viewers bring a set of assumptions with them and anticipate that these will somehow be met in the viewing experience. Genre thus operates as 'an important means of communicating information about the television text to prospective audiences ... [through] its inscription in publicity, in the listings in the TV guide, in the repertoires of cultural knowledge around individual personalities and other intertextual experiences' (Turner in Hilmes, 2003: 5). But how to theorize this relationship between genre and the television audience would become a central concern for television studies.

Attempts made by scholars to theorize the audience profoundly shaped the television studies' agenda, and was made possible through a wider engagement with the burgeoning field of British cultural studies. Such discussions marked a broader shift away from the text as a fixed site of meaning, often associated with authorial intent, to a polysemic one open to multiple interpretations. Here the text only has meaning in the act of reading. Much of the ethnographic work trained attention on television viewing pleasures and consumption, and aimed to understand the context in which a text was produced and consumed. Genre as a popular cultural form played a key role here. Given that British cultural studies was rooted in a post-Marxist concern with the subversive capabilities of cultural practices and reclaiming the experience of those not normally represented (working class, women, ethnic minorities) and given that genre had long been a derided form associated with mass production, commercialization and being formulaic; it seemed the perfect form for re-evaluation.

Feminist scholars in particular looked to genre to question gendered pleasures, television consumption and the interplay between reality and fiction. Modleski (1979; 1983), for example, sought to understand the relationship between daytime television soap opera and women's everyday lives. Reclaiming a generic form previously dismissed as trivial, her analysis identifies the rhythms of television as similar to those of domestic labour. Patterns of distraction and disruption are replicated within the episodic, multi-linear narrative form of soap opera she argues. Ang's 1985 ethnographic study of Dutch viewers watching American top-rated soap opera *Dallas* offers an alternative interpretation of the text-reader relationship, defining it as active, critical and selective. Such work has led the way for further studies that combine an understanding of audience pleasures with genre analysis: Stempel Mumford (1995) interrogates her own pleasures for the soap genre that displays various oppressive tendencies like racism, class-ism and hetero-sexism; while Spence's multi–disciplinary study (2005) examines the varied critical and creative ways in which women viewers use soap operas in their lives.

Genre and the industry

So far discussion has focused on theoretical concepts and audiences, and the interplay between generic structure and readership is often far removed from how the institution of television uses generic forms and formats within its commercial practices. Genre, in fact, guides industrial procedures – how it organizes itself, how it appeals to viewers and how commercial stations deliver audiences to advertisers. Turner contends that genre 'is a means of managing TVs notorious extensiveness as a cultural form' (Creeber, 2001: 5). Developing this idea further, genre not only contributes to understanding how individual texts are classified and produced but also works within the schedules. 'Critics have argued that perhaps the unit of coherence for television is found at a level larger than the program and different from the genre' argues Feuer (1992: 157). So, for example, all possible generic programmes are pitted against each other to match competition, where a comedy may be pitched against a drama on a different channel. Combinations of programmes can be sampled within the same schedule, as with NBC's Thursday night 'must see-TV' line-up or HBO's Sunday evening showcasing of its original programming.

Key to limiting risk when scheduling diverse programmes finds the broadcasting companies depending on generic forms and formats, building on proven formulas to predict future success and launch new programmes. Genre also enables the production teams working on particular series to produce them quickly and more coherently.

Curtin (1995) describes three stages – innovation, imitation and saturation – characterizing the American networks' reliance on genre as they try to attract viewers through a strategy of 'least objectionable programming'. Mittell suggests that it may be overstating the case to identify innovation, as television innovation is less about originality than about recycling old formulas (Cited in Hilmes, 2003: 48). Even the beginnings of television reinterpreted an established cinematic genre like the western to draw audiences to the new medium. More recently, *Deadwood* (HBO, 2003–6) has referenced a longer history of filmic and televisual westerns to create a new, more gritty and profane form than ever before.

Feuer offers further insights on institutional uses of genre, suggesting that the advent of the remote control and multi-channel TV has resulted in a zap culture. This has led to programs being customized to attract an increasingly fragmented audience (1992: 157). But it also has further implications for transmission, whereby genre has increasingly become an important institutional indicator. Entire channels like Comedy Central, Paramount Comedy and Sci-Fi are devoted to particular genres; and the proliferation of cable and pay-TV has been structured around branding and marketing to niche audiences interested in generic types such as sports, lifestyle programming and documentaries.

Industrial dimensions expand generic categories beyond pure theoretical definitions. The demands of commercial practices necessitate that generic forms must somehow 'guarantee meaning and pleasure' in order to locate and retain a sizeable audience to justify a return on substantial investment. But, if as Neale says, 'As far as genre is concerned, expectations exist both to be satisfied, and, also, to be redefined' (1983: 54), then it follows that generic forms must necessarily develop and evolve to keep pace with audience interest. Consider the example of *House, M.D.* (NBC, 2004–present), it has rejuvenated the medical drama through invoking awareness of a rich generic legacy including *M*A*S*H* (CBS, 1972–83), *St Elsewhere* (NBC, 1982–8), *Chicago Hope* (CBS, 1994–2000) and *E.R.* (NBC, 1994–present), but also referencing the new aesthetic innovations associated with the ratings winning procedural dramas from the *Crime Scene Investigation* franchise – *CSI* (CBS, 2000–present), *CSI: Miami* (CBS, 2002–present) and *CSI: New York* (CBS, 2004–present).

Genre: contemporary redirections

Concepts of genre considered above identify the term as about 1) the structural analysis of the text; 2) the audience and how they interpret generic forms and formats; and 3) commercial practices and institutional demands. Taking these three concepts and adapting Altman's classification of socio-cultural theories of genre (1984; 1987; 1996; 1999), Feuer summarizes an approach to studying genre using three categories – the aesthetic, the ritual and the ideological. *'The aesthetic approach* includes all attempts to define genre in terms of a system of conventions that permits artistic expression, especially involving individual authorship … *The ritual approach* sees genre as an exchange between industry and audience, an exchange through which culture speaks to itself … [and] *The ideological approach* views genre as an instrument of control' (1992: 145). Emerging is a theory for studying TV genre that considers the complex and ever evolving interaction between criticism, historical and cultural specificity, audience expectations and industrial demands.

Mittell's recent contribution to the debate has been to argue for genre as not only a theoretical tool but also a methodology. Key to his argument is the notion that analyzing any given genre must take into account 'specific issues and historical moments' as well as 'how genres work at the micro-level of media practice' (2004: xv). He makes the case for suggesting that studying genre is more than about identifying rhetorical similarities and differences, but instead concerns meticulous analysis into the various methods by which television is produced, consumed and theoretically studied.

Genre and hybridity

Box 12.2   Flexi-narrative

'*Flexi-narrative*' is a term identified by Nelson, which he defines as 'a hybrid mix of serial and series forms derived from a prose fiction, distinctive to the majority of TV output today. Flexi-narratives are mixtures of the series and serial form, involving the closure of one story arc within an episode (like a series) but with other, ongoing story arcs involving the regular characters (like a serial). This hybrid form maximizes the pleasures of both regular viewers who watch from week to week and get hooked by the serial narrative, and occasional viewers who happen to tune in into one episode seeking the satisfaction of narrative closure within that episode' (Creeber, 2006: 82).

In Feuer's opinion it is pointless to insist on generic purity in relation to television. Television genre and programming forms and formats are instead notoriously hybridized. Looking at contemporary TV drama, Nelson develops his concept of hybridity in relation to *intertextuality*, 'flexi-narrative' and a media-savvy audience. Operating on several levels, television serials like *The Sopranos* (HBO, 1999–2007) defy easy genre classification. Instead the series mixes generic influences, cinematic and televisual, as well as building on audience knowledge of popular culture, and past media and generic forms. Audience pleasure comes from these intertextual references, in which the text works to assure those watching that they are viewing something that they will like; to make them 'feel superior because they know how this textual genre works and to add an element of playfulness ranging from spotting the allusions made through to a full *post-structuralist* awareness that textuality is all' (Creeber, 2006: 83).

The Case of *The Sopranos*

To illuminate the above we offer *The Sopranos* as a case study. Played out each week in the credit sequence is a meta-narrative that reinvents the gangster type for a media literate television audience. Iconographically Tony Soprano (James Galdofini) immediately codes a more recent generic past, from *The Godfather* (Francis Ford Coppola, 1972) to *Goodfellas* (Martin Scorsese, 1990), more violent, far bloodier than before. The centre of operations has shifted from the city to the hinterland, a place of transience, a no-man's land where bodies are dumped and no questions asked. Chomping a cigar, sporting chunky gold jewellery and a designer Polo shirt he inherits the mantle of the post-classical Hollywood hard man. His bulk never seems to fit the frame, signalling a character larger than life, but also how his authority works – often unseen but always potent. Set up here is a series of iconic conventions already known to an audience based on accumulated media knowledge. But such knowledge also provides an opportunity for disruption. As with the jittery camerawork and jump cut editing style which signals that the gangster's power might not be as assured as first imagined. Quite soon it reveals that our latter-day mobster is seeing a psychotherapist because he feels that his life is spinning out of control. Tony acknowledges his generic crisis early on when he tells Dr Jennifer Melfi (Lorraine Bracco), 'Lately I've been getting the feeling that I came in at the end. The best is over' ('Pilot', 1: 1). As Creeber stresses, 'Tony's depression is symptomatic of a character who unconsciously feels he exists at the wrong end of a long and illustrious tradition (literally in the form of the Mob and metaphorically in the form of the gangster genre)' (Lavery, 2002: 126). Of the self-reflexive referencing of past generic influences on *The Sopranos* he continues that it 'implicitly critiques the "televisionization" of the gangster genre – parodying its gradual development ... from cinematic epic to standard video or television fare' (Lavery, 2002: 125).

Looking further at the credit sequence gives us insight into how generic hybridity has gendered implications. Driving away from the city signals a departure from the traditional urban space where the gangster is most closely associated, a movement from a male generic space to the more female generic territory defined by the leafy New Jersey suburbs where the Soprano family live. It signals a series where the mobster finds himself in unfamiliar generic territory characterized by mundane chores and domestic worries, with women playing an important role in referencing the new generic spaces through which the Mafia don progresses. Long denied an authoritative voice within the self-contained cinematic world of male violence and defined action (Sacks, 1971: 9; Warshow, 1962), women subtly shape the serial arc. Using strategies associated with soap opera and family drama (Feuer, 1984; Seiter, 1982) – listening and confession, gossip and silence, talking-heads and inter-personal skills – women like Livia Soprano (Nancy Marchand) and Carmela Soprano (Edie Falco) may be constantly negotiating Tony to carve out authority for themselves within uncompromising (male) generic conventions and (patriarchal) narrative worlds that tell them they have none. But the feminising forms rejuvenate the filmic gangster genre brought to television.

Critics have long identified the difficulties involved in demarcating one generic form from another, yet the generic hybrid functions to exploit repetition and regulate difference in the same product around audience pleasures and industrial expediency.

Genre and the politics of representation

Box 12.3   Second-wave feminism, post-feminism and third wave feminism

Second-wave feminism, politically motivated, and identified with consciousness-raising women's groups, is interested in how ideology works to construct gender and the idea of woman as Other.

(Continued)

Post-feminism is a hotly contested term. One definition is that post-feminism speaks of the 1980s' right-wing media backlash against feminism and feminist activism; another sees feminism as no longer relevant, arguing that gender equality has been achieved; scholars like Lotz (2001) contest that academic post-feminist thought is marked by 'confusion and contradiction', partly due to changing theoretical contexts (second-wave feminism, post-feminism, third-wave feminism), partly because of competing labels (liberal feminism, radical feminism, cultural feminism), and partly because of confusion over terminology (one woman's feminism is not necessarily another's); and others such as Hollows (2000), and Moseley and Read (2002) understand post-feminist contradiction as about articulating the 'experiences of being female, feminist, and feminine in the late-twentieth and early-twenty-first centuries' (2002: 240).

Third Wave feminism – sometimes labelled post-feminism – is often described as a movement of young feminists who grew up with a sense of feminist entitlement, and who not only confront but positively embrace political and personal contradiction. Offering their definition, Heywood and Drake explain it as follows: 'Third wave feminists often take cultural production and sexual politics as key sites of struggle, seeking to use desire and pleasure as well as anger to fuel struggles for justice' (2003: 4).

Feminist scholars have long looked to genre as a means of understanding the politics of representation and, combining textual analyses with an awareness of production conditions and the socio-cultural ideological context, have mapped out a dense social history of post-war femininity. Rabinovitz contends that American networks took advantage of the emergent and lucrative female demographic, to develop a new trend of feminist programming with a sub-genre of sitcoms like *The Mary Tyler Moore Show* (CBS, 1970–7), *Maude* (CBS, 1972–8) and *Rhoda* (CBS, 1974–8). Rabinovitz claims, 'A generic address of "feminism" became an important strategy because it served the needs of American television executives who could cultivate programming that could be identified with target audiences whom they wanted to measure and deliver to advertising agencies' (1999: 146).

Haralovich (2003: 69–85) pays close attention to how American sitcoms like *Leave It To Beaver* (CBS, 1957–8; ABC, 1958–63) and *Father Knows Best* (CBS,

1954–5 and 1958–62; NBC, 1955–8; ABC, 1962–3) 'sold' suburban middle-class family life, in the way it naturalized class and gender identities through patterns of consumption and the spatial layout of the home, to the female consumer. Interest in how television accommodated social change – incorporating dissent and turning it into consensual representation that preserves dominant patriarchal ideology – has proved another area of discussion. Bathrick (2003), for example, deliberates on how the sitcom form of *The Mary Tyler Moore Show*, the first to center on an unmarried career woman, and initially aired in 1970 at the height of second-wave feminism, worked in fact to preserve patriarchal values. Other contributions like Rabinovitz's analysis (1994: 3–19) of 'single mom' sitcoms (for example, *One Day At A Time* (CBS, 1975–84) and *Kate and Allie* (CBS, 1984–8)), and Bodroghkozy's (2003: 129–149) situating of the black sitcom *Julia* (NBC, 1968–71) – in the broader socio-political context about black single mothers (Julia lost her husband in the Vietnam War) and the politics of civil rights in 1960s America – determine how gender was (re)produced and institutionalized by television and its representational practices; and how those gendered meanings corresponded with, or else opposed, broader areas of women's changing experience and culture.

Genre hybridity appears perfect for scholars attempting to understand the contradictory nature of gendered politics in the post-feminist age (Akass and McCabe, 2004). Mixing musical forms, feminine identities and generic styles, the credits for *Sex and the City* (HBO, 1998–2004) offers us a post-feminist joke narrative. Accompanied by modern jazz rhythms, Carrie Bradshaw (Sarah Jessica Parker) wanders through New York City delighting in the sights – the Chrysler Building, the downtown skyline, the World Trade Center (replaced by the Empire State building after 9/11) and the Manhattan Bridge. Like classic slapstick, however, the viewer soon knows more than Carrie. A wheel drives through a puddle, the camera pulls back and for the first time we glimpse our heroine's outfit – a white tulle skirt and pink vest. A Metropolitan Transit Authority bus carrying her sexy sophisticated image – the 'naked' Donna Karen dress that she wears when planning to have sex (and does when she first sleeps with Mr Big [Chris Noth]) – has given the fairy princess a soaking. Four shots later and the punch line is delivered. A reworking of the classic pie-in-the-face gag finds our heroine looking horrified and embarrassed while a Japanese male tourist observes her soggy humiliation with a wry smile.

Feuer points to the *ideological flexibility* of genres in which generic forms are cyclical rather than linear (1992: 155). What is meant here is how forms and formats get recycled to give representation to current ideological struggles rather than offering something radically new. Certainly *Sex and the City* self-reflexively references the romantic comedy genre, and in particular the classical Hollywood screwball, as well as the enduring television tradition of sub-generic sitcoms focusing on the single girl in the city, like *The Mary Tyler Moore Show* and *Rhoda* (with Valerie Harper, who played the smart witted Rhoda Morgenstern, and turns up in 'Shortcomings', 2: 15). Carrie is a worthy inheritor with her sharp witty dialogue and pratfalls. But just as the series repeats while transforming past generic codes and structures, the opening joke structure comically plays with these generic elements to give representation to fantasies of the feminine self, gender identities and gendered cultural performance. If post-feminist theory contests that feminine identities have become multiple, contradictory and complex then the opening credits of this postmodern, post-feminist series plays with the generic forms of fairytale narratives, romantic comedy, screwball, sitcom and sex comedy to convey the heroine's uneasy relationship to the fairy-tale romance and happy-ever-after glamour and the pursuit of the perfect body.

Box 12.4   Genre, HBO and original programming

Six Feet Under (2001–5) had its debut on HBO (Home Box Office Entertainment), the American premier pay-for-view cable channel, at 10 pm, on Sunday 3 June 2001. It was the first drama series launched by the channel since *The Sopranos* – and HBO were under pressure to repeat its success. The series was created by Alan Ball, fresh from Oscar winning success for best screenplay with *American Beauty* (Sam Mendes, 1999), and made by the production company Greenblatt Janollari Studio, with whom Ball had signed a three-year television development deal. Ball initially met with Carolyn Strauss, senior vice-president for original programming at HBO. Inspired by her interest in producing a show about running a funeral home, he wrote the pilot. HBO bought the concept and gave him a thirteen-episode commitment – and *Six Feet Under* was born (or so the story goes).

   Set in a Los Angeles funeral home, the series focuses on the dysfunctional Fisher family that runs it. In the pilot the Fisher patriarch, Nathaniel (Richard Jenkins) dies in a road accident when a city bus ploughs into his hearse. The family is left bereft and the brothers – Nathaniel Jr (Peter Krause) and David

(Michael C. Hall) – are charged, along with restorative artist and long-time employee Federico 'Rico' Diaz (Freddy Rodriguez), with continuing the family business. Each episode starts with a death and concludes with the burial. Each death brings the Fishers some business, and often it sets the tone for that episode.

Six Feet Under premièred only months before the terrorist atrocities of 9/11 and thus was well positioned to respond to the haunting elegiac-ness of a nation in mourning. The series was thus grounded in this uneasy cultural Zeitgeist obsessed with death and tragedy. Arguably, American culture has long been obsessed with death – with guns, violence and killing. We may be able to bear the cause–effect logic of a mobster whacking a miscreant in *The Sopranos*, but are far more uncomfortable with the fatal consequence of that violence – the cool quiet of death.

Just as the *Six Feet Under* characters are drawn from the post-Vietnam, post-feminist, post-civil-rights, post-Watergate eras of social upheaval, which rendered patriarchal authority suspect; the aftermath of 9/11 has led to another period of introspection and a questioning of American patriarchy – its foreign policy, the Bush administration and the Republican agenda. Many episodes struggle with this contemporary post-patriarchal dilemma – the middle-aged, post-menopausal widow coming to terms with her adult children who no longer need her, the teenage-daughter searching for her identity, the eldest son suffering an existential crisis; the younger one negotiating his way out of the closet.

Six Feet Under was laid to rest in 2005. Over its five seasons it fulfilled the HBO agenda of challenging conventional television wisdom and representing that which had rarely before been seen on our screens. But even so, it pushed HBO to its limits: it is difficult to place in institutional and generic terms; it walks a fine line between comedy and tragedy; it teeters on the edge of unbearable poignancy before tipping over into corny melodrama. Structurally it deals with the space between death and burial; thematically it focuses on cultural taboos – homosexuality, mental illness, old age, sickness, drug addiction, adolescence, race and class – which in turn are used to revisit traditional cultural certainties like religion, marriage and the family – and it questions who we are.

Neale has written, 'It should be recognised that categories such as 'narrative' and 'fiction' – even 'film' and 'television' – are generic in nature, that there is a generic aspect to all instances of cultural production, and that these instances are usually multiple, not single in kind' (2003: 3). Adapting his thinking here, could it not be argued that genre in the new television era, which places emphasis on diversity, innovation and competitiveness, and is driven by among other things consumer demand and customer satisfaction, can be used to define a brand identity for a broadcasting company (Epstein, Reeves and Rogers, 2006: 15–25). In the age of brand marketing and niche audiences, HBO, it would seem, uses genre not only to assert its brand identity within an overcrowded market place, but also to make sense of the diversity of its original programmes.

Superficially at least, the programmes that HBO label 'original' have nothing in common with each other. A generically disparate bunch – a gangster series, a sex comedy set in Manhattan, a family drama involving morticians, a magic realist tale concerning a travelling circus, a western, a prison drama, an historical drama set in Ancient Rome, a 'realist comedy' about a man's struggle with the quotidian and a drama about a polygamist and his three wives. And yet, a closer look reveals that HBO's original programmes are a more coherent group than it first appears.

Neale contends that all genres are predicated on repetition and difference, but it is the work of narrative to regulate such logic. What is meant here is how genre emerges through the way in which the narrative organizes and handles specific structural components and discourses. A telling example of this is when David Milch approached HBO with a drama about order without law in Ancient Rome. The executives may have liked the script but *Rome* (2005–2007) was already in pre-production. Undeterred, Milch re-set the drama in a frontier town in 1876 and *Deadwood* was born (Havrilesky). Looking closely at the narratives of HBO's original programmes, what emerges is a generic theme of, and structuring around, the melodramatic male. From *The Sopranos* through to their latest offering *Big Love*, the narratives often focus on beleaguered men struggling with 'family' demands and work pressures. McArthur (1972) understands genre as about a culture talking to itself, and what unites these original programmes from *Six Feet Under* to *The Sopranos*, regardless of setting or historical specificity, is a different, perhaps darker, response to the American dream based on a destabilised patriarchy and conflicted histories.

How original programming give representation to the illicit – profane language, violence, sexuality and nudity – coheres the diverse offering. HBO has doubtless not discovered any new taboos, but it has defined new rules and conventions for representing the illicit. Straining the limits with its use of profane language, graphic images of nudity and violence, original programs use the illicit as a crucial narrative component in creating innovative and ground-breaking television. Suggested here is that the freedom granted at HBO goes beyond writing brutal violence and lurid language, but it is about telling stories in unconventional ways that surprise audiences. Latitude to tell stories differently, creative personnel given the autonomy to work with minimal interference and without having to compromise, has become the trademark of HBO – how they endlessly speak about and sell themselves, how the media talks about them and how their customers have come to understand what they are paying for.

Returning to Neale's (1983) theory of genre is useful in understanding the television audience. Drawing from psychoanalysis he suggests three basic principles in how genre produces and regulates subjectivity: First, the subject is motivated by a desire to repeat a past pleasure despite the impossibility of fulfilling that initial state of enjoyment; second, conferring identity is always predicated on the Other; and third, identity is never stable but always in the process of becoming (1983: 48–55). Viewers have long come to expect controversial themes, provocative subject matter and thought-provoking television from HBO. Anticipating innovation, adult themes and edgier drama, rather than a particular format, repeatedly lure back the audience who must pay a monthly subscription to view the programmes. HBO must, for commercial survival, differentiate its products and build a distinct reputation to attract its audience. Key to its market strategy is the promise to deliver difference not only from the networks but also in terms of its own programme content.

Hess understands the formulaic repetition of generic convention as rooted in the economics of business practices (cited in Grant, 1977: 54). For her, meaning is limited to supporting the production company ethos. Doing different (setting itself against what is prohibited on network television) emerges as a crucial institutional strategy for HBO. Its audacious marketing slogan 'It's not TV. It's HBO' signals its intent. Freed from a reliance on sponsorship and censorship including FCC (Federal Communications Commission) regulations, the subscription-only cable company has built its reputation around original programmes different from what can be seen elsewhere in the television flow. But HBO is a branch of the Time Warner Empire, which also includes Warner Bros. Television, producers of *E.R.* and *The West Wing* (NBC,

1999–2000). HBO can push itself into new and often controversial television territory precisely because it is part of a vast economic conglomerate demanding difference within the same company.

Conclusion

Generic forms provided a fruitful site of academic inquiry in the 1980s and beyond, in part because the trend to reclaim popular cultural forms gained greater prominence, in part helped by post-structuralist approaches to genre analysis, and in part because new interdisciplinary approaches better enabled scholars to theorize representational ambivalence. The history of genre criticism has shifted away from initial categorizing to theorizing a complex interaction involving criticism, cultural specificity, audience expectation and industrial demands.

Summary

- Studying TV genre is inherently problematic because it is already a contentious term.
- 'Genres are made not born' (Feuer, 1992: 114).
- Genre frames audience expectations.
- Ryall stresses, genre can help us understand the historical and cultural conditions of production and consumption (1978: 11–12).
- Industry depends on generic forms and formats for its organization and attempts to attract audiences.
- TV genre and programming forms and formats are notoriously hybridized.

GOING FURTHER

Creeber, G. (ed.) (2001) *The Television Genre Book*. London: bfi Publishing.
This is an accessible introduction to the study of television genre, identifying generic forms and analyzing the various categories, like soap opera, drama and news, with close textual readings.

Edgerton, G. and Rose, B. (eds) (2005) *Thinking Outside the Box: A Contemporary Television Genre Reader*. Kentucky: University of Kentucky Press.

This edited collection brings together recent scholarship on television genre. It begins with an historical and theoretical overview of the term, before analyzing in depth various generic forms popular on American television.

Neale, S. (1983) *Genre*. London: bfi publishing.
Although focusing on the cinema, this seminal text is one of the first attempts to theorize genre. Drawing on psychoanalysis, Neale provides an invaluable insight into the interplay between film-makers and audiences, history and society, and industrial demands.

Feuer, J. (1992) 'Genre Study and Television', in R. C. Allen (ed.) *Channels of Discourse, Reassembled: Television and Contemporary Criticism*. North Carolina: The University of North Carolina Press. pp. 138–59.
A key text for students studying television genre, offering a comprehensible history of genre criticism, before providing a close reading of the sit-com.

Mittell, J. (2004) *Genre and Television: From Cop Shows to Cartoons in American Culture*. New York and London: Routledge.
Introduces students to various methodologies by which genre can be studied and understood.

Newcombe, H. (ed.) (1976) *Television: A Critical View*. Oxford: Oxford University Press.
One of the first attempts to map out the field of television studies, including an early definition of genre as applied to television.

STUDENT ACTIVITY 12.1

1. Deconstructing the title sequence of *Desperate Housewives*, discuss what it has to say about contemporary gender politics.
2. Deconstructing the title sequence of *Six Feet Under*, identify its genre.

References

Akass, K. and McCabe, J. (eds) (2004) *Reading Sex and the City: Critical Approaches*. London: I.B. Tauris.
Altman, R. (1984) 'A Semantic/Synctactic Approach to Film Genres', *Cinema Journal*, 23(3) (Spring): 14–15.

Altman, R. (1987) *The American Film Musical*. Bloomington: Indiana University Press.

Altman, R. (1996) *Genre: The Musical, A Reader*. Jefferson, North Carolina: McFarland.

Altman, R. (1999) *Film/Genre*. London: bfi Publishing.

Ang. I. (1985 [1996]) *Watching Dallas*. London: Methuen.

Bodroghkozy, A. (2003) '"Is This What You Mean By Color TV?" Race, Gender and Contested Meaning in *Julia*' in J. Morreale (ed.) *Critiquing the Sitcom: A Reader*. New York: Syracuse University Press. pp. 129–49.

Creeber, G. (ed.) (2006) *Tele-visions: An Introduction to Studying Television*. London: bfi Publishing.

Curtin, M. (1995) *Redeeming the Wasteland: Television Documentary and Cold War Politics*. New Brunswick: Rutgers University Press.

Epstein, M. M., Reeves, J. L. and Rogers, M. C. (2006) 'Surviving "The Hit": Will The Sopranos Still Sing for HBO' in D. Lavery (ed.) *Reading The Sopranos: Hit TV from HBO*. London: I.B. Tauris. pp. 15–25.

Feuer, J. (1984) 'Melodrama, Serial Form and Television Today', *Screen*, 25(1): 4–16.

Grant, B. (ed.) (1977) *Film Genre Theory and Criticism*. New Jersey: Scarecrow Press.

Han Jauss, R. (1982) *Towards an Aesthetic of Literary Reception*. Minneapolis: University of Minnesota Press.

Haralovich, M. B. (2003) 'Sitcoms and Suburbs: Positioning the 1950s Housewife' in Joanne Morreale (ed.) *Critiquing the Sitcom: A Reader*. New York: Syracuse University Press. pp. 69–85.

Havrilesky, H. 'The Man behind *Deadwood*', Salon.com: http://dir.salon.com/story/ent/feature/2005/03/05/milch/index.html?pn=1

Heywood, L. and Drake J. (eds) (2003) *Third Wave Agenda: Being Feminist, Doing Feminism*. Minneapolis: University of Minnesota Press.

Hilmes, M. (ed.) (2003) *The Television History Book*. London: bfi Publishing.

Hollows, J. (2000) *Feminism, Femininity and Popular Culture*. Manchester: Manchester University Press.

Lavery, D. (ed.) (2002) *This Thing of Ours: Investigating The Sopranos*. New York: Columbia University Press.

Lotz, A. D. (2001) 'Postfeminist Television Criticism: Rehabilitating Critical Terms and Identifying Postfeminist Attributes', *Feminist Media Studies*, 1(1): 105–21.

McArthur, C. (1972) *Underworld USA*. London: Secker & Warburg/bfi Publishing.

Modleski, T. (1979) 'The Search for Tomorrow in Today's Soap Operas: Notes on a Feminine Narrative Form', *Film Quarterly*, 33(1): 12–21.

Modleski, T. (1983) 'The Rhythms of Reception: Daytime Television and Women's Work' in E. A. Kaplan (ed.) *Regarding Television: Critical Approaches – An Anthology*. University Publications of America. pp. 67–75

Moseley, R. and Read, J. (2002) '"Having it *Ally*": Popular Television (Post-) Feminism', *Feminist Media Studies*. 2(2): 231–49.

Neale, S. (2003) Studying Genre, *The Television Genre Book*, ed. G. Creeber. London: BFI Publishing. 1–3.

Neale, S. and Krutnik, F. (1983) *Popular Film and Television Comedy*. London: Routledge.

Rabinovitz, L. (1999) 'Ms.-Representation: The Politics of Feminist Sitcoms' in M. B. Haralovich and L. Rabinovitz (eds) *Television, History, and American Culture*. Duke University Press. pp. 144–67.

Rabinovitz, L. (1994) 'Sitcoms and Single Moms: Representations of Feminism on American TV', *Cinema Journal*, 29: 3–19.

Ryall, T. (1978) *Teachers Study Guide No. 2: The Gangster Film*. London: BFI Education.

Sacks, A. (1971) 'An Analysis of the Gangster Movies of the Early Thirties', *The Velvet Light Trap* 1: 5–11.

Stempel Mumford, L. (1995) *Love and Ideology in the Afternoon: Soap Opera, Women and Television Genre*. Bloomingdale: Indiana University Press.

Spence, L. (2005) *Watching Daytime Soap Operas: The Power of Pleasure*. Middle town: Wesleyan University Press.

Warshow, R. (1962) 'The Gangster as Tragic Hero', in *The Immediate Experience. Movies, Comics, Theatre and Other Aspects of Popular Culture*. New York: Doubleday and Co. Inc. pp. 127–33.

From Family Television to Bedroom Culture: Young People's Media at Home

Sonia Livingstone

DEFINITIONS

Bedroom culture – especially for young people, a set of conventional meanings and practices closely associated with identity, privacy and the self has become linked to the domestic space of the child's bedroom in late modern society.

Risk society – in late modern societies, knowledge of and calculations regarding risk and uncertainty have become central to most or all social, economic and technological arrangements.

Introduction

In this chapter, I identify and analyze the role played by the media in underpinning the recent historical shift from a model of family life centred on the collective space of the living room to one dispersed throughout the home and, especially, located in the bedroom. It is argued that the domestic media introduced into Western homes over the past half century or more are first conceived as communal but then, as they become cheaper and more portable, they are reconceived as personal media, particularly by children and young people. In sociological terms, this reflects an underlying process of *individualization*, by which it is meant that traditional social distinctions (particularly social class) are declining in importance as determinants of people's (especially young people's) life course, resulting in a fragmentation of (or perhaps liberation from) traditional norms and values. This process is linked in turn to the emergence of the *risk society*, a term by which Beck (1992) points to the recent (post-second World War) development of modern society as it faces vast yet uncertain and unmanageable risks of its own making; childhood has become one key site of just such risks and anxieties. In the present chapter, it is argued that as 'outside' spaces are seen as ever more risky for children, 'home' takes over as the focus of their safety, identity and leisure. Within this, the bedroom, and hence *bedroom culture*, is becoming a central location – both physically and symbolically – of media use and the mediation of everyday life.

Public and private leisure spaces

At the turn of the twenty-first century, 'the home is now commonly accepted as providing personal fulfilment and satisfaction as well as the means of recuperating from the pressures of the working day' (Allan, 1985: 57). It was not always thus. The model of the single family home emerged strongly in the middle-classes in the early twentieth century, with a strict separation of public and private spheres, and with the private constructed as a refuge, a place for nurturing positive values and for the socialization of children: 'home sweet home ... is the household interior, an over-decorated and embellished space held in the highest value' (Segalen, 1996: 400).

With the growing significance of domestic mass media in the second half of the twentieth century, two distinct trends regarding the home can be identified. These help us understand the difference between childhood in the 1950s when television arrived, and childhood at the turn of the twenty-first century now that computers and the Internet have made similar inroads into the home. The first trend concerns the shifting boundary between the home and outside, altering the balance between life in the community and family privacy, as symbolized by the changing significance of 'the front door'. Extending this spatial framework, the second trend concerns the shifting balance between communal family life and the private life of the child, as symbolized by the growing significance of 'the bedroom door'.

To take the first trend then, children's lives are defined by the ways in which:

> adults seek to impose or negotiate rules and limits, adjusted over time, aimed at reconciling children's freedom and security ... The nature of the local environment and the availability of formal recreational services, ranging from parks to clubs, crucially affect how children negotiate their relationships and use of space outside the home. (Hill and Tisdall, 1997: 93)

There has been a gradual shift from children's leisure time spent outside (in the streets, woods or countryside) to that spent primarily at home, both reflecting and shaping cultural conceptions of childhood over the past half century. Interviews with parents about their own childhoods reveal a dominant image of a carefree childhood spent out of doors (Livingstone, 2002). Idealized and nostalgic though this may be, historians of childhood confirm a 'shift from a life focused on the street to one focused on the home'. Further, 'this was accompanied by a change in the social organization of the home. Parents, and in particular fathers, became less remote and authoritarian, less the centre of attention when they were present' (Cunningham, 1995: 179).

The second trend has been fuelled by the continual multiplication of media goods at home, fostering a shift in media use from that of 'family television' (Morley, 1986) to that of individualized media lifestyles (Flichy, 2006) and, for children and young people, of 'bedroom culture' (Bovill and Livingstone, 2001). First the television, then the hi-fi, video recorder, computer, and now the Internet, entered the home for communal use in the living room and were then gradually relocated to kitchens, bedrooms, even hallways. So, new media today enter the home in a similar fashion to the television before them, the decision is no longer whether to have any of these goods but rather how many to have and where to locate them in the home. This *multiplication* of domestic media goods is facilitated by the reduction in price for media goods, by the growth of mobile media (for example, mobile phone, walkman, MP3/iPod), by the continual process of innovation in the design and marketing of existing technologies, and by the *diversification* of media forms (which encourages the multiplication of goods through upgrading and recycling existing technologies through the household).

For many young people now, a personalized media environment is taken for granted, in striking contrast with their parents' upbringing. In interviews with children, some have lost track of their possessions. One six year old boy told us, 'I've got two computers in the house, I've got Sega, and a Nintendo. No, I've got three, Sega, Supernintendo and the normal Nintendo'. In another family, the children disagreed on the number of television sets they possessed – was it 9 or 11, they wondered? – although they were clear that every room, especially the bedrooms, contained a set (Livingstone, 2002).

These two domestic boundaries, marked by the two doors, raise questions about the role of the media in the changing relations between parents and children, and between public and private (Livingstone, 2005). The two are also linked. The creation of a media-rich home tends to be justified by parents in relation to the decline of safe public spaces. Outside spaces are increasingly seen as dangerous, the range and quality of public services has declined, and media use at home is increasingly construed as educational as well as entertaining (Buckingham, 2001). More practically, since much leisure time is spent at home, and since family members' tastes are increasingly segmented, there are also concrete advantages to the multiplication of media goods at home.

In what follows, I shall elaborate the argument just sketched above, drawing on findings from the *Young People, New Media* project (YPNM). This project interviewed and surveyed children and young people (aged 6–17) and their parents across the UK in spring 1997, asking them about the media in their home, their leisure time use, including time spent on each medium, media-related attitudes and tastes, social contexts of media use, parental guidance, family communication, and so on (Livingstone, 2002; Livingstone and Bovill, 2001). A follow up study, *UK Children Go Online* (UKCGO), interviewed and surveyed children and young people (aged 9–19) and their parents across the UK in spring 2004 (Livingstone and Bober, 2005).

The decline of street culture

I think it's got a lot to do with society. In our day it used to be 'Watch for the bad man', but now it's 'Watch for the bad man, and the bad woman and the bad policeman and the little boys and girls'. You cannot trust anybody. It's a horrible thing to say, but you cannot.
(Working-class mother of a 9-year-old daughter)

James et al. (1998) draw on Beck's (1992) theory of the risk society to examine how the spaces for young people's leisure activities have changed in meaning over the past half century. Ennew (1994) argues that British children's lives are ruled by 'the idea of danger', which she sees as having taken a new twist at the beginning of the 1990s. One consequence of the growing fears regarding children's safety is a growth in adult management of children's leisure space and time. For example, Hillman et al. (1990) found that while in 1971 80% of 7 and 8-year-old children walked to school on their own, by 1990 this figure had dropped to 9%.

Parents recall with nostalgia their own childhood freedoms to play out of doors, convinced that they cannot allow this for their children, and so the home is construed as the haven of safety. Fears of the outdoors are expressed by parents in urban and rural areas, and reports of harm to children on television and in the newspapers often figure in parents' accounts. The YPNM survey showed that only 11% of parents with children aged 6–17 say the streets where they live are 'very safe' for their child, compared with 56% thinking this about the neighbourhood where they themselves were brought up.

The perception of public space as relatively unsafe appears to be a particularly British view.[1] Britain is often popularly described as a 'child-unfriendly culture', where many social codes exist to manage the separation of spaces for children and adults, and many others exist to regulate children's participation within those adult-designated, or adult-defined 'family' spaces. However, observing parallel trends in America, Coontz (1997: 17) comments that:

> People talk about how kids today are unsupervised, and they often are; but in one sense teens are under more surveillance than in the past. Almost anyone above the age of 40 can remember places where young people could establish real physical, as opposed to psychic, distance from adults. In the suburbs it was undeveloped or abandoned lots and overgrown woods ... In the cities it was downtown areas where kids could hang out. Many of these places are now gone.

Societal desire to keep children safe is paralleled by the desire to keep society safe from 'youth'. As Hill and Tisdall (1997: 194) comment, 'our fears about children's crime in public places exemplify society's requirements for an 'indoors child', which will not only keep children but also the public safe'.

The retreat to the home

> There's nothing to do really ... 'cos they've just gone and closed down the [club].
> But there's nothing here now.
> (15-year-old girls living in rural area)

Writing in the mid-1970s, Corrigan (1976) contrasted the potential unpredictability of street corner culture with the alternatives of Mum and Dad in the rather formal front room or the known environment of the youth club. If those were the alternatives to the street corner of the 1970s they had changed by the 1990s. For many young people we interviewed, the youth club has closed down and the front room has been replaced by a multimedia home and, particularly, a multimedia bedroom. In the YPNM survey, 66% of children and young people aged 6–17 said that there was not enough for them to do in the area where they live. Crucially, then, the decline of street culture and the rise of the media-rich home are related.

Both parents and children explicitly link restrictions on the child's access to the world outside to increased media use within the home. In an extreme illustration of this, a 13-year-old boy, living in an area with a high level of unemployment and violence, told us that 'Mum gets us a video or a computer game if we have to stay in because of the fighting'. More often, though, the link between street culture and domestic culture is implicit, reflecting not only a shift in perceptions of public space but also in perceptions of the home. Where once the home was highly rule-bound, with codes for eating at the table, activities in the bedroom, behaviour in the living room, and so forth, today it is going out which is heavily hedged about with rules and expectations. Here a middle-class mother living in a rural location talks about her 10-year-old son:[2]

Interviewer: You see television as playing a different role in Leo's life than it did in yours?
Mother: Oh yes, definitely. I can remember playing outside in the street for hours on end and having a lot more freedom to play out. They haven't got that as children now ... he's in more than we ever were as children.

Her son confirms the importance of media in his life, telling us that he spends a lot of time with the television, hi-fi and a games machine in his bedroom, and that while he would like to go out more often, the garden is too small and he is not allowed to play football there.

Thus, children face not only practical and material but also discursive constraints on their lived activities, all contributing towards a historical shift towards the privatization of leisure (Williams, 1974). At home, it is screen media that emerge as the easy way of keeping the family entertained, notwithstanding the doubts parents have regarding the media as 'time-wasting'.

One consequence was to force the realization that home and family are not necessarily one and the same. Ironically perhaps, the privatization of leisure throws family members together precisely at a time when the cultural shift towards individualization means that children and young people are ever more encouraged to pursue their own individual tastes and interests (Buchner, 1990). Their media preferences decreasingly shared with their parents, for 'the modern family ideology [promotes] families in which the goal of individual self-realisation overshadows community solidarity and stability' (Gadlin, 1978: 236).

And there are ever more media contents and sources tailored – indeed, targeted – to their age group. This growing individualization fuelled our second trend, as we explore below.

From family television to bedroom culture

Interviewer: Do you think that there are any advantages or disadvantages to Charlie having TV in his bedroom?

Mother: Advantages are that we can watch programmes in here when Charlie wants to watch something else and –

Father: Disadvantages are that it, err, discourages family life because it separates people [...]

Interviewer: So is spending time together as a family important to you?

Father : Yes, of course, the family is the most important thing.

(Working-class family with 12-year-old boy)

If public spaces in the second half of the twentieth century witnessed a decline in access for children, the private, domestic realm has also undergone changes. The arrival of the television set into the family home transformed the spatial and temporal rhythms of family life (Scannell, 1988). Historical studies of the arrival of television suggest that far from fitting into the home, television transformed the structure of the home by prompting a considerable re-arrangement of domestic space (Spigel, 1992). As each room had pre-defined activities associated with it, television posed a new problem, namely where to put it. In most UK homes, the decision was made to put this proud new object in the once adult-only front room or parlour of the post-war British home, transforming this room in the process into the 'living' room, this itself being part of a wider trend towards the creation of the open plan living space (Oswell, 1999).

Today, only relatively wealthy homes keep a room for 'best', most family homes having 'knocked through' from the best room into the dining room to make a large multifunctional space – the family room – in which the media play a central role. 'Family television' encapsulates a site of both conviviality and power plays, in which the family share interests, pleasures and conflicts. As recently as the mid-1980s, Morley (1986) described the family gathering in the main living room to co-view the family television set, thus providing an occasion for the operation of traditional generation and gender inequalities – Ang terms them 'living room wars' (1996) – in which Dad monopolizes the remote control, sport wins out over soaps, women's viewing is halted when the husband wants to see 'his programme', and children's preferences come last.

As the media at home have multiplied, no longer a scarce resource for the family, the social practices which surround and accompany viewing have altered. A common solution is to transform bedrooms into private living rooms, leaving the family living room only for those times when the family chooses to come together, enforced conviviality being a thing of the past for all but the poor. Thus today, most homes have been reorganized, the dominant principle no longer being that of 'front' and 'back' (Goffman, 1959) but rather than of communal space and personal spaces. How far along this path to go represents a central dilemma for families as they decide whether and when to acquire and locate televisions, computers etc., thereby shaping the particular balance between a communal or individualized model of family life.

The culture of the bedroom

What do these newly privatized, media-rich spaces mean to children? By the end of the 1990s, many young people had media-rich bedrooms, reflecting not only an intrinsic fascination with the media but also the unsatisfactory nature of the available alternatives. Other social changes, including central heating, smaller family size, and continual upgrading of domestic technological goods all had their part to play (Allan, 1985), but the result is a new kind of place for children's leisure which we are just beginning to explore and which is filled with ever more media goods for ever younger children.

The YPNM survey (Livingstone, 2002) showed that in British children's bedrooms music media are the most popular: 68% of 6–17 year olds have a personal stereo, 61% have a hi-fi and 59% a radio. Screen entertainment media follow close behind: 63% have their own television and 21% have a video recorder, while 34% have a TV-linked games machine and 27% have a Gameboy. Just a few years on, the 'UK Children Go Online' project, in updating this work, found that 19% have Internet access in their bedroom (Livingstone and Bober, 2005). As is common, the Internet is no more equally distributed across the population than other media: while one in five have the Internet in their bedroom, this is the case for 22% of boys versus 15% of girls, 21% of middle class versus 16% working-class children, and 10% of 9–11-year-olds versus 26% of

16–17-year-olds. Moreover, this emergence of the media-rich bedroom as a child-centred and private space has its own developmental trajectory. Not only are media-rich bedrooms more common among teenagers, but interviews with children and young people reveal how the meaning of the bedroom alters with time.

Convenience

Children younger than about 9-years-old are relatively uninterested in bedroom culture, although a well equipped, 'media-rich' bedroom is occasionally provided as a way of ensuring the parents' privacy. Indeed, younger children prefer the family spaces, especially when parents are present, by contrast with teenagers who also like to use the space and facilities of the living room but mainly when their family is absent. Six-year-old Belinda told us that she doesn't normally play in her bedroom, but prefers to bring her toys downstairs to play where others are. Hence, these children are less likely to have media in their bedrooms, and family life is heavily focused on the multi-functional, child-centred, media-rich living or 'family' room.

Yet even by this age, children's bedrooms will often contain media-related collections, not just of china animals and foreign coins but also Disney memorabilia, *Pokemon* cards or the paraphernalia of a Manchester United football fan. Ten-year-old Rachel and her friends all collect, but 'they collect different things', suggesting the link between collections and personal identity (Rochberg-Halton, 1984). Part of the convenience of the bedroom, then, is its role in the safe storage of valued objects. As these collections are generally recognized as transient, 'a stage' children go through, children's bedrooms house not only the current enthusiasm but also previous enthusiasms, making for series of partial collections which tell the story of a child's development.

One may see in these collections a legitimized form of consumerism. Generally encouraged or even initiated by parents, the practices associated with adding to and displaying the collection is construed by parents as specialist, serious, knowledgeable. We see this positive assessment of 'the collection' in the narrative spun for John, aged 7, by his mother, a lower-middle-class single parent. She first introduced the 'collection' to explain her son's video viewing, linking his interest in animals with her views of videos as educational and, perhaps, portentous of his future.

> We have got a lot of the Walt Disney videos because we collect those because I think they are a collectable item and John is very much into marine life and the *Free Willy* video, anything to do with animals … In actual fact, the teacher in school said to him something about the whale that was in *Free Willy* and said to me 'if your son doesn't become a marine biologist then I will eat my hat'.

Already, through these collections, through their emerging fandoms, and through the associated theming of wallpaper, bed linen, decoration, etc., children's identities are being constructed and, simultaneously, commodified. In early to middle childhood, the objects collected vary widely, but often take the form of media-related merchandising (Kinder, 1999). By the teenage years, objects being actively collected are more directly media goods – discs, music files, videos, computer games, magazines, and so forth. This transition is noted by Kathy's (15) parents:

> Mother: Oh well, she used to collect all those little whimsies that we once got from a car boot sale (laughter) … little animals that she collected.
> Father: She doesn't collect anything now though, apart from music, not seriously anyway.

As with John, above, Kathy's collection of some 200 tapes is judged 'serious'. Possession and safe storage is no longer key to the enjoyment of these goods, for media require time spent with them. Associated with the transition to media goods is a transition in the use of the bedroom – no longer primarily for convenience but now also for escape (into individualized media use) and for identity (requiring an investment in media use to promote self-development and self-expression).

Escape

> She's got all these comics on the bed, and she likes to read them, and she's got a computer next to her TV so if she gets bored she can just move around quick, and she's got like a computer booklet on computers and TV, and she's got a telephone with a hi-fi midi system sort of thing.
> (9-year-old girl living in a middle-class family and talking of her ideal bedroom)

From middle childhood, children – particularly girls – become more interested in their bedroom, and start to want their own television/computer/hi-fi. This is

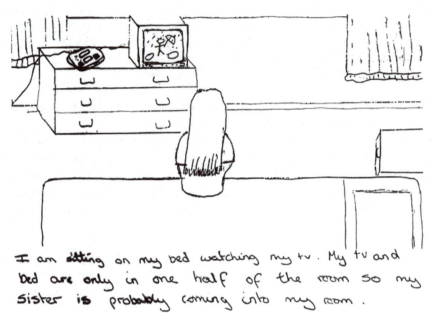

I am sitting on my bed watching my tv. My tv and bed are only in one half of the room so my sister is probably coming into my room.

Figure 13.1   A girl's drawing of 'myself watching television'

Source: Young People New Media project, http://www.lse.ac.uk/collections/media@lse/whosWho/soniaLivingstonePublications3.htm

largely for pragmatic reasons, particularly being able to choose and watch their own programmes uninterrupted. Over and again, children described how irritating it is to be interrupted – when watching television for example – by siblings or parents, suggesting strongly that for them, being alone means welcome respite from family life, especially for the 72% who do not share a bedroom with a sibling (Livingstone and Bovill, 1999). Here, a 10-year-old girl explains: 'I like being on my own ... [I can] watch what I want to watch instead of watching what my sister wants to watch or what my mum wants to watch.'

The image of freedom, or perhaps also of isolation, is well captured in Figures 13.1 and 13.2, drawn by children when asked to depict themselves watching television. In that task (see Livingstone, 2002), about half drew themselves in their bedrooms and half drew themselves in a family space. Perhaps this trend towards bedroom culture is particularly 'British'? European comparisons show that British children and young people generally own more screen media especially than do

Figure 13.2   A teenage boy's drawing of 'myself watching television'

Source: Young People New Media project, http://www.lse.ac.uk/collections/media@lse/whosWho/
soniaLivingstonePublications3.htm

their counterparts in other countries (with the exception of America; Roberts et al., 1999), though they do not necessarily spend more time in their rooms. The advantages of convenience do not appear to encourage isolation from the family but rather, they provide some control over *when* to be sociable or alone (Bovill and Livingstone, 2001). Wanting to escape, then, marks a transition from *having* personal 'stuff' and so needing somewhere safe to put it, to *being* a distinct individual and so needing somewhere private to express this.

Identity

In adolescence, this concern with the self is of pre-eminent importance. The significance of the bedroom is now primarily centred on identity, as young people take a growing interest in how their bedrooms are furnished, arranged and equipped. By the early teens, these psychological reasons are easily as important as the practical ones as children and young people seek to identify, protect and embellish their own spaces distinct from adult scrutiny and intervention. The bedroom provides a flexible social space in which young people can experience their growing independence from family life, becoming either a haven of privacy or a social area in which to entertain friends, often listening to music, reading magazines, playing a new computer game or watching a video together. Listen to the satisfaction with which 15-year-old Joanne, from a working-class family, describes her room:

> I'm usually in my bedroom ... I think that I like to be by myself really. I don't know. I suppose it's just because at the moment I have got all my furniture arranged like in a sitting room area, a study room area and my bedroom and it is just, like, really cool and I just like to go there because I know that that is my room ... I mean I have decorated it how I want it and it's just like a room I don't think I will ever move out.

Personal ownership of media dramatically increases in the early teenage years, part and parcel of the development of identity. From the perspective of the social psychology of adolescence, 'valued material possessions, it is argued, act as signs of the self that are essential in their own right for its continued culti-vation, and hence the world of meaning that we create for ourselves, and that creates our selves, extends literally into the objective surroundings' (Rochberg-Halton, 1984: 335). Lincoln (2004) suggests these material possessions are orga-nized in terms of zones, with a fluid set of physical arrangements structuring the social activities that take place in the bedroom in order to enact the 'unique-ness' of its owner.

Notably, images of self-sufficiency and control figure strongly in young people's talk of their bedroom. In this context of self-sufficiency and control, unwarranted interventions by others can be experienced as a significant viola-tion of privacy:

> Last year I went to Austria and erm, I came back and I nearly had a heart attack because my mum had completely cleaned my room ... She had completely blitzed my room and I was so angry about it ... It is my own private space and I really don't like her touching it ... She just goes on and on about me cleaning it and I mean, I try to tell her that it is my personal space and let me have it how I want.
> (Middle-class girl aged 15)

Emler and Reicher (1994) explore how the management of spatial boundaries, and the constraints on this, frames the everyday management of identities. Behind this lies the social psychological argument that identities must be enacted, and these enactments must be situated in locations with particular spa-tial and temporal structures. Madigan and Munro (1999: 70) identify the partic-ular difficulties posed by the structure of the home for women in resolving the tension between 'the socially sanctioned goal of family togetherness, sharing, equality and the goal of individual achievement, self-identity'. While they suggest that for women this is more often achieved through the management of time than space, for children the bedroom is provided as a spatial solution.

Most simply, whether children can keep their friendships distinct in space and time from their family relationships is crucial to sustaining multiple, possibly distinct, identities. Hence, the widespread irritation occasioned by siblings intruding into spaces in which friendships are conducted, media are engaged with, or privacy enjoyed represents an irritation not simply due to the interruption of an activity or conversation but a clash of identities. The irritation is not alleviated by the younger sibling promising to be quiet, or not interfere, for it is a symbolic intrusion, a clash of one identity with another, a loss of freedom to reinvent oneself for oneself. Similarly, the persistent untidiness of many children's rooms, and the high degree of tidiness of others, may reflect more than a concern, or lack of concern, with order. For an untidy room is hard for an adult to walk around, and a very tidy room will show signs of intruders. The effect is to make the room both child-friendly and adult-unfriendly. By contrast with the traditional hierarchies of the living room, the bedroom is fundamentally a heterarchical space – perhaps the only place where children can dictate the rules of engagement to their parents.

Conclusion: bedroom culture

The bedroom becomes meaningful through the conjunction of all three rationales above. It provides a convenient location in which personal goods can be gathered and maintained. It provides a means of escape from the interruptions, interference and gaze of others. And it facilitates the routine (re)enactment of a desired identity. Steele and Brown (1994) describe teenage 'room culture' as the place where media and identities intersect through the bricolage of identity-work objects on display in young people's rooms. They see adolescents' rooms as 'mediating devices' by which they express who they are and who they want to be – a safe, private space in which experimentation with possible selves can be conducted (see also Frith, 1978). Thus the media-rich bedroom in the 'juxtaposed home allows teenagers to remove themselves from adult supervision while still living with their parents' (Flichy, 1995: 165).

Bachmair (1991) talks of the bedroom as a text within which the television programme is interwoven as one central element among others. This complex text of the bedroom provides a key site for the construction of identity and a position from within which to participate in a shared peer culture. This participation takes two forms, for the bedroom is both a location in which children and young people can entertain friends and also a place in which they can experience their connection to the peer group even when alone, particularly through the use of media valued by peers.

The media are used in various ways to manage these boundaries of space and identity, especially by young people who not only sustain multiple identities but whose identities are often experimental, temporary, available for making over, and the symbolic resources of the media provide the content – images, representations, themes – as well as the material means of managing boundaries (the walkman, the loud music in the bedroom, the total absorption in a computer game) – the 'deafness' parents complain about is more due to identity considerations than to media addiction.

'Bedroom culture' in this sense is very much a Western phenomenon, being dependent on a high degree of modernization, individualization and wealth. As such, it represents a new opportunity for targeted advertising and marketing, as the media-rich child's bedroom is both a site of reception for commercial messages and a location for the display and use of consumer goods. While the bedroom is a key site for the increasing commercialization of childhood and youth, it also supports the development of identity in ways that may be, but are not necessarily, exploitative. For example, McRobbie and Garber (1976) and Frith (1978) emphasized how teenage girls' search for identity through self-presentation and the development of 'taste' has been led by powerful commercial interests in the fashion and music industries, though others (Fornas and Bolin, 1995, Lincoln, 2004; Steele and Brown, 1994) see mediated consumer images as providing the raw materials with which young people creatively construct 'their' style.

Summary: living together separately

This chapter has traced the shift from public to private, first in the decline of street culture and the retreat to the home, and second, in the shift from 'family television' to 'bedroom culture'. The argument may be summarized as follows.

- Today, much privatized media use is centred on the bedroom, once a rather chilly and uncomfortable, even forbidden place in which to escape the demands of family life, but now a positively valued opportunity for socializing and identity work, saturated with media images, sounds, technological artefacts and other media products.

- Although children and young people value spending time with media, often alone – despite adult worries about 'isolation' or 'wasting time', this need not mean that social contacts are being replaced with social isolation, for media offer new means for social interaction, albeit often peer- rather than family-focused (Livingstone, 2005).
- Still, it does appear that within the home, the multiplication of personally owned media facilitates children's use of individual, privatized space, as opposed to communal family space. Rompaey and Roe (2001) calls this the increasing 'compartmentalization of family life' as a result of the individualizing effect of ICT combined with teenagers' desire for privacy within the family context. Similarly, Flichy (1995) calls it 'living together separately' in his characterization of the role of media in family life.

  However, I have argued that privatized bedroom culture is also the result of the progressive exclusion of children and young people from public places, together with a growing priority on 'the home' as the centre of a screen-entertainment focused, privatized and individualized leisure culture.
- Intriguingly, as leisure becomes increasingly media-dominated and as rooms (or people) rather than the household become the unit for acquisition of screen media, today's parents cannot rely on their own childhood experiences to guide them in managing the spatial, temporal and moral structures of domestic and family life.
- Rather they must figure out for their own family how to accommodate, regulate and enjoy the plethora of media goods now widely available. This they generally do together with their children as part of a sometimes co-operative, sometimes conflictual negotiation, within a broader context which pits a discourse of new opportunities and consumer choice against one of parental duties to manage appropriately the social development of their children in the face of increasing potential harms.

GOING FURTHER

Coontz, S. (1997) *The Way We Really Are: Coming to Terms with America's Changing Families.* New York: Basic Books.

An engaging account of how family life has changed in the past century, written for a popular audience.

Bovill, M. and Livingstone, S. (2001) 'Bedroom Culture and the Privatization of Media Use' in S. Livingstone and M. Bovill (eds) *Children and Their Changing Media Environment: A European Comparative Study*. Mahwah NJ: Lawrence Erlbaum Associates. pp. 179–200.

Presents original empirical material on children and young people's use of media in their bedrooms, compared across 12 European countries.

Flichy, P. (2006) 'New Media History' in L. Lievrouw and S. Livingstone (eds) *Handbook of New Media: Social Shaping and Consequences of ICTs*. Updated Student Edition. London: Sage. pp. 187-204.
Examines the relations between the spread of new media and the individualization of family and social life through the twentieth century.

STUDENT ACTIVITY 13.1

Make a list of the media that your parents, and then your grandparents, had at home (if you can ask them, do so). Compare this with the media you yourself grew up with and then with that of children today. Think especially about which media, if any, were situated in the bedroom, and which in the living room. Think also about the other activities that took place in these two domestic spaces, and the rules that determined who could do what? Again, you may need to ask people of different generations, as the answers can be surprising.

Then identify the similarities and differences over time. What continuities and differences does this suggest for what children can do, and for what is meant by, or expected of, 'childhood' or 'the family'? For example, do different arrangements of media (spatial, temporal, symbolic) influence the things that people (parents and children, children with their friends) share in common? Does it make it easier to pursue individual tastes?

References

Allan, G. (1985) *Family Life: Domestic Roles and Social Organization*. Oxford: Blackwell.

Ang, I. (1996) *Living Room Wars: Rethinking Media Audiences for a Postmodern World*. London: Routledge.

Bachmair, B. (1991) *Reconstruction of Family-Systems in a Media Negotiated World – The Social and Interpretive Functions of TV*. Paper presented at the Fourth International TV Studies Conference.

Beck, U. (1992) *Risk Society: Towards a new modernity*. London: Sage.

Bovill, M. and Livingstone, S. (2001) 'Bedroom Culture and the Privatization of Media Use' in S. Livingstone and M. Bovill (eds) *Children and Their Changing Media Environment: A European Comparative Study*. Mahwah NJ: Lawrence Erlbaum Associates. pp. 179–200.

Buchner, P. (1990) 'Growing up in the eighties: Changes in the social biography of childhood in the FRG' in L. Chisholm, P. Buchner, H. H. Kruger and P. Brown (eds) *Childhood, Youth and Social Change: A Comparative Perspective*. London: Falmer Press.

Buckingham, D., Scanlon, M. and Sefton-Green, J. (2001) 'Seeing the Digital Dream: Marketing Educational Technology to Teachers and Parents' in A. Loveless, and V. Ellis (eds) *Subject to Change: Literacy and Digital Technology*. London: Routledge. pp. 20–40.

Coontz, S. (1997) *The Way We Really Are: Coming to Terms with America's Changing Families*. New York: Basic Books.

Corrigan, P. (1976) 'Doing Nothing' in S. Hall and T. Jefferson (eds) *Resistance Through Rituals*. London: Hutchinson and co. pp. 103–05.

Cunningham, H. (1995) *Children and Childhood in Western Society Since 1500*. London: Longman.

Emler, N. and Reicher, S. (1994) *Adolescence and Delinquency: The Collective Management of Reputation*. Oxford: Blackwell.

Ennew, J. (1994) *Childhood as a Social Phenomenon: National Report – England and Wales* (Vol. 36). Vienna, Austria: European Centre for Social Welfare Policy and Research.

Flichy, P. (1995) *Dynamics of Modern Communication: The Shaping and Impact of New Communication Technologies*. London: Sage.

Flichy, P. (2006) 'New Media History' in L. Lievrouw and S. Livingstone (eds) *Handbook of New Media: Social Shaping and Consequences of ICTs*. Updated Student Edition. London: Sage. pp. 187–204.

Fornas, J. and Bolin, G. (1995) *Youth Culture in Late Modernity*. London: Sage.

Frith, S. (1978) *The Sociology of Rock*. London: Constable.

Gadlin, H. (1978) 'Child discipline and the pursuit of self: An historical interpretation' in H. W. Reese and L. P. Lipsitt (eds) *Advances in Child Development and Behavior*. New York, Academic Press. 12: 231–61.

Goffman, E. (1959) *The Presentation of Self in Everyday Life*. Harmondsworth: Penguin.

Hill, M. and Tisdall, K. (1997) *Children and Society*. London: Longman.

Hillman, M., Adams, J. and Whitelegg, J. (1990) *One False Move ... A Study of Children's Independent Mobility*. London: Policy Studies Institute.

Home Office (1994) 'Children as victims of crime, by type of crime 1983 and 1992 (i.e. abductions and gross indecency)', *Central Statistical Office: Special Focus on Children, 1994*. London: The Stationary Office.

James, A., Jenks, C. and Prout, A. (1998) *Theorizing Childhood*. Cambridge: Cambridge University Press.

Kinder, M. (ed.) (1999) *Kids' Media Culture*. Durham: Duke University Press.

Lincoln, S. (2004) 'Teenage girls' bedroom culture: Codes versus zones' in A. Bennett and K. Harris (eds) *After subculture: Critical studies of subcultural theory*. Hampshire, Palgrave/MacMillan. pp. 94–106.

Livingstone, S. (2002) *Young People and New Media: Childhood and the Changing Media Environment*. London: Sage.

Livingstone, S. (2005) 'In defence of privacy: Varieties of publicness in the individualised, privatised home' in S. Livingstone (ed.) *Audiences and Publics: When Cultural Engagement Matters for the Public Sphere* Bristol: Intellect Press. pp. 163–86.

Livingstone, S. and Bober, M. (2005) *UK Children Go Online: Final report of key project findings*. London: London School of Economics and Political Science.

Livingstone, S. and Bovill, M. (1999) *Young People New Media*. London: London School of Economics and Political Science.

Livingstone, S. and Bovill, M. (eds) (2001) *Children and their Changing Media Environment: A European Comparative Study*. Mahwah, N.J.: Lawrence Erlbaum Associates.

Livingstone, S., Bovill, M., & Gaskell, M. (1999) 'European TV kids in a transformed media world: Key findings of the UK study' in P. Lohr & M. Meyer (eds) *Children, Television and the New Media*. Televizion: University of Luton Press.

Madigan, R. and Munro, M. (1999) '"The more we are together": domestic space, gender and privacy' in T. Chapman and J. Hockey (eds) *Ideal Homes? Social Change and Domestic Life*. London: Routledge. pp. 61–72.

McRobbie, A. and Garber. (1976) 'Girls and subcultures' in S. Hall and P. Jefferson (eds) *Resistance Through Ritual: Youth Cultures in the Post War Britain*. Essex: Hutchinson University Library pp. 209–22.

Morley, D. (1986) *Family Television: Cultural Power and Domestic Leisure*. London: Comedia.

Oswell, D. (1999) 'And what might our children become? Future visions, governance and the child television audience in postwar Britain' *Screen*, 40(1): 77–105.

Roberts, D., Foehr, F., Rideout, V. and Brodie, M. (eds) (1999) *Kids and Media @t the New Millenium*. Menlo Park: Henry J. Kaiser Family Foundation.

Rochberg-Halton, E. (1984) 'Object relations, role models, and the cultivation of the self', *Environment and Behavior*. 16(3): 335–69.

Rompaey, V. V. and Roe, K. (2001) 'The home as a multimedia environment: Families' conception of space and the introduction of information and communication technologies in the home', *Communications*, 26(4): 351–69.

Scannell, P. (1988) 'Radio times: The temporal arrangements of broadcasting in the modern world' in P. Drummond and R. Paterson (eds) *Television and its Audience: International Research Perspectives*. London: British Film Institute.

Segalen, M. (1996) 'The industrial revolution: From proletariat to bourgeoisie' in A. Burguiere, C. Klapisch-Zuber, M. Segalen and F. Zonabend (eds) *A History of the Family: The Impact of Modernity* (Vol. 2). Cambridge: Harvard University Press. pp. 377–415.

Spigel, L. (1992) *Make Room for TV: Television and the Family Ideal in Postwar America*. Chicago: University of Chicago Press.

Steele, J. R. and Brown, J. D. (1994) 'Studying media in the context of everyday life', *Journal of Youth Adolescence,* 24(5): 551–76.

Williams, R. (1974) *Television: Technology and Cultural Form*. London: Fontana.

Notes

Acknowledgements: Thanks to Moira Bovill and Shenja Vandergraaf for their comments on an earlier version of this chapter. This chapter draws on material published in Chapter 5 of *Young People and New Media* (2002, London: Sage).

1 British parents' fears are not without foundation. Home Office statistics (1994) on child victims of crime report twice as many cases of gross indecency with a child in 1992 compared with 1983 and a fourfold increase in child abductions. Nonetheless, surveys conducted on both European crime rates and fear of crime show that while in Britain crime rates against children are relatively high, fear of crime is disproportionately high among British parents (Livingstone et al., 1999).

2 Throughout this chapter, names have been changed to protect participants' identity.

Fan Culture – Performing Difference

14

Jeroen de Kloet and Liesbet van Zoonen

Introduction

The usual textbook introduction on theoretical concepts like 'audience', 'fandom' or 'culture' starts with a definition of the key issue. In our chapter about fan culture, we hesitate to give such a clear-cut characterization of 'fan', 'fandom' or 'fan culture'. The reason for our reluctance is that the term 'fan' tends to be loaded with negative connotations of hysteria and pathology, whereas when one looks at the actual cognitions, investments, practices and interactions involved in being a fan, one sees many similarities between the fan of popular culture, the 'connaisseur' of literature and classical music, the collector of art, the ideal citizen in democracy and even the scholar doing academic research. This may seem too radical an assertion to begin with, but consider the following scenes taken from our immediate circle of friends and colleagues:

- A dinner party with an *haute cuisine* five-course meal. The hosts discuss their passion for Wagner's *Ring* cycle and lengthily recount their feelings at a recent performance, which, in its full length, lasted for 15 hours and for which they took a full week off.
- A political party meeting celebrating its electoral victory. The party leader arrives surrounded by cameras and microphones, and the gathered party members burst out in loud cheers, chanting her name.
- A media scholar studying *Big Brother*, immersing himself in hours of television, streaming video and internet forums; discussing the ins and outs of the programme with academics worldwide; and only half-jokingly calling its inventor John de Mol 'God'.

The Wagner connoisseurs will probably not describe themselves as fans, and most likely, they will not be pleased to be called so. Neither will the citizen or the scholar appreciate a comparison with fans. Terms related to high-cultural fandom, to public participation, and to knowledge work – connoisseur, citizen, scholar – differ significantly in connotation from fans. Yet, these seemingly different groups share extensive and detailed knowledge of their object; they are heavily emotionally connected to their object; they spend large amounts of time on it and deeply appreciate it to exchange their experience with other like-minded people. But whereas the connoisseur, the citizen and the scholar are praised for their intensive investments, the fan is more regularly accused of having silly pleasures, of leading vicarious lives and losing their mind over their idols or favourite programmes. Such pathologizing notions of fandom have dominated public discourse in which fans are portrayed, according to Jenson (1992), as either the obsessive individual (for example, the fan Mark Chapman who shot John Lennon four times on 8 December 1980) or the hysterical crowd (the 'bewildered' audience of, say, Robbie Williams).

Why do fans have such a bad reputation, what is gained by these pathologizing notions of fandom, and what 'real' experiences go on behind public stereotypes of the fan? These are the questions that we will discuss in this chapter, using recent cultural studies work on fandom. While media psychology would provide another possible perspective to discuss fandom, it tends to focus primarily on the relation between the individual fan and his or her text (see Box 14.1). In our understanding of fandom it is particularly the social-cultural context and social interaction of fandom that negates the public concern around obsession and other pathologies, and that makes it possible to compare fandom to the other cultural, political and knowledge practices we just discussed.

We will examine three important dimensions in fan-studies. First, the *cultural dimension*, referring to studies in which fans were taken seriously and their fandom read as acts of cultural production, if not resistance (Lewis, 1992; Jenkins, 1992; Fiske, 1992). Second, the *performative dimension*, which shifts the focus from the ideological discourse on power and resistance towards the cultural *practices* of fandom. Fandom is a performative act that should be read in conjunction with pivotal indicators of difference – gender, age, sexuality, class and ethnicity (Hills, 2002; Lancaster, 2001). Third, the *local dimension*, which emerges in the context of debates on globalization and in connection to the Anglo-Saxon bias of fan-studies, inspiring research that is more sensitive towards the specific cultural context of fan cultures (Chow and De Kloet, 2005; Meers, 2006). Before embarking upon this journey into fan-studies, in which we move from the cultural to the performative and finally local dimension, it makes sense – despite our hesitations – to briefly explore which definitional notions of the fan have been proposed, and point at the complications we meet when we try to define fandom.

Box 14.1   Notes on fan psychology

Two concepts are crucial within media psychology to understand fandom: identification and parasocial interaction (PSI). The latter term stands for the social interaction between audiences and media figures as if in a typical social relationship (Giles, 2002). Cohen (1999: 329) defines PSI as a relationship in which 'the viewer is engaged in a role relationship with a television persona.' Although most PSI research focuses on television, the concept can also be applied to pop stars and movie actors. While in early studies PSI was often considered to compensate for a lack of 'real' social contacts (Rosengren and Windahl, 1972), later studies showed how PSI does not correlate to loneliness or escapism (Rubin and McHugh, 1987). Perse and Rubin (1989) showed that people use fundamentally the same cognitive processes in both interpersonal and mediated communication. Rubin and McHugh (1987) distinguished three types of attraction in PSI: social, physical and task attraction. They found that social attraction (i.e. the media figure could be a friend) was most important.

Apart from PSI, Cohen (1999) mentions three other possible ways of relating to media personalities: First, identification, characterized by the sharing of perspective. Second, wishful identification, characterized by the desire to emulate the figure with which we identify in general or specific terms. Third, affinity, referring to the liking of media characters without identifying with them, or forming a parasocial relationship. (For a lucid meta-study on PSI, see Giles, 2002.) However useful this terminology can be for analyzing fandom, in focusing solely on the relationship between a person and the text, it largely fails to account for the social dimension of fandom. In particular, fans constitute vibrant interpretative communities.

Defining fandom

'Fan' is an abbreviation of 'fanatic' a word that comes from the Latin word 'fanaticus'. While the term originally meant, quite simply, 'of or belonging to the temple, a temple servant, a devotee,' its meaning quickly slipped towards more negative connotations, including 'frenzy', 'madness' and 'obsessive' (Jenkins, 1992: 12). Cultural studies' approaches to fandom have usually tried to debunk such associations and present less value-loaded analyses of fandom. One problem most authors encounter is that fandom cannot be pinned down to a singular definition as expressions and performances of fandom change over time and place. Many authors come up with distinctions within the general category of fans. Tulloch and Jenkins (1995: 23), for instance, make a distinction between 'followers' and 'fans', along the axis of engagement with the object of fandom. Unlike a 'follower', a fan claims a social identity. Brooker and Brooker's (1996: 141) distinction in 'admirers', 'fans' and 'cult fans' echoes a similar mode of distinction (see also Meers, 2006).

Abercrombie and Longhurst's (1998) taxonomy of audience involvement is arguably the most extensive example of such attempts at refinement. They have proposed to consider fandom as the first degree of intensity with which one can relate to cultural texts. In a continuum of audience involvement, they distinguish between mere consumers on the one extreme and petty producers on the other, with fans, cultists and enthusiasts in the middle.[1] While it does make sense to distinguish between different kinds of audience involvement, their proposal is problematic for its overhaul of common academic and common sense concepts. Abercrombie and Longhurst explain that the fan in previous studies resembles most closely their definition of a cultist, but as Hills (2002: ix) observes, 'It seems faintly unhelpful to produce a taxonomy in which the definition of "fan" is at odds with the use of this term in almost all other literature in the field.' Hills continues to approach cult fandom as a 'particular (enduring) form of affective fan relationship' (Hills, 2002: xi).

While these authors start from different degrees of involvement in cultural texts, Fiske (1992: 37–38) has made a distinction based on what people *do* or *perform* with their fandom. He distinguishes three levels of productivity: first, at the level of *semiotic productivity*, consumption of popular culture entails 'the making of meanings of social identity and of social experience from the semiotic resources of the cultural commodity' (1992: 37). At the second level, that of *enunciative productivity*, the meanings made at the first level are 'shared within a face-to-face or oral culture' that take a public form. This level includes the fervent fan talk, the sharing of experiences and styling of, for example, hair and outfit, in other words, the appropriation and development of a specific subcultural style. The third level of fandom concerns *textual productivity*, 'fans produce and circulate among themselves texts which are often crafted with production values as high as any in the official culture' (1992: 39). Dutch fans of *Lord of the Rings*, for example, do not only gather every month in a special tavern, they also develop new story lines, learn and develop the languages invented by Tolkien and dress up as Hobbits, Elves and Orcs to engage in role-playing games in Dutch forests (van Romondt-Vis, 2004). With the rapid emergence of the Internet over the 1990s, and the related introduction of new technologies, including all kinds of digital media-tools (Photoshop, Garageband, Blogging etc.), textual fan-production has proliferated and globalized significantly. Today, fans are, even more so than in the past, also producers (Shefrin, 2004).

Fiske sensitizes us to the intimate relationship between the fan and the object of fandom, and his categorization reveals how delicate the line between fan and non-fan is – how often are we not involved in enunciative and at times even textual production ourselves?[2] The level of participation through active appropriation of the object of fandom hints at the performative dimension of fandom. Fans perform a sense of distinction through the accumulation of what Thornton (1995) terms, echoing the work of Bourdieu, subcultural capital. While fan studies often challenge the explicit or implicit high-low distinction that produces derivative accounts of fan cultures, it is becoming increasingly important to take issue with the hierarchies that are produced within the domain of popular culture: fandom of Britney Spears, for example, remains a more contested type of fandom when compared to fandom of U2. Studies consequently need to be sensitive to these more subtle patterns of distinction *within* popular culture.

The tactics of distinction (vis-à-vis other fan cultures or within the same fan culture) all revolve around claims to authenticity – of being the true fan. Fandom can consequently be read as a performative politics of identity in which the authentic self wishes to differentiate him or herself from the inauthentic other. This notion of the performance of 'difference' makes it especially possible to compare the fan to connoisseurs, citizens and scholars, all of whom can be seen as agents of consecration that contribute to the formation of a collective belief surrounding the value of symbolic goods (Shefrin, 2004: 270). The fan's quest for authenticity produces inauthentic Others – the non-fan – just like the connoisseur of high culture looks down on dim pop culture fans, just like the citizen condemns the politically disinterested consumer, and the scholar defies the everyday, non-systematic knowledge of journalism. All these cases involve quite a vicious war of positions (Jancovich, 2002).

Authenticity of fans is produced through a deep commitment to popular texts, ranging from Elvis to the *X-files*, from *Star Trek* to *Lord of the Rings*. These appropriations are often closely linked to the classic indicators of social difference: class, gender, age, sexuality and ethnicity. For example, Beatlemania was very much a girl culture (Ehrenreich et al., 1992), whereas gay men form fan communities around the Eurovision song contest (Lemish, 2004). Fans produce an identity that borders on the acceptable, since the objects of fandom are considered trivial in dominant discourse. But, as Hills also observes, the more important issue is not whether fandom can be perceived as a mode of popular resistance, or whether fandom is 'good' or 'bad,' but to explore '*what fandom does culturally*' (Hills, 2002: xii, original italics). We agree with Hills that in order to approach this question it is crucial to depart from singular studies on specific fan cultures, as well as to think beyond simplistic binaries of resistance versus complicity. We need to move towards a broader understanding in which different and partly overlapping fan cultures are integrated so as to grasp the cultural dynamics that propel the global rise and decline of fan cultures. But before delving into the performative dynamics of fandom, it is crucial to go back in time to the early 1990s, when the first ethnographic studies on fans were published.

The cultural dimension

Jenkins (1992), Fiske (1992) and Lewis (1992) can be considered the key representatives of the cultural dimension in fan-studies. Their work has been greatly influenced by De Certeau's 1984 classic *The Practice of Everyday Life*. The poaching metaphor is employed by De Certeau to account for the active act of reading. De Certeau describes readers as nomads who travel through the media-landscape, picking and choosing, using and abusing what is to their liking. The cultural dimension is thereby driven by a fundamental debate in fan-studies: are fans duped by a consumerist culture industry, or are they active agents who shape their own life in an original fashion? This resistance versus compliance dualism propels most of the studies that follow the cultural approach of fan-studies. Its proponents firmly opt for a resistant reading of fandom: fans are anything but duped by the culture industry. Instead, they are active agents, or poachers, that appropriate media texts to make sense of everyday life. In his book *Textual Poachers*, Jenkins (1992) distinguishes five characteristics of fan cultures:

First, fandom concerns a particular mode of reception. 'Fan viewers watch television texts with close and undivided attention, with a mixture of emotional proximity and critical distance' (Jenkins, 1992: 277–8). Following Fiske's levels of fan-productivity, reception involves fierce discussion with others over the text, up to the level of textual production. Second, 'fandom involves a particular set of critical and interpretive practices' (1992: 278). Becoming a fan implies becoming accustomed with the preferred reading within the fan community, to become skilful in including playful references to the text and to establish links between one's own life and the text. Third, fandom constitutes a base for activism. Since fans are the ones to speak back to the networks and producers, according to Jenkins, they give a voice to the invisible audience. In the words of Shefrin (2004: 270), fans contribute 'to the evaluation of a cultural producer's symbolic capital'. Fourth, 'fandom possesses particular forms of cultural production, aesthetic traditions and practices. (...) Fandom generates its own genres and develops alternative institutions of production, distribution, exhibition and consumption' (2004: 279). Fandom hence constitutes an alternative economy outside the mainstream. Fifth, fandom functions as an alternative social community. Fans try to establish a 'weekend-only world' outside dominant cultural values of work. Fandom constitutes a space 'defined by its refusal of mundane values and practices, its celebration of deeply held emotions and passionately embraced pleasures. Fandom's very existence represents a critique of conventional forms of consumer culture' (2004: 283; see also Meers, 2006: 71).

Studies in this line of research tend to offer a rather celebratory ethnographic insight in fan cultures. The insistence to analyze what fans do with media, rather than what the media do with fans, remains an important story to be told. It counters both traditional models of effect research as well as pathologizing approaches to fandom. Ethnographic fan-studies also move beyond an inversion of the 'fan as duped by the culture industry' narrative by focusing on the mundane and everyday realities of fandom. One more recent example along this line of research comes from Hodkinson (2002), who presents an ethnographic insiders account of Goth culture, in which he fiercely debunks the (postmodern) claim that collective identities and subcultures are increasingly becoming fragmented. He shows how offline and online fan practices strengthen group ties and help produce a spectacular subculture. In recent years, everyday fandom has become increasingly digitalized, when the Internet provides a new way to align with fans nationally and globally (see Box 14:2 for a study of online fandom).

Box 14.2   Tune in, log on: Soap, fandom and online community according to Baym

Taken from van Zoonen (2000).

Baym's (2000) case study of the Internet community that evolved around the American soap *All My Children* is highly illustrative for online fandom. Baym participated in the Usernet news group and observed the interaction between its participants between 1990 and 1993. She returned to the group in 1998 to see whether the development and greater availability of the Internet had changed the practices in the group. The conversations between the participants – mainly women – were primarily concerned with the interpretation of soap stories and characters. Fans process the soaps, for instance, by relating them to their own lives or by speculating about future events. As Baym shows through extensive quotes from the multitude of postings in the group, these interpretations emerged in dialogue and deliberation, which have both a playful and an emotional component. Part of the pleasure of the news group was in the common evaluation of the quality, realism and underlying messages contained in soap texts.

The participants proved to be a highly competent audience expressing critical assessments of the show that often surpassed the knowledge of the producers. Some long-time fans felt they knew the characters and their fictional community better than the writers and were struggling – as it were – with the writers about the ownership of the series. Baym showed how participants came up with new and better storylines, which they exchanged among themselves in a humorous display of creativity and wit. The deliberation around these new stories was conducted in a general sphere of friendliness and consensus seeking. The fact that these participants were mostly women certainly contributed to the group atmosphere, according to Byam. However, it was not gender alone that was an explanatory factor here, but its articulation with the specific textual features of the soap operas that call for diverging meanings and interpretations. In her analysis, Baym thus links fandom to the specificity of a medium (the Internet), to gender (women) and to genre (soap).

During the 1990s, the paradigm of fan-studies has moved increasingly beyond a romanticisation of fandom. Fan cultures are increasingly seen as incoherent, to quote Jancovich (2002: 315): 'in fact, cult movie audiences are less an internally coherent "taste culture" than a series of frequently opposed and contradictory reading strategies that are defined through a sense of their difference to an equally incoherently imagined "normality", a loose conglomeration of corporate power, lower middle class conformity and prudishness, academic elitism and political conspiracy.' To follow a resistance versus compliance dualism is therefore inadequate. According to Hills, fandom is necessarily contradictory, 'fans are both commodity-completists and they express anti-commercial beliefs or "ideologies"' (Hills, 2002: 44). Fans hence oscillate between consumerism and 'resistance'. Their identity is constructed in the never-ending dialectic inside and outside commodification.

The performative dimension

In the attempt to think beyond a resistance versus compliance model it is important to focus on different *practices* of fandom, to unpack their performative repertoires and take issue with the underlying struggles for and over power. 'Thinking of fans as performers means displacing an emphasis on the text-reader interaction, and focusing instead on the myriad ways that fans can engage with the textual structures and moments of their favoured cult shows, reactivating these in cultural practices of play' (Hills, 2002: 41, see also Lancaster, 2001). Performance studies can be traced back to two distinct schools, one focusing on performativity, the other on performances. First the philosophical school, in which authors like Austin (1962) and Butler (1990), among many others, analyze how words impact upon reality. Butler argues that not only is gender a construction, it is a performative construction. We perform our gender in our everyday lives. While performance may evoke connotations of false or fake, Butler takes a Foucauldian position, namely what is left behind the performative mask is a void, or subjectivity is nothing but performance. Subjectivity is constituted through discourse, and once we define discourse as inherently performative (as signalled by Austin's notion of *speech acts*), subjectivity is turned into a performative act.

The second school in performance studies comes from sociology (Goffman, 1959), anthropology (Turner, 1988; Fabian, 1990; MacAloon, 1984) and theatre studies (Schechner, 2002). Here, the attention moves away from phenomenological questions on subjectivity towards a more down-to-earth approach in which everyday social life is perceived as a performance. It can be read in line with Shakespeare's clichéd phrase that 'all the world's a stage'. Studies along this line of thinking involve analyses of the dramaturgical rules that guide performances, and are highly sensitive to the social context in which performances occur.

When we apply a mix of the theatrical and phenomenological approaches of performance studies to fandom, we are able to delve deeper into its social implications. Fandom can be a way to perform sexual preferences, for example, when gay men go together to bars to watch the Eurovision song contest (Lemish, 2004). It can be a way to perform gender, for example, when men go to football matches dressed up in special outfits to support their team (Brown, 1998). It can be a way to perform ethnicity, for example when the black fans of *50 Cent* gain street credibility through their intense involvement with their object of fandom.[3] And it can be a way to perform political involvement, for example, when fans cheer along with their favourite politicians while wearing the colours of their political party (van Zoonen, 2004).

Fandom often involves conspicuous consumption of collectors' items like first editions, bootleg tapes, and all sorts of paraphernalia. Fan cultural capital has gained economic value over the past decades. According to Hills, consumption has a strong performative dimension: 'media fandoms presuppose consumption and are expressed through consumption – it is hence both an act and an iteration-without-origin' (Hills, 2002: 159). The performative dimension becomes most apparent at the moment of impersonation, according to Nightingale (in Hills, 2002: 160): 'Impersonation generates another experience [the experience of "improvisation"], a re-creation of the star not as an image but as a story about capitalism, often as the story of a contradiction in capitalism. As the "star's" personal narrative is recreated and explored by the impersonator, another performance, another personal narrative is pursued – the impersonator's life as the star.' Through impersonation and improvization, the fan oscillates between his 'self' and the 'other', between intense 'self-reflexivity' and 'self-absence' (Hills, 2002: 171). Fandom involves the performative embodiment of such contradictions, blurring the line between self and other (see Box 14.3).

Box 14.3   Buffy Fandom

Buffy the Vampire Slayer has rapidly gained a cult fan following since the series started in 1997. The series directly and deliberately speaks to the experience of outsiderdom, an experience very much shared by fan cultures (Williamson, 2005: 296). The vampire Spike represents an otherness that fans recognize in themselves. Spike encourages a fannish immersion in the text, he 'becomes meaningful to fans because of the existence of a cross-textual, cross-generational sympathetic vampire which transcends him and through which he can be read' (Williamson, 2005: 299). James Marsters, the actor playing Spike, can be considered a subcultural celebrity, according to Hills and Williams (2005). His performance merges to a large extent actor and character, he appears fan-like, thereby disrupting the distance between 'fan' and 'celebrity'. Key to this intervention is Marsters' self-styled accessibility to his fans. His discursive blurrings of character/actor identities, combined with his availability for fans, 'feed into the fans' positive interpretations of Spike' (Hills and Williams, 2005: 354).

Both the deliberate intertextuality encoded in the series as well as the conflation of Marsters with Spike – of the actor with his character – are illustrative for the performativity of fandom. The intertextuality of *Buffy the Vampire Slayer* – consciously encoded in the text – encourages new readings that, in particular

(Continued)

in a social context, can be read as playful performances of the fan to express, that is; construct and display, his or her fan-cultural capital. The merging of the actor Marsters with the vampire Spike hints at the performativity of both the persona as well as the character. The audience is drawn into the series, encouraged to engage in intertextual performances that include real life role-playing games, both online and offline. Such acts of textual production destabilizes the boundary between self and other, between real and imagined. Through role-playing games, fans are involved in a process of perpetual becoming: becoming the Other, becoming the vampire, becoming Spike.

In particular, digital performances of fandom have proliferated tremendously over the past decade. Technological developments facilitate new performative modes of fandom. For example, during *Idols* contests, television viewers participate in the show by SMS voting (Reijnders, et al., 2006). Media audiences increasingly become participants. This may result in what can be termed 'SMS democracy'. In China, the *Supergirl 2005* contest, based on the *Idols* format but restricted to female contestants, became one of the nation's media hypes of 2005. For the first time in China's history, its citizens were allowed to vote through SMS for their favourite contestant. Three and a half million Chinese voters chose Li Yuchun to become the winner and a rising pop star in China (Anonymous, 2005, online).[4] Li Yuchun's stardom is produced by her fans, rather than the other way round. This example is also telling for yet another important aspect of fan culture: the voting system is of particular relevance in the Chinese context, since it offers a fundamentally democratic model and potential to subvert an authoritative political regime, whereas in a Western context, SMS voting practices can be and are being criticized for their capitalist logic. In other words, this example points to the importance of locality, which brings us to the last dimension in fan-studies.

Box 14.4   Marco versus Leon – The Netherlands versus Hong Kong (Chow and de Kloet, 2005)

Amidst American domination of the global pop music scene, an increasing number of people choose a local artist as their star. In a comparative study of fans

(Continued)

Plate 14:1 The fans of Marco Borsato and of Leon Lai, in configuring their local communities, in characterising their local stars, have succeeded in claiming their own space, their own preferences and values, even if the world is said to be flattened out by globalising forces. Pictures reproduced by kind permission of Paciwood Music and Entertainment Ltd © and Loe Beerens ©.

of Hong Kong pop idol Leon Lai and his Dutch counterpart Marco Borsato, Chow and de Kloet (2005) found striking differences in both localities. In general, while the Dutch fans see Marco as an ordinary human being, the Hong Kong fans characterize Leon as an extraordinary worker. The Marco fans' notion of ordinariness, with its associated constructions of having feelings, being authentic and accessible, also leads to articulations of strong emotional ties to his music – entirely absent in the discourse of the Leon Lai fans. Besides his good looks, Leon Lai's most remarkable character trait is work rather than charity – his hardworking perseverance and constant attempt to seek improvement and honour. The different characterizations, the authors argue, are in turn informed by the dominant discourse on being ordinary, emotionally honest and humanitarian in the Dutch society at large, as well as that on being more than ordinary, hardworking and proud in the Hong Kong context.

The fans of Marco Borsato and of Leon Lai, in configuring their local communities and in characterizing their local stars, have succeeded in claiming their own space, their own preferences and values, even if the world is said to

(Continued)

be flattened out by globalizing forces. They are empowering their local stars as much as they are empowered in negotiating their experiences not only in the pop music world dominated by global icons such as Madonna, but also in the larger context of global culture, global economy and global politics. Even when the music of Marco and Leon sounds not unlike that of global counterparts, even when they look not unlike their global counterparts, their local fans perceive them differently.

The local dimension

Fandom can also be a way to express and construct locality. However, locality has remained an understudied topic of research in fan cultures, which continues to show a strong Anglo-Saxon bias. While fandom is taken as a 'response to specific historical conditions' (Jenkins, 1992: 3), the studies undertaken so far by and large fail to reflect upon cultural specificities and therefore run the danger of producing a homogenizing discourse in which fan is turned into a universal label. Under the current conditions of increased globalization, this lack of sensitivity to the importance of place is rather surprising and motivates us to pay particular attention to fandom as *a performance of locality*. The debate on globalization is characterized by two opposite poles: one school argues that globalization is flattening our world (Friedman, 2005), with the US as the cultural, political and economical epicentre of our world. Here, globalization is seen as a process of homogenization or 'McDonaldization' (Ritzer, 2000). The apocalyptic undertone of this argument often includes a harsh critique on the US, in particular, its alleged dream-factory, Hollywood.

The other end of the debate interprets globalization as a process of increased heterogenization, with new cultural elements being cut and pasted with already existing cultural patterns, producing creolized cultures (Hannerz, 1987), or propelling the indiginization of 'foreign' cultural forms (Appadurai, 1996). Similar cultural icons can therefore have different readings, and therefore produce different fan cultures, in different cultural contexts. Along the same line, local stars are appropriated by local fan cultures to produce a sense of locality (cf. Appadurai, 1996), or to construct a *heimat*, a feeling of home (Morley, 2001) – see Box 14.4. For example, Kuwait youth appropriates *The Fresh Prince of Bel-Air* to express a sense of cultural anxiety combined with a longing for modernity (Havens, 2001). Japanese Hip Hop is an expression of a middle-class club culture, rather than an ethnic lower-class street culture as in the US (Condry, 2000). Not only are cultural genres appropriated differently in different parts of the world, but so to is similar text read differently. A study by Liebes and Katz reveals how cultural background greatly influences the reading of the soap opera *Dallas* (Liebes and Katz, 1993). Similar cross-cultural studies for fan cultures are, however, scarce.

One recent study that involves a cross-national comparison focuses on audiences of *Lord of the Rings*. A total sample of 24,648 respondents filled in an online questionnaire. On a decreasing 5 point-scale, they valued the movie, on average, very high (1.4). Meers (2006: 76) further distinguishes them in three types: the *Lord of the Rings* fan, the fantasy fan and the blockbuster fan. Whereas the first group uses the books as their point of reference, the second group uses fantasy films and the third group takes blockbuster films as their reference points. The depth of their engagement with the text is highest for the *Lord of the Rings* fan, and lowest for the blockbuster fan. When comparing the quantitative data of the study, De Kloet and Kuipers (2006), however, discovered no clear or systematic differences between countries, or between clusters of countries. Following Beck (2002), they label the movie as a case of 'banal cosmopolitanism'. Their argument resonates with the homogenization thesis; the *Lord of the Rings* fans are like banal cosmopolitans whose fan alliances move beyond national and cultural boundaries.

Conclusion

Our description of the three dimensions of fan-studies may suggest neatly demarcated approaches. As we indicated in the introduction of this chapter, the pathologizing discourse on fandom is still in currency, particularly in popular discourse. The cultural dimension, which is driven by a desire to counter this discourse, remains of crucial importance. The performative dimension shifts the focus from reading fandom in terms of compliance versus resistance, towards a reading of fandom as a shared cultural practice. The last dimension sensitizes research to local particularities and cosmopolitan possibilities of fandom. Rather than reading these dimensions as contrasting paradigms, we wish to stress that they are complementary and can be combined in a singular study. By way of conclusion, we discuss two more points: one regarding the importance of the objects of fandom, and the need to study fan cultures in combination with a study of star-texts, the other referring to the political economy underpinning fan cultures. Here we return to a classic cultural studies position: reception analysis should go hand-in-hand with a textual and production analysis.

First, fan cultures are formed around specific cultural texts and the nature of these texts is what distinguishes fans from connoisseurs, citizens and scholars, not their cognitions, emotions, behaviour and everyday lives. Ideally, fan-studies should involve, therefore, a more thorough analysis of the object of fandom. There can be no fan without an object of fandom. However simplistic such an observation may sound, fan-studies do run the danger of ignoring the particularities of the text, and dismiss the ideological and economical intertwinement of production and consumption. It remains, therefore, important to study the object of fandom in conjunction with its surrounding fan culture. The work of Dyer on stars (1998) helps to analyze what can be called the *star-text*. Stars are, according to Dyer, not only characters, they are also real people. The star-text involves not just the cultural texts produced by the star, but also his or her personal life. Stars-texts are deeply polysemic, while stars operate as spectacular signifiers. According to Dyer, 'star images function crucially in relation to contradictions within and between ideologies, which they seek variously to "manage" or resolve' (1998: 34). According to Ellis, a star is 'a performer in a particular medium whose figure enters into subsidiary forms of circulation, and then feeds back into future performances' (1992: 91). Ellis continues to observe that stars are 'at once ordinary and extraordinary, available for desire and unattainable' (1992: 91). Studies of stars should hence involve a wide array of texts in which the star appears, both in his role as performer (actor, musician, etc.) as well as in report on his 'real' life, and be sensitive for the multiple meaning and contradictory ideologies embodied in stars. Such a textual analysis will facilitate a deeper understanding of the fan's involvement with the star. Again, here lie the commonalities with other cultural practices such as art and politics; especially in the latter field, the celebrity-politician has become an icon of perversion of democratic and deliberative values with little appreciation of the potential for meaning and involvement that they offer (cf. van Zoonen, 2005).

Second, the politic-economical context in which media texts are produced and consumed is of crucial importance (Mansell, 2005; Golding et al., 1997), and is too often ignored in fan-studies. In his study of cult movie fandom, Jancovich observes how this fandom grew out of a post-war process in which selective film markets were created that were defined as different from mainstream, commercial cinema. 'Indeed, it is the very ideology which insists that these markets are free from economic criteria which needs to be criticized' (Jancovich, 2002: 317). The positioning of non-mainstream cult cinema can be read as a marketing tactic, one that resembles the portfolio marketing strategies in the music industry in which specific units develop and promote specific music genres (Negus, 1999). Andrejevic's study (2002) expresses a similar concern, referring to participants and audiences of reality TV as savvy consumers whose ideas on self-realization, consumption and pleasure are manufactured by a culture industry that is driven by the logic of global capitalism. The earlier mentioned study on cross-cultural differences in fandom of *Lord of the Rings,* and the lack thereof, also hints at the power of the culture industry that produces similar readings of specific products targeted at worldwide audiences. In a perverse way, fans are constitutive, in their disavowal of the culture industry, in their ingenious and passionate fabrications of an 'authentic self', of the cultural mainstream (see also Hills, 2002, in particular, Chapter 1). A study of fandom brings us finally back to a classic debate in sociology: the debate between agency and structure. Studies of fans should be sensitive to the structural and cultural conditions that both produce and contain fan cultures, while keeping a close, committed, ethnographic eye on the cultural practices of fans in their everyday lives.

Summary

- The knowledge, investments, practices and interactions involved in fandom are not fundamentally different from those related to art, politics and scholarship. What distinguishes these relations to culture is the nature of the textual object. Fans are active consumers who use media texts as a way to construct their identity and make sense of everyday life.
- Fandom is a way to accumulate fan cultural capital and helps to produce an authentic self.
- Fandom can be perceived as a performative act, in which fandom can be interpreted as spectacular performances of gender, age, ethnicity, sexuality and class.
- Under current forces of intense globalization, fandom is an important way for the production of locality, in which fan cultures either emerge around particular local stars or produce specific local readings of global stars.
- Studies of fan cultures need to include analyses of the object of fandom and be highly sensitive to the political economy that produces star-texts and fan cultures.

GOING FURTHER

Baym, N. (2000) *Tune in, Log on: Soap, Fandom and Online Community*. London: Sage.
Presents an in-depth, qualitative longitudinal study of an online community of soap opera fans [See Box 14.2].

Dyer, R. (1998 (1979)) *Stars*. London: Routledge.
Classic study of the importance of stars in our everyday life, lucid example of the possible strengths and insights provided by textual analysis, focus is predominantly on movie stars.

Hills, M. (2002) *Fan Cultures*. London: Routledge.
Provides the best overview of fan studies currently available, strongly inspired by earlier studies, but refuses to get trapped in a resistance versus compliance dichotomy.

Jenkins, H. (1992) *Textual Poachers - Television Fans and Participatory Culture*. London: Routledge.
Classic fan-study which is theoretically inspired by the work of Michel de Certeau, with valuable insights into the active engagement of fans in media, and its potential political implications.

(Continued)

Lewis, L. A. (ed.) (1992) *Adoring Audience - Fan Culture and Popular Media*. London: Routledge. Reader with key texts on the cultural dimension of fandom, presents together with Jenkins the academic start of fan studies.

STUDENT ACTIVITY 14.1

Today's global stars like Robbie Williams and Kylie Minogue all have their own fan-websites. Select the message-board of the fan website of your favourite star and analyze the first 50 postings. Give examples of the cultural, the performative and the local dimension of the postings, inspired by the theory provided in this chapter.

References

Abercrombie, N. and Longhurst, B. (1998) *Audiences: A Sociological Theory of Performance and Imagination*. London: Sage.

Andrejevic, M. (2002) 'The Kinder, Gentler Gaze of Big Brother: Reality TV in the Era of Digital Capitalism', *New Media & Society*, 4(2): 251–70.

Anonymous (2005) *China Rockin' to 'Super Girl'*. Retrieved 20 May 2006, http://www.chinadaily.com.cn/english/doc/2005-08/30/content_473432.htm

Appadurai, A. (1996) *Modernity At Large – Cultural Dimensions of Globalization*. Minneapolis: University of Minnesota Press.

Austin, J. L. (1962) *How To Do Things With Words*. Oxford: Oxford University Press.

Baym, N. (2000) *Tune in, Log on: Soap, Fandom and Online Community*. London: Sage.

Beck, U. (2002) 'The Cosmopolitan Society and its Enemies', *Theory, Culture & Society*, 19(1–2): 17–44.

Brooker, P. and Brooker, W. (1996) 'Pulpmodernism: Tarantino's affirmative action' in D. Cartmell, I. Q. Hunter, H. Kaye and I. Whelelan (eds) *Pulping Fictions: Consuming Culture across the Literature/Media Divide*. London: Pluto. pp. 89–100.

Brown, A. (ed.) (1998) *Fanatics! Power, Identity and Fandom in Football*. London: Routledge.

Butler, J. (1990) *Gender Trouble: Feminism and the Subversion of Identity*. London: Routledge.

Chow, Y. F. and de Kloet, J. (2005) *Stars in a Star Spangled World – A Comparative Study of Pop fans in The Netherlands and Hong Kong*. Paper presented at the International Association for the Study of Popular Music – Making Music Making Meaning, Rome (25–30 July).

Christenson, P. G. and Roberts, D. F. (1998). *It's not only Rock & Roll – Popular music in the lives of adolescents*. Cresskill: Hampton Press.

Cohen, J. (1999) 'Favorite characters of teenage viewers of Israeli serials', *Journal of Broadcasting and Electronic Media,* 43: 327–45.

Condry, I. (2000) 'The social production of difference – Imitation and authenticity in Japanese rap music' in U. Poiger and H. Fehrenbach (eds) *Transactions, Transgressions, Transformations: American Culture in Western Europe and Japan.* New York: Berghan Books. pp. 166–84.

de Certeau, M. (1984). *The Practice of Everyday Life.* London: University of California Press.

de Kloet, J. (2001) *Red Sonic Trajectories – Popular Music and Youth in Urban China.* Amsterdam: PhD Dissertation – University of Amsterdam.

de Kloet, J. and Kuipers, G. (2006) 'Banaal kosmopolitisme en *The Lord of the Rings* – Over de conceptualisering van de natiestaat in vergelijkend communicatiewetenschappelijk onderzoek', *Tijdschrift voor Communicatiewetenschap,* 34(1): 88–110.

Dee, A.-C. and Williamson, M. (2005) 'The vampire Spike in text and fandom – Unsettling oppositions in *Buffy the Vampire Slayer*', *European Journal of Cultural Studies,* 8(3): 275–88.

Dyer, R. (1998 (1979)) *Stars.* London: Routledge.

Ehrenreich, B., Hess, E. and Jacobds, G. (1992) 'Beatlemania: Girls Just Want to Have Fun' in L. A. Lewis (ed.) *Adoring Audience – Fan Culture and Popular Media.* London: Routledge. pp. 84–106.

Ellis, J. (1992) *Visible Fictions: Cinema, Television, Video.* London: Routledge.

Fabian, J. (1990) *Power and Performance: Ethnographic Explorations through Proverbial Wisdom and Theater in Shaba, Zaire.* Madison: University of Wisconsin Press.

Fiske, J. (1992) 'The Cultural Economy of Fandom' in L. A. Lewis (ed.) *Adoring Audience – Fan Culture and Popular Media.* London: Routledge. pp. 30–49.

Friedman, T. L. (2005) *The World is Flat: A brief history of the twenty-first century.* New York: Farrer, Straus and Giroux.

Giles, D. C. (2002) 'Parasocial Interaction: A review of the Literature and a Model for Future Research', *Media Psychology,* 4: 279–305.

Goffman, E. (1959) *The Presentation of Self in Everyday Life.* New York: Doubleday Anchor Book.

Golding, P., Murdock, G. and Garnham, N. (1997) 'The Political Economy of the Media', *European Journal of Communication,* 12: 548–49.

Hannerz, U. (1987) 'The world in creolisation', *Africa,* 57(4): 546–59.

Havens, T. (2001) 'Subtitling Rap – Appropriating The Fresh Prince of Bel-Air for Youthful Identity Formation in Kuwait', *Gazette,* 63(1): 57–72.

Hills, M. (2002) *Fan Cultures.* London: Routledge.

Hills, M. and Williams, R. (2005). '"It's all my interpretation" – Reading Spike through the subcultural celebrity James Marsters', *European Journal of Cultural Studies,* 8(3): 345–65.

Hodkinson, P. (2002) *Goth – Identity, Style and Subculture.* Oxford: Berg.

Jancovich, M. (2002) 'Cult Fictions: Cult Movies, Subcultural Capital and the Production of Cultural Distinctions', *Cultural Studies,* 16(2): 306–22.

Jenkins, H. (1992) *Textual Poachers – Television Fans & Participatory Culture.* London: Routledge.

Jenson, J. (1992) 'Fandom as Pathology: The Consequences of Characterization' in L. A. Lewis (ed.) *Adoring Audience – Fan Culture and Popular Media.* London: Routledge. pp. 9–29.

Lancaster, K. (2001) *Interacting with 'Babylon 5': Fan Performances in a Media Universe.* Austin: University of Texas Press.

Lemish, D. (2004) '"My Kind of Campfire": The Eurovision Song Contest and Israeli Gay Men', *Popular Culture,* 2(1): 41–63.

Lewis, L. A. (ed.) (1992) *Adoring Audience – Fan Culture and Popular Media.* London: Routledge.

Liebes, T. and Katz, E. (1993) *The Export of Meaning: Cross-Cultural Readings of Dallas* (2nd edn). Cambridge: Polity Press in association with Blackwell.

MacAloon, J. J. (1984) *Rite, drama, festival, spectacle rehearsals toward a theory of cultural performance.* Philadelphia: Institute for the Study of Human Issues.

Mansell, R. (2005) 'Social informatics and the political economy of communications', *Information Technology & People,* 18: 21–25.

Meers, P. (2006) 'Fandom en Blockbusters. Aanzet tot een typologie van *Lord of the Rings*-fans', *Tijdschrift voor Communicatiewetenschap,* 34(1): 69–87.

Modleski, T. (1991) *Feminism Without Women: Culture and Criticism in a Postfeminist Age.* London: Routledge.

Morley, D. (2001) 'Belongings – Place, Space and Identity in a Mediated World', *European Journal of Cultural Studies,* 4(4): 425–48.

Negus, K. (1999) *Music Genres and Corporate Cultures.* London: Routledge.

Perse, E. M. and Rubin, R. B. (1989) 'Attribution in social and parasocial relationships', *Communication Research,* 16: 59–77.

Reijnders, S., Rooijakkers, G. and van Zoonen, L. (2006) 'Global entertainment and local celebration: appropriations of the Idols TV programme in Dutch festivity culture', *European Journal of Cultural Studies,* 9(2): 131–48.

Ritzer, G. (2000) *The McDonaldization of Society.* Thousand Oaks: Pine Forge Press.

Rosengren, K. E. and Windahl, S. (1972) 'Mass media consumption as a functional alternative' in D. McQuail (ed.) *Sociology of Mass Communications: Selected Readings.* Harmondsworth: Penguin. pp. 119–34).

Rubin, R. B. and McHugh, M. (1987) 'Development of parasocial interaction relationships'. *Journal of Broadcasting and Electronic Media,* 31: 279–92.

Schechner, R. (2002) *Performance Studies: An Introduction.* London: Routledge.

Shefrin, E. (2004) '*Lord of the Rings, Star Wars,* and Participatory Fandom: Mappng New Congruencies between the Internet and Media Entertainment Culture', *Critical Studies in Media Comunication,* 21(3): 261–81.

Thornton, S. (1995) *Clubcultures: Music, Media and Sub-cultural Capital.* Cambridge Polity Press in association with Blackwell.

Tulloch, J. and Jenkins, M. (1995) *Science Fiction Audiences: Watching 'Doctor Who' and 'Star Trek'.* London: Routledge.

Turner, V. (1988) *The Anthropology of Performance*. New York: PAJ Publications.

van Romondt-Vis, P. (2004) *In de Ban van de Ring – Een onderzoek naar fans van 'The Lord of the Rings'*. MA thesis – University of Amsterdam, Amsterdam.

van Zoonen, L. (2000) 'Book review of *Tune In, Log On*', *The European Journal of Communication Research*, 25(2): 210–12.

van Zoonen, L. (2004) 'Imagining the Fan Democracy', *European Journal of Communication*, 19(1): 39–52.

van Zoonen, L. (2005) *Entertaining the Citizen: When Politics and Popular Culture Converge*. New York: Rowan and Littlefield.

Williamson, M. (2005) 'Spike, sex and subtext – Intertextual protrayals of the sympathetic vampire on cult television', *European Journal of Cultural Studies*, 8(3): 289–311.

Notes

1 Their definitions of these three categories are as follows: '*Fans* are those people who become particularly attached to certain programmes or stars within the context of a relatively heavy media use.' (Abercrombie and Longhurst, 1998: 138), '*Cultists* are more organized than fans. They meet each other and circulate specialized materials that constitute the nodes of a network.' (Ibid: 139) '*Enthusiasts* are, in our terms, based predominantly around activities rather than media or stars.' (Ibid: 139).

2 Jeroen, for example, is a fan of Chinese popular music, a fandom he has translated towards a PhD project (de Kloet, 2001), just like Liesbet's lifelong admiration of the Tudor Queen Elisabeth I of England (1533–1603) has resulted in a not really necessary paragraph in her latest book *Entertaining the Citizen* (van Zoonen, 2005). For the problems related to this hybrid scholar-cum-fan position see Modleski (1991), Hills (2002), Jancovich (2002) and Dee and Williamson (2005).

3 Whereas white suburban fans of Hip Hop are labelled as cultural tourists whose performance involves either a negation of or a longing for a marked ethnicity (Christenson and Roberts, 1998).

4 Due to her androgynous performance and ambiguity regarding her sexual preferences, she quickly turned into a national gay icon as well.

Community Media and the Public Sphere

Kevin Howley

DEFINITIONS

Public sphere: The concept associated with the work of German social theorist Jurgen Habermas from his influential *Structural Transformation of the Public Sphere (1989)*. Informed by Enlightenment philosophy, the public sphere is, according to Habermas, instrumental in the constitution of liberal democratic society. In Habermas's formulation, the public sphere is a realm characterized by reasoned debate among equals, in which members of a public discuss matters of common concern.

Community media: Participatory media organizations that provide local populations with access to communication technologies. Community media organizations such as Manhattan Neighborhood Network, public access television in New York City (US), *The Issues Magazine*, a street paper in Dublin (IR), and Bush Radio, community radio in Cape Town (SA), are instrumental in supporting popular participation in public discourse.

Subaltern counterpublics: Members of oppressed, subordinate or marginalized groups – women, working people, immigrants, people of colour, homeless people, lesbians and gays – who form alternative discursive realms for purposes of promoting group solidarity and challenging social, political and economic relations of dominance and subordination.

Introduction

Few concepts have greater relevance to contemporary media studies than Habermas's (1989) notion of the *public sphere*. A German sociologist, Habermas is associated with the Frankfurt School of media criticism that figured prominently in debates regarding the relationship between mass culture, capitalism, and authoritarianism throughout much of the twentieth century. In Habermas's formulation, the public sphere is integral to the constitution of civil society; it is an arena distinct from the institutions and operations of the state, the market economy, and the domestic sphere of the home, where private individuals constitute themselves as a public.

Within this public realm, deliberation based on reason, logic and persuasive argumentation – what Habermas describes as 'rational-critical debate' – rather than the rank or status of individual speakers, provides the basis for political discussion, consensus formation and democratic decision-making. Although Habermas privileges face-to-face communication in the formation of public opinion, his historical account acknowledges the vital role played by print media – newspapers, pamphlets, journals and the like – in the emergence of the public sphere in late eighteenth and nineteenth century Europe.

With the advent of large-scale social organization, the instruments of modern communication (film, radio and television broadcasting, computer-mediated communication) assume still greater importance in sustaining public discourse. But for Habermas and other critical theorists associated with the Frankfurt School, the culture industries – with their penchant for commercialism, entertainment and spectacle – are implicated in the eclipse of civil society, the rise of consumer culture and the attendant degeneration of the public sphere as a site for deliberative democracy.

Despite Habermas's profound reservations, the concept of the public sphere foregrounds the centrality of media institutions in providing a discursive space for the polity – participating members of a formal social or civil group – to debate and deliberate upon important matters of the day (Garnham, 1992). For students of media, then, the public sphere's significance is two-fold. From a theoretical perspective, the public sphere highlights the fundamental and decisive relationship between democracy and modern communication systems. If, as democratic theory holds, democracy requires a well-informed and engaged citizenry, then the media must provide the resources – news, information, and opinion – for a self-governing people to identify and work towards matters of common concern.

In turn, this requirement presents a host of very practical problems, chief among them being the character and conduct of public discourse in a highly mobile and heterogeneous society. Put differently, in societies marked by ethnic, religious and cultural diversity, partisan politics, and economic stratification, the prospects for achieving consensus on matters of public policy seem remote. To further complicate matters, contemporary media systems – characterized by unprecedented consolidation of ownership and control on the one hand, and the fragmentation of mass audiences into ever smaller 'niche markets' on the other – makes issues of access to and participation in public discourse equally problematic.

We can better appreciate the centrality of the public sphere to media studies by asking several pertinent questions. For instance, how are matters of 'public interest' or 'common concern' determined? Who sets the terms of the debate? Are different viewpoints, perspectives and opinions presented fairly and accurately? Are some discursive forms and practices deemed more legitimate than others? And finally, do all interested parties have access to the channels of public communication? In theory as well as practice, then, the public sphere encompasses a number of relevant topics in media studies including agenda setting, frame analysis, political economy and representational politics, to name but a few.

The argument developed here illustrates the value of *community media* in considering these key issues in media studies. By community media, I refer to locally oriented, participatory media organizations that provide groups and individuals, whose voices and perspectives are excluded from mainstream media, with access to the tools of media production and distribution (Howley, 2005). Dedicated to promoting local cultural expression, civic engagement and social integration, community media come in many forms: access radio, so-called 'open channel' television, alternative newspapers, ethnic and indigenous peoples' broadcasting, as well as community-based computer networks. Significantly, these local initiatives have assumed global proportions: community media are increasingly common in post-industrial and so-called developing societies alike – a theme explored in detail by Karim in the final chapter of this book.

Throughout this chapter, I want to suggest that community media democratize the structure and discursive practices of modern communication systems and in so doing, support popular participation in public discourse. In taking up this argument, I review some of the academic thinking on the public sphere, especially as it relates to the field of media studies. Here, I describe the basic features of contemporary media culture that have prompted questions regarding the very existence, let alone the viability, of the public sphere. Throughout, I draw upon the work of scholars who challenge Habermas's historical account of a single, inclusive public sphere, but who, nevertheless, acknowledge the concept's utility to social and democratic theory.

This discussion provides an appropriate context to evaluate community media's role in constructing discursive spaces for groups and individuals marginalized by dominant media institutions and practices. In so doing, community media serve as a resource for *subaltern counterpublics* to articulate their interests and concerns. Here, I draw on three case studies to illuminate community media's significance in a variety of geo-cultural contexts. These observations underscore the relevance of community media to contemporary media studies. What's more, these insights offer an opportunity to re-conceptualize the public sphere in ways that promote communicative democracy in the twenty-first century.

The public sphere and modern media

Habermas's historical account of the emergence and disintegration of what he describes as the 'liberal bourgeois public sphere' has generated considerable academic attention (for example, Calhoun, 1992; Robbins, 1993). We can distill the broad contours of this scholarship in terms of debates surrounding (1) the accuracy of Habermas's history; and (2) the utility of the Habermasian ideal for democratic theory and practice.

For some critics, Habermas's account is deeply flawed insofar as its claims to universal access and participation are greatly overstated. Revisionist histories of the bourgeois public sphere reveal the exclusivity of this discursive realm: in actual practice, participation in the public sphere was strictly limited to white bourgeois men. A related critique takes issue with the Habermasian ideal which suggests that in order to identify and work towards issues of common concern, private individuals must abandon their self-interest and ignore or 'bracket' differences in socio-economic status and life history. Such a requirement seems at odds with human nature and discounts the diversity of human culture and experience.

Still other critics find Habermas's account lacking inasmuch as it fails to acknowledge the existence of parallel discursive spaces created by proletarian classes, women and other groups who were excluded by or otherwise prohibited from participating in the bourgeois public sphere (Negt and Kluge, 1993; Ryan, 1992). Criticism of this sort underscores the problem of conceptualizing the public sphere as a single, inclusive and comprehensive discursive space. Rather, this scholarship recognizes the existence of multiple, overlapping public spheres that provide different groups with the material and symbolic resources to forge a common identity and articulate their particular interests, perspectives, and concerns (Fraser, 1992; Meadows, 2005).

For our purposes here, we should acknowledge the shortcomings of Habermas's emphasis on face-to-face communication and in turn recognize the indispensable role mass media play in modern democracies. That is to say, as an idealized concept, the Habermasian requirement for face-to-face communication is laudable, perhaps even desirable. However, in contemporary society, embodied conversation and dialogue is quite unrealistic; today, public discourse is mediated within and through print, visual and electronic media.

Notwithstanding these criticisms, Habermas's formulation continues to inform the theory and practice of deliberative democracy. As a normative ideal, then, the public sphere provides a useful set of criteria for evaluating media behaviours and performance. Furthermore, as we shall see in the following section, Habermas's work serves as a conceptual framework to establish more democratic media systems. A Habermasian assessment of contemporary media culture, therefore, would consider the extent to which modern communication systems enable as well as constrain participation in public life.

Wither the public sphere?

At first blush, we might conclude that modern media provide unrivaled opportunities for every strata of society to learn about and participate in matters of common concern. Indeed, the proliferation of media channels, coupled with the global reach and instantaneous relay of information allows us to 'bear witness' to world historic events as well as life's more prosaic moments. Even for the casual observer there can be little doubt regarding the sheer volume of news and information available to the public. The question remains: is all of this information accurate, useful, and relevant to a self-governing people?

For some critics the answer is as clear as it is disturbing: contemporary journalism is in a profound state of crisis (Marsh, 2004; McChesney, 2003). According to Habermas's normative ideal, news should do more than simply inform a public. Rather, to serve the public interest, journalism must encourage civic engagement with issues of common concern and promote popular participation in public policy debates. In this way, journalism promotes deliberative democracy, not simply by reporting on important issues, but by providing opportunities and resources for citizens to identify and address these issues and concerns.

There is little evidence to suggest that contemporary journalism fulfills this role. To the contrary, in an increasingly competitive media environment, the pressures of the market come to dictate news routines and practices. As a result, news organizations conceive of their audiences as consumers, first and foremost, rather than as citizens in a democracy. In such an environment, where media outlets seek to deliver audiences to advertisers, the 24-hour news cycle places a premium on speed not accuracy and all too often style triumphs over substance. The result is a form of journalism that lacks context and perspective, and blurs any meaningful distinction between information and entertainment. The rise of so-called 'infotainment' is, perhaps, most evident in the realm of 24/7 news channels such as Time Warner's CNN and News Corporation's Fox News (US), Sky News (UK), and Star News (India) (Thussu, 2004).

In addition, contemporary journalism has grown increasingly dependent upon 'official sources' from government and the business sector. While these sources certainly lend credibility to news reports and provide a semblance of objectivity to journalistic practice, the ritual use of what journalist Jonathan Alter (1985) describes as 'the usual suspects' limits the number of voices and range of perspectives available in public discourse. Media watchdog groups like Fairness and Accuracy in Reporting (FAIR) find source bias to be a persistent problem: most recently during the lead up to the Iraq War (Rendell and Broughel, 2003). Rather than provide a robust forum for popular participation in public discourse, source bias of the sort that pervades current journalistic practice excludes alternative voices and perspectives from important policy debates (Croteau and Hoynes, 1994).

Small wonder, then, that whole segments of the population retreat from public life. Nowhere is this tendency more evident than in the realm of electoral politics. In an era dominated by visuals and the 8-second sound bite, politics is reduced to a spectator sport. Political candidates are assessed less as a matter of their positions, platforms and philosophies and more upon the efficacy of their campaign strategies and tactics. This 'horse race' approach to political reportage serves only to alienate voters who, quite rightly, view the entire process with equal measures of skepticism and apathy.

More critically, press coverage of this sort effectively denies citizens of any sense of political agency. That is to say, when politics is cast as a contest between a select group of powerful individuals, rather than the collective efforts of the citizenry, journalism fails to provide a forum for a self-governing people to make informed decisions about matters of common concern (Hackett and Zhao, 1996). In the absence of a collective sense of political agency, elite interests exercise social, economic and political power to achieve desired outcomes irrespective of the public interest.

Key to the success of these elite interests is the skillful use of advertising, marketing and especially public relations in so-called 'perception management' campaigns. Based on insights gleaned from behaviourism, psychoanalysis, and social psychology, the public relations industry has developed sophisticated techniques to manipulate public opinion in the service of elite interests (Stauber and Rampton, 1995). For instance, business leaders and politicians routinely employ public relations professionals – so-called 'spin doctors' – to influence the news agenda and shape journalistic interpretations of public policy and decision-making processes.

Contrary to Habermas's emphasis on the role of rational-critical debate to deliberative democracy, the field of public relations purposively manages public opinion in order to serve the narrow interests of government and corporate power in a process Lippmann (1997) aptly described as the 'manufacture of consent'. For Lippmann and his colleagues, the mass public had neither the inclination, nor the intellectual capacity for self-governance. Instead, self-appointed experts would manage public opinion in such a way as to secure popular compliance to the agenda of economic and political elites. From a Habermasian perspective, the expert management of public opinion severely constrains popular participation in public discourse. Furthermore, the calculated manipulation of public opinion has deleterious effects on the quality and character of rational-critical debate and as such is completely antithetical to deliberative democracy.

In the early twentieth century, as the modern public relations industry took shape in the US, so too did the nascent broadcast industry begin to coalesce around the principles of private ownership and profit accumulation. From the outset, commercial broadcasters were beholden to federal legislators for a regulatory environment that legitimated and supported private operation of the public airwaves. Furthermore, commercial broadcasters grew increasingly reliant upon advertisers for financial support. Not surprisingly, then, commercial broadcasters were reluctant to take up adversarial positions vis á vis corporate and government interests; rather the media industry assumed interests that were consistent with those of both the market and the state (Bagdikian, 2004). For Habermas, the encroachment of corporate and state interests in the realm of public communication signaled the demise of the public sphere.

The commercial media environment that developed in the US stood in stark contrast to the public service ethos that guided the development of broadcasting in other industrial democracies. Informed by the principles of universal access and civic responsibility, public service broadcasting (PSB) begins from the premise that a media system should cultivate a sense of citizenship within a national political community. For the better part of the last century, public broadcasting in Australia, Canada, and across much of Europe was insulated from marketplace pressures on one hand, and state interference on the other, in an effort to create a common culture and forge a shared sense of national identity.

None of which is to suggest, however, that public broadcasters are immune from substantive critique. Public broadcasters have long faced charges of elitism and a failure to respond to the interests and concerns of its users, especially racial, ethnic and cultural minorities within their respective national context. Over time, this lack of accountability undercut public broadcasting's status, legitimacy, and popularity (for example, see Connell and Curti, 1986). In recent years, political and technological forces have further undermined public service broadcasting across much of the industrialized world (Tracey, 1999).

Today, public broadcasters no longer enjoy monopoly positions within their respective national media landscapes, but instead must compete with an array of domestic and transnational commercial services. In response, public broadcasters have adopted the forms and practices associated with their commercial counterparts. For instance, Britain's vaunted BBC recently instituted a new mandate that places a premium on entertainment, rather than news and information programming (Lyall, 2006).

For some, these developments signal the demise of public service media and the triumph of a privatized communication environment. Summarizing this troubling new condition, Garnham observes how media deregulation and technological innovation have fundamentally altered 'the balance in the cultural sector between the market and public service in favor of the market and to shift the dominant definition of public information from that of a public good to that of a privately appropriable commodity' (Garnham, 1992: 363).

The commodification of news and information and the attendant emergence of a digital divide between the information rich and poor, threatens to limit popular access to and participation in public discourse within and between nation-states (Norris, 2001). Thus, the decline of public service broadcasting exacerbates the problems associated with corporate media culture outlined above. Left to the demands of the marketplace, public discourse reflects a rather narrow (and exclusive) range of interests.

All of this has profound implications on deliberative democracy, the public sphere, and the prospects for global civil society. In an era when a handful of transnational media conglomerates – Time Warner, Bertelsmann AG, News Corporation, Disney, and Vivendi Universal – dominate global media flows, the interests and perspectives of local communities are rarely heard, and their participation in public discourse is severely constrained. What follows is an appraisal of community media in light of the ascendancy of commercial media forms and practices and the attendant diminution of public service broadcasting. Throughout, I suggest that community media represent local interventions into contemporary media culture that encourage popular participation in public discourse.

Community media and communicative democracy

The previous section took a political economic approach to understanding media behaviours and practices (e.g., Chomsky and Herman, 1988; McChesney, 1999). By highlighting the structural factors that help determine contemporary media culture – chief among them media ownership, advertiser-supported content, and the rise of the public relations industry in managing public opinion – critical political economy of this sort reveals the threat that corporate media poses to public discourse and democratic self-governance.

Assessing this condition, Herman observes, 'If structural factors shape the broad contours of media performance, and if that performance is incompatible with a truly democratic political culture, then a basic change in media ownership, organization, and purpose is necessary for the achievement of genuine democracy' (1996: 116). This observation provides a useful starting point to consider the role community media play in challenging the structure and discursive practices of modern media systems. To that end, the following case studies reveal community media's ability to democratize communicative form and practice and in doing so, revitalize the public sphere.

Case study 1

Downtown Community Television

Founded in 1972, Downtown Community Television (DCTV) is one of the longest running, most highly honoured media arts organizations in the US. From its modest beginnings documenting the lives and experiences of immigrant groups in New York City's Lower East Side, to its groundbreaking investigative

---

documentaries for broadcast and cable television, DCTV's principle focus has been to provide marginalized groups and individuals with access to the tools of television production.

Like their peers in the guerrilla television movement of the late 1960s and early 1970s, DCTV co-founders Keiko Tsuno and Jon Alpert were impressed with the intimacy and immediacy afforded by the then new technology of portable video (Boyle, 1992). Over time, Alpert and Tsuno began to realize video's potential to support community-organizing efforts and facilitate inter-cultural communication within the ethnic and racially diverse neighborhoods of lower Manhattan. Working closely with immigrant groups and community activists, DCTV addressed a host of local issues – housing, health care, edu-cation, sweat shop labour, drug abuse and gang violence – issues that deeply affect the working class and immigrant communities of lower Manhattan but which nevertheless receive scant attention in mainstream media.

Taking their cameras, playback units, and TV monitors directly to the people of Chinatown and the Lower East Side – in community centers, union halls, school auditoriums, and on street corners – DCTV encouraged popular partici-pation in television production and distribution. This participatory philosophy continues to shape and inform DCTV's 'house style' – a video verite approach that is committed to communicative democracy and social justice. Through video production workshops, free and low-cost equipment rentals, and public screenings of independently produced video, DCTV champions a form of com-munity journalism that resonates with marginalized populations across New York City and beyond.

DCTV's commitment to challenging the structures and practices of modern media systems is perhaps most evident in its educational programmes for young people. The voice of youth is all too rare in contemporary public dis-course. Despite the fact that young people have an enormous stake in public policy decisions, from education and military spending to labour issues and reproductive rights, youth are often excluded from active participation in the public sphere. Moreover, when young people are presented in mainstream media, they are typically depicted as alienated, uninformed and apathetic. Youth media programmes such as DCTV's Pro-TV counteract this by providing young people with the tools and techniques to create discursive spaces wherein their interests and concerns, as well as their hopes and fears, are granted cur-rency and legitimacy.

A highly competitive pre-professional programme, Pro-TV requires participat-ing students to commit to a two-year programme of study that includes video production training, as well as instruction in media aesthetics, history and theory. During the first year, students receive comprehensive training in television field and studio production techniques. Upon successful completion of a first-year project, students are given the opportunity to pursue an overseas reporting assignment. In recent years, Pro-TV students have travelled to Russia, India, and Mexico, among other locations around the globe, to cover breaking news or produce an investigative report from a youth perspective.

The results of the programme are uniformly impressive and sometimes deeply affecting. For instance, in 2004, as Pro-TV students Daniel Howard and Terrence Fisher began work on a documentary about gun violence in the Bedford-Stuyvesant neighbourhood of Brooklyn, one of their friends, Timothy Stansbury, was shot and killed by a New York City police officer. Press coverage of the shooting was predictable inasmuch as the all-too-familiar narrative of a promising life cut short dominated newspaper and television reports. Applying routine journalistic formulas to the shooting, press accounts reduced Stansbury's life to little more than a caricature and glossed over the long-term consequences the killing had for a neighbourhood plagued by poverty, violence and neglect.

Howard and Fisher's documentary delved deeper, defying the staid conventions of the mainstream press by inhabiting the physical, social and emotional spaces of a grieving community. As freelance reporter Rachel Morris noted: 'The Pro-TV students and the professional TV crews filmed similar moments, but the students thrust the viewer into the story while the mannered news stories hold us at a distance' (2004: 37). Foregrounding their relationship to the victim and the community as they did, the Pro-TV students captured the frustration and anguish of the neighbourhood in a manner unparalleled by conventional news coverage. The result is a compelling counternarrative that challenges the veracity, authority and legitimacy of mainstream press reports.

Case study 2

Street Feat

During the 1990s, street newspapers became a distinctive feature of urban culture throughout much of the industrialized world. A cursory examination of the International Network of Street Newspaper's (INSP) website reveals the global dimensions of the street paper movement: *L'Itineraire* (Montreal), *Novy Prostor* (Prague), *Ocas* (Sao Paulo), *Real Change* (Seattle), *Flaszter* (Budapest) and *The Big Issue* (London, Glasgow, Melbourne, and Johannesburg).

Produced and distributed by homeless and unemployed people, street news-papers provide modest, but nonetheless vital economic opportunity for the poor. Equally important, street papers enable homeless people, the unem-ployed and the working poor to participate in the public sphere. That is to say, like other marginalized groups, the poor are often excluded from participating in policy decisions that directly affect their lives. Street papers constitute a dis-cursive space for the poor to identify their interests and communicate their con-cerns to wider publics.

Encouraged by the success of street papers across North America, local activists Michael Burke and Roberto Menendez launched *Street Feat*, 'the voice of the poor' in Halifax, Nova Scotia in 1997. Economic recession during the mid-1990s swelled the ranks of the homeless and unemployed in the Canadian port city. So-called welfare 'reform' measures at both the provincial and federal level threatened to exacerbate the problem even further. Burke and Menendez rea-soned that a street newspaper could not only provide employment opportuni-ties for the working poor, but also promote greater public awareness of the deleterious effects neo-liberal economic policies were having on the people of Halifax.

Street Feat's commitment to communicative democracy is evident in its will-ingness to publish news, information and opinion that vigorously challenges the conventional wisdom of political and economic elites. *Street Feat* does this by routinely publishing first-person accounts of people living in homeless shelters, volunteering at the local food bank, or waiting in line at one of the city's over-crowded soup kitchens.

For instance, one of *Street Feat*'s most prolific and accomplished writers, Peter McGuigan, writes on a variety of topics – economic redevelopment schemes, labour issues, the rising costs of higher education, and tenants' rights – all from the perspective of an able-bodied, university-educated man who nevertheless has difficulty finding gainful employment. Unlike mainstream media then, whose uncritical reliance upon 'official sources' limits the public's comprehension and awareness of enduring poverty, *Street Feat* values the 'native reporting' of those whose lives are marked by economic deprivation, social isolation and political exclusion.

Although the quality of this writing varies, these first-person accounts, news features and opinion pieces share a common feature: they reassert the funda-mental human dignity of the poor. In doing so, native reporting of this sort explodes the stereotypes of the homeless and the poor – stereotypes that are reinforced and legitimated within and through dominant discursive formations, including mainstream press reports. Like other street newspapers, then, *Street*

Figure 15.1 Street Feat – an example of community media from Canada. Reproduced with kind permission © Street Feat

Feat counters what anti-poverty activist Jean Swanson (2001) refers to as the 'poor bashing rhetoric' that has become a distinguishing feature of press coverage of the homeless and unemployed in recent years.

In addition to this emphasis on first person reporting, *Street Feat* publicizes the activities of social workers, policy analysts and community activists whose work receives scant attention in traditional media outlets. For example, writing in *Street Feat*'s debut issue, Jeanne Fay, a legal aid worker at Dalhousie University, published a stinging critique of the provincial government's efforts to 'reform' social assistance programmes. Fay's report chronicled the government's reluctance to permit community members – most notably public health workers, social service representatives, anti-poverty activists and welfare recipients – with an opportunity to comment upon, let alone participate in policy deliberations.

Calling attention to the government's furtive deliberations, *Street Feat* helped generate support for the Community Advocate Network (CAN), a grass-roots organization that closely monitored the government's reform efforts. Publicizing direct action campaigns, street demonstrations, community organizing events and the like, *Street Feat* not only covers under-reported stories, but also serves as a vital resource for various constituencies to forge alliances in the struggle against economic injustice.

Street Feat's emphasis on economic inequality illuminates one of the shortcomings of Habermas's theoretical formulation. As noted above, Habermas suggests that participation in the public sphere requires individuals to bracket or otherwise ignore individual differences including socio-economic status and life history. Rather than ignore these important distinctions, *Street Feat* foregrounds power differentials within and between community members and makes these differences a central theme in much of the paper's reporting. This approach has important implications for the constitution of a more robust and inclusive public sphere inasmuch as economic disparities often exclude whole segments of the population from participating in public discourse. In this way, *Street Feat* reveals the decisive correspondence between symbolic and material relations of power in contemporary society.

All of which is to suggest that *Street Feat*, is vital to the constitution of an alternative public sphere. In an era when commercial and public service media alike provide news and information that accommodates the interests of advertisers, and the affluent audiences they seek, the issues and concerns of marginalized groups – working people, racial and ethnic minorities, and the poor – receive precious little attention.

Conversely, *Street Feat* provides a forum for the expression of oppositional discourses surrounding issues of poverty, housing, labour, and economic justice. Tapping into the physical and social spaces inhabited by Halifax's poor – the city's shelters, soup kitchens and street corners – *Street Feat* plays a decisive role in constructing a discursive arena for subaltern publics to challenge economic and social policies that demonize the poor and criminalize the homeless.

Case study 3

DDS Audio Initiative

The Deccan Development Society (DDS) is a grassroots NGO operating in the Medak District of the southern Indian state of Andhra Pradesh. The society works closely with women's 'sanghams', or voluntary associations, to promote economic and gender equity for 'dalit' women (untouchables): perhaps the most marginalized group in all of Indian society. With an emphasis on enhancing the autonomy of rural communities, DDS promotes local access and control over natural resources, food production, markets and media systems.

Although the women are non-literate, dalits have formidable skills in agriculture, animal husbandry, health care and, as it turns out, audio production. Traditionally, dalit women travelled throughout the district's 75 villages sharing their knowledge and insights with members of the local sanghams, and providing expertize to those who needed medical, financial, or agricultural assistance. Leveraging the women's rich oral tradition, DDS trained the dalits to use microphones and audio-cassette recorders to document their everyday experience, record interviews and stories, and to share their perspectives with women throughout the Medak district.

For a population whose principal radio service, the state-operated AIR Hyderabad, does not broadcast in the local dialect, the DDS Audio Initiative provides a service heretofore unavailable to these women. Equally important, this grassroots radio project acknowledges the value of dalit women's local knowledge and makes this invaluable expertize available to the broader community. In doing so, the DDS Audio Initiative has played a crucial role in promoting local autonomy across the Medak district and legitimating dalit participation in community affairs.

Despite changes in Indian telecommunications policy that affirmed public control of the airwaves, policy-makers have been slow to license community radio stations owned and operated by local populations. Instead, commercial interests have been encouraged to proliferate in the wake of recent moves to deregulate the Indian broadcast sector. The reluctance of policy-makers to establish provisions for a viable community radio sector has not deterred DDS from using radio for purposes of community communication, however.

In the absence of a broadcast license, DDS promoted narrowcasting of the sort that uses the public spaces of the sanghams as a venue to playback finished programmes. These sessions provide a discursive space for dalits to discuss matters of common concern such as farming, reproductive health, domestic violence and childcare, in a safe and secure environment. Not surprisingly, these discussions provide the raw material for subsequent radio programmes. In this way, DDS promotes an interactive and iterative approach to audio production that is unique to dalit culture.

With the support of UNESCO's 'Women Speak to Women' project, DDS began operating an FM radio station in 1996. Since that time, 'barefoot journalists' equipped with audio recorders and, more recently, video cameras, have been creating their own media, using the regional dialect, and addressing local issues and concerns. In 2001, the women formed a new collective: the DDS Community Media Trust. Like the radio station before it, the community media center is managed and staffed by rural women. As a result, programming produced under the auspices of the community media center reflects the ethos of dialogue, cooperation, and empowerment that informed the earliest efforts of the DDS Audio Initiative.

Conclusion

Despite their local orientation, community media are rarely parochial. Rather, community media are a distinctive feature of an emerging global media culture. As we have seen, community media are common in post-industrial and so-called 'developing' societies alike. And while different community media organizations make use of a variety of communication technologies, these initiatives share the same basic impulse: to provide local populations with the opportunity to participate in civil society; to promote social integration and community cohesion within geo-cultural communities; and to sustain local forms of cultural expression.

The proliferation of community media around the globe supports Steiner's helpful insight regarding the character of contemporary public discourse: 'There is no single public sphere and because no single medium is perfect, agency in the public sphere requires many people using many technologies. No single mechanism can fully support deliberation among publics' (2005: 330–1). As students of media, then, we would do well to consider community media's role in promoting a more democratic media culture and appreciate the modest, but decisive role these organizations play in the constitution of discursive spaces locally as well as globally.

Summary

- In contemporary society, media constitute a 'discursive space' for people to address issues of public interest and concern.
- The concentration of media ownership limits popular participation in the systems of public communication and narrows the range of permissible discursive forms and practices.
- Unlike their commercial and public service counterparts, community media promote innovative cultural practices and cultivate a more dynamic, inclusive and expansive public discourse.
- By opening up public communication channels to various under-represented groups and constituencies, community media promote the formation of alternative or oppositional discursive arenas.
- Community media constitute a nexus of multiple, overlapping public spheres that are essential for creating a more just, equitable, and democratic society.

GOING FURTHER

Chanan, M. (2005) 'Documentary, Public Sphere and Education: New Video Documentary in Argentina', *Journal of Media Practice* 6(2): 113–116.
This brief essay discusses how the advent of low-cost video cameras has engendered the production of documentary work that addresses the issues and concerns of populations typically marginalized by corporate and state-run media.

DeLuca, K. M. and Peeples, J. (2002) 'From Public Sphere to Public Screen: Democracy, Activism, and the "Violence" of Seattle', *Critical Studies in Media Communication* 19(2): 125–151.
This provocative essay promotes the concept of the 'public screen' as an important supplement to Habermas's public sphere. The public screen metaphor acknowledges the undeniable significance of images, image-making and image events in contemporary politics.

Herbst, S. (1994) *Politics at the Margin: Historical Studies of Public Expression Outside the Mainstream.* Cambridge: Cambridge University Press.
Historical case studies reveal the ingenuity of subordinate groups in creating discursive spaces that address the needs, interests and concerns of marginalized publics. Herbst vividly demonstrates the ingenuity of marginalized groups in creating a sense of group identity and community solidarity through communicative forms and practices.

Land, J. (1999) *Active Radio: Pacifica's Brash Experiment.* Minneapolis: University of Minnesota Press.

This informative and engaging account of Pacifica Radio relates the turbulent history of America's leading progressive radio network. Despite external threats and infighting, Pacifica continues to serve as a model for non-commercial, community-oriented radio across the US and around the world.

STUDENT ACTIVITY 15.1

Compare and contrast the way in which a public service broadcaster, commercial media outlet, and community media organization cover the same news story or event (for example, health care, labour dispute, environmental issue, political protest). Consider the similarities and differences between the respective reports. To what extent does each report reflect the interests and concerns of disparate constituencies wrestling with matters of common concern? Are some opinions given greater 'weight' or 'authority' than others? How does each report address the audience? Put differently, is the audience positioned as spectators or participants, consumers or citizens?

References

Alter, J. (1985) 'News Media: Round Up the Usual Suspects', *Newsweek*. 25 March: 69.

Bagdikian, B. (2004) *The New Media Monopoly*. Boston: Beacon Press.

Boyle, D. (1992) 'From Portapak to Camcorder: A Brief History of Guerrilla Television', *Journal of Film and Video* 44(1–2): 67–79.

Calhoun, C. (ed.) (1992) *Habermas and the Public Sphere*. Cambridge, MA: MIT Press.

Chomsky, N. and Herman, E. S. (1988) *Manufacturing Consent: The Political Economy of Media*. New York: Pantheon.

Connell, I. and Curti, L. (1986) 'Popular Broadcasting in Italy and Britain: Some Issues and Problems' in P. Drummond and R. Patterson (eds) *Television in Transition*. London: BFI. pp. 87–111.

Croteau, D. and Hoynes, W. (1994) *By Invitation Only: How the Media Limit Political Debate*. Monroe, ME: Common Courage Press.

Fraser, N. (1992) 'Rethinking the Public Sphere: A Contribution to the Critique of Actually Existing Democracy' in C. Calhoun (ed.) *Habermas and the Public Sphere*. Cambridge, MA: MIT Press. pp. 109–42.

Garnham, N. (1992) 'The Media and the Public Sphere.' in C. Calhoun (ed.) *Habermas and the Public Sphere*. Cambridge, MA: MIT Press. pp. 359–76.

Habermas, J. (1989) *The Structural Transformation of the Public Sphere*. Trans. T. Burger and F. Lawrence. Cambridge, MA: MIT Press.

Hackett, R. and Zhao, Y. (1996) 'Journalistic Objectivity and Social Change', *Peace Review* 8(1): 5–11.

Herman, E.S. (1996) 'The Propaganda Model Revisited', *Monthly Review* (July 1996). pp. 115–28.

Howley, K. (2005) *Community Media: People, Places, and Communication Technologies.* Cambridge, UK: Cambridge University Press.

Lippmann, W. (1997) *Public Opinion.* New York: Free Press.

Lyall, S. (2006) 'New Mandate for the BBC: Put Entertainment First', *New York Times* 16 March: B1.

Marsh, K. (2004) 'Power, But Scant Responsibility', *British Journalism Review* 15(4): 17–21.

McChesney, R. (1999) *Rich Media, Poor Democracy: Communication Politics in Dubious Times.* New York: New Press.

McChesney, R. (2003) 'The Problem of Journalism: A Political Economic Contribution to an Explanation of the Crisis in Contemporary Journalism', *Journalism Studies* 4(3): 299–329.

Meadows, M. (2005) 'Journalism and Indigenous Public Spheres', *Pacific Journalism Review* 11(1): 36–41.

Morris, R. (2004) 'The Shooting', *Columbia Journalism Review* (Sept/Oct): 35–37.

Negt, O. and Kluge, A. (1993) *Public Sphere and Experience.* Minneapolis: University of Minnesota Press.

Norris, P. (2001) *Digital Divide: Civic Engagement, Information Poverty, and the Internet Worldwide.* Cambridge: Cambridge University Press.

Rendell, S. and Broughel, T. (2003) 'Amplifying Officials, Squelching Dissent', *Extra!* FAIR May/June. Available: http://www.fair.org/index.php?page=1145 [Accessed 30 March 2006].

Robbins, B. (ed.) (1993) *The Phantom Public Sphere.* Minneapolis: University of Minnesota Press.

Ryan, M. (1992) 'Gender and Public Access: Women's Politics in Nineteenth Century America' in C. Calhoun (ed.) *Habermas and the Public Sphere.* Cambridge, MA: MIT Press. pp. 259–88.

Stauber, J. C. and Rampton, S. (1995) *Toxic Sludge is Good For You: Lies, Damn Lies and the Public Relations Industry.* Monroe, ME: Common Courage Press.

Steiner, L. (2005) 'The Feminist Cable Collective as Public Sphere Activity', *Journalism* 6(3): 313–34.

Swanson, J. (2001) *Poor-bashing: The Politics of Exclusion.* Toronto: Between the Lines.

Thussu, D. K. (2004) 'Live TV and Bloodless Deaths: War, Infotainment and 24/7 News', *Imperium.* Available: http://www.imperiumjournal.com/0pages/40014.html [Accessed 8 May 2006].

Tracey, M. (1998) *The Decline and Fall of Public Service Broadcasting.* New York: Oxford University Press.

Media and Diaspora

16

Karim H. Karim

DEFINITION

The word 'diaspora' is derived from the Greek *diaspeirein*, which refers to the scattering of seeds. In the past, it usually referred to the existence of Jewish communities around the world; now the term is used to designate various kinds of dispersed communities. Diasporas are viewed as comprising members of ethnic, cultural, linguistic and religious groups who reside in a number of countries to which they or their ancestors migrated. The identities of individuals and groups within specific diasporas are formed over time by complex historical, social, and cultural relationships within the group and with other groups. Retention of ancestral customs, language, religious practices and marriage patterns, and the ease of communication between various parts of the dispersed community, help determine its characteristics.

Global migration over several centuries has produced transnational diasporas around the world. The mass migrations of the eighteenth, nineteenth and the early twentieth centuries led to growth in the New World, while displacing indigenous economies and communities. These included movements of slaves from Africa, indentured labourers from Asia, and settlers from Europe. As slavery and indentured labour became illegal, laws were passed to make it difficult for non-Europeans to migrate to Northern countries. Following the lifting of restrictions on race-based immigration in the 1950s and 1960s, Asians and Africans once again could settle in North America, Australasia and Europe. There has also been substantial migration from Latin America into the US. Much of this has been driven by Northern countries' demand for labour. Among the individuals and families who move to other lands are migrant workers and asylum seekers and refugees fleeing persecution or conflict.

Diasporas generally exist in small numbers in scattered communities within countries and across continents. The movements of people to different parts of the planet have shaped communities that are layered by period of migration, the extent of integration into societies of settlement, and the maintenance of links with the land of origin as well as with other parts of the transnational group. There exist, as a result of this layering, wide variations in connections and attachments within world-wide networks.

Often viewed through the lens of migration from the Southern to the Western parts of the world, the term 'diaspora' has frequently been limited to 'non-white' people who remain distinct as minorities in their new countries of residence. But even though some European immigrants, like the Irish, may find it relatively easy to assimilate into 'white' host countries, their cultural identity frequently remains resilient – especially in literary, music and dance forms. Hence, contemporary discourse also refers to diasporas with origins in Europe.

Box 16.1   Globalization and diaspora

The role of ethnic media in global communication flows is steadily growing. However, this development is not usually discussed by most commentators in the context of globalization, and requires us to distinguish globalizations from above and below. Globalization-from-above is reflected in the transnational activities of international organizations, states and corporations, while globalization-from-below is carried out by civil society, development, professional, and diaspora groups that operate across national boundaries. Whereas the former is characterized by massive flows and transactions, the latter usually takes place with less intensity.

Disaporas help to form intricate networks of trading and cultural links across the planet. They use the same transportation and communications infrastructures as the agents of globalization-from-above, but they employ them for different purposes. Communities scattered around the world have wanted to establish contact with the homeland and with each other. Various modes of communication have been utilized for these purposes. Postal services, the telegraph, the telephone, radio, telex, fax, film, television, audiotape, videotape, and the Internet have all been used over time by diasporic members to keep in touch.

Introduction

Diasporic communication has emerged as a major topic of discussion in media studies over the last two decades. Several books and numerous articles have been published on this issue (for example, Karim, 2003; Gillespie, 1995; Naficy, 1993), which is also frequently discussed at scholarly conferences. Previously, ethnic media operated by minority groups in various countries were treated as being of marginal academic interest. The recent attention to these media activities has been a factor of the significant rise in the global communications networking by diasporas. Ethnic media operated by community groups have increasingly become channels for transnational media flows.[1]

The dispersed nature of diasporas within countries and across continents has spurred them to adopt cutting-edge media technologies in order to develop links between themselves. Diasporic members have been increasingly able to participate in a 'globalization-from-below'[2] as the wealth of these worldwide communities has grown and media like satellite television and the Internet have become more widely available. Live or same-day programming is available from the homeland for its diasporas living around the world. Migrants who previously lived in the same neighbourhood are also able to reassemble in cyberspace. But whereas the new technologies are becoming prevalent around the planet, diasporic individuals living in developing countries have less access to them than their fellows in the West. The growing corporatization of what were previously community-run ethnic media is also, increasingly, leading to the commercialization of diasporic media content. Nevertheless, this 'globalization-from-below' does provide an alternative to the long-standing Western dominance of international media flows.

Nation and diaspora

The nation-state is a fairly recent phenomenon in the history of humankind. It has its roots in the Peace of Westphalia signed in 1648 by several European powers. The treaty laid the basis for inter-governmental relations between states which were posited as exercising exclusive sovereignty over the persons and resources in the specific territories which they controlled. With this, the relatively porous borders hardened and were mutually recognized by signatories of the treaty. However, it was not until the nineteenth century that either rules for multilateral relations between states or international organizations began to emerge. It is significant for students of international communication that among the earliest bilateral and multilateral agreements dealt with the regulation of cross-border communications such as the postal service, the telegraph, and intellectual property. By the beginning of the twentieth century, the international system had spread from Europe to every other part of the world – mainly through colonization. Hard borders had been drawn to divide all the land masses of the planet into individual states.

The concept of the nation-state was loosely based on the idea of a shared ethnicity of the population that lived within a particular territory. *Ethnos*, the Greek word from which ethnic is derived, means 'nation'. The idea of the nation-state brings together ethnicity and territory to imply the existence of an ancestral homeland belonging to a particular people who have kinship ties that are reflected in a common culture and language. National mass media systems reinforce the concept of the nation-state as the primary and natural form of political organization. They play this role with their continual highlighting of national symbols ranging from the prominent portrayal of national leaders in regular news bulletins to the frequent retelling of tales gleaned from the national mythology in dramatic programs. Images of the map of the country in relation to others clearly demarcate the citizens of countries as Canadians, Kenyans, Indians etc. A nation is presented in these ways as a naturalized political, economic, geographic, and ethno-cultural entity, which is distinct from all other nations in the imagination of not only its own residents but that of others.

However, the increased recognition of ethno-cultural diversity within national borders under policies of multiculturalism has seriously challenged the idea of a nation as ethno-culturally homogenous. Multiculturalism is redefining the nation as comprising an ethnically pluralist polity, but one whose leaders strive to unite the population in a common adherence to a set of core civic values. In practical terms, this new approach seeks to contain conflicts between competing ethnic groups within a country and to harness their skills as well as their intellectual and economic resources for national goals. Long-standing ethnic diversity, which was often not valued previously, is now often seen as a vital national asset and showcased to the world.

This transformation of the concept of the nation is occurring in an era in which the means of transnational communications are affording individuals and groups the ability to remain increasingly in contact across countries and continents. The Internet, satellite television, telephonic systems, among other media, provide for intricate linkages among members of ethnic groups living in various parts of the world, making their cultural assimilation into national populations more difficult. These diasporas or transnations stretch out across borders through the means of contemporary global communications.

Diasporas are also often viewed as deterritorialized nations, in contrast to the traditional concept of the nation as linked to an ethnic group's placement within a particular geographic location. Forced or voluntary migrations diminish the physical links of those who leave the homeland; but they take with them the mythical and linguistic allusions to the ancestral territory, which they invoke in nostalgic reminiscences. Some hold on to a hope of eventual return. This creates the demand for cultural products that maintain and celebrate the links of the diaspora with the homeland. The dispersed settlements of transnations exchange symbolic goods and services, including media content, among each other, thus sustaining global networks.

Ethnic media

In previous times, most migrants tended to lose touch with their homeland and with other members of their diaspora. Some were almost completely assimilated into the larger societies into which they settled. The range of communications technologies and the relative ease of inter-continental travel available today have enabled the retention of communal ties. Even members of earlier generations who had lost touch with their diasporas are now reviving them with the use of new media.

Human beings seem to be driven to communicate with those with whom they share a common set of cultural meanings. Cultural and linguistic references from commonly-held myths, legends, stories, music, art, architecture, design and clothing are the bonds that hold together the members of a community. They feel a sense of fellowship with others who use similar cultural allusions, turns of phrases and symbols. Such references provide comfort to migrants who feel isolated in places where they have difficulty understanding the dominant culture.

Even as individuals begin to integrate into their new places of settlement and absorb aspects of the local culture, they continue to maintain a number of their ancestral customs and traditions. It is normal for people to blend various cultures to produce hybrid forms of musical and artistic expressions. This has been a central characteristic of human civilization over the many centuries during which groups of varying backgrounds have interacted with each other.

However, there is often resistance from the dominant society to provide space to emergent cultures in the national public sphere. The mass media, which usually look to serve the largest demographic groups, tend to exclude the cultural expressions of the smaller ones. On their part, some migrant groups may also seek to preserve what they view as the essential aspects of their heritage by establishing distinct media organs to serve their members. These 'ethnic media' are viewed as serving two primary purposes – they contribute to cultural maintenance and ethnic cohesion and they help members of minorities integrate into the larger society. Among the scholars who have studied this topic are Husband (1994) and Riggins (1992).

Box 16.2   Diasporic Chinese newspapers

There are estimated to be some 55 million 'overseas Chinese' living outside China. Their combined annual economic output has been compared to that of the entire population of China itself. They are well-served in Chinese languages by a variety of media, such as newspapers, radio, television, video, film, recorded music and the Internet. These media include those that are run locally, in various countries, and those that operate internationally.

Chinese diasporic newspapers such as *Ming Pao, Sing Tao,* and *The World Journal* have been among the most successful in developing transnational readerships. Not only are they consumed in different countries, some of their ownership structures also tend to be international. The Ming Pao Group, which is headquartered in Hong Kong, is owned by Tiong Hiew King, a Malaysian Chinese businessman, who has close trading ties with China. Sing Tao News Corporation is also based in Hong Kong. The Torstar corporation bought 50 % of the Canadian Sing Tao in 1998, and supplies Canadian news to its Vancouver and Toronto editions. The World Journal, which claims to be the biggest Chinese newspaper in the world, is produced by the United Daily News Group of Taipei, the corporation that publishes an influential newspaper in Taiwan.

Newspapers are the most common form of ethnic media. There are hundreds of ethnic newspapers in countries around the world. They usually tend to be in the language of the group which produces and consumes them, but some are also published in the language of the country of settlement. There are large variations in the form, quality and frequency among ethnic newspapers. Some

Plate 16.1 Chinese diasporic newspapers such as *Ming Pao* have been among the most successful in developing transnational readerships. Image reproduced by kind permission.© The Ming Pao Newspaper Group.

are well-staffed, established dailies that compete with mainstream papers; these print media usually have full-scale production facilities and strong advertising revenues. Others may be very small outfits run by enthusiastic individuals out of their homes. Such ventures tend to have fairly irregular production cycles and do not have a long life. They appear and disappear quickly, only to be replaced by other similarly short-lived publications.

It is generally easier to establish a newspaper than a broadcast station. Governments strictly control the use of the electromagnetic space for radio and television broadcasting, and there is strong competition for licenses to enter this field. When ethnic broadcasters manage to obtain small time slots on the schedules of existing stations, it is often at the most inconvenient times for their potential audiences. In a number of countries, community and campus stations have proved to be more accommodating. Certain governments like those in Canada and Australia have taken initiatives to ensure the presence of the cultures of minorities on the airwaves.

In Canada, the government has steered the federal broadcasting regulatory agency towards facilitating the development of radio and television programming for minority communities. The Canadian Radio-television and Telecommunications Commission has an ethnic broadcasting policy which specifies the conditions under which the dissemination of ethnic and multilingual programming can be carried out. Radio, television and Internet content is distributed by the publicly-owned Special Broadcasting Services of Australia in some 70 languages. The largest Spanish-language (commercial) US television network has hundreds of affiliates and is available to the vast majority of Hispanic households in the US. In a time of fragmenting audiences, niche marketers in an increasing number of countries look upon advertising on ethnic electronic media as a way to reach growing minority populations. Dávila (2001) has conducted a critical examination of these developments.

Diasporas and satellite television

The relatively small and widely scattered nature of communities they serve have encouraged diasporic media to seek out the most efficient and cost-effective means of communication. Technologies that allow for narrowcasting to target specific audiences rather than those that provide the means for mass communications have generally been favoured. Ethnic media have frequently been at the leading edge of technology adoption due to the particular challenges they face in reaching their audiences.

Whereas governments in developing and developed countries had expressed fears that digital broadcasting satellites would erode their sovereignty by transmitting foreign programming to their populations in unregulated manners, this technology is providing remarkable opportunities for diasporic communities. Ethnic broadcasters, previously having limited access to space on the electro-magnetic spectrum in Northern countries, are finding much greater options open-ing up for them through digital broadcasting satellites. For example, France's main broadcast authority, the Conseil Supérieur de l'Audiovisuel, was actively encouraged by a centre-right government to exclude Arabic stations from licensed cable networks in the 1990s. The response of a significant number of Maghrebi immigrant families was to subscribe to digital broadcasting satellite services which provide them with programming from North African countries from across the Mediterranean Sea (see Hargreaves and Mahdjoub, 1997).

Diasporic programming using this technology has grown exponentially in the last decade, well ahead of many mainstream broadcasters. Even as mainstream networks in Europe were making plans to introduce digital broadcasting, the Arab-owned and operated Orbit TV in Rome had begun by 1994 to provide extensive programming via digital broadcasting satellites to Arab communities both in Europe and the Middle East. Al Jazeera has appeared in recent years as the most popular transnational Arabic-language broadcaster. One of the most fascinating uses of digital broadcasting satellite technology in the Middle Eastern context is MED-TV, a Kurdish satellite television station. This is a case of a diaspora within and without the divided homeland attempting to sustain itself and to counter forceful suppression with the use of communications tech-nology. MED-TV has faced resistance not only from governments of various states straddling Kurdistan, but also from anti-terrorist police forces in the UK, Belgium and Germany. Hassanpour (2003) has examined the Kurdish diaspora's uses of satellite in the context of nationalism.

Box 16.3   Bollywood in diaspora

The commercial success of 'Bollywood', the film industry centred in Mumbai in India, is comparable to that of its American counterpart in Hollywood. It has become know for annually producing the largest number of films in the world. And since the vast majority of these are musicals, there has grown, over the last century, a massive recording industry around Bollywood. Television in India extensively uses Bollywood film, reviews, retrospectives, music and gossip as fodder for entertainment programming.

(Continued)

India has been exporting movies to its diaspora for a long time. Audiences of Bollywood in other parts of Asia and in Africa, Europe, Oceania, the Americas and Australasia have used film as a means to maintain contact with the culture of the homeland. The plots of popular films going back several decades, and their actors, directors, music and playback singers comprise a common diasporic memory shared by Indians around the world. With the growth in the size and wealth of the emigrant communities, the box office receipts of some movies are larger outside India, especially in Europe and North America. Bollywood has responded by including storylines and characters that reflect the Indian diaspora.

Television programmes produced in India are broadcast around the world. Strong diasporic subscriber bases exist for competing channels such as Zee, Sony, Star Plus and B4U, all of which carry material from 'Bollywood' (see Box 16.3). South Asians with origins in India, Pakistan, Bangladesh, Sri Lanka, Nepal and Afghanistan are avid viewers. These communities include significant proportions of middle-class and upper-middle-class households who are able to pay for multiple subscriptions to Indian satellite channels. They are carried by international networks like Sky in Europe and Asia as well as others such as DISH and ATN in North America. Cable and satellite television providers in Northern countries have realized the viability of ethnic channels and are making them an integral part of their services.

Univisión and Telemundo, the two largest Spanish-language networks in the US, have been more successful than mainstream American networks in exporting programming to Central and South America. They are available on almost every cable system in Latin America. In some of the poorer countries, local television stations often simply tape stories from Univisión or Telemundo's nightly newscasts for their own use. This gives these Hispanic US networks a high degree of visibility and credibility. The picture that Latin Americans see of American society in these North–South news flows is very different from that presented by mainstream US television and global TV news agencies. Univisión and Telemundo adhere to Latin American news values that favour greater analysis than that offered by mainstream American television.

Diasporas in cyberspace

Internet-based media seem especially suited to the needs of diasporic communities. Apart from the increasing numbers of linguistic fonts that can be accommodated through developments in software, the structures of electronic systems are able to support ongoing communication in the widely-separated transnational groups. The decentralized nature of online networks stands in contrast to the highly regulated and controlled model of broadcasting. Technologies like the Internet are also interactive, relatively inexpensive and easy to operate. They facilitate non-hierarchical organization and lateral communication as opposed to the generally rigid, top-down structures of the mass media. In addition to extensively using online media like email, Usenet, Listserv, and the World Wide Web, diasporic groups are also publishing content on off-line digital media like CD-ROMs. Members of the transnational communities who live in the West, where they generally have access to greater technological and financial resources, are producing CD-ROMs containing the group's religious literature for worldwide marketing to those adherents using this medium. For example, CD-ROMs titled *Al-Quran al-Kareem*, containing the recitation of the Islamic holy book, and *Scriptures and the Heritage of the Sikhs* have both been published in the US. The simultaneous availability of text, sound and graphics provide not only an excellent interactive reference but also a superior learning tool for spiritual communities for whom the precise pronunciation of their scriptures is of vital importance.

The contents of diasporic electronic communications largely consist of cultural, heritage, genealogical, religious, and institutional information. A vast amount of space in digital networks is devoted to genealogy. It is of special interest to those members of diasporas whose ancestors migrated several generations ago. They are finding the Internet to be a remarkable tool in their efforts to reconstruct family trees. Genealogical news groups are organized on Usenet according to family names, places of origin and immigration, ethnicity, and historical events (particularly wars that led to large-scale migrations). The websites designed to locate people of European ancestry are the most numerous, but it is technically possible for individuals of any background to add their personal home pages as links to the sites, which act as genealogical registries. One Netherlands-based service offers assistance to people of mixed South Asian and European origins, providing access to records from churches, cemeteries, military regiments, and community associations. The popularity of online genealogical searches has given rise to commercial websites that provide information for a fee.

Recent migrants separated from family and friends are placing notices on news groups giving particulars of individuals with whom they want to re-establish contact or to search partners for marriage. A number of websites have established global directories of community members. Some of these are organized according to alumni of institutions such as colleges. Global community directories of professionals and businesses have also been compiled online. In certain contexts, the creation of diasporic directories is a matter of life and death. The medical necessity to find human marrow donors from one's own ethnic group for the treatment of more than 60 blood-related diseases has extended these searches into cyberspace. Under the aegis of the National Marrow Donor Program in the US, community organizations of African, Asian, Pacific Islander, and indigenous people are maintaining websites to find suitable marrow donors for patients from their communities. Information on registries in countries of origin is also provided; however, the potential of digital networks to maintain global donor lists does not appear to have been fully exploited.

Although some diasporic websites do carry scholarly and archival material, their major strength lies in functioning as interactive repositories of cultural knowledge. In facilitating global accessibility to Asian, Latin American and African views of the world, community online networks provide a small but important counterweight to the enormous production and export capacities of the cultural industries of developed countries. This becomes a way to mitigate the effects of cultural imperialism and to foster a worldwide cultural diversity. A primary motivation for immigrant communities to go online seems to be survival in the face of the overwhelming output of the dominant culture and the limitations of immigrants' access to the cultural industries in their countries of settlement. Isolated members of diaporas who are using online media can participate, to some extent, in cultural production rather than merely consuming media content. While cyberspace does not allow for the same level of interaction as face-to-face meetings, it enables communication to a much greater extent than that which has previously been possible for scattered groupings of people. Indeed, information about reunions, festivals, and worldwide locations of community institutions facilitate the physical gathering of diasporic individuals. Current events and new publications of materials relating to the transnational group are regularly discussed in online news groups. More recently, members of diasporas are increasingly turning to blogs (web logs) to engage in discussion with each other on contemporary political and cultural issues. All this adds to the growing knowledge base of the diaspora as it interacts within itself and with others.

Members of diasporic groups in the West are among the most active in producing electronic cultural resources. There appears to be an attempt by diasporic participants in cyberspace to create a virtual community that eliminates the distances that separate them in the real world. The global dispersion from the home country over a period of several generations is seemingly reversed by bringing together disparate members of the ethnic group to interact in an electronic 'chat room'. Time and space are seemingly held in suspension in this effort to reconstitute the community and to exchange cultural knowledge held in the diaspora. Several online services catering to Sindhis, a South Asian ethnic group whose members were dispersed by the partition of colonial India and by migration patterns outside the sub-continent, are seeking electronically to recreate their community. A Hong Kong-based website contains Sindhi history, philosophy, spirituality, culture, language, literature, poetry, organizational structures, reunions, directories, and even Sindhi recipes and jokes. Information for Sindhis of Muslim, Hindu, Sikh and Christian backgrounds is provided in other sites, some of which invite contributions from virtual visitors with the stated intention of reuniting the diaspora in cyberspace. A website operated from Germany provides extensive hypertext links to Iranians on the Internet. It electronically brings together universities, research organizations, information resources, cultural industries, literature, art collections, media, sports groups, businesses, political and religious organizations, government agencies, discussion groups, and individuals, located inside and outside Iran. The restrictions of national borders therefore appear to be partially overcome in this alternative form of globalization.

Diasporic cybercommunities centred around very specific topics attempt to bring communal knowledge to bear on contemporary issues. News groups such as soc.culture.sierraleone, soc.culture.jewish, and alt.religion.zoroastrianism allow for people interested in these topics to communicate from any place where they have access to the Internet. 'Shams' is a news group that enables discussion of issues relating to the rights of women in Muslim law, 'Bol' is a Listserv for issues of gender, reproductive health and human rights in South Asia, and 'KoreanQ', also a Listserv, caters to lesbian and bisexual women of Korean heritage. Co-operative arrangements between students and professionals of recent Chinese origins working in high technology sectors in Canada, the US and the UK have led to the emergence of online magazines that express their particular concerns. These new arrivals feel that their information needs are not met by the content of the thriving print and broadcast Chinese ethnic media, which is produced largely by older groups of immigrants. Despite being separated by large distances and, in most cases, not having met each other, the virtual editorial teams are electronically publishing regular issues that cover events happening in the homeland and in the Chinese diaspora.

A number of diasporic websites are designed to correct what are considered misperceptions by outsiders and to mobilize external political support. Several web pages of the transnational Roma ('gypsies'), who have been vilified for centuries in a number of countries, function in this manner. Guillermo Gómez-Peña, a Mexican commentator on issues of cultural hybridity, has extended his post-modernist literary and artistic criticism to cyberspace in a deliberate effort to confront the hegemonic structures of knowledge production and to respond to their globally dominant images of Chicano identity. The Council on American-Islamic Relations and the Canadian Islamic Congress run electronic mailing lists that provide updates on issues affecting Muslims, and encourages subscribers to lobby relevant media, community and government organizations to redress what it views as unjust treatment. Several groups also use online media to challenge hate propaganda and to carry out polemics against other websites. Some anti-government organizations have taken even more strong action with the use of electronic technology. One Tamil group electronically disabled the websites of several Sri Lankan embassies that it viewed as disseminating propaganda. The speed of simultaneous, worldwide demonstrations in March 1999 by Kurdish protestors, who reacted immediately to the capture of a guerrilla leader by Turkish forces, was a result of the Internet links maintained by that global community.

Conclusion

The production and dissemination of diasporic cultural materials in transnational contexts act as unique alternatives to the domination of the cultural industries by global corporations. Print media, satellite television and the Internet have provided unique opportunities for inter-continental communities to develop worldwide communication networks. However, the extensive presence of the communications conglomerates that are increasingly buying up diasporic print and broadcast media, and the growing commercialization of online media, are having an effect on the tenor of the material that they carry. Whereas the improvements in infrastructure and software may benefit transnational groups, commercial contingencies may overwhelm community considerations in the organization of communication networks and in the production and distribution of content.

Diasporic communities living in wealthier parts of the world have considerable access to media technologies, but such access is often hard to come by in developing countries. Therefore, one should not assume that there is equal participation by all members of a global diaspora. Additionally, there are certain sociological realities that act as limits in the use of communication technologies. For example, it is not possible for a large number of netters to engage effectively in discussion in an Internet chat group. Therefore, while this medium does allow for far-flung acquaintances to come together in cyberspace, the entire diaspora cannot fit into the virtual chat room.

A development to watch is the growing control that governments are exerting over online networks; this may affect the ability of global communities to maintain and extend effective electronic links. Additionally, as governments seal national borders more tightly in order to prevent terrorism, transnational movement is becoming increasingly difficult for migrants from non-Western states. Immigrants' affinities for homelands are also coming under suspicion. There is renewed pressure on the layered and hybrid identities of diasporic members to conform to the older models of a culturally monolithic nation-state.

Nevertheless, the momentum generated by globalization and technological development make it difficult to erase the identities of minority groups or to corral them within borders. Diasporic connections have become integral to the networks of transnational trade and have become an intrinsic feature of contemporary international relations. Even as diasporic media are piggybacking on the communications infrastructures established and maintained by states and corporations, they are also engaging in the further development of the means of global communications. Their determined pursuit of innovation in transnational communication has made them key participants in the contemporary unfolding of modernity.

Summary

- Diasporas have emerged as deterritorialized nations that exist across countries and continents.
- Ethnic media exist in many countries where they contribute to cultural maintenance of minorities and to their integration into the larger society.
- Diasporas are at the leading edge of adopting communications technologies that enable them to link up their relatively small and far-flung communities.

- Inter-continental diasporas can regularly watch common programming via satellite television.
- Diasporas have developed strong global communication networks by using Internet-based media.
- The growing linkages between worldwide diasporas are contributing to globalization-from-below.

GOING FURTHER

Braziel, J. E. and A. Mannur (eds) (2003) *Theorizing Diaspora*. Malden, MA: Blackwell.
Several other views on diaspora appear in this edited text. Issues of modernity, globalism, identity, sexuality, gender and cultural production are addressed by various authors. This is a critical reader on the theories underlying the concept of diaspora.

Bunt, G. (2000) *Virtually Islamic: Computer-mediated Communication and Cyber Islamic Environments*. Cardiff: University of Wales Press.
Bunt addresses the use of the Internet by Muslims in majority and minority contexts. He shows how websites and email have become a primary source of news and communication about Islam.

Mandaville, P. (2001) *Transnational Muslim Politics: Reimagining the Umma*. London: Routledge.
Mandaville's work indicates that translocal entities, using these technologies, are leading globally to the emergence of a broader Muslim public sphere in which traditional sources of Islamic authority are being challenged.

Bunt, G. (2003) *Islam in the Digital Age: E-Jihad, Online Fatwas and Cyber Islamic Environments*. London: Pluto Press.

Cunningham, S. and J. Sinclair (eds) (2002) *Floating Lives: The Media and Asian Diasporas*. Lanham, MD: Rowman and Littlefield.
This edited volume examines how ethnic communities negotiate hybrid identities and cultures in the context of media usage. The contributors study consumption of video film and music by Chinese, Vietnamese, Indian, and Thai communities in Australia.

Cohen, R. (1997) *Global Diasporas: An Introduction*. Seattle: University of Washington Press.
Provides an overview of several major global communities and attempts to develop diasporic categories. Jewish, African, Armenian, Indian, British, Chinese and Lebanese experiences are examined.

Gillespie, M. (1995) *Television, Ethnicity and Cultural Change*. London: Routledge.
A pioneering work that addressed the consumption of media content by an ethnic community. It presents the results of the author's ethnographic study of the use of Indian video and television by

South Asians living in Southall, in South London. The book uncovers the complex negotiation of cultural identities in the context of consuming media texts.

Karim, K. H. (ed.) (2003) *The Media of Diaspora*. London: Routledge.

This book explores the ways in which diasporic communities on six continents have sustained local and transnational ties with uses of film, satellite television, video, and the Internet. This book's chapters address historical, social and cultural dynamics within Aboriginal, Arab, Armenian, Assyrian, Chinese, Ghanaian, Greek, Hispanic, Indian, Iranian, Jewish, Kurdish, Macedonian, Muslim. Rhodesian, Turkish and Vietnamese groups. The authors in this interdisciplinary collection use a number of methodologies to understand how contemporary diasporas have adopted particular kinds of media to enable intercontinental connections.

Kolar-Panov, D. (1997) *Video, War and the Diasporic Imagination*. London: Routledge.

Writing about the Macedonian and Croatian communities, Kolar-Panov studies how video technology has had a key role in the reconstruction of identities in these diasporic groups.

Hargreaves, Alec C. and McKinney, Mak (eds) (1997) *Post-Colonial Cultures in France*. London: Routledge. This is a study of broadcasting, film, music and comics among Minorities in France. The various chapters on television, press, film, music and cartoons are enriched by their placement within historical, political and cultural contexts.

The various chapters on television, press, film, music and cartoons are enriched by their placement within historical, political and cultural contexts.

Naficy, H. (1993) *The Making of Exile Cultures*. Minneapolis, MN: University of Minnesota Press. This explores the ways in which cultural productions prompt resistance to the social values of host societies while at the same time acting as vehicles for the absorption of those very values.

Latinos Inc by Arlene Dávila ((2001) Berkeley: University of California Press) views Spanish-language television in the US through the perspective of advertising and programming professionals. She explores how Latino identities are shaped by the corporate and market mechanisms that work through the media.

Shukla, S. (2003) *India Abroad: Diasporic Cultures of Postwar America and England*. Princeton, NJ: Princeton University Press.

India Abroad looks at media and literature in the lives of Indian diasporas in the US and the UK. This anthropological work situates the discourses of nation across different cultural spheres including festivals, business, fiction, autobiography, newspapers, music and film.

Sun, W. (2002) *Leaving China: Media, Migration and Transnational Imagination*. Lanham, MD: Rowman and Littlefield.

Leaving China addresses the connection between Chinese emigrants to Australia and those who remain in the home country through their interpretations of media content. It views the differences between the two groups by examining their consumption of television and Internet content.

STUDENT ACTIVITY 16:1

Identify an ethnic medium (print, broadcast or Internet-based) operating in your vicinity. Conduct a study of this medium by examining its structure and content. Attempt to answer questions such as: What are the identities of the persons operating it? What are their objectives? Does the medium's content reflect ethnic concerns within its geographical area or does it attempt to link itself to a broader diaspora? Is there any evidence of reader/audience use such as letters to the editor or other feedback? What sense of communal identity do the medium's operators and its readers/audiences have of themselves with respect to ethnicity, nation, diaspora and citizenship? How does the medium locate itself within the territory where it exists? How does its content compare with that of a mainstream medium in its location?

References

Braziel, J. E. and A. Mannur (eds) (2003) *Theorizing Diaspora*. Malden, MA: Blackwell.

Bunt, G. (2003) *Islam in the Digital Age: E-Jihad, Online Fatwas and Cyber Islamic Environments*. London: Pluto Press.

Bunt, G. (2000) *Virtually Islamic: Computer-mediated Communication and Cyber Islamic Environments*. Cardiff: University of Wales Press.

Cunningham, S. and J. Sinclair (eds) (2002) *Floating Lives: The Media and Asian Diasporas*. Lanham, MD: Rowman and Littlefield.

Cohen, R. (1997) *Global Diasporas: An Introduction*. Seattle: University of Washington Press.

Hargreaves, A. G. and McKinney, M. (eds) (1997). *Post-Colonial Cultures in France*. London: Routledge.

Hassanpour, A. (2003) 'Diaspora, Homeland and Communication Technologies' in Karim H. Karim (ed) *The Media of Diaspora*. London: Routledge. pp. 76–88.

Kolar-Panov, D. (1997) *Video, War and the Diasporic Imagination*. London: Routledge.

Mandaville, P. (2001) *Transnational Muslim Politics: Reimagining the Umma*. London: Routledge.

Shukla, S. (2003) *India Abroad: Diasporic Cultures of Postwar America and England*. Princeton, NJ: Princeton University Press.

Sun, W. (2002) *Leaving China: Media, Migration and Transnational Imagination*. Lanham, MD: Rowman and Littlefield.

Notes

1 Appadurai's (1996) ideas about global cultural flows with respect to what he calls 'medias-capes' and 'ethnoscapes' has had a significant impact on theorization of diasporic connections.

2 Falk has distinguished between 'globalization-from-above' and 'globalization-from-below'. He identifies the former as reflecting 'the collaboration between leading states and the main agents of capital formation' (1993: 39). 'Globalization-from-below', according to Falk, is carried out mainly by organizations that do not have strong links with governments or large corporations. Karim (2003) extends this form of globalization to diasporas.

Index